Living with the Word

A Collection of
Speeches, Commentaries, Letters, & Poems

by

George Connor

Preface by Frederick Buechner

Edited and Introduced by Charles Thornbury

Cover Photograph (ca. 1966) by Bob Lanza

Living with the Word is published in connection with The George Connor Society.

The proposal for creating the Society was initiated by Dr. Clif Cleaveland in early
2003, and it materialized because of his dedicated and devoted work
and that of Carolyn Mitchell, Rick Govan, and Herbert Thornbury.
Former UTC Chancellor Dr. Bill Stacy and Dr. Craig Barrow, the present holder
of the George Connor Professorship of American Literature, have made possible
an essential partnership with the Society.

The purpose of the Society is to celebrate and honor the life of
George Coleman Connor
through annual programs that reflect the social, intellectual, and personal
concerns that his life exemplified and to which he dedicated himself.
The Society is a non-profit organization affiliated with the
University of Chattanooga Foundation.

ॐ

Living with the Word is published with grateful acknowledgement for funding from
The George Connor Professorship of American Literature at UTC
and the Lyndhurst Foundation

Of all the many changing things
Words alone are a certain good.

W.B. Yeats

e.e. cummings once said, "Better worlds are born, not made, and their birthdays are the birthdays of individuals." If you tell me that this is a moral
judgment and that my use of it implies a moral aim for education, I shall
agree with you heartily on both points.

I always assume that the aim of education is a better world, a world in
which peace and justice and equality under the law and the fullest possible
development of every human being are not only our highest dreams but also
our clearest possibilities.

I am aware that more than education is required to achieve this world, but I
am also aware that education – and the best possible education – is required
to achieve it.

George Connor, June 5, 1963

I'm no theologian, but all this is vital to me, and I feel it's vital to you.

Flannery O'Connor, 1959

I put my pen down, round me the world is dark and all men lie asleep.
But I have written urgently for this beloved person, and indeed for all
beloved persons. . .
And indeed for all persons, whoever may find something in these words.

Alan Paton, 1954

TABLE OF CONTENTS

Writers

Part III - Christian Faith and Life

On Being Christian

Aspects of Christian Life

The Church

Preface

When George Connor turned 75 on September 1, 1995, I was unable to be on hand for the feast that was held in his honor, but I did write him a letter which I'm told was read aloud, among others, by his great friend and former student, Douglas Hale. The first half of it was waggish. I felt that since everybody else was obviously going to say only the most complimentary things about him, it was up to me, at least initially, to strike a discordant note, and I therefore managed to recall a few minor incidents from the past which, by grossest distortion and wildest exaggeration, I was able to cite as illustrating several of his more serious character defects.

I cannot resist quoting the one that pleased me most, whose miniscule kernel of truth is that on his flight north to visit us in Vermont one summer, he somehow got coffee spilled on him. I ascribed this to "the altercation you engaged in with an unfortunate airline stewardess" and then went on to say, "I cannot recapture at the moment just how it was that you provoked it – would I be wrong in supposing that you stuck your foot out into the aisle just as she was passing by with the refreshment cart? – but I know there was a good deal of coffee thrown around before it was over because when you got off the plane, the sorry state of your clothes made it look as though you had recently been involved in jungle combat." The reason that so slender a pleasantry continues to rejoice my heart, I think, is that it so utterly misrepresents this most courtly, considerate, and civilized of men who is the very model of a southern gentleman.

Once I got the waggishness behind me, I decided that it was time to speak the truth. "Dear George," I wrote, "it can't have been much less than ten years since you and I met for the first time. When you and Rick Govan picked me up at the Atlanta airport, I knew within less than ten minutes that I had made a great new Old Friend who would be part of my life from that moment on. And I was right. We laugh ourselves silly over the same things. We agreed about Reagan and Bush just as we agree now about Gingrich and Dole. We have made friends with each other's dogs and with each other's friends. We were born into the same decade and into that same lost, pre-World War II world that all these years later seems so much simpler and kinder and happier and more hopeful than the world that has replaced it. And I believe that we think about Holy Things in much the same way too and that in church and out of it the same kinds of things leave us cold while other things bring tears to our eyes and make our hearts beat faster. I do not believe such friendships happen by chance. I believe they happen by grace." I did not know until I read it in this present volume how unwittingly I was echoing a poem he wrote in 1963, years before I met him, whose first stanza goes,

> There was, as best I can recall
> No outward sign at our first greeting
> That supernatural forces were at work;
> But surely grace was in our meeting.

In other words I want to make it clear from the start that these prefatory remarks to *Living with the Word* are not for one moment intended to be objective and unbiased. The best thing about this book, for me, is how wonderfully well it manages to convey the rare charm of his mind and spirit.

Over the years George Connor has been a teacher, a writer, an inveterate reader of books, a soldier, an active participant in community affairs, a man with so many friends that you wonder how he has managed to keep up with the whole pack of them for so long, a devoted churchman, and above all, or under girding all, a True Believer who at one point in his career seriously considered entering the Episcopal ministry. Charles Thornbury has done his editorial work well in gathering together and organizing here over fifty years' worth of writings from each one of these categories, and among many other things that we learn from them is the fact that, as George himself would never have dreamed of saying out loud, he was awarded a Bronze Star for "meritorious service in connection with military operations against enemies of the United States in Germany" in 1945. It was also news to me that for a time he worked as a cryptographer encoding and decoding messages concerning troop movements on which hundreds of lives depended. He recounts too how during this same period he overheard a group of Military Police brutally beating an African-American soldier with clubs at Fort Riley, Kansas, and later records a visit he made to Buchenwald at a time when some of the survivors were still receiving treatment from American medics there. Such is his reserved and decorous nature, however, that in both cases he makes no attempt to describe in any detail the horror of what he witnessed, but his very silence has its own eloquence.

In a welcoming address to the University of Chattanooga's first English Institute he says several things that not only set forth his view of what the ideal English teacher should be but also give a glimpse of the kind of English teacher he himself was. "The teacher cannot communicate a vision which he does not have," he says, "he cannot spread the contagion of his enthusiasm for poetry if he has no such enthusiasm," and I remember to this day how once when he was driving me somewhere or other during a time I was with him in Tennessee he didn't have to talk for more than maybe ten minutes or so about his beloved Flannery O'Connor, whom up to that point I scarcely knew, before I was firmly determined to read everything she had ever written as soon as I could lay my hands on it, and she has been one of my heroes ever since. In the same English Institute address he also says, "The task of communicating the wisdom of the past to each new generation – and this is the essence of education – is a task which is very largely borne for a great many people by the high school teacher of English." In other words, he was always well aware that his calling as an academic was a great deal higher and holier than simply to see to it that his students read their weekly assignments.

There is also a generous assortment of short pieces on religion among these pages, and they are full of such clarity, conciseness, and common sense as are to be found in "A Statement of Faith," which contains one of my favorite passages. "Mine is a faith strengthened by the certain knowledge that whatever may happen in the affairs of men, the purpose of my life will remain unaltered and unalterable. Since that purpose is to know and love and serve God, the only possibility for real tragedy is the possibility of alienation from Him. My happiness then, for the present and for the future, does not depend upon cheerful headlines or news reports." Just the titles of some of the others – "In Defense of Rest," "On the Ordination of Women" and "Christian Golf, Anyone?" – suggest something of the tone and range of them all, and they also include an occasional aside which in itself is worth the price of admission. A classic among them alludes to the time when an unidentified lady said to him, "When you come right down to it, there are not more than a handful of good Christians in all of Chattanooga," to which George adds only, "None of us who heard that comment dared ask her who the others were."

There are also, among other things to be found here, letters, poems, tributes to old friends, and more, but since the purpose of a preface as I understand it is simply to open the front door rather than to conduct a guided tour of the whole establishment, I will content myself with saying only one further thing. When I picked up the manuscript for the first time, my chief worry was that the magic of the man himself might somehow have gotten lost in the shuffle, but that is far from being the case. The sound of him, the look of him, the sense of his presence, permeate pretty much everything here, and so, praise be, does the utter joy of his wit – dry, understated, unique, and irresistible. Let a single example of it suffice. In discussing the writing of military citations for courage and gallantry, a great many of which crossed his desk in army days, he mentions one in particular which "for unadorned eloquence and force . . . can hardly be surpassed." And then he gives it.

"At this point in the action, Lt. Colonel Smithfield personally threw a hand grenade."

The door now stands open. Come in and make yourself at home.

Frederick Buechner

Introduction

We did not plan it, in collaborating on *Living with the Word*, but George and I fell into the orderliness of meeting for lunch on Tuesdays. We met mostly in the summer months of 2000 and 2001 in Chattanooga, still my home after having set out some years ago on a series of adventures that took me from Alaska to Europe to Minnesota. I teach English at a liberal arts college in Minnesota, and that I teach at all, I owe to my undergraduate professor and mentor, George Connor. Literature and writing found me out, but George made the finding intellectually exciting and emotionally present.

In my last year at the University of Chattanooga in 1964, I did an independent study with him on the poetry of T.S. Eliot. I didn't realize it at the time, but those evenings of our reading Eliot's poetry aloud (a music that's "heard before it's understood") changed the direction of my life – and I found a friend in the bargain. I still have the thirty-page paper I wrote 40 years ago that a friend typed beautifully for me: "This student," George wrote on the cover page, "is fortunate to have had a good teacher and an excellent typist" and below that an *A*.

Like Mitch Albom, who nearly 20 years after his graduation, got a one-on-one class with his undergraduate professor Morrie Schwartz, I was in a tutorial again, but now with a friend and colleague. As all friends of George will appreciate, he did most of the talking, but never was he dull or tedious. Invariably, he told at least one new, often hilarious, story, and one or two I had heard before. But even the old stories were fresh in George's retelling. When I suggested to him a rough parallel between our project and *Tuesdays with Morrie*, he pointed out that he was not dying, "in so far as any of us are not dying." I remembered his wry humor with some melancholy when he died, on a Tuesday, August 20, 2002, eleven days before his 82nd birthday.

Our lunches were quite ordinary, in a leisurely southern way; we had fried okra with our entrées, and George always ordered two servings. We talked about what was going on with his friends, his scorn for a mediocre bureaucrat ("one wonders how he found the way to his office each day"), the errands he needed to run that afternoon, the latest good report from his doctor Clif Cleaveland, the stash of letters and pictures he discovered in boxes that were hiding in his closet. In our conversations, we discovered boxes of ourselves, as though each had been packed in haste several decades before and we had not labeled them. Without knowing what we were about, we delighted in locating something familiar, something forgotten.

Part of that unpacking for me has been the freedom to select and arrange something of George himself. We had begun modestly with the idea of a collection of his speeches, but I was frustrated that, good as these were, they represented only a part of his life and work. There were numerous commentaries, a pile of essays, reviews, and poems, and a mountain of letters. About two-thirds of this book was selected before he died; after his death, I chose additional pieces that give greater scope and depth to his work and reveal more of the paradoxical, and sometimes impossible, person he was.

In his address "The Craft So Long to Learn," George points to directions of his personal, intellectual, and moral compass. The occasion was a "Last Chance Lecture" series in 1964, the premise being that this was his last opportunity to speak to his university community "of subordinating the urgent to the fundamental." Like a compass, which has 32 points and not the four most might think of, George maintains that a reliable sense of direction discerns nuances and contours and perceives hints on the horizon and the blade of grass at one's feet. His fundamentals were less complex: his north was loyalty and duty; his south was relationships and listening; his east, teaching and learning; his west, how to live a thoughtful, compassionate, and useful life.

"What kind of guy inhabits this poem?" I hear George say in quoting one of his favorite poets, W.H. Auden. One might ask what kind of guy inhabits this collection. I asked the committee who helped support bringing *Living with the Word* into print for a description of the man himself. All agreed on his paradoxical personality: "sensitive/intimidating; compassionate/prickly; kind/acerbic; generous/aloof." Less paradoxical descriptions spoke of his charm, praised his values, and admired his intellect and insight: "graceful, loyal, thoughtful, critical, sardonic, witty, a 'yellow dog' Democrat, a Christian, well-read, interesting, superb story-teller, engaging, had incredible timing, a powerful memory, and was provocative, eloquent, and wise." To this list of inspiring qualities, one might add that a collie was one of his companions most of his adult life and that he was an avid Atlanta Braves fan.

His speeches, about a third of this collection, have that rare quality of revealing something of the man himself. There was slender difference between his private and public voice. In each his sentences were fluid and urbane, never halting or faltering. When George was asked to speak on behalf of the community or someone's family – honoring a colleague, dedicating a library, or giving a eulogy – he spoke to the occasion publicly *and* personally and was wise and fully himself in telling stories. There was a sort of sway in his public voice, a resonance, pace, and tone that was, like his description of his mentor

Rev. Thorne Sparkman's preaching style, "quiet," "restrained," "understated": "He [Sparkman] never tried to do with voice or gesture what the thought and the words would not do." Like his mentor, who had "an incomparably beautiful speaking voice," George "never played tricks with his voice" either.

George seemed to have been born speaking words, or it least it seemed so after ten minutes of conversation with him. "A civilization lives in great part by words," he writes, "a people realize their identity and destiny very largely in language." His passion for words was at once secular and theological (*Logos*), a wish to figure human experience, in Robert Frost's sense of the "figure" a poem makes. He had a passion for thinking things over – no cant, psychobabble, or vapid slogans. For all his authority in speaking fluidly and precisely, he recognized that experience cannot be fixed in words. He sidles up to an experience; he interrogates an idea and backs away. He persuades with reason and authority, but, like the writers he admires, he also speaks of the struggle to express experience in words.

George had a genius for citing the felicitous quotation (I cannot resist mentioning that I learned that melodic word "felicitous" from George when I was an undergraduate). "Sometimes a single sentence uttered by some thoughtful and contemplative person," he writes, "will provide us with the opportunity and the inspiration for almost endless meditation." The sentence in this case was Walker Percy's in one of his letters: "Who is onto the secret? – that the mystery is to be found in ordinary things in an ordinary room on an ordinary Wednesday afternoon?" Like Percy, George spoke often of ordinary things, the small things that become extraordinary in ordinary life: "A cheerful word spoken to a friend or acquaintance, or for that matter a perfect stranger, a letter of encouragement and good will, a simple gift or act of thoughtfulness to mark some occasion – such little things can have an effect beyond our most extravagant expectations."

The concluding section of *Living with the Word*, "Among Family and Friends," is less a coda than a well-spring in George's life and work. "From those nearest and dearest to us, to those whom we may know and deal with only casually," he says, "we discover and manifest the love of God in loving service." Those who knew George are thankful for his loyalty, indeed his extravagance, in friendship, and his friends, properly, cannot be arranged to fit into one section of this book. Isobel Griscom, Dorothy Hackett Ward, and Paul Ramsey in the section "A Passion for Learning" and David Parker in "Christian Faith and Life" might be placed in "Among Family and Friends" as well. As Rick Govan, a friend and former student of George's, said recently, "I never knew anyone who worked so hard at friendship. He greatly valued his many friendships and worked passionately at maintaining them." (Sadly, nearby friendships, like that with Rick, do not promote the writing of long letters, and some close friends are not represented here as they should be. Perhaps a collection of their memories of George will be published one day.) Of all the friends in his life, mentioned or not in these pages, George would join Yeats in saying: "Think where man's glory most begins and ends, / And say my glory was I had such friends."

   "The art of teaching," said Mark Van Doren, that great teacher, scholar, and poet at Columbia College, "is the art of assisting discovery." George taught by example, but the most important things he taught by indirection. Whenever a student raised a question about a poem or a novel, invariably he answered with a story, another passage in the same text, or passages from other poems and stories. It was part of his craft, this assisting, and, like his talent for words, he seems to have been born with the insight. That insight of *attending* to discovery was the foundation his teaching. To many students, he was a teacher in another sense: he was a fixed point in a confusing and tumultuous world for a young adult in the 1960s. The world is no less confusing in 2004, and this collection makes me realize how, in the best sense, his life and work are fixed points. But more than fixed points: as testimony to his teaching, they are refuges to which one returns and homes from which one departs.

   "Death ends a life," Morrie tells Mitch, "but not a relationship." Several days before Morrie died, he suggested that they might continue their conversation when Mitch visits his grave, and, he added, "You talk, I'll listen." Before George died, I had written for this introduction that he was "vigorous and vital at the age of 81, and his many friends and colleagues still delight in his wit, his openness, his generosity, his wisdom, his friendship." It makes me glad that he read every word and responded warmly to them. George frequently quoted T.S. Eliot's lines,

   These are only hints and guesses,
   Hints followed by guesses; and the rest
   Is prayer, observance, discipline, thought and action.

George meditated upon the hints and guesses most of his life, and his own experience and Eliot's are seamless in that regard. George turned most often to the third line: "prayer, observance, discipline, thought and action." At the end of my paper 40 years ago, I spoke of Eliot's poetry as, in his own words, the "hint half-guessed, the gift half-understood." George might have half-guessed often enough – better his than many guesses one might think of – but the gift of his life and work – his own prayer, observance, discipline, thought, and action – is more fully understood in the pages that follow.

On the occasion of the 45th anniversary of his high school reunion in 1983, George spoke of not mourning deeply those "departed classmates who led useful and productive lives." "The value of a life," he said, "surely is measured not in its length but in its significance and intensity, its openness and aliveness. Perhaps the best memorial any of us can have is the impact we have upon other human beings – our friends, our families, our associates. If we really live every day of our lives, we will have made a difference in the world." This passage is now a fitting epitaph for one who truly made a difference in the world.

Charles Thornbury

Part I

A Passion for Learning

"There is never a time in this fleeting life when you will be able to say,
I know all I want to know, I understand all I want to understand."

(GC, December 18, 1980)

GC in his home library, May 1977.

Learning

The Craft So Long to Learn

Last Chance Lecture, 1964

An invitation based upon the hypothesis that underlies this lecture – that this is my last opportunity to address the University community – is one which I suppose few of us could resist; certainly I could not. But I am bound to confess that if in sober truth this *were* my last opportunity, I should probably limit myself to the strong admonition to remember whatever I have said worthy of remembering during the past several years. But that clearly will not do, and so I acknowledge that both the greatest challenge and in the long run the greatest pleasure in the assignment comes from the necessity of sorting out, of assigning priorities, of subordinating the urgent to the fundamental.

I am grateful for this forceful reminder that the "unexamined life is not worth living," and for the opportunity, made imperative by this invitation, to submit my own life and thought and work to examination. My life, unlike J. Alfred Prufrock's, is not measured out in coffee spoons but in committee meetings, in conferences, in the daily struggle to leave the student in somewhat better intellectual condition than I find him or her. It is only too easy in the rather hectic circumstances in which we all live to neglect the task of thinking about what we do.

My preparation for this lecture, therefore, in the several weeks since the invitation was given me, has consisted not in the reading of documents, but in the thinking of thoughts, in the contemplation of what one would say if this were indeed one's last chance. During these weeks I have spent as much time as I could in the routine, ordinary, undemanding tasks that leave the mind free: raking leaves, trying to civilize a frivolous young dog, cleaning out a long drainage ditch. (I am perhaps one of the few who in one season have combined college teaching with ditch-digging.) As I have thought about what I should say on this occasion, nothing has amazed me more than the fact that I am here, in this position, with an invitation to say anything. Nothing has struck me with greater force than the fact that my own student days here *seem* to have ended so recently. To paraphrase a little article I once saw in a London newspaper, anything that happened in, say, 1940 is to my students, antiquity; to me, the day before yesterday.

I doubt that anything quite so decisively separates youth from age as this attitude towards time because this attitude is so pervasive, so certain to color our response to experience of all kinds. At the age of most of our present students, life seems an endless adventure, all opportunities seem to remain perpetually

2

open, every path can be explored. But the day inevitably comes when we must acknowledge that doors do close, that many choices once made cannot be unmade, that time has moved inexorably forward. This is surely one of the most persistent and poignant themes in literature. In Dylan Thomas's poem "Fern Hill" in which he recreates the beautiful and imaginative world of childhood, in which a little boy can be "prince of apple towns" and where even "the calves sang to [his] horn," there is also the sober reminder

>that time allows
>In all his tuneful turning so few and such morning songs
>Before the children green and golden
>Follow him out of grace.

Much of the same realization of course is embodied in Robert Frost's poem "The Road Not Taken." When the inhabitant of that poem reaches a place in the autumn woods where the road divides, he chooses, carefully but regretfully, one way over the other. Though he may wish otherwise, he knows it is not likely that the choice can be reopened.

>Oh, I kept the first for another day!
>Yet knowing how way leads on to way,
>I doubted if I should ever come back.

Our maturity, even our wisdom, begins the moment that we first recognize that "way leads on to way," and that painful as it may be, choices must be made. I suppose we can never accept this truth without some feeling of regret for what we must exclude from our lives; after all, Frost's poem is called "The Road *Not* Taken." But if the acceptance of our human limitations in one sense disappoints, in another it surely enhances the value and the pleasure of those things we do choose.

From one point of view, at least, I should think the most important contribution of the college years is to develop in the student the capacity for making wise choices. It is the merest cliché to point out that the college career is the beginning of one's education, but the fact that it is a cliché does not make it any less true. We cannot hope to give students the knowledge and the attitudes and the opinions they will need for the rest of their lives; these things are the work of a lifetime. We can do no more, I think, than to communicate to the student the passion for learning and the means for educating himself and herself. We can help the student to see that to develop as a human being, as a child of God with unique gifts and abilities and interests, is the highest and noblest and most diffi-

3

cult of callings. Chaucer's words would be a fit motto for any college community: "The life so short, the craft so long to learn."

The late Stephen Leacock, that wonderful old Canadian economist and humorist, speaks in one of his essays about those fortunate ones "who come to college and never go away, whose lot it is, thrice blessed, to stay at college all their lives." And we are thrice blessed, indeed, because among other things most of us would acknowledge that for us a life spent in learning the craft and teaching it to others is a form of self-indulgence. We are usually candid enough to acknowledge also that we are the very heart and center of the university. There is a famous story – I am told it is grounded in fact – that a distinguished citizen who became for a time the president of a great American university, once saw fit to lecture the senior professors of that university in a rather condescending way. At one point he said, "What you men must understand is that the university wants. . ." but one of the more venerable among his audience interrupted him: "Pardon me, Mr. President, but we *are* the university." And there is enough truth in that remark to make it worth saying because the heart of any educational institution is the teaching and learning that take place in it. But it is also a perilously over-simplified view. The presence of not only faculty but also of deans and presidents, trustees and buildings seems to presuppose also the presence of students. Inconvenient and restrictive as it may sometimes seem, I hardly think it possible to have a first-rate university without students.

What is the proper aim of the university for these students? What do we hope to accomplish in and for and through the students? Or, to put the question more humbly and more realistically, what do we hope to encourage the students to do and to become? I should answer this complex question with the simple statement that we hope to encourage the student to acquire a thorough liberal education; whatever specialization he or she may later pursue, the student must have first an education fit for free men and women in a free society. Commenting on this point, an excellent little book called *General Education in School and College*, published in 1952, says, "Education designed to free individual human beings from the limitations of ignorance, prejudice, and provincialism makes sense only in a free society and can flourish only within such a society." I do not know a better description of the liberally educated man and woman, than that which this little book sets forth:

> The liberally educated man [and woman — the masculine pronoun should be understood in this quotation as feminine as well]

is articulate, both in speech and writing, he has a feel for language, a respect for clarity and directness of expression, and a knowledge of some language other than his own. He is at home in the world of quantity, number, and measurement. He thinks rationally, logically, objectively, and knows the difference between fact and opinion. When the occasion demands, however, his thought is imaginative and creative rather than logical. He is perceptive, sensitive to form, and affected by beauty. His mind is flexible and adaptable, curious, and independent. He knows a good deal about the world of nature and the world of man, about the culture of which he is a part, but he is never merely "well-informed." He can use what he knows with judgment and discrimination. He thinks of his business or profession, his family life, and his avocations as parts of a larger whole, parts of a purpose which he has made his own. Whether making a professional or a personal decision, he acts with maturity, balance, and perspective, which come ultimately from his knowledge of other persons, other problems, other times and places. He has convictions, which are reasoned, although he cannot always prove them. He is tolerant about the beliefs of others because he respects sincerity and is not afraid of ideas. He has values, and he can communicate them to others not only by word but by example. His personal standards are high; nothing short of excellence will satisfy him. But service to his society or to his God, not personal satisfaction, is the purpose of his excelling. Above all, the liberally educated man is never a type. He is always a unique person, vivid in his distinction from other similarly educated persons, while sharing with them the traits we have mentioned.

This formidable catalog of virtues for the liberally educated person will seem to many too idealistic, demanding too much. Perhaps there are few persons by this definition who could fully qualify as liberally educated. But unless we keep before us a vision of what we ought to do, we are not likely to build here even a moderately good institution, much less a great one.

I hope the fact that I have chosen to spend most of this lecture in discussion of what a university community ideally should be will not seem to you narrow and parochial. For the future of our society, for the future of our civilization,

I can hardly think of a more important subject. Within this context, one can discuss almost everything which is of genuinely lasting significance.

First of all, I believe that a university community should be so organized, its activities so directed, as to provide what Alfred North Whitehead has called the "habitual vision of greatness." The whole college experience – and I mean far more than what takes place in the classrooms – should expose the student unrelentingly to the first-rate in every department of human achievement. It is not too much to say that the student should be saturated in excellence. The student's first encounter with such excellence should be in the very architecture of the college buildings; surely it is not too much to hope that the architecture will manifest a happy union between utility and beauty, that it will suggest dignity and our highest aspirations, that it will take note of the fact that we are living in the twentieth century.

But far more than buildings are involved. Literally nothing is so small or insignificant that it should not contribute to the student's experience of the first-rate. Every ornament, every piece of furnishing, every appurtenance should be a thing of grace and beauty. Why should a textbook be bound in an ugly cover? Why should so many of our parking signs be both unattractive and illegible? Why should the Student Center be embellished with artificial flowers (call them by whatever name you wish) or hung with pictures more reminiscent of Kress than Cress? This is all much more than a question of what some misguided people call "mere aes-

GC speaking at his second "Last Chance Lecture," November 1981. Lisa Huggins wrote in The University Echo: *"Hearing Professor George Connor speak is like listening to the oral version of a research paper. It is very organized, very precise – each point falls into place as outlined, so that when the lecture is through, the whole makes perfect sense. Sound tedious and dull? Nothing of the kind. The man is fascinating. Hawked on the five or six Xeroxed signs that give notice of the lecture as 'In Retrospect,' Connor's talk contained a quote from a 1952 publication called* General Education in School and College *(again, it sounds dull, but… you should've been there), which was repeated from the English professor's last Last Chance Lecture, given in 1964. 'Certain things were true in 1952,' he said, 'indeed, they were true in A.D. 52, and they remain true in 1981.'" Photograph courtesy of UTC Archives.*

thetics"; it is a question of the beauty of form, of the fit appearance of things in the college community, of our use of every opportunity to inculcate standards of excellence.

I will go even further. Many years ago I came upon a reference to a young British army captain in the First World War who was given a military decoration because he shaved every day in the front lines. This seemed to me an unspeakably silly reason for giving someone a medal, but I have long since come to understand the importance of the gesture – and of the captain's appearance. Appearance does matter, and there are appropriate and inappropriate modes of dress in the college community. I am too much of a sacramentalist not to believe that outward appearance both expresses and directs inner attitude. By virtue of the electronic miracles of our age, many of us recently saw a negative illustration of this point in the Richard Burton version of *Hamlet*. What the director thought he was accomplishing by dressing his characters as he did, I cannot imagine. The men looked like prosperous bankers who were impersonating college boys. College boys, in turn, often look like college boys who are impersonating unemployed circus performers. Surely there must be some simple minimum standards for the apparel of both student and teacher; if we fall below those standards, I think we are inviting contempt for the work we are here to do.

Our appearance is important because it does so easily color not only attitude but behavior as well. There is every advantage in our remembering that we may all reasonably be expected to conduct ourselves as ladies and gentlemen, that in every way our dealings with each other should show the kindness and tact which are the essence of good manners. Yeats's poem "A Prayer for My Daughter" concludes with a stanza, "And may her bridegroom bring her to a house / Where all's accustomed, ceremonious"; and he goes on to ask, "How but in custom and in ceremony / Are innocence and beauty born?" Try thinking of those lines the next time you walk through the Student Center.

But I have been talking of form, the outward appearance rather than the inner essence of the college community. And while I would vigorously defend these things as important parts of our common life, they may indeed be no more than empty forms if we are not seriously addressing ourselves to the task of intellectual development. Surely it is here that we as faculty have the greatest responsibility to provide the student with the "habitual vision of greatness." We cannot really teach him or her successfully unless we provide every student with examples of the first-rate, day in and day out. It is our duty to call constantly to the student's attention the best that has been thought and written in our respective fields. The real test of our success in the classroom is probably beyond our power to measure – how much have we stimulated each student's interest, whetted his or her appetite for the first-rate? How many books will students read on their own initiative? How deeply is the student committed to his or her own intellectual nourishment?

Our responsibility to stimulate the student as reader and thinker inevitably suggests another responsibility for the university: it is our clear duty to maintain the fullest possible academic freedom, the freedom of inquiry, the right to read widely and think freely and discuss openly. It is also our clear duty *not* to establish an official orthodoxy and penalize every heretical student who deviates from it. There is a clear distinction between education and indoctrination, and we must never lose sight of that distinction. There is a wonderful German proverb that says "a professor is a man who thinks otherwise." I am suggesting to you that it is our duty to think otherwise, to urge the consideration of alternatives, to be fair-minded and dispassionate, to challenge and scrutinize our own most cherished beliefs. I have heard it said that Adolph Ochs, to whom Chattanooga and this university have so many causes to be grateful, would not allow the use of political cartoons on the editorial page of *The New York Times* because, he said, they leave no room for saying, "on the other hand. . . ." There is perhaps no attitude as helpful to the maintenance of academic freedom as the recognition that one may possibly be wrong.

One sometimes hears academic freedom spoken of as though it were a pleasant luxury and not a real necessity. The careful nurture of academic freedom is not simply good policy; it is a matter of the health and well-being of the college community and ultimately of the society of which that community is a part. I submit that academic freedom is the most basic of all freedoms, incomparably more important than political freedom, or economic freedom, or even religious freedom; without freedom of inquiry, freedom of thought, we cannot possibly know enough to make the choices that the other kinds of freedom involve. What good is free speech if you have nothing to say? What good is the freedom to vote if you have no understanding of the issues? What good is freedom of worship if you cannot use the mind God gave you to seek to understand Him?

We should make no mistake about it: there are numerous forces in our society that regard academic freedom with suspicion and hostility. There are those who are profoundly distrustful of an education that gives the student the opportunity to examine conflicting points of view. It is the habit of vested interests to want to go on being vested interests, and they will often go to great lengths to insure their own predominance. Sometimes their distrust of free inquiry takes the form of legislation: in Tennessee the law forbids the study of the Darwinian theory of evolution in tax-supported schools. Sometimes the distrust takes the form of economic pressure, or social disapproval, or public ridicule; there are many weapons but the objective is always the same.

Still other enemies of free inquiry are more insidious because they are less obvious. These are the enemies who would subvert the whole educational process by substituting slogans for thought, spot commercials for political essays, three-color billboards for careful argument. In the political realm alone, this is enough to imperil the health of a free society. Certainly the easy substitute for hard thought is a genuine threat to the freedom of inquiry.

A college community should withstand all such threats, whether from the enemies of freedom or from those who recognize a profitable market in persons unable or unwilling to think for themselves. In every way we can, in class and out, it is our duty to encourage a continual and vigorous discussion of the truly fundamental issues. The fashionable word just now for this sort of discussion is, of course, *dialogue*, but I am interested in the activity, not in what the activity is called. And I must confess that I miss this kind of discussion on this campus; I hear very little of it among students and not nearly enough among professors. The students' lack of political concern and sophistication is truly appalling; very little of the campus political discussion in the campaign just ended rose above name-calling and empty clichés. We are somehow failing to inspire in our students an interest in important questions.

Perhaps this shortage of serious discussion stems from our fear of controversy, perhaps a legacy of the McCarthy era not yet exorcised. Surely among the most tiresome phrases in contemporary American life are the phrases "controversial figure" and "controversial opinion." Such silly phrases should have no place in college life; if we avoid the controversial, we are avoiding the educational. Nothing is more pervasive in the history of our country than controversy; yet in the current canon I should think we would call Henry David Thoreau a controversial figure and the Declaration of Independence a controversial opinion. I have heard the word *controversial* used to describe the distinguished publisher of the Atlanta *Constitution*, Mr. Ralph McGill, apparently because on the subject of race relations he holds views that are unacceptable to the enthusiasts for white supremacy. Every American should read his book, *The South and the Southerner*, a moderate, rational, and profoundly Christian book. When a man of Ralph McGill's stature, a son of Hamilton County, a graduate of McCallie School, a distinguished citizen not only of the South, not only of the United States, but of the world, when such a man as this can be treated as somehow suspect, then something is seriously wrong.

When I hear some misgiving or fear expressed that we may be contaminated by something "too controversial," I often think of a little story I heard several years ago, a story that long since in my mind has taken on the quality of parable. The poet, critic, and teacher Allen Tate was once invited to lecture at a Roman Catholic girls' school. At dinner beforehand he was seated next to a nun who had written a master's thesis on the poet Hart Crane, a tragic and perhaps rather bizarre figure in American literature. "Mr. Tate, I understand that you knew Hart Crane?" she said to him. Tate acknowledged that he did. "Do tell me about him; not what I can read anywhere but the sort of thing that doesn't get into books." A bit startled, Tate said, "Sister, I'm afraid Hart Crane's private life isn't something one can talk about in a convent." Her reply made the only point worth making: "Nonsense," she said; "it's the only safe place." If the college campus is not safe for controversy, what place is safe for it?

Controversy is safe on the college campus because the campus, at least ideally, is far more than a collection of buildings where one can study history, or read a book, or play ping pong; it is, I hope, at its truest and best, a community of scholars – with all that the word *community* implies in the way of common interests, common beliefs, common goals. Those of us who, in Leacock's phrase, are thrice blessed are privileged to spend the greater part of our lives in this community. And for the student it is a community which for four years opens wide its hospitable gates, giving each student the kinds of opportunities and experiences which will make his or her life profoundly and significantly different forever after.

I am perfectly aware that so far as our campus is concerned – and to some extent so far as any campus is concerned – I am speaking of the ideal. But this university can never afford to lose the ideal, the vision of what such a community can be despite all the imperfections in our life as we know it. At the moment, there are many obstacles to our achieving the community that we ought to have. One of these obstacles is a certain kind of bargain basement attitude toward education which is very widespread in our society and from which we on this campus are by no means free. I mean the attitude which seems to suggest that since earning power greatly improves with every year of education completed, the trick is to cram as much as possible into as little time as possible and graduate in the shortest possible time. I always feel unutterably weary when students tell me how essential it is for them to graduate in three years, outlining for me the program by which they must do so. It always involves summer school, of course, and various other strategies by which the process can be speeded up. The point is that the process of acquiring an education cannot in reality be speeded up, except in a very limited way. Any education worthy of the name must include the leisure so essential to thought and reflection, to the development of our understanding, to the slow and painstaking synthesis which we must all make for ourselves.

Another obstacle to our maintaining a real community is the number of our students who work ten, twenty, forty hours a week at off-campus jobs. While this may often be a matter of simple economic necessity, it nevertheless militates against the kind of community life that one ought to experience in one's college years. But often it is not really a matter of economic necessity at all; it is a matter of boredom, or misdirected energy, or the indulgence in some luxury that the student could not otherwise afford. I suspect that more students are working to support their automobiles than are working to support themselves.

Whatever the argument for working, it is a great pity to divert so much time from study, reading, conversation, and the other activities which are also important parts of the college experience. A college career in which students must spend a large amount of time with an eye on their watch is an impoverished college career. Surely among the important opportunities of college are the associations we form and the friendships we make. In his convocation address at the opening of the fall term in 1959, President Martin admonished the students to spend some time – and even some money – in getting to know their teachers outside the classroom. While both student and teacher may often say things that convey the impression that they are natural antagonists, we both know better. We do have a community of interest and endeavor; we are quite genuine companions in the educational enterprise. It is not true, of course, to say that we come to the task as equals, but we have each our distinctive function.

The teacher's function is nothing less than to make education come alive, to show it to be vital, relevant, indispensable. In *The Aims of Education*, Alfred North Whitehead has written:

> The justification for a university is that it preserves the connection between knowledge and the zest of life, by uniting the young and the old in the imaginative consideration of learning. The university imparts information, but it imparts it imaginatively. At least, this is the function which it should perform for our society. A university which fails in this respect has no reason for existence. This atmosphere of excitement, arising from imaginative consideration, transforms knowledge. A fact is no longer a bare fact: it is invested with all its possibilities. It is no longer a burden on the memory: it is energizing as the poet of our dreams, and as the architect of our purposes.

And from a later section of the same book, one more sentence: "The whole point of a university, on its educational side, is to bring the young under the intellectual influence of a band of imaginative scholars."

To make the point more effectively than Whitehead makes it in these two passages would be difficult work indeed. Another writer has suggested that the essence of the educational process is the impact of personality upon personality, a statement which helps to illuminate Whitehead's meaning. The understanding and enthusiasm of someone else adds immeasurably to our own perception and appreciation; and it is this function which the teacher performs. I still remember a crude illustration of this point from my own high school days. Probably without ever having thought about it, I assumed that once the trees lose their leaves in the autumn, they were hardly worth looking at again until the leaves came back in the spring. Then once on a mountain hike in the dead of winter, a teacher said, "Nothing is more beautiful than a bare tree against the sky." All of us can multiply examples, simple or complex. I never encountered a flesh-and-blood human being in the Old Testament until I studied it under a scholar for whom Isaiah might well have been a next-door neighbor. And when I studied the American novel under Arthur Mizener, I felt that I had seldom before read a novel with any understanding or appreciation. I hope the time will never come when this university becomes so large that we lose the sense of immediacy, of companionship between student and teacher.

Almost inadvertently, I have begun to sound again as though the only thing of any value in the college community is your course work. I am far from holding such a view, though I should hope that genuinely educational aims would underlie all you do here, whether curricular or extra-curricular. But there are a great number of activities which lie outside your course work that can immeasurably enrich your development as a student and as a human being. I can even speak charitably of the bridge table and the television room in the Student Center if you will remember the bookstore, which maintains a first-rate collection of paperbacks. I can take vicarious pleasure in your Greek-letter loyalties, in your athletic and social activities, if you will also remember the library, the art gallery, the University players, the musical concert, the lectures. Standards of excellence are relevant not simply in the classroom but everywhere in the community of scholars. I learned as much about those standards in the University players and on the staff of the *Echo* as I learned in most classes; there is no place in college life for the shoddy and second-rate in any field of endeavor.

I would hope that in four years you would become so accustomed to the first-rate, so imbued with the "habitual vision of greatness" that you will never in your life be satisfied with less. I would hope that you would come so much to love good books, good conversation, good friends, good deeds, that nothing will diminish your commitment or lessen your enthusiasm. "The life so short, the craft so long to learn." I would hope that your minds and spirits would be so touched with imaginative fire that you would happily acknowledge that these years are only the beginning of your education, that your search for knowledge and truth and beauty would be, quite literally, the task of a lifetime.

November 1964

Decision and Farewell
Commencement Address, 1980, UTC

Vice President Prados, Chancellor Drinnon, University colleagues, members of the graduating class, ladies and gentlemen: Though I am the veteran of many commencements, I am cast today in a quite unfamiliar role. I begin by expressing my thanks to Chancellor Drinnon for his invitation to deliver this commencement address, an invitation I hope he will have no cause to regret. The occasion is made for me, and for all of us, more poignant by the fact that it is Chancellor Drinnon's final UTC commencement. I want therefore to take this opportunity, as one member of the faculty, to thank the Chancellor for the leadership he has provided and for the progress the University has made under that leadership.

And because it is in ceremonies like this that the University community perhaps best knows itself, I take note also of the death yesterday of Professor Isobel Griscom. Miss Griscom retired from the English Department in 1963 after forty-

99th Commencement at UTC, December 18, 1980.
Left to right: Dr. John W. Prados, Vice President for Academic Affairs;
Maria Cocke Mitchell, Graduate with the highest GPA;
Dr. James Drinnon, Chancellor; and GC, the speaker.

13

one years of service to the University. She had a long and rich life and I do not mourn her, but I mourn for those faculty members who never knew her as a colleague, and I mourn for those students who never knew the excitement of her classroom.

A commencement address under any circumstances is a difficult assignment; it is made more so when the university is one's own. I have a distressingly clear memory of sitting many times where my faculty colleagues are sitting today and listening to their comments, often delivered through clenched teeth, comments not always marked by the warm sympathy and charity which are otherwise so characteristic of our profession. But the chief reason for the difficulty of the assignment is that there is not a single audience but at least three audiences. In addition to one's university colleagues, there are the graduates, and there are their families and friends who have come, in pride and pleasure, to see their degrees conferred upon them. I have chosen to solve this problem of multiple audiences by the simple expedient of addressing myself primarily to those who are graduating this morning. This commencement is, after all, their occasion, and the rest of us are here because of the way in which we relate ourselves to them – as their families, their friends, their teachers and administrators.

For almost ten years now, we have held here at UTC an annual ritual called student evaluation of faculty and courses. To discuss here the strengths and weaknesses of this procedure would be a thankless and graceless task. I mention the subject only to say that sometimes in conversation among faculty members, some of us have speculated about what might be the results of these evaluations if they were done not during a course, not even during the student's enrollment, but five years, or ten years, or twenty years later. One result might well be that the former student could no longer remember the teacher, or the course, or a single thing he or she had learned. Such a condition itself would be a clear evaluation. But what of those courses and teachers the student did remember? Would the student's judgment not be far sounder twenty years after the fact? Would he or she not be far better able to sort out the trivial from the significant, the transient from the enduring, the flashy from the solid? I believe that student would; I believe his or her judgment would be far more reasoned and therefore far more reliable. Lest you think I am mounting an argument for discontinuing the student evaluations and substituting something many years hence, let me make clear that I think the evaluations are here to stay. I say this with no regret, even if one of my own students last year did write complainingly on the form, "He acts like he's teaching a college class or something."

But I *am* saying that these evaluations during the course and during your

University enrollment are less significant than similar judgments which might be made a number of years later. I will go further. I believe that the quality of your life – say in the year 2000, twenty years from now, when most of you will be in early middle age – I believe the quality of your life will be the surest measure of the success of your University career, and the quality of that life will be a judgment both of you and of us.

I trust that nothing you have experienced in your University days, nobody with whom you have had to deal, has given you the notion that when a few minutes from now you walk across this platform, diploma in hand, your education will be complete. Surely you have discovered by now the simplest and deepest truth about education: it is never complete. There is never a time in this fleeting life when you will be able to say, I know all I want to know, I understand all I want to understand. A few weeks ago, one of my brightest and ablest students, a young man who looks forward to graduation in May, told me that he has recently realized that there are regrettable gaps in his knowledge. I congratulated him on this important discovery and assured him that the time will never come when he will see no such gaps. In one of Tennyson's best-known poems, Ulysses says:

> I am a part of all that I have met;
> Yet all experience is an arch wherethrough
> Gleams that untraveled world, whose margin fades
> For ever and for ever when I move.

This is the essential point: the margin does forever fade, and each new discovery not only diminishes our ignorance but also gives us a glimpse of new areas yet to be conquered. It is our human lot, thank God, never to be satisfied with what we know, never content to say, my education is now complete.

Nobody has understood these conditions of human life better than the poets. W. H. Auden reminds us that we reach those crossroads in our lives which he calls "places of decision and farewell," and this commencement is such a time, a break with what has gone before, a turning point, a moment for celebration. But what you who are graduating properly celebrate is not the completion of your journey but your arrival at one of the resting places that mark our progress. The main point is brilliantly dealt with in Richard Wilbur's poem "Year's End"; in that poem Wilbur uses the coming of the new year to make some observations on our wish always to have more time to complete the task of shaping our lives. He contrasts our human lot with the things in nature that can use almost unlimited time to become what they finally are. For example:

There was perfection in the death of ferns
Which laid their fragile cheeks against the stone
A million years.

After the last example of what can happen in the natural world, Wilbur contrasts our human longing:

And at Pompeii

The little dog lay curled and did not rise
But slept the deeper as the ashes rose
And found the people incomplete, and froze
The random hands, the loose unready eyes
Of men expecting yet another sun
To do the shapely thing they had not done.

These sudden ends of time must give us pause.
We fray into the future rarely wrought
Save in the tapestries of afterthought.
More time, more time. Barrages of applause
Come muffled from a buried radio.
The New-year bells are wrangling with the snow.

One hundred and twenty-eight meager hours, or whatever number of hours you may have accumulated, are never enough. "More time, more time" is the human cry out of the human longing to think of ourselves as civilized, to consider ourselves in some sense educated. If at this stage of your life you are dismayed to think how little you actually know, you can also be heartened to realize that you have the rest of your lives to complete the task of your education. It is for this reason that I suggested earlier that an evaluation twenty years from now may tell you and us something far more valid about your University experience than any current evaluation could have told us. Twenty years from now there will be with respect to your education two crucial questions to ask yourself: First, how well did your University experience awaken in you a passion for learning? Secondly, how well did it teach you how to go on educating yourself for the rest of your life? By these two questions your college experience deserves most to be judged.

At this moment, so recently having completed graduation requirements, you may still be reacting too vividly to term papers and final examinations to open your mind to your own educational future. But in a few days or a few weeks, these academic chores will have faded from your immediate consciousness, and it is then that you must take thought about what comes next. I hope you will discover then that your relationship with the University of Tennessee at Chattanooga is not forever terminated but that it has simply entered a new condition. You go out from here today as alumni of the University, a fact that carries far more significance than you may now imagine. Many years ago at a national conference on adult education, I heard a speaker say that Iowa has a higher literacy rate than any other state in the union. "But," he said, "if the records in the registrar's office of the state university should be destroyed, a lot of illiterate people would be walking around in Iowa." I hope you will have better proof of your own literacy than the record of hours you have earned, the diploma you are about to receive.

I hope you will establish and validate your own literacy by a continual participation in the University's life. And let me make clear that I am talking about far more than your attendance at athletic events or specifically alumni gatherings. These things certainly have their place, but they are by no means the heart of your experience as alumni of the University. I remind you of the library, the art gallery, the concerts and plays and lectures – and indeed the regular courses – which will be open and available to you.

Moreover, under the aegis of Continuing Education there will be an increasing number of attractive educational opportunities in which you can participate; liberated from any worry about examinations or credits, you can indulge yourself in the pure pursuit of learning for its own sake.

A second measure of the quality of your life will be the soundness of the judgments you are able to make with respect to the moral, social, and political issues that confront us. Will you think your own independent and tough-minded way through these questions, or will you give yourself over to the ever-willing opinion-makers who will be only too eager to furnish a ready-made judgment for your individual use? One of the most depressing features of the press is the publication of best-seller lists as a not-so-subtle recommendation of what ought to be read; such lists are filled with the titles of books not worth the paper they are printed on. I hope your education has given you some ability to recognize a sound book when you see one; there is certainly no shortage of forces seeking to thrust upon you the second- or the tenth-rate.

A few weeks ago the *New Yorker* ran a chilling series of articles on what is happening in the publishing industry (the very use of the word *industry* is surely ironic); the series was the most melancholy thing I have read in the *New Yorker* since John Hersey's account of the destruction of Hiroshima was published in 1946. The articles detailed the increasing tie-ins with movie production and television promotion and paperback rights; there is an increasing use of procedures which militate against quality and work to the benefit of glittering trash. Promoters can calculate almost to perfection how much an author's appearance on a television talk show will increase the sale of any given book, or non-book, whatever its quality.

The damage from television talk shows unhappily does not end there. I suspect an impressive case could be made for the contention that the hosts of the television talk shows, and probably a good many of their guests, are among the most persuasive shapers of opinion in our society. Most of these persons, to put the matter as charitably as possible, are moral and intellectual lightweights, by no means fitted for the role in which circumstance seems to have cast them. Their revealed wisdom apparently derives from anecdote and statistic, rarely from careful thought or deep principle. The result is a moral world in which chaos waits just beneath the surface.

We are now living in a time – I hope we shall somehow survive it – in which almost total emphasis is placed on the individual and his or her pursuit of whatever happens to attract that person. "What's in it for me?" is an almost universal question, "doing one's own thing" a widely practiced art. This absorption in self to the almost complete neglect of common concerns and common values seems depressingly characteristic of our time. Set against this hedonistic preoccupation is the saying from Heraclitus that T. S. Eliot used as an epigraph for the first of the *Four Quartets*: "Although the Word [Word is capitalized, the *Logos*] is common to all, most men live as if they had each a private wisdom of their own." Or in a paraphrase suggested by one of Eliot's commentators: "Though the law of things is universal in scope, the average man makes up the rules for himself." One result of making up the rules for ourselves is that we often denigrate the truly valuable and give our deepest admiration to the meretricious.

One distinguished theologian has suggested that modern society resembles a shop window where some mad man has exchanged all the price tags, making cheap things very expensive and the expensive things very cheap. This mad man has been greatly abetted by the television talk show, the shoddy book, and the sloppy thinker. In Auden's poem "The Shield of Achilles," he pictures dramatically some of the least attractive features of our civilization. In a clear reference to the political oppression which uses a stark militarism as its instrument, he writes:

> Out of the air a voice without a face
> > Proved by statistics that some cause was just
> In tones as dry and level as the place:

No one was cheered and nothing was discussed;
Column by column in a cloud of dust
They marched away enduring a belief
Whose logic brought them, somewhere else, to grief.

I beg you to remember that no cause can be proved by statistics to be just. I hope you will confirm the worth of your college experience by refusing to be intimidated by mere numbers. Sexual promiscuity, for example, remains exactly that no matter how many statistical surveys there are, or how many magazines make promiscuity into what they are pleased to call their philosophy. (James Thurber once in a quite different context observed that the word *philosophy* is surely capable of higher flights than that!) Cheating on income tax for another example, remains exactly that, whatever the numbers involved and whatever rationalizations people are able to create. I hope your education has taught you to call a spade a spade and that you will continue to call it that no matter what pretentious disguises others may employ.

A third way in which the quality of your life can be measured is by your reaction to the malaise of gloom and pessimism which seems increasingly to characterize our common life. No great talent is required to produce a list of formidable problems which weigh heavily upon us: the problem of arms control, of energy, of population growth, to mention only three universal concerns. But sometimes we give such exclusive attention to these and other problems that we seem unaware that they have been balanced by enormous achievements. To a recent issue of *The American Scholar*, the historian Barbara Tuchman contributes an interesting essay titled "Mankind's Better Moments," from which I quote an early passage: "Amid a mass of worldwide troubles and a poor record for the twentieth century, we see our species – with cause – as functioning very badly, as blunderers when not knaves, as violent, ignoble, corrupt, inept, incapable of mastering the forces that threaten us, weakly subject to our worst instincts: in short, decadent."

"The catalogue is familiar and valid," Mrs. Tuchman goes on to say, "but it is growing tiresome. A study of history reminds one that mankind has its ups and downs and during the ups has accomplished many brave and beautiful things, exerted stupendous endeavors, explored and conquered oceans and wilderness, achieved marvels of beauty in the creative arts and marvels of science and social progress; has loved liberty with a passion that throughout history has led men to fight and die for it over and over again; has pursued knowledge, exercised reason, enjoyed laughter and pleasures, played games with zest, shown courage, heroism, altruism, honor, and decency; experienced love; known comfort, contentment, and occasionally happiness. All those qualities have been part of human experience, and if they have not had as important notice as the negatives nor exerted as wide and persistent an influence as the evils we do, they nevertheless deserve attention, for they are currently all but forgotten."

Mrs. Tuchman goes on to catalogue instances of ingenuity, imagination, skill, and courage, reminding us in a variety of examples how splendid human achievement, individual and corporate, has sometimes been. Surely such a reminder from this distinguished historian helps to restore the balance in our thinking, to remind us that enormous difficulties are not new in human experience. Surely a society which has placed men on the moon and brought them safely back to earth again is capable of solving the energy problem.

But only an incurable optimist can forget that our lives are beset with troubles. Given the kind of uncertain and often oppressive world we are living in, what is the role of the individual, how can the individual properly react to the forces one finds arrayed against us all? I knew a college chaplain once who liked to preach from a text in the eleventh Psalm: "If the foundations be destroyed, what can the righteous do?" His thunderous answer was invariable: "They can go right on being righteous!" And indeed what other answer is there? When we are confronted with difficulty or peril, or tragedy, what can we do except exert our very best effort to deal with these things, and as far as we may be able, to conquer them? How you respond to these vicissitudes of life is surely one of the most important tests of your education.

I offer you as a model an obscure Englishman who is memorialized in a church near London. A plaque in the church proclaims his significance:

> In the year 1653, when all things sacred in the kingdom
> Were either profaned or demolished,
> This Church was built by Sir Robert Shirley, Baronet,
> Whose singular praise it was
> To do the best things in the worst times
> And hope them in the most calamitous.

A few weeks ago the first University play of the year, Thornton Wilder's *Our Town*, was presented in the Dorothy Hackett Ward Theatre by a superbly talented cast. In a moment of great poignancy late in the play, Emily, the young heroine, says to the Stage Manager, "Do any human beings ever realize life while they live it? – every, every minute?" "No," he replies. "The saints and poets, maybe; they do some." On this commencement day, this momentary pause on your way to fuller education, this high holy day of the spirit, I suggest to you that we are all of us called to be saints and poets, called to confront the world we live in with the best intelligence and the highest courage of which we are capable, called to do the best things in the worst times and to hope them in the most calamitous. For that high venture, I bid you Godspeed.

December 18, 1980

Education for Freedom*

A Six-Year Report (1952 – 1958) for the Adult Education Council
of the Chattanooga Area

"The years teach much which the days never know."
– Ralph Waldo Emerson, "Experience"

Introduction

I offer in this report an interpretive account of our efforts in Chattanooga to build a vital and enduring organization committed to a program of liberal education for adults. I was present at the first public meeting called in connection with the project, and since my appointment in March 1952 as the Adult Education Council's executive director, I have been deeply and continually involved in its work. An astonishingly great number of documents have been at my disposal. But human behavior has a way of defying and outrunning the records, which tell little of the atmosphere, the feelings, the enthusiasm, the frustration of the endeavor.

I have tried neither to magnify success nor to camouflage failure. I have talked with many persons who have played important roles in the Council's development and whose comments and criticisms often showed me a clearer perspective. I hope that my use of personal pronouns will not strike the reader as graceless. In part, this is a matter of style and taste; I myself have grown thoroughly weary of reading documents which sound like the products of disembodied ora-

---

*Editor's note: In an effort to make this seventy-three-page report friendlier to a general audience, I have edited and cut some of it. I include the document, abridged as it is, because it describes so well not only a major effort to enrich the intellectual and cultural life of the Chattanooga community but also GC's fundamental philosophy of administration, learning, and teaching.

cles. But perhaps more often I have used "we" to indicate that every achievement (and alas, every failure) has been the result of the effort of many people. After describing the necessary background information, I have chosen to discuss separately four aspects of the Council's work: organization, program, participation, and finance.* I hope this report makes clear that all of these elements are deeply interrelated.

If circumstances force us to concede that the necessary money cannot be found, and the Council ceases to exist, much will be lost to this community. But not everything. The loyalty and cooperation of so many people, the significance and validity of the program which they have made possible, will not fail to have their influence. If our program has touched and helped to illuminate vital, enduring human issues, we must be content with whatever the future holds.**

Background

Adult education in Chattanooga did not begin with the emergence of the Adult Education Council. An important human enterprise, no matter how widespread or all-embracing it becomes, can almost always be traced to the interest and devotion of a single individual or to a small group of individuals. In the late forties, the League of Women Voters committee on adult education, under the chairmanship of Mrs. W. B. Richardson, who had been long interested in the field, conducted a selective survey of adult education opportunities available in Chattanooga through established organizations. The survey sought to discover what subject areas were being covered, what was needed which was not being provided, and how the community program generally could be strengthened.

Perhaps the most valuable thing the survey did was to inspire thought and concern about the educational opportunities open to the adult citizens of Chattanooga. Certainly it helped to develop an interest in adult education among the members of the League. In May 1951, more than a year after the survey report was issued, Mrs. Richardson and others attended a League convention in Knoxville, where they met Miss Anna Lord Strauss, who was on the board of directors of the Fund for Adult Education, a corporation newly established by the Ford Foundation. Recognizing a propitious opportunity, Mrs. Richardson told Miss Strauss about the Chattanooga League's hope that a sound community adult education program could be developed. Would the Fund for Adult Education be

---

*Editor's note: The section on finances has been omitted in this abridged version.
**Editor's note: For a view of the future of the Adult Education Council, see GC's later address in 1985, "What Is It That Makes a City Great," pages 282-286.

interested? Miss Strauss suggested an inquiry and in July 1951, Chattanooga was selected as one of the participants in the Fund's Test Cities project.

At least two universal propositions about an adult educational program do not alter from one city to another: as a unique human being, every person has both the right and the responsibility to develop to the fullest possible capacity, and because every American citizen has the right to cast a free ballot, each has the responsibility for making the wisest choices of which he or she is capable. The validity of these principles is not affected by the place of residence, the economic status, or the educational background of the individual American citizen.

While these factors do not alter the principles on which a program is built, they obviously do have direct relevance to questions of organization and strategy. An appropriate plan for translating principle into program in one city may be wholly or largely unworkable in another. What we have learned in six years of work in Chattanooga, therefore, must be understood against the background of the kind of city Chattanooga is.

Chattanooga

In December 1839, Chattanooga was incorporated under its present name, only one of the many place names in Tennessee which continually remind us that this was Indian territory. While there are several theories about the meaning of "Chattanooga," the authors of a recent history of the city identify the word as a phonetic rendering of a Creek phrase which means "rock that comes to a point," a reference to Lookout Mountain.*

Chattanooga, ca. 1965. The Tennessee River and the three Bridges, Walnut Street, Market Street (Chief John Ross Bridge), and Olgiati with Lookout Mountain in the background. Photograph courtesy of Chattanooga-Hamilton County Bicentennial Library, the Paul A. Heiner Collection.

*G. E. Govan and J. W. Livingood, *The Chattanooga Country*, New York: E .P. Dutton and Co., 1952.

By the time of the Civil War, Chattanooga was a small but important rail junction community, and the area became one of the war's notable battlegrounds. Following the war, ex-Confederates and ex-Federals joined together to develop and build a city. A pro-Union sympathy that existed here before and during the war explains at least in part the fact that Chattanooga is not as obviously Southern as, for example, Nashville or Atlanta. While there was great hardship during the period of reconstruction, Chattanooga was spared the harshness of military occupation and its divisive consequences. One historian has observed that the vicissitudes of the reconstruction period account in large part for the lack of a firm educational tradition in the area.

Chattanooga lies in the extreme southeastern corner of Tennessee. With mountains to the south and west, with Missionary Ridge to the east, and with the Tennessee River winding through the town, there is a natural beauty perhaps equaled in few American cities. Within the corporate limits, the population is approximately 142,000 and in the metropolitan area perhaps 250,000. The trade area is made up of 34 counties located in Tennessee, Georgia, and Alabama. One experienced organizational worker has referred to Chattanooga as a city of 'manageable size,' and the phrase is apt. The city is large enough to support a variety of activities but not so large as to hinder the success of an educational program – communication can be carried on in many informal ways and need not depend upon the elaborate mechanisms of large metropolitan centers.

According to the census of 1950, only about 1,100 foreign-born persons were living in the city. Negroes comprise approximately 30 percent of the population and very few live in the metropolitan area outside the city limits. With the single exception of Birmingham, Chattanooga is the most heavily industrialized city in the southeast. According to a research report of the Chattanooga-Hamilton County Metropolitan Planning Commission, the manufacturing payroll accounts for virtually half of the total metropolitan area payroll.

A variety of competent observers have noted that Chattanooga has a small middle class. Perhaps the two most widely used criteria for determining who belongs to the middle class are economic and educational status. According to the 1950 census, the educational level completed by persons 25 or older in the metropolitan area is an average of 8.7 years. Approximately 53 percent of the adult population have only a grade school education or less. Eleven percent have one or more years of college (as against thirteen percent in the country); only five percent graduated from college.

Despite these limitations and shortcomings, there is considerable vitality in the cultural and intellectual life of the community. In *The Chattanooga Times*, the city has a distinguished newspaper, a claim that can be matched by few American cities. Adolph S. Ochs and his heirs have owned this newspaper since 1878, almost twenty years before Mr. Ochs went on to buy *The New York Times*. The close relationship which still obtains between the two newspapers has been a great benefit to Chattanooga. The University of Chattanooga, a privately endowed liberal arts college founded in 1886, has been another important influence. In addition to the two public school systems, two independent schools for boys and one for girls are located here; parochial schools and church-related colleges in Chattanooga and the area have also made their contributions. The library, the opera association, the symphony, the Hunter Art Gallery, and numerous other institutions and organizations provide some measurement of the considerable interest in cultural affairs.

Chattanooga is a city of contradiction. The visitor is bound to be impressed both by the great beauty of the city's natural setting and the relatively little effort to build a city which will take advantage of that beauty or be worthy of it. In approaches to the city, for example, one can choose between highways which move through industrial and slum areas, or through unsightly, neon-lighted strip developments. Mayor P. R. Olgiati, the incumbent at City Hall, has often said that Chattanooga now has the best plan for its development it has ever had because it is the only such plan it has ever had. Certainly there is a new vitality discernible in our affairs; an ambitious urban renewal project, railway relocation, and the expressway system are all parts of the effort to develop Chattanooga into the city it can become.

Organization

Under the chairmanship of Miss Elizabeth Edwards, Librarian, the planning committee was comprised of representatives of the thirteen organizations which sponsored the public meeting of November 6, 1951, plus representatives from the Jewish Community Center, McKenzie College, and *The Chattanooga Times*. Information and advice were solicited from cities like Denver and Cincinnati, where adult education councils had been operating since the early thirties; from school systems, public libraries, and chambers of commerce; from the Adult Education Association of the USA; and from any other source which the committee felt to be promising. But no member of the committee expected to find anywhere else in the country the ready-made solutions to Chattanooga's problems.

Surely it is fair to begin with the question, "What purpose is the organization to fulfill?" With this question in mind, on January 8, 1952, the constitution of the Adult Education Council of the Chattanooga Area listed eight purposes for which the Council was formed:

1. To organize a representative group of citizens who can interpret and express the needs and interests of the people of the Chattanooga area in respect to adult education.

2. To promote the idea that education is a lifelong activity.

3. To serve as a clearinghouse for ideas and information in the various fields of adult education through the collection and dissemination of pertinent information, through discussion, and through other means.

4. To assist adult education activities already in operation and when existing agencies are unable to meet specific needs of the area, to seek to call into existence new agencies to meet these needs.

5. To conduct educational activities which are of such nature that they can best be handled as cooperative enterprises, initiated and sponsored by member agencies through the Council. The Council shall be slow to take over the direct management of community services and shall do so only when such a course is clearly to the advantage of the community and approved by a majority of the member agencies.

6. To aid, assist, and advise individuals who desire to continue learning.

7. To exchange experience, ideas and research findings with other communities and adult education councils.

8. To do all things which shall be necessary and proper for executing the foregoing purposes.

The basic question the newly formed Council faced was how to achieve a significant role in the educational life of the community. Should the Council be chiefly a *coordinating* agency or an *operating* agency? It seems to me fair and accurate to say it was intended to be both. But an important problem remained to be solved: what kind of coordination? Taken on the simplest possible level, *coordination* consists perhaps of no more than a calendar listing of events to avoid an overcrowded community schedule. A higher level is the joint efforts of many groups to provide leadership training, or to procure information, or to carry out some other common objective. A still higher level of coordination is the systematic attempt to achieve a coherent pattern in the community program of adult education so that gaps may be filled and duplication avoided. This coordination is largely a matter of keeping organizations informed about each other and providing the mechanism for an exchange of information. Given the size of Chattanooga, it is not difficult for one organization to know what another is doing. Moreover, there is not much evidence to suggest that duplication of services or programs has ever been a serious problem in this community.

A tension has existed from the beginning between the Council's coordinating and operating functions, perhaps a valuable corrective. Certainly our coordinating function has kept us from competing with other organizations and from planning programs without full regard for what other groups are doing. Out of this tension has come an operating principle based on a concept of creative coordination, which is admirably suited to this community.

Affiliation

In each participating community, the Test Cities project would be vested in an institution or organization already established, called a "sponsoring agency." The agency would house the project, furnish equipment and supplies, and undertake to find the necessary local funds for the second and third years. The Chattanooga Public Library made the first approach to the Fund; in Miss Edwards, the library had a person of great energy and dedication who spent considerable time and effort on the organization of the Council. It was natural that the library should come to be regarded as the most appropriate sponsoring agency in Chattanooga. To be identified with the library's work undoubtedly conferred a status on the Council which it could not have achieved independently for many years. Moreover, the library's facilities were open to all citizens, another fact of considerable consequence. But if the Council derived prestige and strength from its relationship with the library, as it certainly did, it also proved difficult to establish in the public mind that a new and separate organization with distinctive functions had come into existence.

In the fall of 1953, the approximate mid-point of the three-year test period, the Council had reached a position in its development when larger and more suitable quarters seemed desirable. In view of the need to raise money, we felt that the Council should be more visible, and it was chartered by the State of Tennessee as a non-profit, public welfare corporation. The agreement between the Council and the library was dissolved by mutual consent and with the Fund's concurrence. On February 17, 1954, the Council moved to its new center at 865 McCallie Avenue.

Membership

From the earliest movement to establish the Council in Chattanooga, the conviction was firmly and widely held that the largest possible number of persons should be encouraged to participate in its administration and its program. This feeling underlay the arrangements for the first public meeting, the appointment of the planning committee, and the provisions made in the constitution for Council membership.

By specifying that a representative's vote did not bind his or her organization, the planning committee went a step further in seeking to assure organizations that the Council was a voluntary and cooperative enterprise that offered not the slightest threat to their autonomy. While this provision clearly weakens the Council's ability and authority to act in the name of its member organizations, it helps to guarantee that the Council does not become a battleground for the competing purposes and views of all its member agencies. The Council has been extremely fortunate in this regard.

The problem, I think, is that the membership provisions do not define membership sharply enough to give it any real meaning. What rights and duties does membership involve? It is specified, for example,

GC, front right, and the Adult Education Council at a board meeting in Chattanooga, ca. 1955.
Photograph by Oscar and Associates, Chicago.

that the Council is to meet five times a year and that "the Council must approve all new policies and new undertakings." But these hardly add up to a clear definition of membership. The meaning of individual membership is even vaguer. The only qualification required of an individual member was an interest in adult education; the vote of a single person in the Council was of the same weight as the vote of a person representing an organization of several hundred.

At the end of its first year of operation, the Council had 75 organizational and perhaps 350 individual members. The Council began with the feeling that we should have as large a membership roll as possible; recruitment was done on that basis and, I am afraid, without very much thought about how this large membership would function. Perhaps we confused a desire for wide participation with a desire for large membership. To establish and maintain lines of communication with 75 organizations is a very demanding job indeed.

I suggest the Council needs certain reforms. The adult education organization in a community (at least in this community) should be an association, not a Council. The association could have both organizational and individual members, but organizational members should probably be confined to those organizations doing public programming rather than programming only for their own membership. This would mean the inclusion of library, college, community center, YMCA, YWCA, et al., but not of the civic club and the social agency. I do not intend to suggest a policy of exclusion. There are certain practical questions that would not be difficult to apply. Is the organization maintained for wide community benefit, in its program and other activities? Is the organization capable of significant interest in education?

Board of Directors

To provide the necessary leadership for an adult education program, any one of three basic approaches is possible. A great many programs – especially those maintained by public school systems or institutions of higher learning – are staffed almost entirely by paid professional workers. At the other extreme, many programs may be the work entirely of volunteers. The third method of course is to use a combination of volunteer workers and professional staff, and it is this approach to which the Adult Education Council of Chattanooga is committed.

If such a program is wholly a staff matter, if lay people are involved only in a vague and general advisory capacity, the program easily loses touch with the community of which it is meant to be a part. This seems especially likely where a budget is underwritten by a sponsoring institution; onerous as fund-raising can be, it is still one of the useful means of discovering whether an organization is in vital touch with the community. At the other end of the scale, if the program is wholly the work of volunteers, it runs the obvious risk of lacking continuity and consistency, of dissipating its efforts through lack of leadership. I suggest that a program which is the joint responsibility of professional staff and lay citizens is a far more promising enterprise.

From the beginning of my term of office, there was in Chattanooga an interested and concerned group of citizens with whom I worked, to whom I was responsible, and in whose name I was able to speak. The constitution provided for a board of 16 persons (a reasonable number for a city of this size), one of whom was the official representative of the Chattanooga Public Library so long as there was an affiliation between the Council and the library. The other fifteen directors were chosen at large; they were not required to be organizational representatives of any sort. Their terms were fixed at three years and, having served a full term, they were ineligible to succeed themselves. The board was responsible for electing its officers from its own membership.

Board membership has largely been made up of persons in the second rather than the first rank of community leadership. To use the sociological term, very few board members have been chosen from the power structure in the community. This fact is especially notable in the small number of those in business who served in the first two or three years. I do not suggest that everyone in the business community is automatically a part of the power structure; I do suggest that in a heavily industrial community, a private agency should have on its board a good representation of those in business. I do not offer those comments as criticism of the original nominating committee's work. The most desirable board member is one whose very presence on the board will give it prestige and authority in the community but one who also accepts an active role in the management of the organization, and whose sympathetic interest and understanding would insure their vigorous efforts on behalf of the new organization.

It is not difficult to find examples of community organizations that have deteriorated over a long period of time because of continual service by a few persons. It is only too easy for a board member of long, uninterrupted service to grow weary of his or her assignment and to put little thought or energy into it. For this reason the principle of rotating this membership is unquestionably sound as the means of getting fresh views and new abilities; it should not become the means of excluding all those who have ever served from serving again.

Professional Staff

One of the important tasks to which the original board immediately addressed itself was the appointment of the executive director. After long and presumably careful consideration, the board chose me to be the executive director and I assumed these duties on April 15, 1952. For several years prior to my appointment, I was employed by the Chattanooga Public Schools, most recently as a teacher of English and speech at Chattanooga High School. I had a deep interest in adult education and a strong conviction of its necessity, but I was wholly without professional knowledge or training in the field. Any hesitation or misgiving which the board felt in making its appointment, the past six years have taught me to regard with understanding and sympathy.

What is required of an executive officer, I think, is the ability to achieve a genuine working relationship with the board, a relationship in which one neither wastes the board's time with trivia nor in which one takes the board for granted. The natural tendency of organizations, it has been widely remarked, is to widen function, raise the budget, and increase staff. This tendency towards empire-building is difficult to resist, and it is perhaps especially so for a new organization which must demonstrate its worth as quickly as possible or perish. But a budget which covers the salaries only of an executive director and a secretary is a healthy corrective; it is quite difficult to build an empire out of this material. But in the face of this, I must record my own conviction that one of our problems has invariably been a shortage of staff.

Committee Structure

As Council procedure has become more firmly established, there has been increasingly less need for a great variety of committees. Often they have been created when we faced new problems of administration or new areas of operation and discontinued when the problem was resolved or an adequate policy established. A major portion of the Council's activities has been carried by committees – administrative, program, and special committees.

The most vital work of the organization has been the work of the program area committee. More than two months before I assumed my duties, the board established two program committees, "world affairs" and "family life." Mrs. W. B. Richardson chaired the world affairs committee and Professor Haskell Miller, then head of the University of Chattanooga's sociology department, chaired the family life committee.

Three other program area committees were established within the next few months: public affairs, economics, and humanities. Though similar in many ways, I do not wish to suggest that these committees have developed with equal vigor or have managed comparable achievements; there has been considerable unevenness. The economics committee, for example, has never advanced beyond the paper stage.

As I look back after several years to this period of the Council's development, I have two major regrets. The first is that I should have found myself in such deep disagreement with persons who contributed so vitally to the organization and for whom I had and still have the warmest regard. But it is wise to remember that human beings usually disagree sharply only over questions which concern them deeply; the disagreement itself in this matter was evidence of commitment. The second regret is that after the FPA grant was expended and Mrs. James A. Bryan Jr.'s term was over, the Council was unable to provide the committee with programming funds or with staff help. This was entirely a matter of money. In the comparatively carefree days of 1953 (the reader will kindly note the adverb) we had hoped and believed that we could raise sufficient funds to divert a significant amount of money to the world affairs committee. But having done our first general community fund-raising campaign in the spring of 1954, we were obliged to be much more realistic in our expectations.

The briefing of committees seems to me often neglected in organizational enterprises. We have always tried in our work to provide a committee with the necessary information which will permit the understanding of its role and the effective performance of its duty. A committee ought not to have to guess what its function is; even though it is most probably required largely to chart its own course, it should be given some framework of policy and procedure in which it is expected to operate. That so many men and women have demonstrated their dedication and commitment by their work as members of the board of directors or of various committees must be counted among the Council's most solid achievements. There is finally only one question worth asking: What is the result of this work in terms of the Council's program? The machinery, however simple or complex, has no lasting significance unless it makes possible a vital and imaginative program.

Programs

The most casual glance at the field of adult education in the United States will reveal an almost incredible variety of activities which can properly be called "adult education." Carried on under enormously diverse institutional auspices, these activities embrace liberal, vocational, remedial, recreational, and many other kinds of education, but some lines of demarcation are absolutely essential.

So far as we are concerned in Chattanooga, our concentration on liberal education is desirable for two reasons: the imperative necessity in a free society for the highest possible level of public understanding and the comparative neglect of programs which might be expected to develop this understanding.

Liberal education can be defined most simply as that kind of education which is appropriate for free men and women, which is indeed essential to their fullest development as human beings and as citizens in a free society. The educational task begins with the recognition that freedom is not something which is once given to us, complete and inviolable, as part of our heritage; it is ours only as we understand, develop, and cherish it. Education is one important means by which this freedom is continually achieved and maintained. Little imagination is required to understand that our freedom is always threatened by the forces of ignorance, prejudice, and parochialism. One is free only in making intelligent choices between the alternatives; one cannot make such choices unless he or she understands the true nature of the alternatives.

Liberal education in its essence, then, is education for freedom, for the wise use of personal and social responsibility, for the fullest understanding of ourselves and the world we live in. But this says more about the aim of an adult education program than it does about its content; there is no simple device by which this aim can be converted into a specific set of activities, a curriculum for adult education. The liberating power of education depends at least as much upon the imaginative skill of the educator as it does upon the subject matter. The study of literature or history is not inevitably liberal, nor the study of cabinet-making merely vocational. Nevertheless, faced with the objective of creating an educational program to enhance human dignity and freedom, an organization has the responsibility to develop the program most likely to produce this result. The special project can excite interest, the discussion group can do much to widen intellectual horizons and discipline the mind, the lecture or the television program can provide information and background. They cannot replace the hard work of private, individual effort.

Four kinds of program offerings make up the nucleus of our work: (1) discussion groups; (2) lectures; (3) institutes, forums, and workshops; and (4) television programming. Everything else has been either a community service of some sort or a special project.

Discussion Groups

Great Books has been by far the most popular discussion program which the Council has sponsored, accounting for 28 groups, ranging from first- to fifth-year programs. Though it tends to be confused in the public mind with other, similar enterprises, it is one of the few programs designed to cover a period of years and with a sequential order carefully built in.

The locally developed programs (except for Introduction to Poetry, which I shall comment on later) were all novel reading programs which made use of the excellent array of paper-bound books which are now so widely available. The first in this series, American Life in the Novel, sought to examine some of the major themes which have absorbed the attention of the American novelist throughout much of our history. The reading list included *Huckleberry Finn*, *The Sun Also Rises*, *The Bear*, *All the King's Men*, and others. The second program offered English and continental novels, and the third a miscellaneous collection. These programs were designed in large measure to undercut the common fallacy that the novel makes no significant commentary on human life.

At least three things, it seems to me, are necessary to a satisfactory discussion group: good materials, competent leadership, and careful preparation by the participant. The discussion group is an educational activity which does not lend itself easily to reliable measurement; it can be a stimulating educational experience, or it can be merely a series of pleasant, aimless discussions, depending largely upon the degree to which these three conditions are present. Many of our groups certainly have been defective in one or more of these three conditions.

Leadership is perhaps the most difficult problem of all in the discussion group. Intellectual ability must combine with such personal qualities as tact and patience as well as a good deal of self-discipline; the number of people, therefore, who make first-rate discussion leaders is not large. It seems to me that no matter how skilled the leader is, he or she must have considerable knowledge of the field the selected program covers. I have heard it argued that the leader need know little about world affairs, or whatever, in order to lead a discussion group in that subject. I regard this view as nonsense; without at least a reasonably good background, how can he or she even know what the relevant questions are?

Lectures

Suitable expressions of regret over the death of the lecture have often been made during the past several years. These expressions, some of which are sincere, seem to me premature. No one can deny that there are problems connected with the lecture, but many of these problems result from change in social habit rather than from the deficiency of the lecture as one educational device.

The Council has managed to use lectures to good effect for several reasons. We have chosen persons whose subjects fitted into our program so that their lectures were not isolated events but closely related to other things we had done and would continue to do. Whenever staff or volunteer personnel have been available, we have tried to arrange workshops covering the general subject of the lecture and held several days before. In every case we have used the utmost precaution to make quite clear that the Council takes no position with regard to the subject matter of any speech, that we simply sponsor the lecture as a part of our public service. Following each lecture there has been a lively discussion, often including sharp cross-examination of the lecturer.

We have not tried, except in rare cases, to make the lectures large and spectacular aspects of our program; we have aimed at the persons with genuine interest in more background and information in world affairs and at those whose concern about a specific crisis can be used to develop a wider interest. Although such programs have had audiences ranging from 40 to 400, an audience of about 100 is typical for most lectures. We think this is a valuable part of our program if only because no other agency brings to Chattanooga anything like this number of persons whose appearances are open to the public.

Institutes, Forums, Workshops

Institutes, forums, and workshops have constituted one of the regular elements of the Council's program. These names are at best imprecise, and the variety among these program elements is quite marked. A program planners' workshop in September 1952 was a Friday evening and Saturday affair, with various kinds of sessions and activities aimed at making clear to the community the Council's role in working with other organizations. Two family living workshops, in 1952 and 1953, consisted of several evening sessions; including both general meetings and discussion groups, these programs concentrated largely on specific areas of family problems. Each concluded with an address by an outstanding figure in family life education.

Another format was used in a workshop called World in Crisis, which the Council and several other organizations co-sponsored in February 1957. Scheduled for late afternoon and evening, this included a dinner speech on the Eisenhower Doctrine, simultaneous meetings of three discussion groups (each using a different kind of material as its point of departure), and a general session to discuss what help local organizations would like from the Council's world affairs committee.

Television

In April, 1954, WDEF-TV went on the air, the first of Chattanooga's television stations. Morris Quave, a participant in numerous Council activities, was appointed program manager for the station. Keenly interested in local programming, Mr. Quave raised the question of the Council's doing a regular television series dealing with community issues. All of these factors influenced the direction of the public affairs committee in making its plans for 1954-55. The committee decided that fall to do a pilot series of four television programs called "Schools in Crisis," dealing with the most pressing needs of the two local public school systems. The purpose of this limited series, of course, was to discover at first hand the problems involved in television programming and to determine whether the Council was able to undertake a regular, long-range series. "Schools in Crisis" was presented bi-weekly in November and December, 1954; the response was deeply reassuring, and the public affairs committee decided to launch a regular program early the next year.

The program was named *Point of View* and was inaugurated on January 30, 1955; except for very brief periods when it has been off the air because of scheduling problems, it has been presented every week since that time. By June 1, 1958, the end of the Council's program year, 161 *Point of View* programs had been presented. It has certainly

GC, moderator of Point of View, *ca. 1957*

become one of the important fixed elements in the Council program and has introduced this organization to a large and miscellaneous audience which it could hardly have reached any other way. Viewer survey figures have seldom fallen much below 30,000.

Point of View has given us wider access to the community than anything else. Most importantly, the program has been a continuing public example of the fair-minded, non-partisan role which the Council plays in Chattanooga. While there have certainly been programs which were not wholly satisfactory, these have invariably been failures of performance rather than of planning or intention. The program's reputation for fairness and responsibility has resulted in a general willingness of governmental, organizational, and civic leaders to appear whenever they are asked. Further testimony to the success of *Point of View* is the fact that both local television stations coming on the air since WDEF-TV have instituted similar programs.

Special Projects

Our special projects, first, were designed to capture community interest and attention. By its very nature education is not an especially glamorous enterprise and efforts to make it seem so are likely to be self-defeating. But the devices which our society has developed for promoting activities of one kind or another are fearful to contemplate; it is hardly possible to be less a hermit than Thoreau and escape the blatant voices which are always competing for our attention.

The success of the special project must finally be judged, I think, in three ways: Has it made an impact on the community? Has it been itself a successful educational experience for those who participated? Has it fitted usefully into the total program pattern by buttressing other Council activities and by stimulating and encouraging people to participate in these activities? In the main, we have been fortunate in the degree to which our special projects have managed to meet these three criteria.

Each of the special projects (United Nations Pageant, Community Leadership Institutes, World Affairs Forum, Town Hall Missions, Conferences on Aging and Education, Our Living Future, and Basic American Issues) shows the Council in its role of providing leadership in what I have called creative coordination. Numerous organizations were involved on all of these projects; without their cooperation, they would not have been possible. In each case the efforts and energies of many groups were joined in common enterprises which none could have managed individually.

United Nations Pageant

Together with the Mayor's Committee for U.N. Day and the University of Chattanooga, the Council through its world affairs committee accepted responsibility for devising an appropriate observance of the anniversary of the United Nations in 1952. Someone who had recently visited the U.N. headquarters and had been deeply impressed by the value of seeing the U.N. at work posed a question: Would it be possible to dramatize the history and function of the U.N. in such a way that its work and value might be clarified for large numbers of people? This innocent question resulted in the writing and production of *There Shall Be Peace*, depicting in drama and music the historic mission of the United Nations. Written by Dr. Edwin S. Lindsey, head of the University of Chattanooga's English department, and produced by Dorothy Hackett Ward, head of the dramatics and speech department, the pageant achieved success beyond our fondest hopes. The cast of *There Shall Be Peace* included several hundred (not counting the goats, donkey, or the dog); another several hundred were involved in production – ranging from a young advertising man who designed the sets, to the carpenters' union that built the flag stands. More than a hundred organizations cooperated in some way; many, for example, took one specific part of the production job, while others provided members of the cast for a given scene. And on Sunday afternoon, November 2, a non-segregated audience of 6,000 persons filled the Memorial Auditorium to witness the moving and memorable performance. The pageant was repeated, again with great success, as the 1954 celebration.

Community Leadership Institutes

The record of the Fund in the Test Cities project is by no means limited to the granting of money. Among its most significant contributions was the holding of two leadership institutes, in the summers of 1953 and 1954, at Bigwin Inn, Lake of Bays, Ontario. The professional head and several lay persons from each Test City spent approximately two weeks in a residential program of liberal education, addressing themselves both to the substance of this education and to the procedures by which it could be vital in the community. In discussion groups, in lectures by distinguished American and Canadian figures, in joint consideration of their common problems, the delegates from each city found new faith and new enthusiasm for the task at home. Any assessment of what has been done in Chattanooga would involve the recognition that these two institutes, through our delegates who attended, enlivened and encouraged our efforts.

World Affairs Forum

Using a part of its FPA programming grant, the world affairs committee sponsored in April, 1954, a forum around the theme of "America's Role in Freedom and Peace." Surely few projects we have ever done have enjoyed such careful and thorough committee preparation. With Mrs. Bryan's able staff work and under the chairmanship of Ralph Shumaker, a large committee composed of individuals and organizational representatives chose the theme, the speakers, the workshop topics, and made every other important decision related to the forum.

Town Hall Missions

A very different sort of project was made possible by Town Hall's sponsorship of two groups of foreign guests who toured the United States in 1955 and 1956; the Foreign Policy Association cooperated by working out the itineraries and providing liaison between Town Hall and the local community organizations. The world affairs committee readily agreed to invite members of the Asian Mission to Chattanooga in 1955, and a special committee under the chairmanship of Mrs. C. P. Kelley was appointed to make the arrangements. Citizens from South Vietnam, Jordan, and India, and the ambassador from Afghanistan composed the group which visited Chattanooga, from Friday evening to Sunday afternoon. An informal reception and supper party were given for them on the evening of their arrival; a seminar on Saturday afternoon and a symposium on Saturday evening were the main features of their stay.

In 1956 a similar Town Hall Mission composed entirely of Israelis came to the United States and four of its members visited Chattanooga for four days in early February. Mrs. Joel Solomon was appointed chairman of the committee set up to handle their visit. Included in the group were a woman doctor, a youth worker, a foreign ministry official, and an officer of the Hebrew University in Jerusalem. Members of the Mission made speeches to the Rotary, Civitan, and Optimist Clubs, to classes at Chattanooga High School and the University of Chattanooga, and the student body of Howard High School. Several women's groups joined in the co-sponsorship of a women's meeting, to which the doctor spoke; another of the guests addressed a large Bible class on the Dead Sea scrolls. The Mission's visit was concluded with a public meeting at which all members participated in a panel discussion called "Israel, 1956."

Given the American tendency to condescension towards foreign peoples, particularly Asians, much of this was probably quite salutary. I still cherish the memory of the Indian making a brief, impassioned speech to a group of substantial local citizens; he quoted his instructions from Nehru before his departure to join the mission: "Tell them we are always willing to discuss international differences, but only on terms of absolute equality; we will accept nothing less." But despite the value of strong speech and firm opinions, we took special care to see that none of these persons could simply turn any meeting into a propaganda session. At least one unique benefit accrues from such visits by foreign guests: it gives us an insight into the lives of their people which no amount of reading can provide.

Conference on Aging

Still another kind of activity is illustrated by Chattanooga's first Conference on Aging, held in September, 1955. This was part of the work which was done under the special grant of $2,000 from the Fund for a Senior Citizens' project. Mrs. Charles Waugaman became a part-time staff associate under the terms of this grant, and the conference was staged under her leadership. In our initial efforts, aimed at discovering the sort of educational programming which might appeal to older persons, we soon learned that the community needed to give some careful thought to issues for the senior citizen.

The conference explored such areas as education and recreation, housing, finance, health, and retirement. We had hoped that the conference would lead to the formal beginning of some sort of city-wide committee or other organization which would operate in the field of the aging. Unhappily, the most diligent efforts to start such a group failed, largely for lack of willing leadership. We could not get the necessary cooperation to begin a limited pilot project involving a day center of some sort.

Conference on Education

Acting in concert with several local organizations, the Council sponsored in April, 1956, a Conference on Education, a follow-up to the White House Conference held the previous fall. The conference posed six basic questions concerning the educational situation on Chattanooga and Hamilton County; committees composed largely of lay persons produced studies of these six questions to serve as a basis for thought and discussion. The conference was inaugurated by a day's workshop where school patrons and other interested citizens met to discuss the six topics. In the following weeks, three regular Council television programs were given over to a discussion of the same questions, and many local organizations were furnished with programs dealing with the school situation. One suburban community arranged 20 discussion groups for one evening as a follow-up of the conference.

Our Living Future

In June, 1957, the Council acted as local sponsor for the urban renewal film-with-commentary, *Our Living Future*. Prepared by *Life* magazine and distributed by *Life* and the American Council to Improve Our Neighborhoods (ACTION), the program depicted the plight of the American city. With slides, still photographs, cartoons, and movies, the program showed what blight, inadequate traffic patterns, conflicting political boundaries, and unwise planning are doing to the American city. In connection with *Our Living Future*, the Council elicited the support of local groups interested in urban renewal and thereby guaranteed an audience. Considerable effort was expended on publicizing the program. We reminded all concerned that the program was simply background information on the general problem which urban renewal is meant to solve, not advice to Chattanooga about what should be done here.

Basic American Issues

The Council's sixth program year was recently concluded with the most ambitious single project which we have yet undertaken. Designed to focus attention on the most fundamental questions which our society faces, the Basic American Issues project was essentially the adaptation of the familiar university practice of the visiting professorship to the informal community setting of adult education. Four men, each representing an important field in human endeavor, were invited to spend a week in Chattanooga to participate in a wide variety of activities. Each delivered a public lecture; granted interviews to press, radio, and television; made informal speeches to civic clubs and other groups; spoke to college and high school students; and held conferences and seminars with persons having special responsibility for or interest in the field which the guest represented. Informal entertainment offered still another opportunity for them

March 1958, GC with John Kenneth Galbraith. During his week in Chattanooga with the Adult Education Council, Galbraith spoke on "Basic Issues in Economics."

41

to meet and talk with local people, for a genuine exchange of thought and opinion. After numerous problems, the following schedule was arranged:

Week of March 16: Dexter Perkins, Professor in American Civilization, Cornell University; Basic Issues on Foreign Policy.

Week of March 30: John Kenneth Galbraith, Professor of Economics, Harvard University; Basic Issues in Economics.

Week of May 18: Francis Keppel, Dean of the Graduate School of Education, Harvard University; Basic Issues in Education.

Week of May 25: George F. Thomas, Chairman, Department of Religion, Princeton University; Basic Issues in Religion.

In addition to the public lectures, there were ten informal speeches and 17 conferences and seminars. Our guests made 16 appearances on television and four on radio. The project figured in 41 newspaper stories, including six editorials and one full-page transcript of a round-table discussion sponsored by *The Chattanooga Times* and the Council during Dean Keppel's visit. Twenty-five organizations participated in the project in some significant way.

*   *   *

Time and effort have been invested in numerous other things which I have not mentioned. In 1956, for example, the Council sponsored the FPA film series, "The Dilemma of Modern Man," composed of eight feature-length films, each exploring some aspect of the human situation. In 1957 we did an adaptation of the FPA program, "Decisions, '57"; a series of five Tuesday evening seminars met to hear a presentation by an area university professor and to discuss the problem about which he spoke. Reading materials were also furnished each participant. The series was especially designed for world affairs chairmen of local organizations, although of course it was open to the public as well. The Council has also sponsored five series of radio programs.

Several years ago the Fund offered to each Test City a grant of $2,000 for producing a discussion program in the field of liberal education, a program which could, with proper revision and development, be distributed as part of its body of discussion programs. We used this money to develop Introduction to Poetry, a ten-session program which sought to show the relevance of the poetic vision to what we are likely to regard as more 'practical' concerns. The program was tested in an experimental group of about 15 persons here in the fall of 1955. While I had chosen to develop this program almost as a self-indulgence and as a means of winning temporary freedom from the telephone and the committee meeting, I was genuinely delighted with the success of the test group. After exhaustive reports were sent to the Fund, Elizabeth Drew, distinguished critic and teacher of literature at Smith College, was commissioned to develop a program which she titled "Discovering Modern Poetry." This is the only program now available from the Fund which developed, albeit indirectly, from that special grant to the Test Cities.

To find weaknesses in the Council's programming structure is not an especially difficult undertaking. Certainly the offering of discussion groups needs to be strengthened. More effort should be made to utilize radio and television as means for doing a stronger program and reaching an ever wider audience. Better ways should be devised for encouraging participation in educational and cultural activities available from many sources in the community. It is especially desirable to arrange programs which will illuminate the immediate issues of the moment by relating them to the central tradition of American society. For every opportunity we have seized and developed, at least one has been neglected.

But when all this is said, it is still apparent, I think, that the program has also had great strengths. We have moved a long way since 1952 towards establishing ourselves as a useful and indeed essential part of the community's educational life.

Promotion and Participation

The need always to demonstrate the program's relevance to basic human concerns, to show that it is important because it touches individual lives in important ways, suggests something about the nature and the method of promotion. If one wishes to promote a circus, it is a fine thing to send an elephant around town. If one wishes to promote an educational program, one is especially careful to choose methods which will give the prospective audience a true notion of what to expect. If the main appeal is something other than a genuine interest in dealing with significant questions and issues, we are asking for trouble.

One of the worst things we can do is to imply that the intellectual content of a specific program will not tax the mind of a cocker spaniel. If a program does not make intellectual demands, there is something wrong with it. Any effort to suggest that participation in a discussion group, for example, is no more demanding than an evening of television will usually result in people's staying at home to watch television.

I doubt that from our experience we can suggest any new methods of promotion. We have used most of the standard approaches, in various patterns and combinations, from the beginning to the present time; almost invariably we have used several methods simultaneously. Beyond the voluntary word-of-mouth promotion by the participant, we have used newspaper stories and pictures, radio and television spot announcements, mimeographed and printed brochures sent to the Council mailing list and to selected institutions, newsletters, and personal letters. A good variety in promotional methods is at least as important as a comparable variety in program elements. If programs are arranged as an integral part of the activities of an organization, this usually precludes any necessity for effort which is purely promotional. While the Council can never limit its work to such situations, programs addressed to an already existing audience both relieve us of promotional chores and provide the means for reaching important segments of the community.

Two Criticisms

Perhaps no criticism of the Council has been made more often than two with regard to participation: that we are reaching the same people repeatedly and that they are mainly the people who are "already educated" and who "don't need it."

While there is undoubtedly some justice in them, neither of these criticisms can be supported by the facts. The influx of new participants has been steady and encouraging, if never sensational. As for the second criticism (which implies that adult education is always remedial and therefore for other people), three points need to be made. The first is that the criticism ignores much of the Council's work. It ignores, for example, the television program, which certainly enjoys a large, miscellaneous audience; those of us who work with the program are continually surprised by comments from the most unexpected sources, from men and women of widely differing educational and social backgrounds. Secondly, it ignores the considerable work we do at the request of, and in cooperation with, other organized groups whose members apparently feel that they are among those who "need it."

The third point in reply is the most important. Any organization with small staff and small budget must impose stern limits upon itself; not to do so is to attempt everything and to end in frustration and failure. When one looks at the American community or at American society itself, one is confronted with the obvious and urgent need for leadership and constructive action in all the major fields of human enterprise. I am not talking about any need revealed by the launching of the Russian satellites or by any other event; I am talking about the need imposed upon us by the nature of a free society. If an educational program addresses itself to this need, there are clearly discernible priorities.

Assessment

I have labored the point sufficiently, I think, that the greatest virtue in our program has been the variety of elements which make it up. Surely it is one of the advantages of liberal education that it enables us to apprehend and cherish the great differences among human beings; surely to ignore these differences in building a program is to that degree to repudiate the validity of liberal education. I think we must be very sure to continue this variety, with increasing effort to design a program of the widest possible appeal. I am especially hopeful that we can expand our efforts to use the mass media and to design intensive programs which can be fitted into the context of professional and organizational activity.

I am never willing to claim more than a good beginning of a long and arduous task. Those persons, professional or volunteer, who commit their time and talent to an organization like this one, must do their work with patience and with a sense of the limitations of human effort. For those who want quick and dramatic results, education is certain to be a disappointment; the results are slow and hard to see. This point was well made in a brief statement which Mrs. Bryan wrote to complete a visual display several years ago:

> What is the ultimate goal of adult education? Wisdom in action, a little more understanding of the world in which we live, of the human situation, and the conduct of life – and a little more, and a little more, and a little more, for a lifetime.

Teaching

"Rather than teaching topics in Religion and Philosophy,
I see myself as teaching students."

A college teacher

GC lecturing at UTC, 1983.
Photograph courtesy of UTC Archives.

Teaching: A Later View

In a 1987 issue of *Context*, edited by Martin E. Marty, there was a truly moving story about a friend and former student of Marty's who has had a twenty-year bout with lymphoma. This friend is himself a college teacher, and I was much interested in one of his comments on the effects of his illness, now fortunately in remission: "Ideas were once most important to me, but now people and relationships take priority. Rather than teaching topics in Religion and Philosophy, I see myself as teaching students. They are more important than the content of my courses. I have also developed a more pastoral attitude toward people, feeling much more sensitive and aware of their pain and sorrow and anxiety."

I was reminded at once of my own interviews, forty years ago, for my first teaching job. The final interview was with the elderly principal to whose junior high school I was being assigned. After assuring himself apparently that I was knowledgeable enough and tough enough to teach seventh and eighth graders (a judgment I myself often doubted in the next several months) he said to me, "Now what will you be teaching?" A little startled by his question, I replied simply, "English." "No!" he cried, bringing his fist down on the table between us, "You'll be teaching boys and girls." This was a popular saying in certain circles in those days and I was full of scorn for it, but in that interview I kept my scorn to myself. Now, a career in the classroom later, I am a good deal less scornful. I would still want to say that if we are teaching students, we are (I hope) teaching them something, some substance. I trust I never forgot that I was teaching English to human beings.

GC lecturing at UTC, 1985.
Photograph courtesy of UTC Archives.

But I understand Marty's friend's newly achieved emphasis in his illness and in his career. Several years ago a young friend and colleague whose marriage was breaking up said to me, a little ruefully, "It has taken me all of my forty years to learn the primary importance of human relationships." Certainly it is a lesson which few people learn early and easily.

January 17, 1988

In Defense of Heresy
Address to the Tennessee College of English Teachers
Lambeth College

It is sometimes the custom in France, I am told, to salute a newly consecrated Roman Catholic Bishop with the words, "Excellency, now you are a bishop. You will never eat a bad dinner or hear the truth again." We are all bishops in some kind of diocese, and no doubt we all have our ways to avoid hearing at least the more unsettling truths. But surely it is equally certain that on occasions like this one we owe it to ourselves, to our institutions, to our discipline to ask ourselves some rather unpleasant questions. We cannot afford forever to leave unexamined the assumptions by which we live and do our work. It is only too easy to take ourselves more seriously than we deserve to be taken.

I cherish a story I heard recently from one of the participants in an international conference of Biblical scholars and theologians, meeting at Oxford. After several of the most learned discourses by members of the conference, the Archbishop of Canterbury was set forth as a featured speaker. He began with a casual statement, "As I was driving over in my automobile and thinking about what I ought to say at this meeting. . . ." I am sure I need not tell you that the distinguished theologians were shocked that the Archbishop should enter on this holy ground without a carefully prepared address. And yet, said my informant, he was of course quite right. He was quite carefully and deliberately putting us in our places, reminding us that we can be curiously remote from the life of the church and the life of individual church people. He was paying his respects, I believe, to what we must confess is the aridity of much that passes for Biblical scholarship. Whether that is what the Archbishop meant to do or not, that was at least the effect of his words upon some of his hearers.

I am not certain who in the academic world is the equivalent of the Archbishop of Canterbury, but we should seek him out and persuade him to be a regular participant in our meetings. Meanwhile, we shall have to provide our own criticisms. As a modest beginning, I want to suggest three ways in which I believe we are professionally vulnerable. The first, and the least important, is the way in which we organize and produce the meetings of our learned and professional organizations. Here, if ever one existed, is an occasion for the demonstration of excellence – excellence in conception, in planning, in performance. But alas, "Between the idea / And the reality / . . . Falls the Shadow." We do not seem very often, at least publicly and officially, to question the purpose and value of these meetings. We go on year after year, assuming that some value does follow from them. If we should ask what their value is, we are likely to answer the question in marginal terms. We go to see our friends, to keep in touch, to show our interest, sometimes to demonstrate to chairmen what dazzling ornaments we would be in their departments. There is nothing really wrong with these motives, but they do seem for the most part to have only an incidental connection with the organized proceedings of such gatherings. But if our motives are peripheral, this fact hardly justifies the almost unbelievable arrangements of the program itself.

Surely the most elementary understanding of the psychology of learning, to say nothing of plain common sense, should suggest that the reading of several papers in quick succession is not an effective educational enterprise. And I speak of only one session; multiply that by the several sessions likely to make up such a meeting, and the mind reels. Some of the papers are clearly worth hearing, though the proportion of chaff to wheat is depressingly high. But if every one of them was a polished gem of wit and intellectual distinction and glittering scholarship, how can we possibly defend a format that sanctions the reading of paper after paper after paper? It should not surprise us that the dazed listener begins after a while to drift from session to session, smiling and nodding in a preoccupied sort of way.

But the most distressing single impression with which I usually come away from such meetings is that no matter how good the papers may sometimes be, their presentation is often incredibly inept. It is not unusual to find oneself unable to hear the speaker, or to understand him; too often he seems totally devoid of the slightest ability to project his voice, or to help his hearer to an understanding of the paper by tone, inflection, and other vocal devices by which we should seek to make our meaning clear. Since we belong to a profession almost wholly dependent upon the word, both written and spoken, this seeming indifference to the quality of delivery is truly shocking.

One is tempted to say that as a profession we are at our worst in learned meetings. Probably the best thing we can do for young persons looking towards a career of teaching and scholarship is to discourage their participation in these pageant rites.

The second vulnerability I want to discuss is our attitude and our consequent tribal customs having to do with what is called 'productive scholarship.' I suppose any of us who have responsibility for the seeking out, interviewing, and employing of teachers must soon develop a sense of great humility; it is, I think, an extraordinarily difficult job to identify with any real certainty those qualities that we covet for the members of our departments. But it is not impossible to identify them, and in largely pragmatic and empirical ways we develop what skill we can in reading the recommendations, and other relevant documents, and in asking the right questions. I am always rather dubious about this phrase 'productive scholarship' with its promise – or threat – of a fairly steady stream of publications. The sacred principle of "publish or perish" has been so widely and relentlessly attacked that it would be graceless to make this one more occasion for its denunciation. And yet I feel impelled to record my own view that very often "publish and perish" would be a better principle. (One distinguished scholar I know, having himself an excellent publication record, thinks it would be desirable if everyone wishing to publish were required to show cause.) Is there anyone here who has not felt, at least occasionally, that the whole matter of scholarly publication has become a ghastly parody? Is there anyone here who has not felt a sense of profound melancholy when he has beheld the trivial and the mediocre works which this system produces? One has not only the right but the duty to wonder, how productive is productive scholarship? How illuminating is the literary criticism available in such great abundance?

From the point of view of the teacher and lover of literature, the more important question is whether we do not sometimes lose sight of the purpose and function of criticism. Productive scholarship seems too often to regard criticism as an end in itself. A wiser view is expressed in Donald Stauffer's book *The Nature of Poetry* in which he says, "The most that criticism can ever do is to help a reader to see more, or to see more clearly, or to see once again." Put in juxtaposition with much of what passes for productive scholarship, this modest statement would seem strangely out of company. Much of what we read and hear hardly seems aimed at sending the reader back to the literature itself; too much criticism reads as though it were an end within itself.

My own impression – it is no more than that – is that our British colleagues do far better in remembering that the deepest purpose of criticism is to send us back with increased pleasure and understanding of literature. When I read reviews in the *Times Literary Supplement*, I very often have the feeling that one thing the reviewer wants to do is express his enjoyment of the book, even to help provide enjoyment for me. Can you imagine a writer for the *New York Review* sitting down to his typewriter with any such purpose in mind? Indeed often the long and learned essays in the *New York Review* seem to have so little connection with the book allegedly under review that I marvel at the ingenuity of the reviewers. I have often read there extremely interesting autobiographical essays masquerading as book reviews.

Perhaps a story from the field of Biblical criticism makes the point most clearly.   When the great German theologian Harnack was occupying a chair in the University of Berlin, his students, half in jest, began to say that in all of Berlin, only Professor Harnack understood the New Testament. When this word reached the old man, he was genuinely distressed and he took an early occasion to say in a lecture, "Gentlemen, the simplest hotel chambermaid who reads her Bible and kneels at her bedside in simple faith knows more about the New Testament than Professor Harnack." The implied analogy breaks down very quickly, but the little story still makes its point. The sophomore who discovers for himself the vast excitement of *Hamlet* knows more about the play that any critic at that moment can teach him.

The third point at which I think we are vulnerable is a clear tendency towards vocationalism in our attitudes and certain of our practices. In the recently published *Letters of C.S. Lewis*, a relevant comment is included in one letter to his brother. He is talking about someone he had recently met in whose conversational resources he felt keen disappointment: "Books – oh yes, editions, prices, suitability for exams – not their contents. . . . Unless I misjudge him he is one of those dreadful fellows who never refer to literature except during the hours they are paid to talk about it. . . . How small a nucleus there is in each liberal profession of people who care about the thing they are supposed to be doing; yet I suppose the percentage of garage hands . . . who are really interested in motoring is about 95." Or the point is made in an old joke from *Punch* which Elizabeth Drew recalls in one of her books. A poet and a professor, the latter with examination questions running in his head, are walking in the woods in the brightness of spring. The poet quotes:

> O cuckoo, shall I call thee bird,
> Or but a wandering voice?

The professor completes the verse:

> State the alternative preferred,
> With reasons for your choice.

We are very willing to think of ourselves as guardians of the humane values which our discipline is peculiarly fitted to record and to pass on to future generations, and we can be quite self-righteous in our attitude to those disciplines that are essentially vocational. But we need to remind ourselves at least once a day that liberal education, with all the traditional values that we claim for it, does not follow necessarily and inevitably from any particular subject matter, not even from literature. Whenever I feel myself on the brink of forgetting this simple but significant truth, I recall the formidable lady whom I encountered once in a discussion of the difficulty of teaching Shakespeare in the high school. "No difficulty at all for me," she assured us; "whenever we study *Macbeth*, I just have my students go through it and underline the introductory adverbial clauses." An admirable plan, I should think, for the study of adverbial clauses, but rather hard on Shakespeare and the study of literature – and certainly hard on any education which aimed to liberate the student from narrowness and prejudice and lack of understanding.

But we cannot laugh too smugly at the lady; we too live in glass houses. There is no reason to suppose that the humanities in general, or our own discipline in particular, will inevitably be liberating in its influence and effect. Language and literature fit parts of a liberal education only if we design our courses for that purpose and resist steadfastly the numerous pressures that militate against their being so. Of all these pressures, I choose two for comment.

The first is the pressure which militates against doing justice to our lower division courses, especially freshman English, whatever its specific content and nature. Simply because of sheer numbers, it is only too easy to neglect these courses. So many students somehow to be brought under some sort of discipline and taught something is a prospect to frighten even the most courageous English department. Nobody can claim that this assignment is not a formidable one. But what saddens one is that we begin to invent reasons for questioning the need for a freshman course. A particularly amusing example of this tendency came recently to my attention. In a certain mid-western state, it has been customary for a long time for the chairman of the English department in the distinguished state university to complain loud and long about the lack of adequate instruction in composition in high schools of the state. Recently in conversation with a high school teacher, the same chairman said that it is quite reassuring how much better students are beginning to write, so much better that his department is now contemplating the abandonment of freshman English. I am sure we can all admire this improvement in so short a period of time.

I am afraid, however, that there is a better explanation of this indifference to freshman English than the improvement in student writing. There are many ways, at varying levels of tactfulness, to make the essential point, but it is neatly summed up in a one-sentence comment by a fully qualified observer of my acquaintance. Speaking of the large English department in which he teaches, he recently wrote to me, "So far as I can see, most of the senior professors don't give a damn about anything except their own little kingdoms." It is not a happy thought; whether it is a fair one, I leave you to judge in light of your own experience.

The second influence which often militates against our making language and literature courses genuinely liberal in effect is the shadow of the graduate school. It is quite natural that we should rejoice to see our ablest and most promising students preparing themselves for graduate work; if higher education is to meet our expectations in this society, there is no reason that we should not do vigorous and continuous recruiting for graduate students. But it is very easy to allow this zeal to influence quite heavily – and I think improperly – the work and organization of the undergraduate department. Is it too much to hope for that the undergraduate student, whatever else he may get, will go out from our departments with a deep and genuine love of literature? I do not see how any teacher without this love can be even passably good. This love and enthusiasm that it engenders can redeem a lot of otherwise pedestrian teaching. I suspect that if we make all our choices, if we make up our reading lists and plan our comprehensives and conduct our classes with an eye chiefly to the student's admission to graduate school, our courses will become increasingly narrow in their scope and purpose, increasingly vocational, increasingly untouched by the joy that should be the student's highest reward.

1967

Teachers

"We must be what we would produce."
A friend of GC's

Fleming James

I was fortunate to have known Dr. Fleming James, dean of the School of Theology at Sewanee from 1942 until his retirement in 1947. Those who knew him at Sewanee and came under his influence there remember him with real devotion; he was a saint, a scholar, and a gentleman. Along with his lovely wife, he gave a great many young men preparing for the priesthood a fuller and more beautiful illustration of the Christian life.

An Old Testament scholar, Dr. James was a teacher of rare power and persuasion. I think I can say that before I studied under him, I had never met a flesh-and-blood

Professor Fleming James, ca. 1940.
Photograph courtesy of
University of the South Archives.

human being in the Old Testament; I was inclined to see them all through stained glass. In the dean's teaching, they came alive. He spoke of Isaiah and Jeremiah as though they were next-door neighbors.

Like the Old Testament prophets whom he venerated, Dr. James had a blazing concern for social justice. In his day on the mountain (I don't know whether it is still true), University people received preferential treatment in various places. He declined to go ahead of the 'mountain people' in the doctor's

53

office; he waited his turn. He gave time and money to the things he believed in, and he was not much worried about whether these things were 'popular.' Small wonder that his students called him, behind his back, 'Flaming Jim.'

Dr. James' most significant scholarly work was the book *Personalities of the Old Testament* (available in the St. Peter's parish library). Though published a generation ago, it still offers genuine and valuable insight into the chief characters of the Old Testament. Happily, he was able to end his long and distinguished career in a final contribution to Biblical scholarship by serving as Executive Secretary for the Old Testament section of Revised Standard Version. He has been dead now nearly twenty years, but through his writing and teaching he is still a pervasive influence.

February 16, 1975

Isobel Griscom: An Appreciation

When Isobel Griscom retired in 1963, it fell to my unhappy lot as the newly appointed chairman of the English department to arrange some sort of observance of the event. I call it an unhappy duty not only because her retirement was a grievous loss to the department, but also because I feared she would prove 'difficult' (a euphemism) in the planning of any sort of public recognition. My misgivings proved to be more than well-founded.

Miss Griscom first took the position that she would not hear of any retirement dinner or other foolishness of that sort. She had had a long and happy career at the University, she said,

Isobel Griscom, 1977.
UC Professor of English (1926-1964).
Photograph by Arlie Herron.

and she wished to leave her post in the same quiet and unobtrusive way in which she had done everything else. Remembering a few occasions when neither 'quiet' nor 'unobtrusive' would have adequately described her behavior, I suggested that a great many people would feel deprived of an opportunity to show their admiration and affection. After negotiations which extended over a period of several months, she finally agreed to a 'small, quiet dinner' with a few of her friends. She firmly stipulated that the occasion must be wholly free of sentimental speeches and that we must not embarrass her by the presentation of a gift of any sort.

All of us who were involved in the planning of that occasion were realistic enough to know that we were obliged to meet her conditions. We therefore submitted as gracefully as we could. Even Miss Griscom agreed that the retirement dinner party, given at the Read House in January, 1964, was in every way both simple and felicitous. But in the several years since that occasion, former students and colleagues have often agreed that we should do something more, that Miss Griscom's long and fruitful career at the University of Chattanooga must in some way be publicly and permanently acknowledged. A number of ideas have been informally exchanged among us; while none of them seemed to be exactly the right plan, we became increasingly determined to discover the most appropriate way to do honor to this remarkable woman.

In January, 1976, a committee was organized to address itself to this task. We called ourselves the I. G. Committee, using the familiar initials with which she has signed almost everything except her checks. Feeling that I had been defeated by her intransigence in 1964, I agreed to serve as chairman of the committee composed of Martha J. Gundaker, Mary Y. Hodge, Mary Glenn Phillips, Rickie Pierce, Arlie Herron, Joseph A. Jackson, and Raymond Witt, Jr. After some discussion of alternatives, we agreed that we would seek to raise a significant but unspecified sum of money for purchase of books in American literature to be given in Miss Griscom's honor to the UTC Library. We also agreed that if funds were available and if she would consent, we would publish a small book of her poems as a further means of homage. On this latter point we were deliberately quite vague in any public statement, not wishing to promise what we might not be able to fulfill or something which she might not approve.

In our preparations for sending out a fund-raising letter, we were the beneficiaries of valuable aid and advice from Ian Sturrock, Director of Development, and members of his staff. I mean this to be more than a routine acknowledgment: without the help of the development office, we could hardly have mounted even our modest campaign. We sent out the letter on July 1, and by the middle of August, we had received contributions of slightly more than six thousand dollars. By any standards, this was a welcome and generous response. Many of the checks were accompanied by letters almost invariably thanking us for the opportunity to give and paying high tribute to Isobel Griscom and what she meant in the lives of many persons.

As we studied the results of the campaign, it was abundantly clear that we had touched a vital memory in many persons who had known Miss Griscom during her long University career, persons whose minds and imaginations she had challenged, persons whose very lives were different because of her teaching and influence. There is simply no way in which the impact of her forty-one years in the English department can be reliably measured, but it can in some ways be documented by even a few brief excerpts from letters received with contributions:

Isobel Griscom with UC student Carleen Davis, 1958.

Indeed I would like to contribute to the Isobel Griscom Fund. I remember Miss Griscom with great fondness, and I am indebted to her . . . for awakening in me a love for reading.

Had it not been for Isobel Griscom, I would not have stayed in undergraduate college. The debt of friendship I owe her is incalculable.

My freshman course in English under Miss Griscom was not only an inspiration for me at Chattanooga but also in my subsequent student days at Vanderbilt and Columbia. She opened vistas for me to the beautiful world of literature.

[We] send this inadequate contribution to the Isobel Griscom Fund with love, appreciation, and admiration for a wonderful person. Thank you for letting us participate.

There were many comments worthy of quotation, but perhaps none quite so well approached the essence as this one from Edith Donaldson Carden:

> Isobel epitomized to me all of the qualities of a great teacher. She was always the perfect lady with her inborn charm, her intelligence, her keen wit, her piquant way of motivating and inspiring, and always with love and gentleness. She had a great influence on me and I love her very much.

Hundreds of her former students would gladly sign their names to those words.

II

A sort of paradox characterized Miss Griscom's University career. She believed as strongly as anyone I have ever known that the teacher's main function is to teach, to give to that teaching the best and truest effort of which the teacher is capable; but her interest in her students as human beings, her concern for them, inside or outside of class, was virtually without limit. I can call this a paradox only by remembering that a paradox is but an apparent contradiction, both terms of which are true. I suspect that almost every good teacher regards the interest in teaching and the interest in students as two sides of the same coin, but I have almost never seen a teacher who kept them in such perfect balance as Miss Griscom has done.

Thinking about her long interest in students and the many friendships which grew out of that interest, I realize what presumption is involved in my trying to comment adequately on her and her career; I am sure there are many who could do as well or better. But at least I can cite for my credentials a friendship covering now almost forty years, beginning with my student days at UC, including a year's service as her student assistant, and embracing also several years at the end of her career as her colleague in the department. During those latter years, I was fortunate enough to share her office, which gave me an excellent vantage point for observing her approach to teaching and to students.

Perhaps the most striking characteristic of her career was its consistency. She has never been one to be blown about by every blast of vain doctrine; I have hardly known a teacher less affected by the shibboleths and sacred words of educational vocabulary. I never remember hearing her use the word 'innovation' but she was the most truly innovative teacher I have ever known. When I speak of her consistency, I certainly do not mean to imply that her methods or even her opinions as expressed in class were always the same. (One former student insists that when any class session needed to be enlivened, Miss Griscom would either praise or attack Edgar Allan Poe, whichever she thought would annoy the students most.) I doubt that she ever went to class with anything that could be called a lesson plan. In my early years in the department, I put a good deal more of such plans in writing than I do now, and I remember her looking once at such a document with polite admiration. But I also felt some reproach in her words; I think she may have felt that if I had been better prepared, I wouldn't need such notes.

Her consistency was clearly not of a simple or superficial sort. She often managed, at least theoretically, to be on all sides of a question in a relatively brief period of time. She would agree with Emerson, surely one of her intellectual heroes, that "A foolish consistency is the hobgoblin of little minds." She could never be accused of that "foolish consistency" because there has always been an undogmatic quality in her mind that required her to turn a question over and over, examining it from various points of view. She has never hesitated to reverse herself from time to time, even from day to day, when her convictions prompted her to do so. Several years ago when Mary Macdonald Reynolds was writing her splendid series of weekly interviews with women in *The Chattanooga Times*, she did one of her columns on Miss Griscom. It was Mrs. Reynolds' only failure in that series that I am aware of; she did not catch the essence. And I think the reason she did not was that she asked Miss Griscom a series of questions, noted the answers, and wrote her column accordingly. Not otherwise knowing Miss Griscom, she did not know what we serious Griscom watchers could have told her – that if she had come back the next day and put the same questions, she would probably have gotten refreshingly different answers. One does not plumb the depths and views of that mind in one interview.

Miss Griscom's consistency as a teacher was the consistency of fundamental aim and understanding of what the educational enterprise seeks to do: to make the student more literate, more humane, more civilized. She was always quite willing to break into any routine or to interrupt any sequence of instruction in order to further the deepest purpose of education. I don't know whether she had ever heard of Robert Frost's assertion that we need to have "something alive" going on in English classes all over the country, but she certainly would have welcomed it and rejoiced to confirm it in her own teaching. An event in the news, a new poem called to her attention, something she had been reading – any of these would serve as the point of departure for a brilliantly stimulating class discussion. I remember one occasion when the prologue to St. John's Gospel was the point of departure; she spoke of it with what I can only call passionate conviction. She told us that we might well find the notion of the Word made flesh a difficult one because it was among the profoundest concepts in human experience.

I cannot remember on that occasion that the idea of the Logos became the center of class discussion and argument; it may have been that even in our smug and callow assurance of our own wisdom, we recognized that the water was over our heads. But usually the heart of the class experience was discussion and it was discussion of an especially searching and disciplined kind. Miss Griscom's method was always basically Socratic, manifesting itself in a series of questions which forced us to define terms, clarify thoughts, and speak precisely. (One of the contributors to the fund spoke of her as "that magnificent Socratic gadfly.")

Never was a teacher less a propagandist: she insisted, by precept and example, that we consider all sides of a question, that we take nothing for granted, that we never settle for easy second-hand answers. She did not scorn the traditional, but she saw to it that we could not take refuge in the traditional without the hard thought which would entitle us to do so.

III

Another quality which her teaching continually demonstrated was selfless-ness. She never sought in the smallest way to dazzle the student with her superi-or learning, nor to score debating points in class discussion. Though I am sure she had no illusions about the depths of our innocence and ignorance, in class she rarely betrayed to us that fact. Rummaging recently among the accumulations of my own distant past, I came upon the carefully preserved themes that I submit-ted to her as a freshman in 1938-39. Quite a number of them make keenly uncomfortable reading because they address themselves with such insouciant con-fidence to the most complicated, difficult and imponderable of questions. Miss Griscom's penciled comments make clear that she did not hesitate to chasten me or hold me accountable, but there is nothing in her markings to make me feel that she was anything other than a sympathetically demanding teacher.

It is only fair to say that some students found in their relationship with her more demand than sympathy, but I am convinced by my own observation that the only student for whom she had no sympathy was the one who did not care, who aimed to get by on the smallest possible amount of work. Even some of these she converted by the contagious exuberance of her interest in language and literature. But most such students usually avoided her, and certainly those who did not often came to regret it. But the dividing line in her treatment of students was not between the bright and the less bright but between those who cared and those who did not. For the indifferent, she had little time; for the concerned, she was always available and helpful. I remember a case in point not long before her retirement. A hefty young football player came into the office one morning when she and I were both there; without wishing to overhear their conversation, I could not help doing so. The team was in mid-season and the boy felt quite over-whelmed; could he defer his papers and quizzes in world literature until the sea-son was over? I winced when I heard his question, but to my amazement she replied, "Certainly. Just let me know when you are ready." After he left, I said, "Isobel, you have the reputation of a tiger, and then you turn out to be the softest touch in the department." She laughed and said, "I'll do anything for a student who really cares."

Her University career can hardly be summed up in a better sentence: she would and did do almost anything for a student who cared. My strongest recollection of her from my own student days is of her sturdy friendship in time of need, especially when that need was for counsel and encouragement. Of course my generation was in college in the innocent days before we knew the importance of a corps of deans and counselors, but I am sure that then, as now, any lack was supplied by sympathetic and imaginative teachers. I suspect Miss Griscom spent about as much time in hearing and discussing students' problems and difficulties as she did in following strictly academic pursuits. She was a wise, understanding, and unsentimental advisor, and I know I am only one of a great number whom she helped through the stresses of their student years. Nor did she limit her encouragement to words. I have been told by more than one person, not including herself, that she sometimes in the Depression years came to the rescue of some students with loans that enabled them to stay in school. They paid no interest; each one merely took out an insurance policy in her favor in the amount of the loan. She sometimes concerned herself also with helping a student find adequate money for graduate school. I am not sure that I have known in my own experience a more generous person.

IV

But I do not mean to make Miss Griscom's life and work sound all so entirely sober. She always had in abundance that essential trait of the good teacher, a lively sense of humor. That humor has illuminated her life at every point, in class and out. She appreciated humor and attracted it. Once in an American novel class we were beginning the study of *The Scarlet Letter*. All ten or twelve of us in the class that day appeared wearing sweaters or jackets buttoned to the chin. When Miss Griscom took her place to begin the discussion, we opened our sweaters or whatever to reveal the large scarlet "A" each of us was wearing. It was at least a more academic joke than some we perpetrated.

One winter a large open space on the ground floor of a main classroom building, the then 'art gallery,' was being used by the Chattanooga Art Association for an antique show. The exhibits were mainly small things – dishes, vases, *objets d'art* and the like. Each item bore a label with its approximate age and its owner's name. The temptation was too great: we bought a cup and saucer at the dime store and lettered the card, "Property of Isobel Griscom. Given to her on the day of her birth. 85 years old." That doesn't seem very funny to me now, but at the time it seemed hilarious. At least our stunt wasn't discovered until the midst of the show's opening night, and the object of our 'humor' was there to share the laughter.

No one who reads these words now or in some long future need feel any great rush of sympathy with Miss Griscom as the object of such juvenile humor; she was always more than able to take care of herself. Not only in verbal wit but in elaborate situation jokes, her often devilish sense of humor expressed itself; it was a nimble student indeed who could keep even with the game. One young male student in one of her classes she thought took himself much too seriously. She arranged a series of telephone calls from an allegedly angry mother, berating him for his heartless unconcern for her young daughter who was madly in love with him. The poor bewildered lad came to Miss Griscom for advice, and she cherished this opportunity to run with the foxes and chase with the hounds.

I once felt the brunt of this playful wit several years after my departure from UC. As a young man I had the young man's usual strong opinions on almost all subjects. One of my strongest was an attitude of scorn toward a local citizen whom I thought to be a drag on civilization. She wrote me when I was in the army, asking what I would think of the University's giving that man an honorary degree. I wrote back a long letter of towering rage, asking how on earth the University could think of such a thing, *etc., etc.* In due course her answer came. "After your reply, I almost hate to tell you that I fostered that honorary degree as an April fool joke."

A year or so after World War II an old army friend from the Bronx paid me a visit. Like many New Yorkers, he was surprised to find the streets paved in Chattanooga, and on this occasion he was clearly astonished by the appearance of Lookout Mountain. I had briefed Miss Griscom and she was fully equal to his naive image of the South. We had hardly seated ourselves in her living room when a car backfired nearby. "Oh dear," she said in unmistakable distress, "I do hope another Indian hasn't been shot!" In answer to his wide-eyed question, she explained that a feud had recently broken out on the mountain over the question of who had better right to wear coonskin caps; the Indians felt that the caps belonged especially to them and that the palefaces had no right to wear them. At that moment an ambulance passed by (for all I know, she may have arranged it) and she said, "Mercy! I hope nobody was killed." As we drove down the mountain, my friend expressed amazement that such an obviously affluent and civilized suburb would be the locale of a feud over coonskin caps.

But delightful as all of these memories are, I am sure that for most of us our recollections of Miss Griscom have as their focus the campus and the classroom. Among my own examples of those visual images that we all store up in our memory is the first time I saw her; she came almost trippingly down the stairs from her office to meet our class, which was gathering in a room at the end of the hall. (That building is now called Race Hall, and the whole floor where her classroom was is now given over to offices.) I had immediately a sense of great energy and almost as quickly a sense of gaiety, of great pleasure in the work at hand. I know now, almost forty years later, that all of us who love teaching go sometimes in this attitude to meet a new class; but the point about Miss Griscom is that she seemed always to meet every class in that spirit. In the last year of her teaching, she did her work with the same energy and the same enthusiasm which she had brought to it for all of those forty-one years. I know few teachers indeed who have matched her unquenchable youthfulness.

A colleague who joined the department late in Miss Griscom's tenure also remembers his initial impression. He first saw her in a department meeting and he thought, "What a beautiful woman," and fell in love with her.

The fact that Miss Griscom loved her work, took great pride and pleasure in the challenges and opportunities of teaching, certainly influenced the atmosphere of her classroom. Class sessions were always characterized by courtesy and mutual goodwill, but they were never in the least stiff or formal. Perhaps like most college teachers, she found it unnecessary to say much about class behavior. She was such a lady herself that she set the obvious tone for all of us. A few crisp – or occasionally withering – words to a student who had been thoughtlessly rude always settled the matter. Once in class someone scornfully commented on another student's view. "That's a typical Roman Catholic position!" "Then, no doubt," Miss Griscom said, "you have the typical Protestant reply?" A gentle rebuke, but enough.

There was of course much more than courtesy in her dealings with students: there was also a quality that can be called by several names, of which tolerance is perhaps one. But I can remember her saying once that to be tolerant, merely tolerant, is a presumptuous thing. "Who am I to be tolerant of another human being?" Perhaps there is in all tolerance except pure indifference an element of condescension. So I look for other names: the quality I mean is a kind of openness to other people, a glad and hospitable acceptance of their differences, a patience with their foibles. Perhaps the best term of all is 'charity' in the theological sense, because this quality involves the basic attitudes that St. Paul is exploring in I Corinthians 13. In the Pauline sense, I think Miss Griscom is one of the most genuinely charitable people I have ever known.

Especially with students, she was always able to look beyond the superficial and transient and to see the promise and possibility that others did not see. Any college teacher is likely to encounter students (and sometimes even colleagues!) who are not very skilled in the social graces, not yet habituated to the civilized life of the college community. Miss Griscom always dealt with such persons with the utmost tact and kindness; I have never heard her utter a word that could be called snobbish. She could sometimes adopt the cause of someone who seemed to others a quite impossible person. A few years before her retirement a young man enrolled at the University after graduating from an out-of-town preparatory school. His abrasive approach quickly made him unpopular with faculty and students alike, but Miss Griscom would have none of the prevailing scorn. "There's quite a lot to that young man," she said; "just show a little patience." Long before this student graduated, he justified her confidence; she was entirely right about him. I have no doubt that he and many others among us, from various student generations, found our way because she believed in us. She has the authority of Marianne Moore: ". . . trust begets power and faith is an affectionate thing."

Through all of her University years – and since – she has been a tireless advocate of women's rights. Though I doubt she finds much to sympathize with in the more strident voices of the current movement, she has always believed deeply in certain basic principles, such as equal pay for equal work. President LeRoy A. Martin once ruefully recalled that Miss Griscom came to see him to complain about the disparity of faculty salaries between men and women. He promised to get the facts, and at a second conference he was pleased to tell her that while the national average for the differential was X percent, at UC it was only Y percent (I forget the exact figures). She brought her dainty fist crashing down upon his desk: "There shouldn't be any differential!"

I have been using largely in this essay some form of the past tense because the focus has been on Miss Griscom's long and distinguished University career. She has certainly not been one of those for whom the zest of life ceased upon retirement. She has maintained her keen and lifelong interest in people and ideas, in books and travel; she has led and participated in informal discussion groups dealing with literature. She has had more time for her own poetry, as this little book bears witness. Hundreds of her students can testify that she was able to leave her University post with a sense of fulfillment and accomplishment. At her retirement she wrote to President Martin:

> I don't believe anyone could have had a luckier, happier life
> than I have. All my days at the university have been filled
> with interesting persons and events. My 'bosses' have been
> scholars and gentlemen; and my faculty friends a constant
> source of enjoyment. Who can say more?

I think it is H.G. Wells who says somewhere that the teacher must be the sower of "unseen harvests." Anyone who invests his or her life in education must be content to remember that opinion and not to expect to see very many measurable results. Yet we are not wholly without evidence of the profound influence Isobel Griscom had on many of her students. The response to the fund and the notes and letters which many people write to accompany their gifts at least suggest how deep was that influence. One former student, herself now a college teacher, has established in her own English department an annual award named for Miss Griscom. Many of us who are her former students are teaching in schools and colleges in various parts of the country; I am sure that our teaching reflects at least our indebtedness to a truly distinguished teacher. But it is of course not only her former students who are now teaching who are in her debt. Another former student commented recently on the vicarious influence Miss Griscom has had on his own children, who have never met her. In the long run, the harvest is indeed unseen; it is also a rich and plentiful harvest.

The *Moccasin*, the University yearbook, was dedicated to Miss Griscom in 1964, the year after her retirement. The editor quoted a sentence from Robert Penn Warren's essay on Robert Frost, and we adapted that sentence for inclusion on the bookplate which will mark each of the books given to the UTC Library in her honor: "She dropped a stone into the pool of our being, and the ripples spread."

Spring 1977

Elizabeth Massey

When I think of what good teaching is, or when I think of those good teachers whom I have known in my own education or more recently as my colleagues, I remember a simple statement that a friend made a number of years ago in a speech about adult education. "We must be," he said, "what we would produce." It is a simple but profoundly significant statement about the educational process. "We must be what we would produce."

As a person and as a teacher, Elizabeth Massey has consistently demonstrated the wisdom and truth of that aphorism. She has known first-hand what are the graces of civilization; she has known and embodied the qualities of heart and mind which are important in human life and therefore in education. Though we may all think up arguments to dissuade students, I suspect we all have a grudging admiration for the student who chooses his or her courses on the basis of who is teaching them. As such students will readily testify, they have their reward. And when that reward has been a year or two under the tutelage of Elizabeth Massey, the reward is rich indeed.

Elizabeth Massey, 1977.

"We must be what we would produce." Elizabeth has been a lady, a scholar, a lover of the language which she teaches. Nobody could know her, in class or out, without recognizing these things. In dress, in manner, in the quiet authority and efficiency with which she has managed her classes, in every way she has been those things she would produce. Can anyone here imagine a student's being rude to her? The grace and beauty of her own manners are too obvious. Can anyone imagine a student who felt ill-at-ease or uncomfortable in her class? With her own warm and genial style, her ready sense of humor, her genuine human concern for each and every student, how could anyone feel other than that he or she is in the presence of something rare and beautiful?

In their invincible innocence, most students assume that the University began its existence the day they registered and will cease the day they graduate. Such students suppose that the evaluation of teachers is something new, first thought up by clever and long-suffering students. Evaluation is as old as teaching. All of us are subject to it, every class we teach, every term we teach. But evaluation does not require elaborate paraphernalia; there is no evaluation as humbling and as effective as that which is involved in the ordinary reactions and opinions of intelligent students and colleagues. Anyone who wants to evaluate can do no better than to go among students at registration time, listening careful-ly. I hardly need a complicated computer form to evaluate Elizabeth Massey's teaching; I can evaluate it very well on the basis of the many comments I have heard, year in and year out. Not one of them has been negative; not one of them has been less than enthusiastic and admiring. This surely registers a five on the Bach-Drinnon scale.

It is a fact, as the current catalog records, that Elizabeth Massey joined the faculty in 1966; but this is a "fact" which falls a good deal short of the truth. She did not come among us as a novice and a stranger barely ten years ago; she has been at least our fellow laborer over the years, accepting part-time teaching assignments in various circumstances, serving as our colleague in numerous enter-prises. But the real point of course is that she became a fully accredited member of this University community in 1939, when she arrived in Chattanooga as Winston Massey's bride. What better credentials than those could she have had? So the year 1966 is quite inaccurate to mark Elizabeth's beginning here; for all these years she has been a member of the goodly fellowship of those who teach and those who learn in this place. And as 1966 was not the real beginning, so 1977 will surely not mark the end of this relationship. Elizabeth Massey is one of the truly elect, whose tenure in our hearts and minds has no discernible limits. We shall continue to claim her as one of us, and our admiration and affection for her will not diminish.

March 25, 1977

Paul Ramsey

For those of us who knew and loved Paul Ramsey, his death last week was a profound and melancholy loss. When Carolyn Mitchell, who wrote the obituary for the *Times*, asked me for a quotation, I ended it by saying, "Our friendship goes back more than fifty years, and I shall remember him in a thousand affectionate ways." I am sure some people probably thought that was hyperbole born of grief, but it is the simple truth. Paul had a way of saying trenchant and memorable things, not only in his poems and his literary criticism but in conversation with friends. I quoted him often in speeches and even more often in conversation – always, I trust, giving him due credit.

A lot of people are fond of talking about godless professors in godless uni-versities, and I'm sure there are some of both. But UTC has not in my time been the sort of place I would call hostile to religion, and Paul Ramsey was one of the people who continually demonstrated that religion and higher learning are not incompatible. I am sure he was always moderate in his comments in class, but it was clear to students and colleagues alike that here was a person who took the faith seriously and who worked at it. (Certainly the readers of his books cannot fail to know that he was a committed Christian.)

For my last fifteen years at the University, Paul and I had offices directly opposite each other in the same suite; thus we saw each other virtually every day, usually being in and out of each other's offices two or three times in the course of a day. I cherish the memory of those many visits, however brief. And seeing the traffic in and out of his office, I was constantly aware of how attentive he was to students and how endlessly generous he was with his time. Sometimes he would seem to be summarizing a whole course for the benefit of someone who was struggling for one reason or another. I never heard a student complain that he was not available, or that he was unwilling to spend with the individual student enough time to be of real use in the student's difficulty. He was little short of a genius in working with his creative writing students; he could see clearly what they wanted to do and make useful suggestions about how they might accomplish it.

Dr. Paul Ramsey, Guerry Professor of English, Poet-in-Residence, and Alumni Distinguished Service Professor (1976-1989). His collections of poems include An Ordinary Place *(1965),* The Doors *(1968), and* No Running on the Boardwalk *(1975). His books of scholarship and criticism include* The Lively and the Just: An Argument for Propriety *(1962),* The Art of John Dryden *(1969),* The Fickle Glass: A Study of Shakespeare's Sonnets *(1979), and* The Truth of Value: Moral and Literary Judgment *(1985). Photograph by Charles Counts.*

A good friend who has been a consistent reader of this page once told me that he thought the columns that have a little vinegar in them may be my best. I must say something of the same for Paul in his comments on the human scene. I remember walking away from a faculty meeting years ago when one of our colleagues had made several windy and unhelpful speeches. Paul said, "I'm sure that X will be right about something some day, but it hasn't happened yet."

I thank God for such a friend, for his life, for his writings. To have known him is one of my life's great privileges.

October 9, 1994

Homage to Dorothy Hackett Ward

I want to thank, on my own behalf and on the behalf of everyone here, Chancellor Drinnon for his cordial support of the appropriate naming of this theatre, support without which this occasion would not have been possible. But I am mainly here today in my capacity as Elder Statesman, a role which I seem to play more and more often these days. So far as I know, I am the only person present here today who was already a member of the University Players when Dorothy Hackett Ward became chairman of the department in 1940. This month indeed marks the fortieth anniversary of the first play produced under her direction, E. P. Conkle's *Prologue to Glory*, a play about the young Abraham Lincoln. We greeted this new era in the University theatre with all the exuberance at our command, and it was considerable. Almost immediately some of us began to call Mrs. Ward, behind her back, Dottie Dear. I am afraid we grew bolder still. I think what happened was that she overheard some of us calling her Dottie Dear, she didn't have apoplexy, so we gradually began – I blush to remember it – to call her Dottie Dear to her face.

Dorothy Ward, faculty member of UC and UTC (1938-1975), Guerry Professor of theatre and speech and chair of the department. Photograph courtesy of UTC Archives (ca. 1950).

But if I have given you the idea that we were just a cozily democratic group, doing our work together without anyone really in authority, let me disabuse you of any such foolish notion. From the moment of Mrs. Ward's arrival in the chairmanship, there was never the slightest question about who was in charge. And I must tell you that there was never a more demanding, hard-hearted, tyrannical director than Dorothy Hackett Ward. She laid out for us the highest possible standards for our work, and when we failed to reach those standards – and I am afraid that was rather often – she called the failure to our attention in polite but vigorous language. It was the custom in the final rehearsals for her to summon the cast after each act for a critique. Critique! Now there is a euphemism if there ever was one. "Excoriation" would have been a better word, or even "blood-letting."

I still remember vividly from April 1941 one such "critique" at the dress rehearsal for *Romeo and Juliet*, the first of many Shakespearean plays which Mrs. Ward did in her long University tenure. On that occasion she regaled us with a rather large catalog of our sins and ended by saying indignantly, "And furthermore this scene took 78 seconds longer tonight than it took last night!" This point was met with a stunned silence, broken after a moment by a young man, unhappily one of those who did not return from World War II, who said, "Well, is that good or bad?"

But still we called her Dottie Dear.

In spite of our smug and callow youthfulness, we knew we were in the presence of something rare and wonderful. In spite of the fact that we affected a blasé attitude toward practically everything, we were serious about the quality of our education, and we knew that our experience in the theatre under Mrs. Ward's leadership was a very valuable part of that education. Despite ludicrously inadequate facilities, she continued to produce through the years a dazzling succession of plays. Through many student generations she provided that kind of civilizing, humanizing

"Dottie Dear" performing and teaching once again at the dedication of the Dorothy Hackett Ward Theatre, November 9, 1980. (GC is seated behind her purse.) Photograph courtesy of UTC Archives.

influence upon all of those who chose to work in the theatre. There are a goodly number of persons present here today who can testify with me to the value of what we learned there; after all these years, I can think of nothing in my own college experience which has proved more valuable. What all of us owe to Mrs. Ward is simply beyond calculation.

In the midst of it all, Mrs. Ward never ceased to be the teacher, and she never allowed us to forget that the theatre was first of all educational. Naturally, we aimed at the best performances of which we were capable, but the first emphasis was always upon the educational value of what we were doing. There is a temporary sign on the brick wall just inside the doors to this theatre, a sign which will be replaced by a bronze plaque now in the works. The plaque will read as follows: "This theatre is named in honor of Dorothy Hackett Ward, who in the life of service to her alma mater was a member of the faculty, 1938-1975, Guerry Professor of Theatre and Speech, chairman of the department." And the plaque concludes with a single line from Shakespeare, the words which Romeo spoke the first time he saw Juliet: "O she doth teach the torches to burn bright!" I should have liked to italicize the word "teach" to emphasize what was always at the heart of Dorothy Ward's purpose.

Dorothy Ward and a group of her drama students during the 1960s.

Today is a University occasion and I have therefore said nothing of the many community enterprises to which Mrs. Ward contributed. I have not mentioned her long years of service to the Chattanooga Opera Association, nor her work since her University retirement with the Festival Players in their superb efforts to bring the delights of theatre to the children and adults of this community. These things too are part of the record.

But today the University community honors one of its own. I count it a very great privilege to speak for all of us who were Mrs. Ward's students and all of us who were her colleagues in paying homage to an extraordinarily gifted teacher and to a rare and wonderful human being.

November 9, 1980

The University Community

University of Chattanooga, ca 1950. Photograph courtesy of UTC Archives.

Introduction to *Light Upon a Hill: The University at Chattanooga, 1886-1996*[*]

"It is, sir, as I have said, a small college,
and yet there are those who love it."
Daniel Webster, arguing before the Supreme Court in the
Dartmouth College Case, 1818

"This dear place"
UC's late classics professor, Dr. Joseph Callaway, in conversation with
President LeRoy Martin

Without question, the most significant event with which John Longwith has had to deal in this centennial history is the merger in 1969 of the University of Chattanooga and the University of Tennessee. Concomitantly with this merger was also that of Chattanooga City College into the UT system. This centennial history, the account that John Longwith has written, is not a public relations document; he is too honest and too good a research man and writer to fall into that

---

[*]By John Longwith. The University of Tennessee at Chattanooga, 2000.

71

trap. Nevertheless, those of us who have known and loved the University in many ways for many years must face the problem of nostalgia.

Several hundred UC alumni live in the Chattanooga metropolitan area; many of them still long for what they think of as the good old days. They are those who have never acknowledged the wider opportunities that the University of Tennessee system offers UTC as one of its major campuses. It is impossible to read this book without recognizing those opportunities that have opened to us as part of the UT system. There are certainly also those alumni,

Entrance to UC from McCallie Avenue, ca. 1963.
Photograph courtesy of UTC Archives.

among whom I count myself, who, given all the circumstances that obtained, accept the merger as both inevitable and beneficial.

Perhaps the more visible advantages the merger made possible were less important than those having to do with educational opportunities in this community, but nevertheless they mattered significantly. If I may be excused for using personal illustrations: when I became chairman of the English department in the summer of 1963, I did not have the convenience of a telephone in my office on the first floor of Race Hall. Dr. Maxwell Smith, who had retired a few years earlier after a long tenure as dean of Arts and Sciences, had an office just down the hall from mine, and he kindly left his office door unlocked so that I could use his telephone.

Nor did I have a dependable typewriter; what I had was an elderly manual typewriter, and when I asked the provost if it would not be possible for me to have an electric typewriter, his laughter was dismissive. Nevertheless within a few days, a portable electric Smith-Corona was delivered to my office. Following the merger, a young IBM sales representative spent so much time on the campus that he was sometimes taken for a new faculty member, hoping for a tenure track position.

A much more important and immediate change was the increase in the enrollment of minority students and the disadvantaged. The merger did not inaugurate the desegregation of UC of course; the graduate programs were desegregated in 1963 and the undergraduate the following year. Sometimes I hear comments that seem to imply that all the faculty and staff were opposed to desegregation, but that is simply not true. My own experience tells me that we had among us very few determined racists. The opposition to desegregation, such as it was, came from certain of the UC trustees; it was they who vetoed an honorary degree for Ralph McGill, editor of the Atlanta *Constitution*, a native son of Hamilton County, a graduate of McCallie School. McGill's sin, of course, was that he was a racial moderate as demonstrated in his columns in the *Constitution*, and more especially in his book called *The South and the Southerner*, published in 1963, a truly seminal book, especially for those who longed to see the influence of the Judaic and Christian tradition brought to bear on public policy in the United States of America.

I think very often of the passion of the two quotations that serve as epigraphs for this introduction: Daniel Webster's love for Dartmouth College and Joe Callaway's affectionate reference to our own campus as "this dear place." Dr. LeRoy Martin during his tenure as president of UC (1959-1966) on more than one occasion expressed public annoyance at being asked at educational meetings and similar gatherings out of town, how large the University of Chattanooga was. I share vicariously Dr. Martin's annoyance. There are far more important questions to ask – the level of intellectual challenge, the striving for excellence, the willingness to try new measures. Many questions are more important than the size of a school.

In a convocation address in Patten Chapel at the beginning of a fall term, early in his presidency, Dr. Martin's speech was as memorable as any I have ever heard on that sort of occasion. He had a great fondness for students; he and Mrs. Martin had two daughters of their own, and he liked young people. He was interested in the life of the mind, and that convocation address 40 years ago was full of sound and affectionate advice. One point he made, as I recall, is that all the administrative machinery, and all the equipment, have as their role to enhance and facilitate the educational experience. That is the reason for their existence. It is a point to keep in mind in reading this book.

John Longwith's history of the university, both UC and UTC, shows us, I think, that Shakespeare's words in *The Tempest* are validated once again: "What's past is prologue." The present state of the University is an outgrowth of the past, of our history and our traditions. The present is the fulfillment of the past, and in a hundred ways the University continues to deserve our loyal allegiance.

Remarks on the Occasion of the Dedication of the New Library at UTC (1974)

UTC Lupton Library, dedicated in 1974 and named in honor of Mr. and Mrs. T. Cartter Lupton in 1985.

To attempt to speak for all of the members of the faculty is a daring enterprise and one normally to be undertaken only with fear and trembling. But on this occasion I can accept the assignment with confidence: all of us rejoice in this handsome building and in the increased scope and usefulness it makes possible for the library of the University of Tennessee at Chattanooga. We are deeply grateful to all of those who have helped to make this day possible.

While this may not be the time for a long discussion of the role of the library in university life, we cannot let the occasion pass without at least reminding ourselves of what that role ideally is. The library is at the heart and center of the campus for the simple reason that the use of the library is at the heart and center of the educational process. The ability to use the library well is surely one of the most important skills which we can help the student to develop. Such use is essential not only to the successful completion of the student's undergraduate studies; it is also essential to lifelong *self*-education, of which the college years are only the beginning.

There is a highly relevant paragraph in an essay called "The Lost Tools of Learning" by that remarkable Englishwoman, Dorothy L. Sayers. "Do you ever find that young people," she writes, "when they have left school, not only forget most of what they have learned (that is only to be expected) but forget also, or betray that they have never really known, how to tackle a new subject for themselves? Are you often bothered by coming across grown-up men and women who seem unable to distinguish between a book that is sound, scholarly and properly documented, and one that is to any trained eye, very conspicuously none of these things? Or who cannot handle a library catalogue? Or who, when faced with a book of reference, betray a curious inability to extract from it the passages relevant to the particular question which interests them?" Surely Miss Sayers' questions are inexorable reminders of the educational importance of the library.

Moreover, the library stands as a symbol and guardian of that academic freedom which is perhaps the most important quality of our common life. The student has not only the right but the responsibility to explore alternatives, to consider diverse and sometimes unpopular opinions. There are always the siren voices to admonish us to take the safe and tested truth – their safe and tested truth – without bothering our heads with anything new or different. The library stands as a stalwart and continual reminder that all human thought is our province.

Finally, the library is one of those chief civilizing influences upon which the tone and quality of university education depend. In spite of all the marvels of our technology, nothing has yet been fashioned to take the place of a book; if we allow students to depart from these walls without at least a glimpse of this truth, we have cheated them. Let no student come through these hospitable doors without visible reminders of what a vast domain he or she has entered. Let students find here not only intellectual challenge and adventure, not only the companionship of the great minds of every age, but let them find here also the pleasure of reading as a means to the imaginative enlargement of their own lives.

If we have a true and lofty vision of the purpose of education, we have also a lofty vision of the role of the library in that education. All of us rejoice today to see this beautiful library so excellently and felicitously equipped to perform its functions.

January 17, 1974

Remarks at a Memorial Service for Dr. Frank Boyer

We are gathered on this occasion not primarily to mourn Frank Boyer's death, although our loss is a grievous one; we are gathered instead to celebrate his life, his goodness, his influence. At its best, the University is a community of those who teach and those who learn, and we are never more conscious of our membership in this community than when we are deprived of one its members through death. But if we should allow this to be a mournful occasion, we shall be unfaithful to that remarkable man whose memory we seek to honor.

It is fitting that for these ceremonies of celebration, we are gathered in Patten Chapel, where so many members of our community have gathered on so many occasions, where we are, therefore, in the words of the King James Bible, compassed about with so great a cloud of witnesses. We can rejoice in the Christian symbols by which we are

Patten Chapel, ca. 1963.
Photograph courtesy of UTC Archives

surrounded. Frank Boyer was himself a serious and committed Christian, active in the life of his own Church but intelligently cognizant of that larger Christian community of which all of us who profess and call ourselves Christians are members. As there are differing styles in every aspect of life, there are certainly differing styles in the way we acknowledge and display our Christian convictions. Frank was not a person to publish his faith, or to embellish his conversation with what C. S. Lewis once called "wearisome piety," but it was a quiet and pervasive faith which was therefore all the more impressive.

My task today is to speak on behalf of my faculty colleagues, always a demanding assignment. But I am confident that in my opinion of Frank Boyer, I *can* speak for all of us, confident that what I found in him, what I observed about him is a matter of very wide consensus in the faculty. There was in him a steadiness, a sameness, an integrity which allowed all of us, in whatever relationship we stood or in whatever enterprise we were engaged, to see precisely the same qualities, the same character. There was a wholeness in Frank to which even the most casual observer must have responded.

I believe that most of us, if we think carefully and candidly about our own education, will agree that one of the most important aspects of the process and environment of education is the impact of personality upon personality, the influence of the mature mind and person upon the less mature. Of course every teacher should be as well-trained and well-prepared as his or her own education and his or her own efforts will allow. But the teacher has far

Dr. Frank Boyer.
Photograph courtesy of UTC Archives.

more than learning to convey to students and indeed also to colleagues; he or she has a character, a set of attitudes, a philosophy of life. I have not encountered, in this community of scholars, a person in whose influence I had more confidence than I had in Frank Boyer's. He was a man whom his students could properly and usefully emulate; he was a man whom his colleagues could wholeheartedly admire.

It seems almost impossible now to realize that Frank was in only his fourteenth year on the faculty; he was so deeply a part of the University, a part of our goodly fellowship, that one easily had the feeling that he had always been here. On several occasions during these fourteen years, when I have had the responsibility of some enterprise and needed the help of someone who enjoyed the complete confidence of the faculty, I turned to Frank. He never declined any of these invitations to be of service, and he brought to whatever the task a grace and a competence all his own.

Two more qualities I shall remember especially about him: his beautiful manners and his sense of humor. He took the old-fashioned view that manners are important, that in the web of our relationships manners make a profound difference. Paul Ramsey has written of "the concept of courtesy as the primary justice due to personhood." I never heard Frank say that he subscribed to the same belief, but every encounter with him made it perfectly clear that he did. He treated other people, I am sure his students as well as his colleagues, with unfailing courtesy.

Frank's delightful sense of humor – an absolutely essential ingredient for any teacher – showed what a sense of humor always shows, a sense of proportion, a recognition of what is important and what isn't. My last conversation with him, at lunch a week ago today, seems in retrospect almost a summing up. He spoke warmly and affectionately of his family, of his wife and his children. We discussed some aspects of the University; we laughed about a good many things. One of his young colleagues told me on Monday how much he will miss Frank's laughter. So shall we all.

To speak of Frank Boyer in the past tense is a melancholy business. Our loss is a grievous loss. And yet it is deeply true that in some real sense, we have not lost him. Because we have known and loved him, because we have had the splendid example of his life so vividly before us, he will continue to exercise upon us significant influence. We shall be inspired by his goodness and heartened by his faithful devotion to this community of scholars, a devotion which I do not for a moment believe that even death can cancel out. As long as we live, we shall remember him with gratitude and affection.

In one of his finest lyric poems, Stephen Spender has taught us a way of celebrating the lives of the "truly great." It is a poem that could have been written for Frank Boyer:

> I think continually of those who were truly great.
> Who, from the womb, remembered the soul's history
> Through corridors of light, where the hours are suns,
> Endless and singing. Whose lovely ambition
> Was that their lips, still touched with fire,
> Should tell of the Spirit, clothed from head to foot in song.
> And who hoarded from the Spring branches
> The desires falling across their bodies like blossoms.
>
> What is precious is never to forget
> The essential delight of the blood drawn from ageless springs
> Breaking through rocks in worlds before our earth.
> Never to deny its pleasure in the simple morning light
> Nor its grave evening demand for love.
> Never to allow gradually the traffic to smother
> With noise and fog, the flowering of the spirit.

Near the snow, near the sun, in the highest fields,
See how these names are fêted by the waving grass
And by the streamers of white cloud
And whispers of wind in the listening sky.
The names of those who in their lives fought for life,
Who wore at their hearts the fire's centre.
Born of the sun, they traveled a short while toward the sun,
And left the vivid air signed with their honour.

October 29, 1980

Alpha Memorial Tribute to Dr. William Henry Masterson

Dr. William Henry Masterson, who became a member of the Alpha Society in May 1967, died accidentally at his home in Austin, Texas, on March 3, 1983. Dr. Masterson occupies a unique place in the history of this institution: he was the eleventh and last president of the University of Chattanooga and the first chancellor of the University of Tennessee at Chattanooga. A year following his retirement from the chancellorship in 1973, he became a full-time member of the History Department. In 1977, he was designated Guerry Professor of History.

For those of us fortunate enough to be here during the entire tenure of Dr. Masterson, certain of his qualities and abilities are unforgettable. He had, for example, a great talent for language, the ability

Dr. William Henry Masterson, the last president of UC (1966-1969) and the first chancellor of UTC (1969-1973), faculty member (1973-1979) and Guerry Professor of history. Photograph courtesy of UTC Archives.

to articulate for all of us the nature and purpose of the university and the profound importance of scholarship. It is fitting that we should be able to remember these things at the annual meeting of the Alpha Society because two of his speeches delivered at annual meetings of Alpha were among the most memorable of his fourteen years on this campus. The first of these speeches was delivered at the April 1967 meeting at the time of his induction into membership and the second on the eve of his retirement in April 1979. Both speeches cut through the secondary and the derivative, the extraneous and the superficial, and they dealt with the true and abiding purpose of the university as a community of scholars. Fortunately the Alpha Society published the second of these speeches and his wisdom and eloquence are therefore a matter of historical record.

But it is for deeds as well as words, deeds of inspired leadership, for which we remember William Masterson. For those of us with a sense of the history of the institution, there are many ways in which he remains a part of our community life. It was his vision which led to the closing of Oak Street in the very heart of the campus, a development of enormously significant consequence. And it was his insistence on the need for a new library which initiated the long planning that led to the present structure; this was a need which he recognized long before the merger with the University of Tennessee.

All of us remember with pleasure the gracious hospitality which obtained in the President's House during Dr. and Mrs. Masterson's years there. They gave us continually a demonstration of the civilized graces, and all of us responded to it and rejoiced in it. We remember Dr. Masterson with continuing gratitude for what he contributed to this society and to the university community; he is forever a part of the development of this institution.

February 24, 1984

Some Thoughts about Excellence

Address at the annual dinner meeting of The Alpha Society
The University of Tennessee at Chattanooga, February 28, 1986

When Jane Austen had completed what most discriminating readers regard as her finest novel – the novel entitled *Emma* – she spoke of having created "a heroine whom no one will like except myself." I am about to deliver a speech of which the same thing can be said; probably no one will like it *in toto*, or certainly agree with it *in toto*, except myself. This will not be my first experience as a minority of one, and I shall try to bear it with Christian fortitude.

For the purpose of making my intentions as clear as possible, I want to begin with three prefatory comments. The first comment is implicit in what I have already said: I have made no effort to find a consensus out of which I can speak. It occurred to me some time ago to put this speech into the hands of several friends who know the University well and who therefore might have been expected to be good and useful critics. But I decided that there would be more disadvantage in such procedure than otherwise. So I want to make it extremely clear: the views I am about to express are wholly my own.

Secondly, I want to assure you that I have no sentimental, nostalgic view that the University of Chattanooga was a perfect institution, without noticeable flaws of any kind. In order to hold that opinion, one would have to be very forgetful.

Thirdly, and perhaps most importantly, I came a long time ago to the simple conclusion that on balance the merger with the University of Tennessee system was desirable and probably, given the circumstances, inevitable. Moreover, I believe the merger has had a far more positive effect than a negative one. Salaries have certainly been improved substantially, and the merger has made available to us vastly increased resources to do what it is our mission to do.

When the news broke in April 1968 that conversations were in progress looking towards a merger with the University of Tennessee, I was a member of President William Masterson's staff as his executive assistant. A few weeks later I was appointed to the merger committee, made up of representatives of Knoxville and ourselves. I mention these facts only to establish that when I speak of the merger and its aftermath, I speak of what I know of first hand. If I seem to depend upon experiences of my own to support my points, it is for the same reason; I speak of what I know. The earliest estimates of our growth as a state institution suggested that by the year 1980 – eleven years after the merger – enrollment on this campus would reach 10,000. Fortunately, and more accurately, that estimate was soon scaled down to 7,500 as the probable enrollment by 1980.

But the earlier figure – the estimate of 10,000 – certainly had its value as a spur to our planning. Soon after that initial announcement, I was on the campus of East Tennessee State in Johnson City for some sort of literary symposium. At that time, East Tennessee State had approximately 10,000 students; during almost two days on that campus, I remember paying careful attention to all of at least the visible aspects of campus life to the end that I might learn as much as I could from their experience, from their successes and their failures. I became more determined myself that we should, by careful and thoughtful planning, avoid as much as possible the curse of bigness. This concern about numbers was one which a good many of us shared in Dr. Masterson's administration; there were several of us who were convinced that we needed to deal with vastly increased enrollment vigorously and imaginatively. But unwiser heads prevailed, and we failed then as I think we have continued to fail ever since, to minimize as far as we humanly can the negative impact of large numbers.

It is certainly not my intention here to argue that all of our problems and infelicities are the result of increasing enrollments. There are certainly additional and multiple causes for any problem one is likely to think of, but my point is that all of these problems are worsened and aggravated by increasing enrollments and our frequent failure to attack the problem directly and forthrightly. I want this evening to address myself to three aspects of university life which in my judgment have been deeply influenced by increasing numbers of students and of faculty. Since the merger with the University of Tennessee in 1969, I think there has been in our common life on this campus a decline in civility, in our sense of community, and in our concern for standards of excellence in many aspects of the university's life.

I begin with civility, and as background I want to describe for you briefly an experience of my own more than ten years ago. In 1974, the University of Mississippi began what has become a distinguished annual conference on the life and work of William Faulkner. Because Professor Arlie Herron, our resident authority on Faulkner, was engaged in summer school and unable to go, I represented the department at the first conference. I had never been on the Ole Miss campus before, nor had I ever thought of the University of Mississippi as one of the intellectual strongholds of the southeast. In that week I certainly got rid of several of my snobbish prejudices; the two or three Ole Miss teachers who lectured to the conference more than held their own amongst the glittering array of Faulkner scholars and critics who were gathered there. But the deepest impression that I carried away from that week was of the civility which pervaded that campus and all the activities of the week. By the Chancellor of the University to the lowliest members of the university staff, we were all of us treated with unfailing courtesy.

A small incident on the first evening of the conference turned out to be a foretaste of things to come. I had no idea of the location of the building where the first conference session was to be held, and I asked directions of a young man, a student, who was employed by the conference. No indeed, he could not tell me; the route was much too difficult and I was bound to get lost. Therefore, he insisted that he transport me there in his own car. I found such solicitude somewhat startling, but it was to be matched again and again during that week.

I ask you to set against that act of courtesy and hospitality an experience on this campus which I became involved in quite by accident. Several years ago one spring afternoon, returning from lunch, I entered the eastern doors of Hooper Hall and at once encountered a couple – husband and wife – whom I knew slightly. I also knew they had sent three children to UTC, all of them distinguishing themselves. The third of these three was a severely handicapped daughter, and because of some federal program from which that young woman benefited, the parents needed from the university a document of some sort. They appealed to me for help with desperation on their faces and in their voices; they had been to five offices in the university and someone in each had sent them to another office. Nobody had taken the time or the trouble to understand precisely what they needed and to give them reliable advice about where to get it. Could I help them? Yes, I could help them because, like many of you, I had learned by hard experience which university offices are helpful and which are not. I took them into the Records Office and introduced them to Natalie Schlack, who, of course, did for them, with her usual efficiency, what needed doing.

(I trust that my old friend will not object to a slight digression here. And yet it isn't a digression because I am discussing the civility which ought to characterize our common life. Because it is often Miss Schlack's painful and thankless duty to tell students what they do not want to hear, she is seldom appreciated, either by students or her administrative superiors, for what she contributes to this university. When she chooses to retire, it will be interesting to see what three persons the university employs to do the work that she does single-handedly.)

If you tell me that all of my evidence for the lack of civility on this campus is anecdotal, I can only agree with you. But what other kind of evidence is possible? I limit myself to one more anecdote, this one also personal. Very late in July, I received a call at home from a young woman in the parking office. Her tone I would describe as firm but polite; "Is it true, Professor Connor, that you have retired from the University?" "Yes, quite true." "As of June 30th?" Again, "quite true." Then she said, with just a touch of accusation in her voice, "You did not clear this office." "Why on earth should I have cleared the parking office?" I asked with just the suggestion of a laugh. The young woman made it clear by her tone that this was no laughing matter. "You still have your decal," she said. "Well, am I not still paying for it?" I asked. No; my final check included a parking deduction only for June; I owed six dollars for July – and the parking decal. Knowing I was wasting my breath, I said to the young woman, "You know, it's this sort of bureaucracy which drives the faculty right up the wall. Last November when I wrote my letter formally expressing my intention to retire, I addressed it to my department head and sent copies to the acting dean, the acting provost, the chancellor, and the personnel office both here and in the university system. I should think someone would have let you in on the secret." "We are always the last to hear," she said plaintively. I decided to play one more card, though I knew I was wasting her time and my own. "You know," I said, "I finished cleaning out my office and turned in my keys on July 3rd. I haven't been near the parking garage since then." She was implacable: "Professor Connor, I must have your decal and a check for six dollars." I put them in the mail that afternoon, very much feeling that it was not a happy way after more than twenty-six years to conduct a final piece of business with the university. Forgive me if I draw the moral yet more clearly: it is not wise or prudent for the university to commit such tactless business to the hands of minor functionaries. Somebody with a little more authority and some sense of proportion should have been involved.

When Charles Temple was here, he had hanging on his office wall the excellent admonition "Think students." That is sound advice for anybody engaged in the enterprise of education. I propose two more signs for as many walls as possible. One should read "Also think faculty" and the other "Treasurers were made for man and not man for treasurers."

I turn now to another aspect of our common life. The sense of community, of collegiality, the sense that we have common allegiances which bind us in a common enterprise – all this has greatly diminished since the merger. I do not believe that I am distorting or romanticizing the circumstances when we were a small private school. We took a keen and lively interest in our colleagues and in the work they were doing and in their families. It seems to me now that there is the most limited sense of community, and the university system seems to use the word 'family' almost wholly for fund-raising purposes. When a major fund-raising drive, the campaign called Tennessee Tomorrow, was launched in 1977, I was

Student inscriptions on the inside cover of The Seven Mountains of Thomas Merton, *by Michael Mott. Boston: Houghton Mifflin, 1984. Given to GC by his Rhetoric and Composition class his last semester before retirement.*

invited to serve as chairman for the in-house contributions on this campus. I made it a condition of my acceptance that we would not call this phase of the campaign the Family Campaign (as it was called on other campuses). We won that minor skirmish by calling our efforts among faculty and staff the Campus Campaign. I will do quite a lot to help raise money for the university, but I will not perjure myself.

Nor was I ever willing to use the gadget introduced into orientation and registration periods. I refer of course to those very large buttons reading "UTC Family, ASK ME." This is gimmickry and nothing more. The newcomer who appears lost is quite as easy to identify as the old hand who obviously knows his way around the campus. One hardly needs a button for these people to identify each other. Nor does my heart leap up when I behold the tacky humor used in labeling members of the Student Orientation Board as SOB's. I don't know who thought up that tasteless acronym, but he should have gone on thinking at least a little longer. More gimmickry. And if a secretary or someone else answering a university phone genuinely wants to be helpful, that fact will communicate itself without the inane question, "May I help you?" When Dot Bradley – God rest her soul – was in the Chancellor's office, I never remember her using that threadbare question "May I help you?" but it was perfectly clear from the tone of her voice and its warmth that she was there to help. And I cannot remember that she ever failed to do so.

There is no formula so clever that it can communicate an interest in and concern for other people unless that interest and concern are genuinely there. My point is that it is often painfully obvious that too few of us are concerned about our colleagues, too few who feel a strong sense of common interests and common welfare. I give you two examples. A few years ago a person whom I regard as an extraordinarily able teacher and faculty colleague was promoted to full professor. I telephoned him to express my pleasure and congratulations. A few months later, he told me that exactly five persons had telephoned or sent their best wishes. All five were persons who had been a part of the University of Chattanooga. My second example is more revealing still. Twice in the past two years I have been present at a funeral for someone in a faculty member's family. On both occasions the members of the department to which the bereaved faculty member belonged were conspicuous by their absence. In one case I did not see one single member of the department concerned.

Such callous indifference – I hardly know what else to call it – can hardly be ascribed to large enrollments or to administrative failure of some sort; failure clearly belongs to the individual faculty member. As faculty members we have by no means taken advantage of our opportunities to express our commitment to the university community. Surely one of the best developments in recent years was the establishment of the Chickamauga Room, the faculty and staff dining room on the second floor of this building. But members of the faculty have simply not taken advantage of this opportunity to see their colleagues informally or to make some effort to enhance the sense of community on campus. Unless things have changed radically this year, I would estimate that not more than one-fourth of the faculty use the facilities of the Chickamauga Room with any regularity. One of the most important things to ask, it seems to me, about a prospective faculty member at the time of his or her appointment is how good a colleague will he or she be? If every faculty member is simply to pursue his or her own interests with scant regard for other persons and their interests and concerns, what we have is not a community of those who teach and those who learn; what we have is the Tower of Babel.

Finally, I turn to the most important aspect of all, the concern for excellence. One of the most distinguished elder statesmen in British education in this century was Sir Richard Livingstone, sometime president of Corpus Christi College, Oxford. In 1944, the penultimate year of the bloodiest and most destructive war in human history, Sir Richard published a little book called *Education for a World Adrift*. In an early chapter he quotes Alfred North Whitehead, himself also a great educational statesman. Whitehead wrote, "Moral education is impossible without the habitual vision of greatness." Sir Richard comments, "It could not be put more strongly–'impossible,' 'habitual' vision (not a chance and occasional glimpse). Outside Plato, there is no profounder saying about education."

Sir Richard goes on to expand the point: "A 'habitual vision of greatness' is necessary not only to moral education, but to all education. A teacher cannot give an adequate training in anything unless he or she knows, and can make the pupil see, what is great and first-rate in it. How can you train a surgeon unless you show him or her the finest technique of surgery; or a teacher, unless he or she knows the best methods of educational practice; or an architect, unless he or she is familiar with the great examples of his art? So, too, with all subjects, from building to farming, from carpentry to Greek prose. Much else may enter the student's training, but there is no stimulus like seeing the best work in the subject which the student studies; he or she will have no standards, no conception of the goal, unless the student sees the best; he or she will slip insensibly to lower levels of ideal and practice, unless it is continually before the student's mind, unless, in fact, he or she has the 'habitual vision of greatness' to attract, direct and inspire."

In a speech done more than twenty years ago under the joint auspices of Blue Key and Mortar Board, I spelled out as best I could what this 'habitual vision of greatness' ought to mean in the university community. I argued then – and I would certainly argue now – that the student's every experience in his or her college years should contribute to this 'habitual vision of greatness,' that every part of the student's college life should help to inculcate the standards of excellence. The student should encounter this excellence in the architecture of the campus buildings, in the beauty of the campus, in everything that is a part of our common life here. Unfortunately we too often confront the student with the meretricious and the third-rate.

In some recent promotional material for several campus enterprises, including the bookstore, the claim was made that the bookstore was, and I quote, "more than just books." "Other than just books" would have been a truer billing, because the books are all but lost amid the sweat shirts and the deodorants. But when one is clever enough to find the books (and I am talking of course not about textbooks, but the other books that are there for our reading pleasure) when one is clever enough to find the books, what a glorious mess is there. Certainly there are some books that one would expect to find in a college bookstore; there are far more that I would be quite unable to justify. One looks at the shelves in dismay and wonders if after all the invention of printing was a good idea. If it is an important part of our function to confront the student continually with the first-rate, then there needs to be a vast cleaning out of the bookstore. If you tell me that every trashy, shoddy book or magazine there is also widely available downtown, I shall not argue with you. But Walden's is not in the business of education; the university is.

If we look for those things which militate against the 'habitual vision of greatness,' a prominent place must be found for the most recent and most costly building on campus. I refer of course to the arena, once named in a ballyhooed contest, the Roundhouse. I am offended first of all by the enormous cost of that building, fifteen and a half million dollars, when there are so many urgent needs elsewhere in the university. Sheer financial necessity makes a certain income necessary to meet financing costs. The result has been a succession of productions which have not exactly contributed to the university's educational aims. I am aware that we can always comfort ourselves that we are not sponsoring the living unicorn, or the tractor pulls, or the more vulgar rock shows. But whether the university in fact sponsors these things or not, its name is always prominent in the advertising and I rather think in the public mind we get full credit. In the midst of all this, I ask you to remember sometimes Whitehead's 'habitual vision of greatness'.

If these remarks have seemed unduly negative to you, I regret it. I have tried to obey St. Paul's admonition to speak the truth in love. I have spent a lifetime in the conviction that the educational experience is a civilizing, humanizing experience. There is much that is good and sound and worthy in this institution. The only way we can make it a truly distinguished university is to look plainly at its faults and take action against them. If we do so, there will be enough work for all of us to find our proper share.

February 28, 1986

"The Goodly Fellowship"

Despite the sometimes contentious nature of college audiences, (after all, the Germans have a proverb, "A professor is a person who thinks otherwise,") I believe I can obtain immediate consensus for one claim: I have made more speeches than anyone should be expected or allowed to make in one lifetime. I say this only as background for telling you that this speech for this occasion has been more difficult for me than almost any speech I can remember.

I suppose the difficulty lies mainly in the fact that for now well over fifty years the University has been one of the chief presences on which my life has pivoted. Thus, I cannot hope to render a full account of what I owe the University as student, alumnus and teacher. Stephen Leacock, that wonderful old Canadian humorist and economist, speaks somewhere in an essay about those fortunate persons "who come to college and never go away, whose lot it is, thrice blessed, to stay at college all their lives." I wasn't quite able to manage that life-long tenure, owing to the Second

GC accepts the Distinguished Alumnus Award presented by Chancellor Fred Obear, 1992.

World War and other distractions, but I shall always be glad that I was able to come home to the University for the last twenty-six years of my teaching career.

These brief remarks will not have the formality of a speech with a thesis and the traditional three points, but I do want the luxury of an epigraph, in this case a brief quotation that I hope will clearly convey the essence of my intentions. I have chosen this epigraph from a short story by one of the most brilliant writers to enrich our lives and shape our perceptions in the post-World War II period. I speak of Flannery O'Connor, and my chosen epigraph comes from her story called "Revelation," which I think is the very finest of her many fine short stories. The protagonist is Ruby Turpin, a no-nonsense sort of woman who thinks of herself, quite rightly, as "a respectable, hardworking, church-going woman." Along with several other people, she is in a doctor's waiting room and the conversation has turned to the subject of gratitude. Mrs. Turpin begins a brief speech on the matter by uttering the sentence that is my epigraph: "If it's anything I am," she says with feeling, "it's grateful." In spite of the shaky grammar, I gladly associate myself with that statement. I will go further: to be ungrateful in a world in which so much is given to us, where we are indebted to so many people for their kindness and beneficent influence is to fail in an important moral responsibility.

When I arrived on this campus as a callow and opinionated freshman in September 1938, I was not so satisfied with myself that I did not look forward to all the opportunities for growth and development that the University offered me. Dr. Alexander Guerry had gone that same fall to Sewanee to be the Vice-Chancellor there, but he left here, I think, a legacy of community from which UC continued to benefit for a long time – indeed from which the University still benefits. We were, all of us, students and faculty, in some measure, shaped by that community, by its size, by its intimate and cordial atmosphere. To paraphrase Daniel Webster when he argued the Dartmouth College case before the Supreme Court in 1818, "It was a small college, but there are those who love it." We were still living under the shadow of the Great Depression of the 1930's, and resources were often limited, but there was assembled here a quite remarkable faculty, and one of the virtues of our smallness was that we all profited from all of those talented people. But I must single out two persons in that faculty to whom my own indebtedness can be acknowledged but never discharged.

One person here this afternoon I want especially to acknowledge is Jim Livingood, whom I always think of as "my" Dean. It was he who invited me to the faculty and certainly always gave me sturdy support and useful advice. I had a class in economics from Jim in my freshman year in the spring of 1939, and if I am wholly ignorant of economics, the blame certainly cannot be assigned to him.

Of the great influence among my teachers, I mention first Isobel Griscom, who spent more than forty years in the UC English Department; thus I am only one of a great company of students whom she helped to civilize and at least to begin to educate, from whom she elicited respect for the language and passion for the literature that she taught. She was the best teacher I ever had at any level; I cannot make the point any more plainly or any more justly than that. In my introductory essay to the little book of Miss Griscom's poems published by the English Department in 1977, I was at least able to make my indebtedness to her a matter of record.

The other great influence of my undergraduate years was Dorothy Hackett Ward, though she was never in the strictest formal sense my teacher. When she came to take command of the theater department in the fall of 1940, I had already taken all the courses then available in that department. But I make a rather pedantic point, I fear, in saying that she was never my teacher in the formal sense. I was in five of the six major productions that Mrs. Ward directed in her first two years in that position, and I can assure you that as director, she was very much, first and foremost, the teacher. It was my happy assignment to be the speaker on a Sunday afternoon in November 1980 when the new theater in the Fine Arts Center was officially designated as the Dorothy Hackett Ward Theatre. Appearing that afternoon in my capacity as elder statesman, I was able to give that capacity audience some notion of the tyranny that she practiced upon us. But I must tell you also that we were a good deal more civilized as a result of that tyranny. We learned a great deal through the discipline of that unrelenting pursuit of excellence that Dorothy Ward simply took for granted.

(We used to wish sometimes that Dottie would suffer some of our shortcomings in silence. But let's face it – silence was never Dottie's strong suit. God knows I will pay for that.)

You must not misunderstand my nostalgic references to the University of an earlier day and far smaller size. Even if it were possible, I would not want the clock turned back. The overwhelming majority of faculty members accepted the merger with the University of Tennessee system and worked to help make the transition a smooth one. I was both in the Chancellor's office at that time and one of the UC members of the merger committee, and as far as I know not a single faculty member resigned as a result of the merger. I rejoice that the increased resources available to us as a member of the UT system have made possible greater service and wider impact in the community. Especially do I welcome now, as I welcomed it in 1969, the opportunity to make the University more accessible to minority students and to the disadvantaged.

If I seem to have said little to this point about students, it is not because I think them an unimportant part of the University community. One officer of the University during his tenure here had a sign on his office wall that read THINK STUDENTS. A very good idea indeed. Though I am tempted to call a few names of students, for obvious reasons, I dare not. One of the greatest advantages of staying put, of living all one's life in the same place, is the opportunity it affords to see how one's students turn out. Many of those students have made and are making for themselves admirable and distinguished careers, and not always those for whom I might have predicted such development. Many of them are here this afternoon. If I am hesitant to identify them and call them by name lest I make painful omissions, they will be happy to identify themselves to any of you who are interested.

Among those great teachers of our time whom I have admired vicariously – through their writing and through other people's testimony – one whom I value especially is Mary Ellen Chase, whose long and distinguished career culminated in twenty-nine years as Professor of English at Smith College. But I mention her now simply to cite with admiration the title of her memoirs, dealing mainly with her teaching experience. She called the book *The Goodly Fellowship*, taking that phrase from the ancient hymn of the church, the *Te Deum*: "The goodly fellowship of the prophets praise thee." The academic community at its best is certainly a goodly fellowship, a community of those who teach and those who learn. And in this community, this fellowship, we are all sometimes teachers and sometimes learners. I learned a great deal from my students, and I certainly learned a great deal from my colleagues. It is impossible to find words adequate to thank all of you, so I conclude very much where I began: "If it's anything I am, it's grateful."

October 30, 1992

Judge and Reverend Sam Payne and his wife Carolyn with
GC at his retirement gala, April 14, 1985. Photograph by Lisa Waddell.

Part II

On Literature and Language

"Literature gives us not instruction, but illumination."

William Temple

The Values and Pleasures of Literature

"For me it is almost impossible to separate the pleasures in reading
from the values derived from it."

(GC, April 1969)

"Gradual Time's Last Gift"

At the end of one of his most poignant poems, William Butler Yeats writes
of literature as ". . .gradual Time's last gift, a written speech / Wrought of high
laughter, loveliness and ease." Often one thinks of those words with an overwhelming sense of irony – when, for example, one is looking at a list of best sellers in the newspaper. Of the fifteen books of fiction listed in *The New York Times*
best sellers, it is a safe guess that two-thirds of them will be forgotten in a year,
certainly in ten years. Number two in the current list (admittedly not a fair example) is Judith Krantz's latest offering. A recent reviewer said of the book that every
page is "related in the most pedestrian, plodding prose. There is not an insight, a
clever line, a hint of humor, a neat turn of phrase, a felicitous description."

Just when I had been musing on the powers of literature (again), a friend
sent me a quotation from Robert Stone. He writes in part: "Fiction is, or should
be, an act against loneliness, an appeal to community, a bet on the possibility of
spanning the gulf that separates one human being from another." The clear implication of those words is that writing is a moral act. What makes so many writers
immoral is not the four-letter words or emphasis on sex; it is, to use the charge
once made against a famous would-be poet, that they are so little above sea level.
At the end of the Stone quotation, my friend writes, "In the absence of *honest* sto-
rytelling, [emphasis added] people are abandoned to the beating of their own
hearts." The use of the word "honest" is very telling.

One of the great values of literature is that it permits us to enter imaginatively into the lives of other people, to see the world as they see it. Thus we come
to know fictional characters sometimes even better than we know other human
beings. But our knowledge of those characters gives us the power of understanding other people better. George Buttrick says of the rich man in our Lord's parable that he did not know Lazarus, that he was not aware of him as a person
(*Interpreter's Bible*, Vol. 8, 289). The rich man knew his own kind of people, and
most of us are prisoners of that condition. Literature, if it is worthy of the name,
helps us to free ourselves.

September 18, 1988

The Relevance of Literature
Annual Meeting of the Alpha Society, April 1969

In the academic world in every age – alas, in every season – certain words achieve such universal popularity that they assume the quality of incantation. In this season such a word is *relevance*, or perhaps more often the adjective *relevant*. In the current educational discussion, more properly known as dialogue, every course, every book, every idea is relevant, or it is nothing. An irascible correspondent in the University *Echo* belabors the Curriculum Committee because it is not sensitive to the problem of relevance, by which he seems to mean that the committee tolerates a curriculum in which even prospective engineers are introduced to the discipline of literature.

I do not wish to be misunderstood. I am not opposed to relevance. I am not opposed to the most searching and critical examination of the intent and structure of the curriculum. But I do find myself wondering what *relevance* means in the minds of some of its warmest advocates. I had a telephone call the other day from a young man whose exuberance seems to be well-supported by intelligence and a sound education. He wished to call my attention to a distinguished educator and scholar whom the University might be able to interest in an appointment. This scholar is the product of distinguished universities here and abroad. For twenty years he has held positions as teacher and administrator in several first-rate institutions. But now at the age of 45, he wishes to give it all up and find something genuinely relevant. Since relevance seems to have eluded him in twenty years of work in an old and honorable discipline, it is surely fair to wonder whether he will be able to find relevance in any position.

It is tempting to speculate as to whether this widespread demand for relevance does not arise from the attitude toward education in which the urgent is more important than the fundamental. In many ways the attitude seems to be a response, and undoubtedly often a healthy response, to the social and political problems that sorely beset us, crying out for solutions. But I doubt whether any education worthy of the name can so fix its attention upon the immediate problem that it denies itself the illumination of the past, the illumination, for example, of history and literature. I doubt that what an urban sociologist published last week, or what the *New York Times* printed today, is more relevant, except in the most superficial sense, than Shakespeare or Dante or the Hebrew prophets. Or, to put the point more defensibly, I doubt that the most perceptive writing about current problems is really meaningful – or relevant – to those who have no genuine sense of the long history of man, of his baseness and his glory, his failures and his achievements.

It is this universal cry for relevance that has persuaded me to address myself on this occasion to the relevance of literature. It seems to me an occasion, as we honor scholarly achievement, for expressing one's deepest educational convictions. My deepest conviction can be simply stated: the reading and study of great literature is profoundly relevant to all of our most significant personal, professional, and social concerns. Much of what I shall say will be more in the nature of confession than argument, but at least I shall have put into the record what I believe about the relevance of literature.

Because I shall be saying more about the values of literature than about its pleasures, I add one more word of preface. For me it is almost impossible to separate the pleasures in reading from the values derived from it. I number among my closest friends a couple, among the most happily married people I know, whose temperaments could hardly be more different. The husband is a concerned citizen, a toiler in worthy causes, a member of many committees. The wife, who also has a career of her own, is inclined in her leisure time to stay at home and read books. One evening several years ago the husband came home from an important meeting to find his wife reading a novel. "My dear," he said reprovingly, "your reading sometimes borders on the recreational." I would hope that our reading does not merely border on the recreational but that it is deeply and genuinely recreational, in the best sense of that term. This itself is no insignificant value to derive from reading, that in the midst of the busyness and the varied demands of our lives, we can find in reading the re-creation and the refreshment of spirit that will send us back to our work with a renewed sense of pleasure and purpose.

Apart from this important recreational value, I shall content myself with three claims for literature. My first claim is that literature reveals both the glory and the cost of our humanness. What happens to any of the great tragic heroes – Job or Oedipus or Hamlet or Othello – matters to us in proportion to our understanding of what superb and majestic human beings they are. In his Nobel acceptance speech in 1950, William Faulkner suggested that the only things worth writing about are "the problems of the human heart in conflict with itself." It is the tension between *is* and *ought,* between desire and duty, between one part of his nature and another in which man is most fully revealed in great literature. The conflict reveals both the glory and the cost. We cannot genuinely encounter the great tragic heroes without a renewed sense that human life is enormously worthwhile, whatever the cost.

One thinks of Job, "none like him in the earth, a perfect and an upright man"; when he appeared in the street, "The young men saw me and hid themselves: and the aged arose and stood up." To see such a man beset by woes which he thinks outrageously unjust and incomprehensible, and with such a wife and such friends as comforters, is to be filled with awe and pity. But Job hardly wins our admiration by his submissiveness; despite the glib phrase "the patience of Job," he is the least patient of men. No person in the Bible casts his complaints so boldly into the very face of God: "Therefore I will not refrain my mouth: I will speak in the anguish of my spirit; I will complain in the bitterness of my soul." The book yields up no neat set of theological or philosophical formulations which explain the relationship between the moral quality of man's life and the prosperity or adversity which he experiences. But one cannot go down into the depths with Job without gaining a fresh understanding of what it costs to be a human being, without some new vision of man's glory.

The glory and the cost of being human is perhaps in few places made so vivid as it is in *King Lear*. It is surely a part of Shakespeare's genius that he never falsifies the human situation, and therefore Lear himself reveals far more than his majesty and authority. He reveals also how jealous and spiteful and petty he can be; all of the most unpleasant qualities of senility are there in full measure. But the glory is also there. Otherwise, we could not be so shaken by the cruelty of his two elder daughters, so profoundly moved by his ability in the midst of the storm to take thought about his own failures and to begin to find redemption. Cordelia speaks for us when she says:

> For thee, oppressed king, am I cast down;
> Myself could else out-frown false fortune's frown.

But Lear at this moment is not in the least cast down. He goes light-heartedly to prison with his rediscovered daughter:

> Upon such sacrifices, my Cordelia,
> The gods themselves throw incense.

It is not of course only in the most firmly established literary classics that this sense of the glory and goodness of life is revealed. It is quite possible to compile an almost endless catalog of characters who by their courage, their goodness, their enterprise, remind us of "what a piece of work is man": Huckleberry Finn, who is willing to go to hell if that is necessary to help Jim retain his freedom; Jeanie Deans in Scott's *Heart of Midlothian*, who walks from her little Scottish village to London to plead with Queen Caroline on behalf of her sister condemned to die; Gatsby and his "heightened sensitivity to the promises of life"; Jane Austen's Emma, who discovers that she is not God (a useful lesson for any human being). The list is long indeed of those works that offer us a renewed sense of the glory, the pain, the possibilities of human existence.

The second claim is that literature has the power to diminish, perhaps very nearly to eradicate, the sense of isolation and loneliness which any human being is certain on occasion to feel. When any student has come to talk with me about a really serious personal problem, I have almost invariably been struck by his feeling that he alone in the vast history of the race has been called upon to face this particular problem. If he is feeling the pressure from his father to elect his father's profession, if he is being misunderstood by the only young woman in the world whose understanding matters, he feels himself absolutely unique. I am not suggesting that on these occasions one can dispense the proper reading suggestions much as a doctor prescribes the proper drugs, although it is worth saying that often one book in which a parallel situation exists can be very healing. What I am saying is that this sense of being cut off from human companionship and consolation can be powerfully diminished by the reading of literature.

There are few of us who can identify with Hamlet in any complete and detailed way. Few of us are the sons of royal fathers, murdered by lecherous and ambitious brothers. But all of us have been dismayed by the irrational behavior of others, by the treachery of those whose loyalty we counted on, the hypocrisy of one who can admonish his son to be true to himself and hence to all other men while he is himself false in almost every deed in the play. I do not believe one can read and study *Hamlet* (I do not mean superficially or pedantically) and be the same person after the experience.

One can argue, I think, that poetry is especially rich in its capacity for reminding us of our common humanity, of underscoring the simple and profound truth that no man is an island, entire of himself. How many disappointed lovers have found some measure of comfort in the recognition they feel when they read Yeats's "A Deep-Sworn Vow"?

> Others because you did not keep
> That deep-sworn vow have been friends of mine;
> Yet always when I look death in the face,
> When I clamber to the heights of sleep,
> Or when I grow excited with wine,
> Suddenly I meet your face.

At least if he does not find consolation there, he finds companionship in the human condition, the notion that he is not unique in human history.

A man cannot feel entirely lonely in his suffering if he knows even a few poems of Gerard Manley Hopkins. When he comforts the little girl who weeps because the autumn leaves are falling, he recognizes for her and for us the fact of mortality as the cause of all our grief:

> It is the blight man was born for,
> It is Margaret you mourn for.

In spite of the reassurance of his faith, that devout Jesuit Hopkins gave almost unbearably poignant expression to his discoveries in what Yeats called "the abyss of himself":

> No worst, there is none. Pitched past pitch of grief,
> More pangs will, schooled at forepangs, wilder wring.
> Comforter, where, where is your comforting?

And later in the same sonnet:

> O the mind, mind has mountains; cliffs of fall
> Frightful, sheer, no-man-fathomed. Hold them cheap
> May who ne'er hung there.

But most of us at sometime have hung there, and we recognize the geography of despair. But we can also recognize another condition in Hopkins because here and there the profound religious assurance does break through, perhaps nowhere more beautifully than in the conclusion of "God's Grandeur," in which the poet has viewed the worst ravages of the Industrial Revolution:

> And for all this, nature is never spent;
>   There lives the dearest freshness deep down things;
> And though the last lights off the black West went
>   Oh, morning, at the brown brink eastward, springs–
> Because the Holy Ghost over the bent
>   World broods with warm breast and with ah! bright wings.

If we can find companionship in the darkness of Hopkins, perhaps we can find it also in that radiant light.

I think often of the experience a friend had in dealing with Robert Frost's

"Home Burial" with a group of boys in an eastern preparatory school. You will remember that the deeply grieving wife in that poem supposes that it is only utter lack of feeling in the husband which allows him to dig the grave for his own dead child. My friend did not find it easy to persuade his students that there might be other ways of regarding the husband's behavior. But one boy stopped after class to say, "Now I understand why my father went to his office the morning my young brother died. He had to do something." This is perhaps a small and limited insight, but let it stand as the symbol of the kind of insight literature can give us of our kinship with nothing less than the whole human race.

My third claim for literature is that it reminds us, continually and unrelentingly, that the human situation is infinitely more complex than it may appear on the surface to be. Especially in the age of mass communications, this is a reminder that we urgently need. The picture magazines, the sunny little digests, the television screen are only too willing and too likely to portray life as a single struggle between the forces of good and the forces of evil. Such a portrayal outrageously falsifies human experience as we know it and as it has been conveyed by literature as long as there has been anything worthy of the name.

The characters of Greek tragedy, the Canterbury pilgrims, the vast gallery of Shakespearean figures are not cardboard constructions whose virtue can be determined by the color of their hats. One reason that I always look forward with something less than total enthusiasm to the motion picture version of any great novel is that the tendency is almost always to divest the novel of its moral complexities. I objected to *Tom Jones* not because it was racy – it already seems quaintly old-fashioned in that regard – but simply because it seemed to me that the character was not Fielding's Tom Jones. With all its lust and 18th century bawdiness, *Tom Jones* is a deeply moral book. It is the story of a charming libertine, but it is also the story of a libertine who undergoes genuine reform, whose good qualities are finally triumphant. Tom for a long time was caught in St. Paul's dilemma: that which he willed not to do, he did; that which he willed to do, he did not. This struggle is crucial to the novel; it was excised from the film version. It was difficult to believe there that any change had taken place; Sophia was simply one more conquest.

Perhaps few human experiences are popularly represented to be so simple and clear-cut as the experience of religious commitment; it seems to consist of making the right choice, of saying the right words, of belonging to the right group. Once a decision is made, so one gathers, everything else is easy. Such a view runs counter to almost unanimously contrary testimony in the Bible and in the writings of the saints in every generation. The passages I read from Hopkins must surely suggest that religious faith is not all pure bliss. Anyone who wants to know the quality and texture of religious experience would do well to avoid the power of positive thinking and read Eliot's "Ash-Wednesday." Nobody can read that great poem and suppose that it is an easy or a simple thing to be a Christian. In the poem of renunciation with which "Ash-Wednesday" begins, the convert has forsaken those things in the past that have beguiled him from the faith, and he says:

> Consequently, I rejoice, having to construct something
> Upon which to rejoice.

And one feels in almost every line the struggle and the self-discipline which that construction involves. There are parts of the poem in which all seems bright and easy because of what Eliot calls elsewhere "this grace dissolved in place"; but these periods are succeeded by further doubt and struggle:

> Will the veiled sister pray
> For children at the gate
> Who will not go away and cannot pray:
> Pray for those who chose and oppose . . .

The poem never comes close to preaching or to arguing the validity of the Christian faith. Eliot is saying instead, this is what it feels like, this is what it means to make a religious commitment and attempt to live up to it.

A modern American novel is also a powerful reminder that the human situation is not a simple one, that things are not always what they seem. I speak of Robert Penn Warren's *All the King's Men*. This book is sometimes referred to as a political novel, a fictional biography of Huey Long, a view both mistaken and imperceptive. No doubt there are striking parallels between the story of Huey Long and the story of Willie Stark, and probably it was Long's bizarre political career that set the creative forces of Warren's mind to work. But Willie Stark is not the chief character, in no way the center of focus. The chief character is Jack Burden, the narrator, and the story is – if one must reduce it to a phrase – the story of his awakening, of his coming to understand something of the complexity of the human situation. The Jack Burden of the beginning of the novel would have made a fit lieutenant for Senator McCarthy – Eugene McCarthy – because he seemed to believe that virtue could be established by proclamation. But the cataclysmic events of the story have a profoundly educational effect upon Burden, and he ends a much wiser and a much more humble and human person. Late in the novel he tries to explain to the young woman he will marry: "I tried to tell her how if you could not accept the past and its burden there was no future, for without one there cannot be the other, and how if you could accept the past you might hope for the future, for only out of the past can you make the future." There is a haunting line in one of Richard Wilbur's poems that says "I dreamt the past was never past redeeming." Jack Burden has redeemed the past by accepting it, with all its complexities and ambiguities, and by his willingness to base the future upon it.

All the great themes, the great virtues, the great values of literature are profoundly relevant to the deepest concerns of the human race in the 20th century. But we cannot abstract these qualities and serve them up as a kind of instant relevance. These qualities do not yield themselves to the impatient and superficial search. We cannot reduce great works to a kind of formula and say glibly that we have found the solution to a complicated problem. One writer has made the essential point: "Literature gives us not instruction, but illumination." It is the glory of literature that it provides the illumination for those who choose not to walk in darkness.

Some Practical Suggestions on Reading Modern Poetry
from *Discovering Modern Poetry** (1961) by Elizabeth Drew and George Connor

Perhaps the greatest obstacle to the intelligent reading of poetry is a feeling that a poem ought to be read as quickly and easily as a short prose selection. Any such feeling is bound to end in frustration. The reading of poetry requires more work, more patience, more concentration, more imagination. The careful reading of a poem requires the best that we can give it, intellectually and emotionally.

No formula can make the reading of poetry effortless, nor is it possible even to make simple, practical suggestions that are useful to every reader. Despite these limitations, this commentary aims to provide some suggestions that some readers may find helpful.

The poem, any poem, is much more significant than what any critic has said about it. As Donald Stauffer has put it, "The most that criticism can ever do

*Elizabeth Drew was responsible for the Introduction and Section I, "Poems for Discussion." GC contributed "Some Practical Suggestions." He also had primary responsibility for choosing the poems in Section II and essays by poets in Section III. In the Preface, they write "The purpose of this book is to make readers and lovers of poetry, especially modern poetry."

is to help a reader to see more, or to see more clearly, or to see once again." In the reading of any poem, then, readers should go just as far as they can under their own power: first the poem, then the comment on the poem.

Even at the risk of laboring the obvious, it may be said that the reader should not go quickly through the poem once and turn immediately to the commentary. The reader who is trying seriously for the first time to understand modern poetry will feel a strong temptation perhaps to do just this. Readers must resist the temptation. Readers begin wherever they can, wherever an opening of any promise occurs. They may wish to strive for a kind of general notion of what the poem is saying, a "feel" for the substance. Or they may begin by looking carefully at what seem to be key figures of speech. Someone has said that you cannot read a modern poem – you can only reread it, and, one might add, with care and concentration several times. And surely when you begin to reread, you notice details, hints, suggestions, possibilities, which you did not notice before.

Let us look at a specific and not especially difficult poem, T.S. Eliot's "Journey of the Magi." How far we can go toward a full understanding of this poem without commentary or collateral materials? The answer is probably that we can go a long way indeed. After all, Eliot is using here the familiar story of the visit of the Wise Men to the infant Jesus. We need, then, little more than the title to give us this initial orientation, this beginning of our understanding of the poem. Also, we see almost at once that this is the personal narrative of one of those who made the journey; he is of course recalling what took place "a long time ago." So much will one careful reading of the poem tell us.

When we begin to look more closely, we see that the first section of the poem is really a kind of abridged diary, setting forth without comment and without directly expressed emotional coloring the vicissitudes of the journey. "Regretted" is really the only word that express the speaker's feelings. The matter-of-fact tone throughout the first section is underlined by the use of the word "and," which occurs fourteen times.

The journey can hardly have been a pleasant one. Not only were the hardships enough to discourage any travelers, but these particular travelers heard "The voices singing in our ears, saying / That this was all folly." Even in this first section, we begin to get the feeling that the trip was, among other things, an exercise in self-discipline.

At first, the second section may seem to be no more than a continued recounting of details, but a little more careful attention is enough to show that the details are no longer so matter-of-fact; numerous New Testament allusions are to be met with here. The "three trees on the low sky" foreshadow Calvary; the white horse figures twice in the Apocalypse; the empty wineskins and the dicing for silver are likewise allusive. But is the emotional tone of the second section different from that of the first? Most readers would probably answer this by saying yes and no. Certainly there is a difference; critics have pointed out that the lengthening lines and the more easily flowing rhythms establish this. At the same time, there is still something of the restraint and emotional neutrality of the first stanza; apparently the best word the narrator can apply to the object and conclusion of the journey is the word "satisfactory." The parenthetical "(you may say)" simply reinforces the restraint.

Only in the third and final section does the speaker state explicitly his reaction to the experiences recounted in the first two sections. He does not doubt the validity of what he saw, and in spite of everything, "I would do it again." But nevertheless there was in the experience a profound ambiguity which made it very painful to the Magi. This is hardly the Christmas-card view of the Magi, ecstatically offering their gifts to the Child. This Birth is like a death, "hard and bitter agony for us," and only his own death can release the narrator from the torture and isolation that he feels.

These suggestions by no means exhaust the possibilities of the poem, but they at least give readers a general grasp, a framework on which they can build a fuller interpretation. If we bring this much understanding to the further reading of the poem, we will find deeper probing and testing all the more rewarding. We will notice that the first five lines are enclosed in quotation marks; why Eliot should have used quotation marks here is perhaps the one question that we (at least the reader moderately familiar with the New Testament) cannot answer without the aid of a note. These lines are almost a verbatim quotation from a Nativity sermon preached in 1622 by Lancelot Andrewes, an Anglican bishop. Few readers indeed could be expected to recognize the source of these words, but our understanding of the poem is not at all diminished by this fact. Often Eliot uses allusions where the effectiveness depends upon our recognizing their original source, but that is not the case here.

We have already seen that the details of the second stanza have a symbolic significance that those in the first do not have. The temperate valley, the smell of vegetation, the running stream and the water mill all carry suggestions of life and vitality. But there are suggestions of death too in the biblical allusions, so that the explicit statement of ambiguity in the third stanza is implicit in the second.

Though it is not essential to our understanding, readers may also wish to look up the New Testament version of the story of the Wise Men (Matthew 2:1-12). The point is not that Eliot falsifies or distorts this account; the story is simply told from a very different angle of vision. (Eliot uses New Testament material in almost exactly the same way in "A Song for Simeon.")

We know already that the biblical story and Bishop Andrewes' sermon made up part of the essential material of the poem, the imaginative background from which it was written. But many of Eliot's commentators have also noted the relevance of the following comment from his *The Use of Poetry and the Use of Criticism*:

> Only a part of an author's imagery comes from his reading. It comes from the whole of his sensitive life since childhood. Why, for all of us, out of all that we have heard, seen, felt, in a lifetime, do certain images recur, charged with emotion, rather than others? The song of one bird, the leap of one fish, at a particular place and time, the scent of one flower, an old woman on a German mountain path, six ruffians seen through an open window playing cards at night at a small French railway junction where there was a water mill: such memories may have symbolic value, but of what we cannot tell, for they come to represent the depths of feeling into which we cannot peer. We might just as well ask why, when we try to recall visually some period in the past, we find in our memory just the few meager arbitrarily chosen set of snapshots that we do find there, the faded poor souvenirs of passionate moments.

The ability to read poetry with intelligence and appreciation is developed by the reading of any poem. Or to put the point another way, the reading of any poem is informed by the previous reading of every other poem. We may say that it is almost impossible to read well in isolation a single poem of any poet; we need to know something of a great many of his or her poems before we can effectively deal with any single poem. But we must start somewhere!

Robert Frost's poetry, on the surface level, is likely to consist of a simple episode, and quite often – indeed almost always – the reader can find a good deal of pleasure just on this level. But when the reader begins to ponder a poem like "Come In," the ripples, to borrow a phrase from Robert Penn Warren, begin to spread.

Now on the simplest level, the poem is perfectly satisfactory, a beautiful lyric. The reader who has only a slight acquaintance with Frost's poetry may be content or even determined to go no further. Many readers even feel that there is a kind of desecration involved in probing and questioning, in examining the particulars to see what more is there than the simple narrative. In his essay on Frost, Warren addresses this objection to a critical reading:

> I know perfectly well that there are some readers who object to this process. They say that it is a profanation, that they simply want to enjoy the poem. We all want to enjoy the poem. And we can be comforted by the fact that the poem, if it is a true poem… will survive all the pinching and prodding and squeezing which love will lavish on it…. Further, and more importantly, the perfect intuitive and immediate grasp of a poem in the totality of its meaning and structure – the thing we desire – may come late rather than early – on the fiftieth reading rather than on the first.

For the attentive reader, "Come In" illustrates the value of reading it in the light of other works by the same poet. Those who are well acquainted with Frost will recognize in this poem the darkness encountered also in "Stopping by Woods on a Snowy Evening," "Acquainted with the Night," "Desert Places," and numerous other poems. The relationship between the man and the thrush is something else which a wide reading of Frost will help to illuminate. For the moment, however, let us content ourselves first with the narrative level of the poem and second with a few simple questions which may help us to achieve a greater appreciation.

Is there anything at the narrative level which needs elucidation? Is there anything in the poem which impels us to read it figuratively as well as literally? What is suggested by the darkness? Does the darkness seem at all ominous? What is suggested by the bird's song? The woods? The poet's being "out for stars"? Is the last verse mere whimsy? What is the contrast between man and bird? Does the darkness affect them in the same way?

It is not surprising that readers who turn their serious attention to poetry for the first time may feel some frustration. The skill to read poetry well is neither easily nor quickly developed and readers may even feel the keenest annoyance that others see so much more in the poem. But if they keep at reading, if they make a determined effort, they will find their ability developing. Most important of all perhaps, there are no short cuts to this ability; it must be achieved by carefully reading and pondering a great many poems.

On Language

The Language of a Poet: Remarks at a Memorial Service for President John F. Kennedy

To judge the quality of a man is always a difficult and daring enterprise. But when we have recognized greatness in him, it is often even more difficult to identify those things upon which his greatness depends. Yet one could not observe John Fitzgerald Kennedy in the thirty-four months of his presidency without the deep conviction that here was a man upon whom the stamp of greatness had been placed. It is our loss, and the world's loss, that he did not live to employ that greatness more and more completely in the service of mankind.

President John F. Kennedy.
Photograph courtesy of the John
Fitzgerald Kennedy Library, Boston.

Of what qualities did his greatness consist? What qualities made it possible for him to occupy with distinction the loneliest and most powerful office in the free world? As he himself observed in his inaugural address, "history [is] the final judge of our deeds," and only history will make possible a final assessment. But nevertheless, some of the qualities which made him what he was are easily identifiable: energy almost without limit, a kind of tough-minded courage, great intellectual endowment, and as Mr. James Reston once observed, "grace under pressure."

Reflecting something of all of these qualities, and deriving from them, was his ability as spokesman of a free and freedom-loving people. It would be difficult to name a great national leader, found in whatever part of the world, who did not have the ability to make articulate and manifest the hopes and aspirations of his fellow citizens. What this country owes to Franklin D. Roosevelt for the buoyant confidence of his public addresses during the dark days of the Depression, or what the whole world owes to the indomitable spirit of Winston Churchill's oratory during World War II, is quite beyond estimation.

We owe now a similar debt to President Kennedy. He was not perhaps a great speaker in the conventional sense of that term; his delivery was sometimes rapid and rather stiff. But the words he spoke on the great occasions were unfailingly words which helped us to see ourselves as a people, words which revived our sense of community and common endeavor, words which gave us a heightened vision of what it can mean to be an American.

Of these great public utterances, I shall always remember three with special admiration and gratitude. The first was his inaugural address, to which I have already referred. By any standards, it was a great speech, a fitting crown and climax for that extraordinarily moving and impressive ceremony. Those who saw it can never forget the spirit of youth and vitality and promise which permeated that occasion, nor the strong and solemn and hopeful words with which the first President born in this century addressed his fellow-Americans.

The second occasion was Mr. Kennedy's speech on the Sunday evening of the desegregation crisis at Ole Miss. It was a tactful and conciliatory speech, but it was also tough and courageous. He compromised no principles, and he did not waver in his support of full opportunity for every citizen. It was the speech of a man who had the courage to believe in the dignity and worth of every human being.

The third speech was his address to the nation on the Cuban crisis in October of last year. To stand at the pinnacle of power at that demanding and decisive moment must have been a dreadful thing, but he did not falter. Here, I think, was the supreme test of his "grace under pressure," and he looked almost calmly at the unspeakable horror which could easily have ensued. He reminded us of our duty, and we took courage from his courage.

We may be sure that it was no mere gesture of politeness that accounted for the presence on his inaugural platform of a distinguished American poet. Mr. Kennedy had a poet's sensitivity to language, and he had a profound and genuine appreciation of a poet's vision. If I seem to make too much of this great ability with words, I simply remind you that a civilization lives in great part by words, a people realize their identity and destiny very largely in language. For a sharpened sense of the high privilege of citizenship in the United States of America, all of us have good cause to hold John Fitzgerald Kennedy in grateful and affectionate remembrance.

November 27, 1963

On the Use of "Who" and "Whom"
Letter to Columnist Bill Casteel*

Dear Bill Casteel,

I hope you will not mind my pointing out that in yesterday's column you make two grammatical errors – really the same error in two forms. For your convenience I have marked them in school-teacher red, and I enclose the column.

The trouble in the first one is that the ear is tricked into thinking that since <u>whom</u> follows the preposition <u>over</u>, it is naturally the right form. But the relative pronoun beginning a dependent clause takes the case from the function it fulfills in that clause. The pronoun is the subject of <u>is</u> and therefore should be <u>who</u>. It is the whole clause that is the object of the preposition.

Later in the column you repeat the error by using <u>whomever</u>. I think of some grammatical rules as school marm rules; e.g., never end a sentence with a preposition, or never begin a sentence with <u>and</u> or <u>but</u>. Those are rules made to be broken as all good writers do, but <u>who</u> and <u>whom</u> deserve to be kept straight.

A good column, though.

With best wishes,

George Connor

Bill Casteel was a reporter for the Chattanooga Times *from 1966-1998; he covered politics and wrote feature stories. His "Byline" column, which he wrote from 1978 to his retirement, was the most popular feature of the paper. He does not recall "the subject of the column in discussion. It was but one of several that Mr. C took the pains to correct my misuse of who and whom." The letter is dated September 30, 1993.*

Writers

"These things I love the more because you loved them first
Who sought the wine of life and gave to me the thirst." (GC, 1940)

To Thomas Wolfe

October 5, 1900 – September 15, 1938

I think I shall not say to you, who now are gone
Into the dark eternal night with no desire
For waking, no expectation of the dawn,
'Rest in peace'; in no such way could I inspire
Your passionate, turbulent spirit to be calm.
Nor shall I fall upon my knees and wail and weep
And hope to find in bitter tears my sorrow's balm.
No, rather shall I seek the earth, the lonely sweep
Of winter limbs across gray sky, the still highnoon,
A rustic wooden bridge, October's golden haze,
A city fast asleep, lit by a waning moon.
These, your visions, shall make less sad my barren days.
These things I love the more because you loved them first
Who sought the wine of life and gave to me the thirst.

GC, June/July, 1940

Remembering Robert Frost
(1963)

During the summer of 1949 when I was doing my first graduate work at the Bread Loaf School of English, Middlebury College, Vermont, an army friend from New York City came to visit me. He was traveling with his parents and a family friend; it was painfully apparent that all considered themselves as beyond the geographical limits of civilization. Intending to prove them wrong, I said hopefully, "If we are very lucky, we may see Robert Frost; he lives just down the road." The family friend spoke for all of them. "And who is Robert Frost?"

If the question was surprising then (as it was), it is surely unbelievable now. It is difficult to think of a literary figure in American history who achieved in his lifetime the standing and the respect – indeed the veneration – which Frost achieved. He was four times the winner of the Pulitzer Prize. He was honored by

110

several resolutions of the United States Senate. Both he and his work have been the subject of countless newspaper and magazine stories, radio and television commentaries. Ten or twelve student generations have heard him lecture and read his poems. And of course he appeared, heartbreakingly but at last triumphantly, at President Kennedy's inauguration. It is hard to imagine any literate American who has not heard of Robert Frost.

So far as I know, Frost was the only serious American poet of the twentieth century who was able to earn his living chiefly by the writing of poetry. And he certainly came closer than any other contemporary poet to winning what T. S. Eliot says every poet wants – a large, miscellaneous audience.

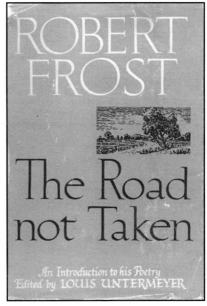

One of GC's collections of Robert Frost's poems, this one signed by Frost.

If Frost's poetry is not read by every reader, and it certainly isn't, it is undoubtedly read by more different kinds of readers than the work of any other serious poet of our time.

In a country where poetry is not exactly the most cherished of the arts, how do we account for Frost's popularity? The question is difficult to answer with any certainty, but there has been no shortage of persons willing to try. *Time* magazine, in the unmistakable accents of infallibility, had this to say in a cover story in October, 1950: "Vermonters here find nothing outlandish or alarming about Robert Frost. Neither do U.S. readers, to most of whom the word 'poet' still carried a faint suggestion of pale hands, purple passions and flowing ties. They understand what he writes – or understand enough of it to like what they understand. In a literary age so preoccupied with self-expression that it sometimes seems intent on making the reader feel stupid, Robert Frost has won him by treating him as an equal." There is some truth in this pompous pronouncement, but I doubt that it was written by anyone thoroughly familiar with the body of Frost's work.

Randall Jarrell, a critic warmly sympathetic to Frost, has written: "Ordinary readers think Frost the greatest poet alive, and love some of his best poems almost as they love some of his worst ones. He seems to them a sensible, tender, humorous poet who knows all about trees and farms and folks in New

111

England, and still has managed to get an individualistic, fairly optimistic, thoroughly American philosophy out of what he knows; there's something reassuring about his poetry, they feel – almost like prose. Certainly there's nothing odd or gloomy about it. These views of Frost, it seems to me, come either from not knowing his poems well enough, or from knowing the wrong poems too well."

If there is any vast body of opinion that Frost is a simple poet, not at all like those nasty moderns who are trying to make us feel uncultured, Frost himself must be assigned some of the blame for this innocent view. He often seemed to go out of his way to foster this impression. I am told, for example, that in a lecture once at Dartmouth, he said, "Sometimes when I'm reading some of these smart moderns, I say, 'So you have a secret, have you? Well, you just keep it!'" Surely all of us who work at being good readers of poetry have felt this sense of frustration, and perhaps Frost was talking mainly about poetry where the difficulty seems conscious and calculated, not where it is inherent in the theme and the mode of expression. Still it is a misleading statement when it is taken too seriously.

There is a lovely postscript to this story from Dartmouth, by the way. At the conclusion of the lecture, the person presiding announced that Frost would be happy to read any of his poems that the audience might like to hear. An innocent freshman arose to ask if he would please read "My Last Duchess." After looking suitably startled, Frost read "West-running Brook," a poem which is certainly not simple, a poem in which any number of little secrets seem to be embedded.

Much that Frost had to say about his own work has contributed to the feeling that his poetry is simple and harmless. His impatience with critics and interpreters is well known and probably understandable. But nevertheless it was over-simplification to the point of distortion to pretend that a lyric like "Stopping by Woods on a Snowy Evening" was all a pleasant little surface narrative told in four stanzas with a tricky rhyme scheme.

Moreover, his own public statements about this very well known poem cannot be reconciled. He was asked once if the last two lines ("And miles to go before I sleep, / And miles to go before I sleep") had to do with Heaven and death. "No," he said, "all that means is to get the hell out of there." But on other occasions he said that the poem contains "all I ever knew." If this is true, he should have been tolerant of the reader who wants to enter fully into the experience of the poem and understand it as well as he possibly can.

But all this gets us no closer to an understanding of Frost's popularity. My own view is that Frost's poetry is almost universally popular because so many of his poems can be taken on a variety of levels. The most primary, literal-sense level of many of them gives the unsophisticated reader something that he can cherish; where the more experienced reader can go from there depends more perhaps upon his limits than upon the poem's. This point was made by Robert Penn Warren, who was talking about "Stopping by Woods":

"Now the poem we are dealing with may be said to be simple – that is, the event presented is, in itself, simple and the poet says, quite simply, what the event presumably means. But this does not mean that the implications of the event are not complex: the area of experience touched upon by the poem is 'suggestive' or 'haunting.' And all good poems, even the simplest, work, it seems to me, in exactly that way. They drop a stone into the pool of our being, and the ripples spread."

It seems to me just this variety of levels on which the imagination can operate in Frost's poetry that gives it such popularity. And it is certainly largely because of this quality that Frost is such a good poet for teaching purposes.

I suggest briefly two other reasons for his popularity. The first is his use of the world of nature, his devotion to trees and brooks and Morgan colts, mountains and pastures. The use he made of these things is hardly at all the traditional use of the nature poet, but the point is that the things of the natural world are plentifully present in the poetry. And there is deep in the consciousness of the American people a warm sympathy for these things, a sympathy which seems to grow warmer and more nostalgic as our society grows more industrial and urban.

Also, many of Frost's poems reflect qualities which we regard (rightly or not) as almost peculiarly American: self-reliance, a kind of independence, a refusal to be frightened or to give up, even against great odds. We respond to the common and admirable humanity of the people who inhabit his poetry.

In all of these comments, I have found it difficult to use the past tense, to realize that Frost is dead, a few weeks short of his 89th birthday. It is difficult now to use hyperbole in speaking of the loss to the nation: it is a grievous loss. Ezra Pound has suggested that poets are the "antennae of the race," more sensitive, more perceptive, more understanding than others. We can ill afford to lose a great poet in whom these qualities were so highly developed.

But it is of course not really true that we have lost him. We have the great body of his work, not a prodigious output but enough to keep us reading and pondering for a long time. The last edition of his *Complete Poems* was published in 1949; presumably now a new and final edition will appear. (It is hard to avoid the feeling that most of his best work was done in his middle years, but of course everything he wrote will continue to be of interest to readers and students of his work.)

Robert Frost in Vermont.
Photograph by Clara E. Sipprell.

We have also sharp and clear memories of him in whatever way we encountered him, in the lecture hall or on the television screen or in some other setting. For my own part, I shall always be glad that I saw him rather frequently at Bread Loaf in the summers that I spent there. The school, which he helped to found and over which he was always a kind of hovering genius, is located only a few miles from Ripton, the little village in the Green Mountains which was Frost's summer home.

When I speak of having seen him frequently, I must be understood to mean at some considerable distance. I was not one of those able to convince himself that he would be a welcome visitor at Frost's cabin, and I never sought out even the road he lived on. But he was often on the Bread Loaf campus, and there were genuflections wherever he went. He always lectured at least once each term, though 'lecture' is a rather formal word for his witty and discursive commentaries that preceded his reading of poems. He always came and listened dutifully to the other lecturers, and sometimes spoke a word of mild reproof or dissent in the question period that followed.

For a long time, the closest I came to Frost was to send him a book of his poems to be autographed. It was the custom of the Bread Loaf book store to sell the *Complete Poems* and to handle the details of getting the copies signed. But I had thriftily taken with me in the summer of 1951 a copy of the collection called *The Road Not Taken*, edited by Louis Untermeyer, and I sent it along to be signed. In due time the book came back inscribed as follows:

> Robert Frost
> to
> George Connor
> Breadloaf Vt
> 1950

What led Frost to mistake the date by one year, I do not know; but since the book was not published until 1951, I am fairly certain that a hundred years from now this inscription will provide a puzzled footnote in some scholarly treatise.

114

Despite all the excellent photographs in existence, I am especially glad to have seen Frost in person often enough to remember how extraordinarily impressive he was in appearance. At a distance he looked like nothing so much as an amiable polar bear. At close range, the piercing look of his eye, the benign but rather wary expression on his face seemed exactly right for the man who wrote "Birches."

I cherish especially the memory of the evening in July, 1955, when I saw him for the last time in a platform appearance. A benefit program had been arranged in Ripton for some worthy civic project, I think refurbishing of the Town Hall. While Frost was the main attraction for most of us, he was by no means the only one: William Hazlitt Upson, the short story writer, lives near Ripton, and he appeared briefly on the program. The master of ceremonies was a distinguished rabbi from Cincinnati, who owns a summer home nearby. But the real focus of interest and attention, at least from the point of view of the natives, was the patriarch of the Dragon family. The Dragons are the leading, or at least the most numerous, family in Ripton, and Daniel Dragon is a notable fiddler and singer of ballads and folk songs. The thing about Frost which impressed me that evening was his determination to stand aside, to defer to his fiddling friend, to do his part but not to occupy center stage. He was capable of being a prima donna and a ham actor, but there was nothing of either in him on that occasion.

I graduated two or three weeks later, and on that evening I finally met Robert Frost. It is a part of the commencement ritual at Bread Loaf, which is a very small and delightful school, to have a reception and a dinner preceding the commencement ceremony. The highlight of the reception was the introduction of each graduate to Frost, at least the introduction of those not brash enough to have sought him out elsewhere. On this occasion Frost moved patiently through the crowded room, escorted by Professor Reginald Cook, the director of the school. (His book *The Dimensions of Robert Frost*, published in 1958, is an excellent study of Frost's work.) My turn came and I was duly presented. Mr. Cook added that I came from Chattanooga. I still remember vividly the firmness of Frost's handshake, the tremendous size of his hand, and the sound of his voice as he said, "Ah, Chattanooga, Chattanooga, Chattanooga," savoring the name as a poet would savor it.

Bread Loaf was buffeted that evening by the marginal winds of a hurricane. Out of necessity commencement was by candlelight, and the rain came down without mercy. The speaker began by saying, "Sakes, it's only weather." The true disciples recognized this as a quotation from the master, and the speech was off to a good start.

Our best memorial to Robert Frost is to remember that his role was to make us more alive, more perceptive, more appreciative of the world we live in. He helped us to see more clearly and to feel more genuinely. He was able to "drop a stone into the pool of our being, and the ripples spread." They will continue to spread for quite a long time.

Published in the *Chattanooga Times*, February 3, 1963

T. S. Eliot

We can hardly suppose, living in the twentieth century, that we are living in an age of faith. It is somewhat surprising, therefore, that so many writers of the first rank in our time are practicing Christians and that their work testifies to their Christian position. Perhaps the most distinguished modern writer who was also an active Christian was the Anglo-American poet and critic, T.S. Eliot. We are all of us in his debt, whether we recognize it or not.

Though born in St. Louis, Eliot sprang from the distinguished New England family of Eliots and was himself educated at Harvard. Following his graduation, he took up residence in Europe and was thereafter never more than a visitor on these shores. Eliot by accident of birth was coming to full intellectual maturity in the years following World War I, and he became one of the voices which most clearly and distressingly articulated the malaise of Western civilization in that era. *The Waste Land* is perhaps the most famous poem of the twentieth century, and it is a poem in which the decline of our society is made apparent.

In the late 1920s, Eliot made two momentous decisions: he became a British subject and he was confirmed in the Church of England. Indeed for those who are willing to take the trouble, his poem "Ash-Wednesday" is something of an emotional record of his own progress toward the faith. But it is a poem and neither a sermon nor an argument. He is not seeking to persuade us of anything; he is rather saying to us, this is what it is like to make a commitment and attempt to live up to it. At the height of his career, before and during World War II, he wrote the *Four Quartets*, surely the great Christian poems of our time.

There are many ways in which one can call others to a faith in Christ. As C.S. Lewis once pointed out, it takes all kinds to make a world and to make a Church. Eliot used the quiet way of the poet and the dramatist as his own means of witness. At the end of the *Quartets*, he wrote:

> We shall not cease from exploration
> And the end of all our exploring

116

Will be to arrive where we started
And know the place for the first time.

And a few lines later, he calls the Christian life

A condition of complete simplicity
(costing not less than everything).

March 23, 1975

Alan Paton: In Memoriam

When Alan Paton died last April (1988) at his home in South Africa, he had completed the second volume of his autobiography, *Journey Continued.* The book was published by Scribner's last summer in this country and a copy has been added to the parish library. For its insights into that incredibly complex and troubled land, I do not know a better book than this one. The book seems to me a balanced and fair-minded review of South Africa society, but it is always perfectly clear that Paton regarded the policy of apartheid with loathing and disgust.

After the publication of his novel *Cry, the Beloved Country* in 1948, Paton was able from the income from that book to devote himself to writing and to politics. He was a member of the Liberal party and served for a time as its chairman. He was throughout his party affiliation kept under close surveillance by the Security Police. With great courage, Paton refused to allow himself to be intimidated into silence by these servants of the status quo; he spoke his mind and he carried on his life as normally as possible. It is only fair to say that his prestige as a best-selling author gave him a certain standing and protection.

Perhaps the most interesting aspect of the book is its depiction of a serious and committed Christian as he dealt with his own life and with the miserable racial conditions in his homeland. Paton was converted to

Alan Paton in the United States in 1954.

117

Anglicanism in his early manhood. One cannot read his books without realizing that here was a truly dedicated Christian, one who believed that the faith had something to say about the whole of life. This is quite clear in his devotional book, *Instrument of Thy Peace*, and it is certainly clear also in his autobiography. He saw every person he met as the child of God, as a unique human being who deserved to be treated as such.

In the news stories following Paton's death, the only one of his books which got anything like major attention was *Cry, the Beloved Country*. While it is undoubtedly a powerful novel, my own preferences among his books are *Too Late the Phalarope* and *Instrument of Thy Peace*.

I first read *Too Late the Phalarope* in May 1957, the year that St. Peter's was established and still a parochial mission of St. Paul's. Those facts are forever linked in my mind with the novel. Something called, I believe, a parish life conference was held at St. Paul's in May and I was one of the chosen participants from St. Peter's. I must have gone reluctantly because the week was one of those groupie things that people dreamed up in the fifties and sixties, and its purpose was to induce us to love each other more.

Each evening after the session I came home and read *Too Late the Phalarope*, which someone had recently given me or lent me. I can hardly remember any novel which has moved me more deeply; I found it, and I still find it, almost unbearably poignant. I learned far more from reading it than I learned from the parish life conference. I have almost wholly forgotten the details of that affair, but *Phalarope* has remained for me a vividly compassionate book. I have lost track now of how many times I have re-read the book or how often I have used it to demonstrate Christian themes in literature. My indebtedness to Alan Paton runs very deep.

Instrument of Thy Peace is a series of meditations based on the familiar prayer ascribed to St. Francis of Assisi. It is a wonderfully thoughtful and imaginative treatment of that prayer and manages to maintain its power and freshness. One of the tests of any book is whether it holds up in re-reading, whether it retains its appeal. I have found *Instrument of Thy Peace* to lend itself very well to repeated use in the penitential seasons or, for that matter, at any other time. Several years ago we did a series of sessions on it in the Barth Bible Class, and I think all of us discovered a power and immediacy in the prayer which we had not discerned before.

Paton took obvious pride in his accomplishments and he does not write of them as though they were matters of fact or accident. But he was never blind to his own faults or inclined to take himself too seriously. In a lecture at Yale in the early 1970s, he spoke these memorable words: "By liberalism I don't mean the creed of any party or any century. I mean a generosity of spirit, a tolerance of others, an attempt to comprehend otherness, a commitment to the rule of law, a high ideal of the worth and dignity of man, a repugnance for authoritarianism and a love of freedom." Those are the words of a Christian citizen and statesman.

Alan Paton has strengthened my understanding of the Christian faith; may his soul rest in peace.

May 1, 1988 and January 8, 1989

"On an Ordinary Wednesday Afternoon": Walker Percy

Sometimes a single sentence, uttered by some thoughtful and contemplative person, will provide us with the opportunity and the inspiration for almost endless meditation. Such a sentence occurs in a recent memorial to the distinguished Roman Catholic Southern novelist Walker Percy, who died last May at the age of 74. The memorial appears in the current issue of *South Atlantic Review*, written by a woman, a teacher who knew and admired Percy and who corresponded with him. In the conclusion of her tribute, she quotes a single sentence from a letter Percy wrote to her in February 1990: "Who is onto the secret? – that the mystery is to be found in ordinary things in an ordinary room on an ordinary Wednesday afternoon?"

The truth that this sentence conveys is not unique to Walker Percy, as he would be the first to say. Percy is saying here in his own memorable way what Frederick Buechner says in *Now and Then*: "Listen to your life. All moments are key moments." Even those moments that occur, Buechner might have added, on an ordinary Wednesday afternoon. Or this is Henry James, responding to a query from a young man who wanted to be a novelist: "Be one of those upon whom nothing is lost." Buechner goes so far in *Whistling in the Dark* as to ask, "Is it too much to say that Stop, Look, and Listen is also the most basic lesson that the Judeo-Christian tradition teaches us?"

What these three writers are reminding us of in these quotations is simple enough: it is one of our human failings to suppose that important discoveries are always attended by shooting stars or other heavenly manifestations. Or at least by spotlights and soft music. We live in a world which often seems to have lost its respect for simplicity, for the quiet and the unobtrusive. Even the episode of the Burning Bush in Exodus would have been much more exciting if it had been more adequately staged. The possibilities of even more dramatic events in the Bible stagger the imagination. The flashier biblical movies help us to realize what might have been.

But Walker Percy lived with a different kind of imagination in a different kind of world. The thrice-used word in the quoted sentence from his letter, the word "ordinary," is used in what is essentially an ironic mode. For the real observer, for the person upon whom nothing is lost, nothing is ordinary. Whatever is taking place in our lives is a part of God's providence and revelation. If we miss what is happening on an ordinary Wednesday afternoon, it is our loss.

November 25, 1990

C. S. Lewis

C. S. Lewis was by profession a scholar and literary historian; most of his teaching career was spent at Oxford and, more recently, Cambridge. But he had a sort of second career as spokesman for the Christian faith, as the writer of books on popular theology (in the best sense of the word "popular"). It seems very doubtful whether any other layman of our time was so well-known or so influential in the life of the Church.

Perhaps Lewis's greatest book is *The Screwtape Letters*, which consists of private correspondence between one of the devil's own and a junior tempter. It is really a manual on how to lead a young and struggling Christian into temptation and sin. It is a Christian classic, and one feels safe in predicting that it will be read for many generations. But there are numerous other Lewis books, and those who do not know them are depriving themselves of lively and interesting reading.

In early December 1978, *Time* magazine, which prides itself of course on what is current and newsworthy, devoted an entire page to a discussion of C. S. Lewis. The story was headed "C. S. Lewis Goes Marching On" with a subtitle "The apostle of *Mere Christianity* converts a new generation." Obviously the focus of the discussion was not on Lewis's primary vocation, which was that of the literary scholar, but on his writings as a lay theologian and one of the great Christian apologists of our time.

C.S. Lewis at work.

120

What makes all this rather remarkable is that Lewis has been dead for fourteen years; he died the same day President Kennedy was assassinated. It is not unusual for a writer's reputation to go into decline in the years immediately following his death; it is rather unusual to witness the kind of attention which is being widely paid to Lewis. His following is by no means limited to Anglicans; he has always had a Roman Catholic audience and, as *Time* points out, one of the centers of Lewis interest and activity in this country is Wheaton College, which is "staunchly Evangelical Protestant."

Even this diverse company is not new for Lewis. At the end of his introduction to his book on the Psalms, he explains that he has written as a member of the Church of England but has "avoided controversial questions as much as possible. At one point I had to explain how I differed on a certain matter from both Roman Catholics and Fundamentalists; I hope I shall not for this forfeit the goodwill or the prayers of either. Nor do I much fear it. In my experience the bitterest opposition comes neither from them nor from any other thoroughgoing believers, and not often from atheists, but from semi-believers of all complexions."

One of the happiest results of the continuing interest in Lewis is the recent publication of *The Joyful Christian*, a selection of 137 excerpts from his

Inside cover and facing page of GC's copy of The Screwtape Letters *(1944), by C.S. Lewis. The prayer, written in GC's hand, brings together two of his intellectual and spiritual heroes, Lewis and William Temple.*

The prayer reads: "O Risen Lord, who didst endure the pain of the Cross as the price of the world's deliverance from the power of evil, and for whom God loosed the bands of death, unite us, we beseech Thee, with Thy purpose and Thy constancy that we may both do what Thou callest us to do and bear what Thou callest us to bear in the sure and certain hope of everlasting life; through Christ, Our Lord."
- William Temple

many books. Such collections can be very disappointing but this one is absolutely first-rate. The selections range in length from one paragraph to several pages, and each one of them is self-contained. But the best thing of all is that the selections send us back to the books themselves and teach us fresh appreciation of a remarkable Christian spokesman.

In his autobiographical *Surprised by Joy*, Lewis describes the culmination of the process by which his mind had driven him from atheism to an acceptance of the faith: "You must picture me alone in that room in Magdalen, night after night, feeling, whenever my mind lifted even for a second from my work, the steady, unrelenting approach of Him I so earnestly desired not to meet. That which I greatly feared had at last come upon me. In the Trinity Term of 1929 I gave in and admitted that God was God, and knelt and prayed: perhaps, that night, the most dejected and reluctant convert in all of England. I did not see then what is now the most shining and obvious thing; the Divine humility which will accept a convert even on such terms. The Prodigal Son at least walked home on his own feet. But who can duly adore that Love which will open the high gates to a prodigal who is brought in kicking, struggling, resentful, and darting his eyes in every direction for chance of escape?"

The "high gates" were indeed opened to him. Let us remember him with gratitude.

December 15, 1963 and January 1, 1978

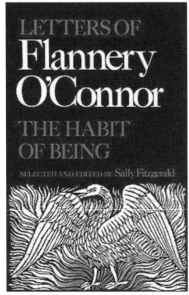

Published by Noonday Press, 1979.

Flannery O'Connor's Letters: A Series of Reflections

One of the most interesting books of recent memory is the collection of Flannery O'Connor's letters published a few weeks ago under the title *The Habit of Being*. It is a hefty collection, running to more than 600 pages, although it includes only those available letters written between 1948 and Miss O'Connor's death in 1964. The letters are fascinating when looked at from almost any perspective as the comments of a writer of fiction, a serious and practicing Christian, a person who probably suspected that she was doomed to an early death.

The earliest letters were written when she was in her mid-twenties, a yet unpublished writer but one who took her vocation as writer – indeed as Christian writer – with deadly earnestness. One of the first letters is to a New York publisher who decided that her novel *Wise Blood* needed the benefit of his editorial wisdom. In a wonderfully candid letter, she puts him firmly in his place: ". . .I am amenable to criticism within the sphere of what I am trying to do; but I will not be persuaded to do otherwise." Those are brave words from a young woman who had not yet published anything. But all of us can be grateful that she went her lonely way and insisted on her own version and her own kind of writing.

Miss O'Connor has sometimes been seen as utterly provincial, a Bible Belt Catholic whose horizons were somewhat limited. That is rather careless reading of the fiction, but just how careless is made entirely clear by the letters. She was a voracious reader and was nourished by Augustine, Thomas Aquinas, Teilhard de Chardin, and a lot of other writers, ancient and modern. She was a writer who knew her own mind. As she writes to one correspondent, "Let me make no bones about it: I write from the standpoint of Christian orthodoxy."

We live in an age when the letter has been largely replaced by the telephone call. Because of her illness and other circumstances, Flannery O'Connor found in lively correspondence an outlet and a means of relationship with many friends. One is struck by how generous she was with her time and energy, both of them limited. She writes sometimes at length to casual acquaintances who have written her about faith or something which was troubling them. That she wrote so wisely and helpfully enriches us all.

April 29, 1979

"A Blessing"

During the weeks of Lent, it is always the custom to devote this page to a series of related articles. This year they will be based on brief excerpts from Flannery O'Connor's letters, published in 1979 under the title *The Habit of Being*; the book is available in both paper and hard cover. Over the past three years I have referred to the book several times on this page; it is a truly remarkable collection of letters. One of the charms is that often in the midst of discussing something else, Miss O'Connor in a sentence or two would provide some keen insight into the nature of the faith and the human condition.

For the last fifteen or so years of her life, Miss O'Connor was suffering from the disease lupus and some related medical problems. She had to be very careful to save the time and strength essential to her writing. A letter to friends in

123

the East early in 1953 contains a very low-key account of her health, the report ending with these words: "I have enough energy to write with and as that is all I have any business doing anyhow, I can with one eye squinted take it all as a blessing. What you have to measure out, you come to observe closer, or so I tell myself."

Miss O'Connor was a good and faithful Roman Catholic, and her orthodox religious views permeate everything she wrote and everything she did. One cannot read this comment on the limitations her illness imposed without being moved by the matter-of-fact acceptance of her life as it had to be lived. Not many of us are capable of this kind of calm and sturdy patience, this willingness to live by the limits God has set for us. Surely it is a measure of her Christian commitment that she could "take it all as a blessing." It would be interesting (but of course impossible) to know how many people were touched or even converted to the faith by the courage and gallantry with which she met her disability.

Surely it is true that what is limited in our lives, what we "have to measure out," takes on for us a more precious value. Surely it is the essence of the Christian faith that we take the raw materials of our lives and do the best we can with them. As one of the rabbinical sayings suggests, we shall not be judged because we are not Moses; we shall be judged because we are not ourselves. Lent is a good time for looking at our lives on the basis of our bedrock Christian beliefs.

February 28, 1982

"Blessed in Our Deprivations"

In a long letter to a friend in August 1956, Flannery O'Connor remarked, almost casually, "Needing people badly and not getting them may turn you in a creative direction, provided you have the other requirements . . . . We are all rather blessed in our deprivations if we let ourselves be, I suppose." In order to judge fairly such a comment as this, it is useful to remember that when O'Connor spoke of deprivations, she spoke of what she knew. During more than a decade at the end of her life (she died at age 39), she was in such uncertain health that she had to discipline herself very carefully to have the strength and energy to do her writing.

Most of us certainly do not respond to deprivations of any kind as though we are blessed in them. We often respond with a feeling of rage that God could be so heartless, or that our family and friends could so lack understanding, or that the world could treat us so shabbily. And clearly there are times to fight back, to

stand up for our rights, to
work to make the conditions
of our lives more tolerable.
But deprivation is a part of
the human lot and unless we
are extraordinarily fortunate,
we are bound to share to
some degree in this common
human condition.

It is in our state of
inevitable deprivation that we
must come to terms with life,
actively seeking for that blessing which can so often accompany the deprivation. All of
us have seen persons afflicted
with the loss of one sense
who have the heightened use
of another; surely the blind

Flannery O'Connor (1925-1964).
O'Connor Collection, Ina Dillard Russell Library,
Georgia College & State University.

person hears much more carefully than the rest of us. But there is far more to
finding blessing in deprivations than this natural compensation. We can resolve
that by the grace of God and our determination we will use our deprivations to
His glory and to the enrichment of our lives. The loss of a dear family member, a
friendship that goes awry, a career that crumbles before our very eyes – every
tragedy or misfortune, in the providence of God, can be used to make us more
sensitive, loving, compassionate human beings.

We begin with the acceptance of our lives as they have been given to us
and shaped by circumstances. And wherever there is deprivation in our lives, we
look actively and hopefully for the ways in which that deprivation can be turned
to the aid of other people, to our own enrichment, and to the glory of God.

March 7, 1982

"I Was at Home"

After her graduation from college, Flannery O'Connor was accepted for
enrollment in the School for Writers at the State University of Iowa, one of the
most prestigious programs for creative writing in this country. Fifteen years later
in a letter to a friend she commented on her church-going habits while she was

there: "I went to St. Mary's as it was right around the corner and I could get there practically every morning. I went there three years and never knew a soul in that congregation or any of the priests, but it was not necessary. As soon as I went in the door I was at home."

Perhaps this brief comment conveys an attitude that all of us would do well to ponder. In order to evaluate her opinion here, one needs to remember that she was a good and faithful Catholic but by no means professionally pious. There are in the letters some wonderfully sharp comments on what she regarded as sentimental and meretricious religious practices. That she could get to Church "practically every morning" is itself interesting because the life of a graduate student is not a leisurely one. But the important point of the quotation, I think, is how at home she felt without knowing anybody, clergy or laity.

Naturally enough, whenever we discuss and debate the health and vitality of St. Peter's parish, one of the questions we ask ourselves, sometimes agonizingly, is how well do we make visitors feel welcome. I want to make clear that I am fully in favor of doing everything we can to demonstrate to our visitors the love and warmth which I think are characteristic of St. Peter's. But I also hope that visitors will feel at home in whatever circumstances; I hope they will recognize this place as nothing less than the house of God where prayers are said and sacraments administered and the Word proclaimed.

Flannery O'Connor's words contain by implication some sound advice for all of us when we are visitors in some parish, perhaps far from home. We do not go chiefly to be greeted and made over and introduced around, though that is very pleasant when it occurs. But surely we go first of all as worshippers of God and in that capacity we ought to be able to find ourselves 'at home' in any parish.

March 14, 1982

"Faith Comes and Goes"

A friend who had been recently received into the Roman Catholic Church wrote to tell Flannery O'Connor (who was probably in part responsible for her conversion) that she was unhappy in the Church and had decided to leave it. O'Connor's reply is calm and measured and she does not attempt to conceal her regret over this news. She makes a point about faith which we would all do well to examine: "Faith is a gift, but the will has a great deal to do with it. . . . But let me tell you this: faith comes and goes. It rises and falls like the tides of an invisible ocean. If it is presumptuous to think that faith will stay with you forever, it is just as presumptuous to think that belief will."

126

Surely there are few principles of the spiritual life more important to remember than this tendency of faith to come and go; if we are at all attentive to our spiritual welfare, we are bound to have observed it. C. S. Lewis in *The Screwtape Letters* (VIII) calls it the Law of Undulation, and he excoriates his nephew Wormwood for his ignorance of so important a law. Faith does indeed rise and fall like the tide; many writers have spoken of the periods of peaks and troughs in our spiritual lives. But it is not a condition which involves only our religious faith; it also involves almost every aspect of our lives: our work, our family, and other human relationships, our recreation, everything.

O'Connor's clear implication is that her friend would have been wise to wait for a time before jumping to the conclusion that her faith was gone for good. She would have been wiser to remember the words of the father of the child with the dumb spirit: "I believe; help my unbelief!" (Or in the words of the Jerusalem Bible: "I do have faith. Help the little faith I have!") There are probably persons far advanced in the life of sainthood who do not experience this coming and going, these undulations, but for most of us the condition is only too familiar.

And what do we do when we find faith lacking? We will to have it back again. We remain faithful to our prayers and other obligations. We do the work at hand, whatever it is. Perhaps most of all, we remember the Law of Undulation.

March 21, 1982

"This Is Vital"

One fact which emerges from Flannery O'Connor's letters is that she was a wise and perceptive theologian. Those people who look upon her as a kind of fundamentalist Bible-belt Catholic just haven't read the fiction very well and they certainly have not read the letters. In a long letter which she wrote in 1959 to a newly acquired Catholic friend, but one who she thought was not very well grounded in the faith, she concluded with this interesting paragraph:

> I am going to send you some books along that may clear up one thing or another. This is one part apostolic zeal and two parts horror at some of your misconceptions . . . . I probably have a lot of misconceptions myself and what I say to you is subject to correction by anybody more in command of the subject than I am; I mean by any competent Catholic theologian. I'm no theologian, but all this is vital to me, and I feel it's vital to you.

Of course what we believe is vital to all of us. One of the commonest heresies on the modern scene is that it doesn't much matter what we believe just as long as we behave reasonably well, love our neighbor, feel occasionally repentant for our sins, and so on. But how we behave depends very much upon our understanding of God and man; loving our neighbor is a vague and many-faceted term which needs the toughness and discipline which theological understanding can give it. And of course if we manage to believe, for example, that pretty much any behavior is acceptable so long as we are truly expressing ourselves, we shall be conscious of very little sin to call us to repentance.

Part of the task of being a serious Christian involves the best grasp we can manage of theological truth. And we are by no means without plentiful help in achieving that understanding. There are sermons to hear and books and articles to read; one of the unsettling facts about this parish is how little use we make of the library. Certainly we do not enjoy a first-rate collection but there are plenty of good books there which most of us are not taking advantage of.

As a point of departure for our own theological understanding, we do well to remember the Prayer Book. The section called "An Outline of the Faith" (pp. 845-862) is an excellent sketch of basic beliefs which we as Christians and Anglicans might be expected to hold. Not everything is here (see the prefatory note on p. 844), but it is an excellent beginning.

March 28, 1982

"Center of Existence"

There is a rather widely known story about a party Flannery O'Connor was taken to during the late forties when she was living in the East. Many of the group were former or lapsed Catholics, and there was a sort of expectation that she would be the Church's spokesman. The party began at eight and ended at one a.m.; according to her own account, she had said nothing. But in a letter dealing with the matter some years later, she quoted her one comment: "Mrs. Broadwater (Mary McCarthy) said when she was a child and received the Host, she thought of it as the Holy Ghost, He being the 'most portable' person of the Trinity; now she thought of it as a symbol and implied that it was a pretty good one. I then said, in a very shaky voice, 'Well, if it's a symbol, to hell with it.' That was all the defense I was capable of but I realize now that this is all I will ever be able to say about it, outside of a story, except that it is the center of existence for me; all the rest of life is expendable."

Since the letters were published three years ago, several persons have discussed that passage with me, often urging me to suggest that O'Connor didn't really mean what she said. I think it's very clear that she did mean it. She was not much given to saying things she did not mean, especially on the subject of religion. I suppose there is some sense in which the Bread and Wine might be considered symbols, but the word would be very tricky to use in such a context. The discussion of the Eucharist in "An Outline of the Faith" (*Prayer Book*, pp. 859-860) does not come close to the word 'symbol.' To the contrary, it says, "The inward and spiritual grace in the Holy Communion is the Body and Blood of Christ given to His people, and received by faith." The Body and Blood of Christ, not symbols thereof.

It is not even possible to charge O'Connor with unduly strong language; she means what she says: "To hell with it." The last half of the last sentence in the quotation is the most important: ". . .it is the center of existence for me; all the rest of life is expendable." For the faithful Christian, it is almost impossible to overstate the abiding importance of the Eucharist. We can indeed let almost everything else go but to this we cling as the life-giving sacrament by which the grace of God is made operative in our lives. That is a thought to keep in our minds as we make our final preparations for Easter.

April 4, 1982

Fred Buechner

Introduction to *Listening to Your Life:*
Daily Meditations with Frederick Buechner
Compiled by George Connor

Frederick Buechner spent a week on the campus of the University of Tennessee at Chattanooga in November 1986 as a participant in one of the programs in observance of the university's centennial year. As chairman of the committee for that program, I was his escort and almost constant companion for that week; I believe that on one public occasion he called me his manager. One happy result – the happiest for me – was that Frederick Buechner and I became friends. We discovered that we look at the world in much the same way; we have many of the same sympathies and, yes, many of the same dislikes. Making new friends is not easy as one grows older, and I look on that week as a gift of grace.

When I was asked to serve as editor of this book of meditations, I readily agreed, both as an act of homage and as a self-indulgence. My admiration for Frederick Buechner as a writer is virtually without limit. If there is a writer with a

"This book is meant to possess, and at the same time liberate, the heart. I'm happy to report it succeeds."
—MAYA ANGELOU

Listening to Your Life

DAILY MEDITATIONS WITH
FREDERICK BUECHNER

Published by HarperSanFrancisco, 1992.

more felicitous style now working in the English language, I do not know who it is.

As an editor, I have tried to be as unobtrusive as possible. Where an introduction to one of the meditations seemed necessary, I have made it as brief as possible. Where there was no title for the selection being used, I have provided one, using as often as possible a word or phrase from the text itself. There are very minor changes here and there from the original text (e.g., a transitional phrase removed, a name or another noun substituted for a pronoun) without the usual scholarly indication that such a change has been made. All of us involved in the book, certainly including Frederick Buechner with whose consent the changes were made, agreed at the outset that we ought not to clutter up the text with footnotes, ellipses, brackets, and the like. But where a lengthy portion has been left out of a passage, I have used an ellipsis. The source for each passage can be found at the back of the book along with a listing of passages from each book used.

I want finally to thank several persons to whom I am indebted for generous help, beginning with Frederick Buechner himself, who was infinitely patient in answering my queries. I have been helped enormously also by my own parish, St. Peter's Episcopal Church in Chattanooga, especially by Hallie Warren, the rector; Patsy Phillips, parish secretary; and the members of the Bishop Barth Bible Class, who spent three sessions discussing the plans for the book and giving me useful suggestions.

Letter to Fred Buechner, October 7, 1988
(The 46th anniversary of GC's entering military service in WWII)

Dear Fred,

Your last letter concluded with the promise of an enclosure. It was something you had seen "months before" and had made lots of copies of because it struck you as so funny. There was no enclosure. Et tu, Brute? As a reward I will

GC and Fred Buechner in Vermont, ca. 1996.

send you something I tore out of the Middlebury alumni magazine, a photograph along with the cut lines. It strikes me as one of the most pretentious items I have seen recently. Just the sort of thing Flannery would have rejoiced in.

As I remember, I wrote you that I wasn't scheduled to teach in the School of Religion next Lent and therefore wouldn't for the moment be doing your fiction. That turns out to be wrong. I will be teaching and I will be doing your novels. What I propose to do is one novel a session; I think this is better (and more within my competence) than to attempt to survey every fictional thing you have written. What I am thinking of doing is the following, in the order given: *The Return of Ag*, *The Final Beast*, *Lion Country*, either *Open Heart* or *Treasure Hunt*, and end with *Godric*. I think *Godric* rather than *Brendan* mainly for length. The participants in the school are pretty good about reading things but I believe they would be more likely to read the shorter than the longer book. Is my list a fair one? I would welcome comments or suggestions. I really am looking forward to it, and I will do a set of tapes for you.

I long since finished Mrs. McCoy's book [*Frederick Buechner: Novelist and Theologian of the Lost and Found* by Marjorie Casebier McCoy and Charles S. McCoy]. I think it is a useful and sensible book, and I certainly don't think she praises you beyond your just desert. She is a little naïve here and there, I think. Once somebody lent me a copy of the raw research which went into a *Time* magazine cover story in the fall of 1950 (or perhaps 51) on Robert Frost. A very interesting document, as you can imagine. The young man who "covered" the story in New England and who therefore interviewed Frost several times wrote at one point, "One can't quite tell what made him a poet" and at another time, "It is difficult to account for his sense of humor." I think Mrs. McCoy is a little too sure that she does understand these things. I also thought of a favorite sentence in a research manual I used with freshmen: "Let the researcher beware lest he find what he is looking for." But I am grateful to her for doing the book and you for your kindness in sending it to me.

This is turning into a letter about Buechner the Writer. Recently some organization in NYC sent me a discussion guide for the film *The Last Temptation of Christ*. (Have you seen it or do you plan to? I doubt that I will. I avoid "religious" films whenever possible.) Anyway, in a list of supplemental readings, what should be listed first but your *Faces of Jesus*. Pretty suspicious, I think. How did you get associated with that dubious enterprise? The Committee on un-Christian Activities may need to look into this.

I have noticed something interesting about readers' reactions to *Whistling in the Dark*. Almost everybody who mentions it has a very favorite entry which is especially meaningful. Doug and Peggy Hale (you remember that Doug drove us to Atlanta on that miserably rainy day now almost two years ago) have a son who is rapidly approaching his thirteenth birthday. Peggy says there are days which she can get through only by frequent recourse to the entry on adolescence. Another friend read some selections from the book to her Sunday school class at the First Baptist Church. One woman in tears stopped after class to say that the discussion of anxiety was surely divinely ordained for her sake. Almost every time someone mentions the book, a particular entry emerges as a favorite.

I assume you saw the vice-presidential debate on Wednesday evening. At last I understood clearly why Bush chose Quayle: it is to ensure our unending prayers, night and day, for Bush's good health. I loved it when Bentsen put the young man in his place about Jack Kennedy. A lady cousin felt that it was very rude of Bentsen, but I take the view that Quayle asked for it and he got it. Clearly he was trying to suggest a parity of ability and background. Isn't it curious that Bush said in his acceptance speech that he wanted a kinder and gentler nation and then set out at once on what seems to me the most low-down presidential campaign I can remember. I think your brother-in-law whom you quoted is wholly right: Bush has no convictions, no principles whatever. He wants to be president because he wants to be president. . . .

I do trust that you are keeping Chattanooga in mind for a visit in January – or whenever it suits your schedule. We can't have two winters in a row like last winter.

I trust that all goes well with you and that your wife is feeling wholly fit again.

Love and peace,
George

Part III

Christian Faith and Life

"T.S. Eliot's 'Ash-Wednesday' never comes close to preaching or to arguing the validity of the Christian faith. Eliot is saying instead, this is what it feels like, this is what it means to make a religious commitment and attempt to live up to it."

(GC, April 1969)

On Being Christian

"I was confirmed in the face of doubt, attracted to the priesthood, nurtured in truth and finally rounded out as a Catholic believer by the simple power of God."

(GC, May 8, 1943)

Toward a Definition of Christian

Sometimes an unexpected question or a chance remark can force us to re-think positions or attitudes we thought we had settled. In a recent letter, a friend was commenting on some literary texts I had chosen for a discussion of Christian literature: "I am even uncertain as to what a 'Christian' is." Obviously it is a word used in a number of senses, not always clearly distinguished from each other; and since my friend belongs to a religious body which prides itself on the lack of explicit creeds, her puzzlement is not surprising.

Yet the question is not an entirely simple one. What indeed is a Christian? What are the definitions that will really hold water? I suggest that for our purposes there are chiefly two meanings, related but by no means identical. (1) A Christian is a person who believes in the unique position of Christ as the Son of God in a sense in which the words cannot be used of any other person. (2) A Christian is a person who makes a sincere and consistent attempt to live according to the teachings of Christ. When we speak of a Christian, we usually mean both things, but the two are not the same. And surely it is possible to be something of a Christian in the second sense without being one in the first sense. But the Christian in the matter of doctrine (first sense) who made no attempt to be a Christian in behavior (second sense) would be an unlovely spectacle indeed.

But what does believing in the unique position of Christ involve? It certainly involves more than looking upon Him as a good man, a great teacher, the foremost of the prophets. He was clearly all of these things, but taken all together, these things do not add up to the full nature of Christ as it is set forth in the New Testament and in the Creeds. In the full Christian view, Jesus of Nazareth was the Christ, the Word made flesh, "eternally begotten of the Father, God from God, Light from Light, true God from true God . . . ." To put the point another way, the Christian believes that at a moment in time, God chose to enter history clothed in human flesh. This is essentially what the dogma of the Incarnation asserts, and surely with respect to Jesus the Christ, it is the basic dogma.

Surely if we believe something of this sort of the historical personage of

134

our Lord, then it follows that we attempt to live our lives in a certain way. What we truly believe is manifested in our behavior, in the way in which we attempt to manage every aspect of our lives.

September 25, 1977

A Statement of Faith: 1942*

The assurance that in my life there is but one great purpose – to know God, to love Him and to serve Him – is the substance of my faith for the future.

Just as I have no intention of trying to define for anybody what God is, neither have I the intention of suggesting to anybody in what particular way one may serve Him. There are, however, certain basic things which I believe all of us must do: we must attempt to understand as nearly and as clearly as we can what God wills for each of us. To do so we must turn to a careful study of the New Testament, since it is probably our best source of knowledge of God. We must learn from the life of Christ Himself the real nature of Christian life, its serenity, its humility, its beauty. We must see in Him the strength and joy of the life devoid of personal ambition, of pride and selfishness. Then, having seen the will of God and the exemplification of Christian living as clearly as we can, we must turn to our daily lives and be college students, or lawyers, or doctors, or whatever, to the glory of God. That, so far as I know, is the only thing worth doing; it is the only way to make the world, socially and economically, a better place to live in; it is the only thing that is big enough to claim the whole energies and talents of man.

Mine is a faith strengthened by the certain knowledge that whatever may happen in the affairs of man, the purpose of my life will remain unaltered and unalterable. Since that purpose is to know and love and serve God, the only possibility for real tragedy is the possibility of alienation from Him. My

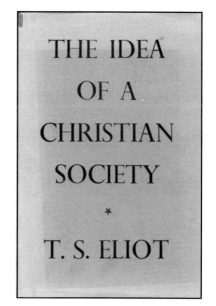

THE IDEA
OF A
CHRISTIAN
SOCIETY

*

T. S. ELIOT

---

*Published in *Motive Magazine*, by Methodist Youth, in a series titled "Statements of Faith." GC, as editor of the *Echo* (the University of Chattanooga student newspaper), was asked to contribute a statement.

135

happiness, then, for the present and for the future does not depend upon cheerful headlines and news broadcasts, but upon a heart and mind turned toward God.

I believe, finally, that man's religious activity must be centered in the church. I have very little sympathy with what Mr. T. S. Eliot in his *The Idea of a Christian Society* (a book which has considerably influenced my thinking) derisively calls "the religion of the blue sky, the grass and flowers." I believe that whatever religious influence can be exerted upon society must be exerted through a body of persons allied to a positive Christian tradition.

It is because of my belief that the chief end of man is to glorify God and that the more important activities which such a concept involves can best be done within the church that I am preparing to take Holy Orders – which seems to me to be the best way to carry out my beliefs.

March 1942

Letter to Isobel Griscom* from Fort Riley, Kansas May 8, 1943

"What progress I have made could not be attributed
either to the power or the vigor of my own intellect; it could be attributed only
to my increasing life of private and common worship." (GC)

This is Saturday night, which is always in the barracks a quiet evening until around twelve, when a considerable number of the personnel come in and pass out. Because it is now unusually quiet, I have been wishing I had someone to talk to. If I were home, I thought, I could drop in to chat with you – so I decided to write you, which is as near conversation as I can come right now.

For some time I have been meaning to write to you at some length about the position as regards religious faith in which I find myself at the present. I imagine this will interest you less than it does me, but I have talked to you so much about what I could believe, at any given stage of my religious development, that I want to tell you something of the position which I have finally achieved.

You may or may not recall (as I *do*) a conversation we had about Christianity when I was a sophomore. "What," I asked, "has Christianity done except make political democracy possible?" That was a very ignorant question, as

---

*Teacher of English and American Literature at University of Chattanooga (1922-1963), GC's mentor, and, as their relationship developed, life-long friend. See also "Isobel Griscom: An Appreciation" in Part I, pages 54-64.

I know now, but you answered it very wisely. You said, "What more would you have it do?" The more I thought about the relationship between democracy and Christianity, the more certain I became that Christianity deserved support and that if I could not honestly embrace the articles of the Creed, I could at least give to the Church my support, by membership, work and money. I don't know whether I described in detail to you my conversation with Mr. Sparkman [rector of St. Paul's Episcopal Church in Chattanooga] a week or so before I was confirmed [March 31, 1940], but I told him at the time that I was choosing to be a member of the Church because I thought democracy depended on the Church for survival. And I further had the unbelievable lack of judgment to tell him that I thought the Church should admit anybody to membership who believed anything at all about God and religion. Fortunately, he listened very patiently and made very thoughtful suggestions. He suggested that if I decided to be confirmed, I should come to Church for a while without trying too hard to believe, that I should listen reverently to the prayers, pray if I could, and participate as much as I could in the life of the Church without forcing myself to do that in which I had no belief or faith. How utterly ridiculous, thought I, that he should expect me to be converted by suspending my mind for a few months, but for some strange reason I followed his advice. I went to church and heard the prayers and tried to pray; I went to Communion determined that anything so superstitious could not possibly nurture my soul and, of course, it never did.

It was not long before I began to feel my affection take hold upon the Church, to feel committed to it in every way except intellectually. I felt unhappy when I couldn't be in church on Sunday morning. Little by little, I began to be impressed by the Church's teachings, to see how really wonderful was Christian doctrine, as it concerns men and their relations with each other. I lived in this sort of attitude for perhaps a year, and during the latter part of the year, I found myself making very strange statements, or admissions: that the Christian religion, once one could accept the belief in God as fundamental, makes the most wonderful and logical sense possible; that I would decide to be a priest if only I could believe in God. This I said to you and Ben in April of 1941; it was less than six weeks later when I told Mr. Sparkman that I felt impelled to take Holy Orders. I cannot account for my taking the step for my progress from April to June, but I must insist that I knew what I did not then believe would, in God's good time, be revealed to me. I "believed" in God; I believed that He is the sum Total of everything Good; that He is Perfect Love.

When I considered that in March 1940, I had talked to Mr. Sparkman about being confirmed and told him how little I actually believed; then in June

1941, that I was convinced that I must take orders, I thought I had made about as complete an about-face as one could possibly make. But when I consider how far I have come since that conversation with Mr. Sparkman, the first evolution of feeling is insignificant.

From the time that I decided to take Orders, I made more and more of an effort to see things from the Christian point of view. But I must say that what progress I have made could not be attributed either to the power or the vigor of my own intellect; it could be attributed only to my increasing life of private and common worship. I wasn't sure of what prayer was (and even today I have no thoroughly satisfactory definition, but then neither can I define 'love' or 'beauty'), but I prayed and the more I prayed, the more I found myself believing. The step-by-step growth of my belief from, roughly, June 1941 to May 1943, is too subtle to trace, and also I don't bother to try since I see relatively little value in such minute analysis. It is enough to say that a year ago I had a strong certainty of God as the Creator and Governor of the universe; I was committed firmly to the Creed because I had either a simple literal meaning or a symbolic meaning for each article. Yes, I believed that Christ was the Son of God, because I believe that in one sense every man is the son of God. I believed, in a way, in the resurrection. I remember agreeing completely with Dr. Tietze when he said a year ago in New Testament (on the day I went to class) that he believed that Christ was risen in every way that could matter for those of us in the 20th century. By this he meant, I think, that Christ's greatness, His power were still transforming lives and that hence He was as alive as if He had actually risen from the grave.

I think I can best explain the greatest change and the most important change in my religious faith by saying a word about my changed attitude toward two fundamental doctrines: the Virgin birth and the Resurrection itself. For three years I worried about the matter of the Virgin birth; I could neither believe it nor see the importance of believing it. Why it took me so long to see the thing in its proper light, I do not know. But, finally it occurred to me that the fundamental question is not, was Christ born of a Virgin, but is He God or is He not? If Christ was God and was sent by His father to redeem the world, why worry about *how*? If God can bless the world by the miracle of sending His Son to redeem it, He can surely also arrange whatever circumstances He chooses for the birth. Likewise, I disposed of the question of the Resurrection. Not, did He rise from the dead, but was He God? If He was God, why bother to ask if He could rise from the dead. I can say with certainty that these questions were settled within my soul before they were settled in my mind. Hence, when my mind suddenly realized that the *One* question was, is He God? I knew already the answer; I knew He was God.

Hence, after starting out to lend my support to the Church so democracy might flourish (how that must have amused God!), I find myself in a position of complete Catholic orthodoxy. I no longer have very abstruse mental images of what the Creed means; I believe it quite literally.

I believe that God created the world (not *a la* Genesis, but just as surely), that Christ was God, who came to earth to save men from sin. I believe that Christ rose on the third day, quite literally, because I don't believe the Christian religion makes complete sense in any other light.

If anyone called upon me for "proof," I couldn't give any at all. But yet I know it is true, as surely and as deeply as if I could measure the facts with a ruler. How can I believe it? To quote you, whether *you* remember or not: "I can easily believe the Christian religion as anything else; the mind can go only so far and no further." I know that there are a great many people who have no sympathy with a position built on certainty of truth that yet cannot be scientifically determined. But my faith stands because I *know* it is true. I can, thus, account for every step in my faith – I was confirmed in the face of doubt, attracted to the priesthood, nurtured in truth and finally rounded out as a Catholic believer by the simple power of God. It is no accident that the Church's life is strengthened in time of a people's greatest sorrows and burdens, and in complete humility, I hope that I am set apart to aid in the Church's great program for these times.

That, in outline, is what has happened to me. I only hope that when I am a priest and am confronted by the same situation by which Mr. Sparkman was confronted in March 1940 that I will be as patient and wise as he was. I have no patience with the religious position which I embraced at any period in my religious growth, yet I hope I will never be so foolish as to be impatient with the people who hold the same opinions. . . .

Anniversary, 1980: A Personal Essay

On Monday of Holy Week, I observed the fortieth anniversary of my confirmation at St. Paul's Church. Forty years are a long time, especially when I remember that I was a brash college sophomore when I went to confer with Thorne Sparkman, then Rector of St. Paul's, and outline for him the terms on which I was prepared to be received into the Church. A good part of my indebtedness to that remarkable man is owing to the patience and courtesy with which he listened to me.

The Christian Century is currently running a series of pieces by theologians and others dealing with ways in which they have changed their minds about

St. Paul's Church, ca. 1960. The Norman-abbey-style building, shaped like a Roman basilica and modeled after Braddon Abbey on England's Isle of Man, was built from 1886 to 1888. Made of brick and native stone, with a tower holding a chime of eleven bells, the nave stands in the center of a complex of offices and meeting rooms. St. Paul's is on the National Register of Historic Places. Photograph by Roy Tuley Photos.

important questions over the past decade. Applying that formula to my own situation, I ask myself in what ways I have changed my mind during the four decades that I have been an increasingly happy Episcopalian. I think chiefly I have changed my mind toward other Christian bodies. Several years ago, a layman from another parish remarked in my hearing, "My idea of the ecumenical movement is that everybody ought to be an Episcopalian." That pretty much sums up my own view of forty or even twenty years ago. But I look at people from other communions who obviously manifest the fruits of the spirit, and I have come to the simple conviction that the Holy Spirit does not operate exclusively in and through the Episcopal Church. My non-Episcopal Christian friends, I know, will want to congratulate me for my perspicacity.

At the same time, I must confess – all this is very personal, for which I hope I may this one time be excused – I must confess that I cannot imagine myself happily a member of any other Christian body. I frankly do not think there is any place else where I could be so well nourished in the Catholic faith in all its fullness and at the same time permitted so much freedom. Moreover, I am temperamentally suited to the Episcopal Church; as a friend once observed, thank God there are not only diverse callings and functions in Christendom but there are diverse styles. I rejoice in the dignity and beauty of the service, in the fact that things are done decently and in order, in the reverence which underlies it all. I thank God most devoutly for these forty years.

April 13, 1980

Fifty Years!

A few weeks ago, I observed the fiftieth anniversary of my confirmation, which took place at St. Paul's on March 31, 1940. Half a century is a long time in the human scheme of things, giving one a vantage point for some measure of summing up. I give thanks for these fifty years and the ways in which the Church has nourished me. In a real sense my life as an Episcopalian has been framed by two experiences at St. Paul's: membership in an organization called the Young People's Forum at the one end and the Thorne Sparkman School of Religion at the other. Intellectual understanding is not everything, but it is an important part of our lives as Christians, and I am grateful indeed for the help the Church has given me in this regard.

The Forum, to which I belonged in the forties and early fifties, was for college age and older; the average age in my time was probably about thirty. Except for Advent and Lent, when we did specifically religious programs, the sky was the limit; we talked about anything and everything. Sometimes we had an outside speaker who made a presentation and sometimes we managed everything ourselves. Thorne Sparkman, then Rector of St. Paul's, was always there; he never dominated the discussion but he set us straight when he thought we needed to be set straight. The Forum discussions impressed upon me as nothing else has that religion has to do with the whole of life, that it is by no means a Sunday-only affair.

I think often of a program we did, I believe more than once. We brought in two or three large circulation magazines and subjected their advertisements to careful scrutiny. The object was to determine which of the Seven Deadly Sins the advertisement appealed to. I think often of this innocent exercise. If one were to play the same game these days with television ads, I believe it would be less interesting – and certainly a good deal more depressing. Lust and greed and envy are used in such obvious and blatant ways that it would be no challenge to identify them. The sponsors of the ads are often – almost always – old, established, and respectable companies who apparently are prepared to use any means whatever to increase sales.

Since the Thorne Sparkman School of Religion is still a live and lively enterprise, it seems unnecessary to say much about it. I have been involved in the school, one way or another, almost from its inception. I have learned enormously from courses I have taken – and even more from those I have taught. Now that Thorne Sparkman is no longer living (he died last year at the age of 84) the school is a most appropriate memorial. He was a truly remarkable priest, to whom my own indebtedness is beyond calculation.

May 20, 1990

Aspects of Christian Life

"What we truly believe is manifested in our behavior, in the way in which we attempt to manage every aspect of our lives." (GC, September 25, 1977)

More Fully Ourselves

In his autobiography published several years ago, the teacher and scholar Mark Van Doren describes a visit he paid to a former student, Thomas Merton, who had become a Trappist monk. Stopping off at the monastery in Kentucky, Van Doren spent some time with Fr. Louis (Merton's monastic name) and at one point laughingly said to him, "Tom, you haven't changed at all." "Why should I?" Merton replied, "here our duty is to be more ourselves, not less." A profound part of the truth of the Christian faith is contained in this simple reply.

Any person who makes any sustained attempt to live according to the faith one professes must be struck at times by the curious view that one's non-Christian friends take of the whole business of the Christian life. They are likely to think that the essence of this life is giving up things, and in a sense of course it is. But this is another of the many paradoxes which characterize the Christian faith: as C.S. Lewis once remarked, everything is taken away from us in order to be given to us again in far more glorious form. Everything we give up of our superficial self brings us closer than ever to our real, essential self.

We have all had the experience in human relationships of knowing those few persons with whom we find ourselves most profoundly and permanently engaged. It isn't simply a matter of congeniality or even love, though both are involved: it is ultimately a matter of a quality in the relationship, which allows us most fully to be ourselves. We turn to these friends without pretense, without a sense of strain or tension, without misgivings or fears. They allow and encourage us to be ourselves.

At its best and most enlightened, this is also what the Christian faith does; it allows and encourages us to be ourselves, to develop the talents God has given us to enjoy the world that He has made, to find the crown and focus of our identity in our worship of Him. St. Augustine admonished us with great simplicity to

142

love God and do as we please. If we love Him enough, we shall find ourselves flourishing in the kind of freedom He gives us, the freedom that makes us more fully ourselves and more fully the children of God.

May 10, 1964

Little Things

One of the pleasures and advantages to be derived from reading *The Interpreter's Bible* is the sudden and frequent appearance of a passage that illuminates some part of human experience. We may be at work in a part of the Bible especially familiar to us, but even there – perhaps especially there – the words of one of the scholar-contributors can give us new and unexpected insight. For some of us, the commentaries on the gospels are especially rewarding in this regard.

Commenting on a point in the Fourth Gospel's passion narrative, for example, the expositor makes what is perhaps a small point but also a fundamentally important one: "Samuel Johnson remarks with truth in one of his wise essays that it is not sufficiently considered how much of human life passes in little incidents; and thinks it is a mistake that the moralists have endeavored to inculcate the awful virtues, without considering the lesser qualities which, though they produce no single acts of heroism nor astonish us by great events, do so much to make the draught of life bitter or sweet."

The writer goes on to make the point that the mistake of neglecting the small gesture was certainly not one of which our Lord was guilty; nor is it one of which the ordinary practicing Christian can be guilty, either. The earnest Christian takes his or her human relationships seriously, quite seriously, knowing that faithfulness to Christ Himself is for most of us most often manifested in our treatment of other human beings. "Inasmuch as ye have done it unto the least of these" are among the most challenging words in the Gospel.

Surely among other things which this attention to little things can mean is that good manners are important for the Christian, undoubtedly more important that they are for the non-Christian. Though the thought may strike us as odd, or even trivial, we do well to remember St. Paul: "Love is patient and kind . . . it is not arrogant or rude" (I Cor. 13:4). That is our standard as Christians; even in our haste or carelessness, even in our persistent desire to Do Good, we cannot neglect or ignore the standard.

One does not mean of course good manners in the sense of etiquette; etiquette has more to do with the use of the right fork or the right response to a formal invitation. Manners have to do with the way we treat other people in the various relationships in which we find ourselves. Someone has said that good manners in this sense consist mainly in treating other people with kindness, and surely that is a thoroughly Christian view.

But of course the "little incidents" of which Johnson wrote are more than merely one's manners: they are the deliberate deeds which people do, good or bad, and which therefore shape the relationship between individuals or groups of individuals. The deed may be something almost trivial in its import. A small act of thoughtfulness toward a neighbor or a casual acquaintance is sometimes worth more than its weight in gold. For someone who is in trouble or need or grief, a positive act of kindness, however small, may have a value and earn gratitude out of proportion to itself. Not surprisingly, Shakespeare makes this point in *The Merchant of Venice*:

> How far that little candle throws its beam!
> So shines a good deed in a naughty world. (V, i, 90-1)

Most of us can judge the validity of Johnson's view by a little careful introspection. Sometimes almost without thought we have done little things for other persons and have discovered consequences far beyond anything we dreamed of. An unkind word may provoke a lifelong enmity, or a good deed may earn us lifelong gratitude. A friend used to say, explaining her neglect of someone or her failure to do a perfectly obvious kindness, "I am not a thoughtful person." Perhaps not, but one might think if she was thoughtful enough to recognize her thoughtlessness, she was at least on her way to being thoughtful. Not to be a thoughtful person is an option the Christian is not free to choose.

In any case, it is not only the large and obvious virtue that is worthy of cultivation. The small gesture also has a powerful influence on the quality of Christian life. Simple good manners are not a dramatic demonstration of Christian discipleship. But they are an important part of the little ways in which the Christian shows forth the love of Christ in a hostile or indifferent world.

May 2 & 9, 1976

On the Matter of Charitable Giving

Charitable giving is a vast and complicated subject. All of us know how persistent fund-raisers can be and how overwhelmed we can feel by the sheer volume of the requests. But we certainly must not allow other people to make our decisions for us; it is our Christian responsibility to use our money to express our own convictions and commitments. Few of us are rich enough to give to everything; we have to make choices, and it is our duty to make those choices as intelligently as we can.

Next to the care for our families and ourselves, surely the church ought to be our main priority. If we make it so, we are managing a kind of structure for our giving that ought to be of help to us in every aspect of that giving. Beyond our basic annual pledge to the church, we have other church-sponsored or church-related channels that we can use with confidence. I thank God, for example, for the Presiding Bishop's Fund for World Relief* (to give its full title); when catastrophes occur, domestic or foreign, the fund is a very sensible and efficient way to make our contributions for the alleviation of human suffering. The administrative costs are taken from the national church's budget; they do not affect the amount of the gift we are making. There are also such local opportunities as, for example, the Community Kitchen and Hosanna, both worthy enterprises indeed.

I do not mean to suggest that valid choices for giving are limited to those under church auspices. Given the way our society is organized, the United Way is crucial to a civilized community. There is no shortage of other possibilities: gifts to cultural and educational concerns, to environmental and health organizations. The list goes on. What we must remember is that we are fully responsible for our own choices; we cannot be excused from that necessity. Whether we have much or little that we can give to worthy objects, we must make the very best choices that we can.

And a final word about whether we have much or little. For most of the decade of the fifties, I worked in an adult education program for which the initial grant came from the Fund for Adult Education, an agency of the Ford Foundation. From day one we had to be concerned about fund-raising. I heard from many people about how many times they were asked to give out of their limited resources and how impossible it was. Of course, one simply cannot do everything. But so often hearing these complaints in our fund-raising efforts, I bought a small notebook to list those persons who had ended up in bankruptcy or some other serious financial embarrassment because of their habits of giving. More than forty years later, I have yet to find a name for that list; the little notebook remains blank.

July 3, 1994

---

*Now re-named Episcopal Relief and Development.

Keeping Sunday

For several years now a number of supermarkets in the Chattanooga area have been opening for several hours on Sunday. Recently a group of stores and shops at Northgate Mall have adopted the same practice. When any business decides to operate on Sunday, it always provides a wonderfully inventive explanation for doing so. The convenience of the customer is often mentioned in reverent tones. In the recent Northgate action, the Sunday openings were said (presumably with a straight face) to be a part of a program to save energy. The reason for Sunday openings is simpler than indicated in these pompous pronouncements; almost always the Sunday opening indicates an overwhelming fondness for the dollar.

What is the proper Christian response to the increasing secularization of Sunday? Some of our Christian brethren are not slow to attack the Sunday openings, but for the most part Episcopalians remain silent. Surely our silence does not mean that we make no distinction between one day and another, that we think Sunday is as good a day for business as Wednesday. We are commanded to keep holy the Sabbath Day, which in Christian terms is Sunday; it is a day set apart for rest and for worship. To use it as an ordinary day is to disobey the plain commandment.

To treat Sunday as a holy day does not mean that we must sit with piously folded hands, as many of us can picture our forebears as doing. There is surely nothing morally wrong with a great many things we can do on Sunday for the refreshment of body and soul: we can read, listen to music, visit our friends, watch television. The Christian point – and it is a sound psychological point – is that Sunday ought not simply to be a day like every other day; it ought to be a day that helps to prepare us to use all other days wisely and productively.

What does this mean in terms of our response to any sort of store open on Sunday? For many of us, it means that as a matter of principle we will not use Sunday as a day of shopping and that we will do what we can to persuade others not to do so. It may also mean that we express ourselves to the management of such enterprises, telling them what we think of their silly and specious claims. The weakest thing we can do is simply to accept the profanation of Sunday as though there were nothing we can do about it. We are clearly commanded to keep Sunday holy.

November 17, 1974

Christian Golf, Anyone?

My life was enriched last week by a friend's kindness in sending me a newspaper clipping which had been sent to her from Louisville or its environs. The clipping recounts the building of a Christian golf course in Valley Station, a settlement somewhat to the southwest of Louisville. What, you may ask, is a Christian golf course? The best answer, I think, is a few quotations from the builder himself. "We'll call the course Gloryland, because it's beautiful and it's something that will give glory to God." According to the article, the design of the nine-hole course includes eight-foot crosses along some fairways.

The builder seems to be in very close touch with our Lord Himself. He tells of being at some other golf course (obviously non-Christian) where he had to wait two hours to play. "Then I heard the Lord's voice. He told me to build a golf course." The family invested everything it had, even its savings, in this enterprise. The builder added, "I designed the course with the Lord's help. I had never done anything like that before. He showed me what to do."

Then the builder adds specific details: "Between the No. 2 and the No. 3 fairways are three crucifixes, like when Jesus was crucified on Calvary. I want to build a Jacob's well, like in the Bible. I want to put a tomb in the back section of the course with a sign saying, 'It's empty. He has risen.'" There are a few other details but you get the idea.

The most puzzling sentence in the story is also a direct quotation from the builder: "It's time Christian people had something to do." I wonder if this does not portend Christian tennis, Christian baseball, Christian football (an oxymoron certainly), *ad infinitum*? I could not help remembering from a good many years ago the visiting football team at UC, a team from a small denominational college to the south. The wife of the college president left a dinner early to go and admonish the team to "beat the stuffing out of your opponents; that is what the Lord wants you to do." Surely some Christians are more Christian than other Christians.

But back to this curious statement, "It's time Christian people had something to do." I should think they have quite a lot to do. I believe, for example, it is our Christian duty to work for peace and justice in this society and in the world at large. That alone is a tall order but it can hardly be said to exhaust our responsibilities. Why should Christian people give themselves to such tacky and futile enterprises as putting up crosses on the fairway of a Christian golf course? I can't believe that builder really understood our Lord. Something was garbled in the transmission.

September 5, 1993

On Aging

Jorge Luis Borges, the distinguished Argentine writer, recently celebrated his eighty-fifth birthday. A newspaper story pointed out that Borges has been blind for almost thirty years; as the story said, "his advancing age has slowed him physically – but not mentally." The truly remarkable thing in the news account, however, was a statement from Borges himself. It is worth quoting in full and pondering:

> Blindness, old age, sickness – you have to think of them as gifts, as a blessing in disguise. You have to turn them into beauty. I'm happier now than when I was young. When I was young I tried my best to be dramatically unhappy, to be Hamlet or Byron. Of course I wasn't. Now I take those things as they are. I'm grateful for things.

I have read almost nothing by Borges and I have no idea what his religious position is, but this quotation seems to be admirably and profoundly Christian. Two points in his statement, one implicit and the other explicit, seem to me perfectly consonant with the Christian faith. The implicit point is that one does not try to evade the fact of growing older; there are surely few things sadder than the older person struggling to maintain the illusion that he or she is still, at most, middle-aged. It is of course a cliché to say that we adore the cult of youth in this country, and a lot of people get rich because a lot of other people attempt to triumph over the very process of growing older.

The explicit point is that we should accept what life brings us, even the pains and weaknesses of age, and use them for our own growth. We simply make the best of these disadvantages and do all we can to rise above them. We have all known persons whose behavior is the very opposite of what Borges is recommending in his birthday statement; they get so caught up in all their aches and pains that they seem to cherish the opportunity to make a bid for everybody's sympathy. I am not for a moment suggesting that we should not invest our sympathy in them, but there is a large difference between gratefully accepting sympathy when it is given us and demanding that sympathy just because we've had a lot of birthdays (or any other reason).

Surely God is saying something to us in the diminishing of our health and energies as we grow older. Perhaps we are being reminded of our dependence upon others, that we are indeed members one of another. Perhaps we are being reminded that this world is a transient home for all of us. Whatever our weaknesses are intended to teach us, surely we do well to remember Borges' words: "You have to turn them into beauty."

September 9, 1984

The Duty of Love

Baccalaureate Address at Susquehanna University (1994)

Verses 20 and 21 of the fourth chapter of the first letter of John: "Those who say, 'I love God,' and hate their brothers and sisters, are liars; for those who do not love a brother or sister whom they have seen, cannot love God whom they have not seen. The commandment we have from Him is this: those who love God must love their brothers and sisters also."

I want to use this brief passage more as a point of departure than as a text. This is not a passage for exegesis. I have no intention of attempting the sermon that all of us have heard more than once, a favorite sermon especially for the young clergy recently graduated from seminary, a sermon that deals in detail with the Greek words for *love* in the New Testament. I want instead to suggest in these brief remarks as precisely as I can how we manifest in our lives the love of God and the love of our brothers and sisters in Christ.

If we are attempting to work out in our own lives, in our own responsibilities and obligations, those ways in which the command to love one another is made operative, we can hardly do better than to begin with Paul Tillich's simple admonition: "The first duty of love is to listen." I suggest that many of us, whenever we may have first encountered those words, may have felt that they were almost too simple, too easy an accomplishment. I sug-

GC and Dr. Joel Cunningham, then President of Susquehanna University. On this occasion, Professor Connor was conferred the Doctor of Humane Letters, honoris causa, "in recognition," the citation reads, "of your exemplary life as a teacher and your dedication to quality in life and literature." May 15, 1994.

gest that the command is more difficult by far than it may appear. But have not most of us in our own experience observed how many of us are not really good conversationalists because we spend the time while the other person is talking, not listening but in devising ways in which we can seize the conversational ball and run with it? Of course none of us here would be guilty of that gauche behavior, but all those other people.

Twenty years ago one of our senior colleagues at the University of Tennessee at Chattanooga was honored at a gala retirement evening, including the production of a one-act play by James M. Barrie in which our honoree had played the leading role before she stood for two hours greeting friends from both campus and community. But all this is merely background for telling you that another colleague, an extremely talented amateur photographer, produced from that evening a truly marvelous album of photographs in which the honoree was shown engaged in conversation with friends, sometimes only one, sometimes in a small group of persons. In all of these photographs, I have never seen so intent, so rapt an expression as that on the honoree's face for that entire evening. And why? Because these people were her friends, some of them the friends of a lifetime, and she was showing them the attention and respect and courtesy that each deserved. "The first duty of love is to listen."

In a brief, but wonderfully suggestive essay on art in Frederick Buechner's book called *Whistling in the Dark*, he widens significantly the command to demonstrate our love by listening. Here is the next-to-last paragraph in that little essay: "And when Jesus comes along saying that the greatest command of all is to love God and to love our neighbor, He too is asking us to pay attention. If we are to love God, we must first stop, look and listen for Him in what is happening around us and inside us. If we are to love our neighbors, before doing anything else we must *see* our neighbors. With our imagination as well as our eyes, that is to say like artists, we must see not just their faces but the life behind and within their faces. Here it is love that is the frame we see them in."

In a world in which so much is forever clamoring for our attention, in a world, to use a line from the first of Eliot's *Four Quartets*, a world in which we are too often "distracted from distraction by distraction," it seems worthwhile to use one more example of the necessity to pay attention that both Tillich and Buechner urge upon us. Here is the comment from that remarkable man, the late George Buttrick, Presbyterian clergyman, ecumenist, eloquent preacher and writer, a comment that is a part of the exposition of the Gospel according to Luke in *The Interpreter's Bible*, of which Buttrick was of course the general commentary editor. He is discussing the parable of Dives, the rich man, and the beggar Lazarus:

"Dives did not see Lazarus. Dives was not an intentionally cruel man. . . . The likelihood is that Dives not only gave Lazarus scraps from his table, but contributed generously to charity. But he did not see Lazarus. He did not say: This man is lonely. This man has pains of conscience and flashes of glory, and longs for God. This man wakes at night and asks 'Why, and whither?' Dives spoke about the colored races, but never saw a Negro who passed his gate. Dives discussed employment statistics but never imagines a man out of work. He did not see.

"He was too much absorbed in himself to be able to see. He was a man of large affairs, and there were problems galore connected with his house and estate; and soon Dives was so close to himself that he could not see Lazarus, though the beggar was as near as the doorstep."

Once we have mastered our lesson from these wise and civilized spokesmen, once we have learned to listen, to see, to be aware, what comes next in our effort to bring our lives more fully under the discipline of love? I do not suggest that all persons achieve their spiritual and moral growth in the same way, by some sort of lock-step progress from one point to another. But if we give ourselves to the task of becoming increasingly aware of all sorts and conditions of human beings, surely then one clear task is to take advantage of our opportunities to be unselfishly of service to others in whatever ways are open to us. When E. E. Cummings delivered a series of talks at Harvard in 1953, later published as *Six Nonlectures*, he told his audience: "Better worlds (I suggest) are born, not made; and their birthdays are the birthdays of individuals. . . . 'He who would do good to another,' cries the poet and painter, William Blake, 'must do it in minute particulars.'"

A cheerful word spoken to a friend or acquaintance, or for that matter a perfect stranger, a letter of encouragement and good will, a simple gift or act of thoughtfulness to mark some occasion

A note from GC to Carolyn Mitchell, February 2, 1976: George faithfully practiced what he advocated. He wrote innumerable letters of encouragement and good will. He gave simple gifts to friends and family frequently; his own acts of thoughtfulness to mark some occasion did indeed "have an effect beyond our most extravagant expectations."

– such little things can have an effect beyond our most extravagant expectations. Henri Nouwen, the Dutch Roman Catholic priest and writer who has lived and taught in the United States for many years, has written frequently about our collective ministry to the lonely and forgotten, to the disabled, to the bewildered and downtrodden, and Father Nouwen is so old-fashioned as to remind us of the power of letters. Especially when he was spending a period of time in Latin America, testing his vocation for service there, he came to see anew the value of letters, how important they are in friendship, how they can diminish loneliness and alienation. He writes in his book *Genesee Diary*: "A good letter can change the day for someone in pain, can chase away feelings of resentment, can create a smile and bring joy to the heart. Some of the most profound insights are written down in letters between people who are attracted to each other by a deep personal affection." Here is a ministry, a way of showing love, open to all of us.

It is certainly not my intention to suggest that all the ways of showing love require of us only simple, elementary tasks, easily accomplished. Sometimes heroic sacrifice is necessary. If you do not know Anne Tyler's novel *Saint Maybe*, published in 1991, I commend it to you. Even if you are familiar with the novel, I commend it to you; it is worth re-reading and pondering with great care. When the novel opens, Ian Bedloe, the protagonist, is a callow high school student, not a hero, certainly not a saint. But in some way he must respond to a whole chain of events: his older brother's death, almost certainly a suicide; a few months later, his sister-in-law's death, also probably a suicide. These deaths leave three young children to be cared for. Both of Ian's parents are elderly, his mother increasingly arthritic. There are no other relatives to whom Ian can turn, and he gives up college – and a great deal else – to help raise these children, none of whom is related to him by blood. Some of his friends clearly think he is demented. He says to one young woman, "I certainly don't plan to hand them over to strangers or anything like that." "What are you, crazy?" his friend asks. "You've got a life to live. You can't drag them around with you forever." But Ian perseveres. When late in the novel, the youngest of the three calls him "Saint Maybe," most readers would surely make a less tentative judgment. Not maybe, but certainly, Ian Bedloe has become a saint. He has listened, he has observed, he has given.

Whatever you are called to do and to be in this life, I wish for you the ability to listen, the ability to see, and the ability to love. And I wish all of you Godspeed.

May 15, 1994

The Christian View of Work

A recent selection of the Episcopal Book Club is a little anthology of selections from the writings of Dorothy L. Sayers called *A Matter of Eternity*. From the publications of this remarkable woman, the editor has chosen passages of various lengths (some quite brief) on more than a dozen topics. One of the most interesting and significant is the topic of work.

Without getting into any argument about the work ethic, we can see quite clearly that the Christian point of view is of the greatest importance. If we take at all seriously the Christian idea of stewardship, which means a great deal more than the mere handling of money, we must surely see the significance that lies in our choice of work. Second only to the choice of what person one marries, there is probably no decision so crucial as the choice of the work in which we shall invest a great portion of our lives.

From the Sayers anthology, a one-sentence statement makes one point which as Christians we dare not forget: "The habit of thinking about work as something one does to make money is so ingrained in us that we can scarcely imagine what revolutionary change it would be to think about it instead in terms of the work done." There are probably few of us who can read that statement without some shock, or at least some puzzlement. Surely work is something one does to make money, we think. And of course, it is – in part; and there is nothing in the statement that suggests that it is unworthy to make money from the work we do. But the statement clearly implies that the money one makes is much less important than the value of work one does.

Any shock we feel in reading this statement perhaps largely results from the fact that we have almost wholly lost the sense of vocation, of being called, to a given kind of work. To be sure we still use the term in this sense, but we think of vocation mainly as it applies to the clergy and perhaps a few other groups – social workers, teachers, doctors and nurses and a few others. But a thoroughly Christian concept of vocation would apply to every sort of honorable and useful work.

One urgent Christian task in the modern world is to re-establish this sense of vocation. Surely the Christian ought to regard it as blasphemy to take the abilities and talents that God has given us and to use them for selfish and unworthy ends. We should be far more concerned with the value of our work than we are with the amount of money we make from it. And surely, provided that the work we do is honorable and useful, we ought to feel some sense of vocation concerning it.

But to say these things is not for a moment to suggest that there are no problems in connection with many kinds of work in a highly industrialized, technological society such as ours. Anyone who has seen an assembly line in an industrial plant must recognize how difficult it is to feel a sense of vocation in a job that requires endless repetition of some limited and often dull operation. This problem is a complex one, but surely two points are worth making. People who do this sort of work should remember that Brother Lawrence found it possible to peel potatoes to the glory of God. Secondly, such work makes all the more necessary the wise and constructive use of leisure time.

A person's attitude toward work is of more influence and importance than the kind of work he or she does. All of us are quite aware that it is possible to do very significant work badly and carelessly. This is reprehensible for any person; for the Christian it is also immoral. There is nothing in the New Testament or elsewhere that says we must be deliriously happy in all that we attempt. It is a part of the reality of life that some jobs are less interesting than others, but even more is it true that in any conceivable job there are times of dullness and routine. But if we can get through such periods of work by prayer and discipline, they too become something we can offer in the service of God.

Someone has suggested that a Christian should be identifiable by the very way that he or she walks down the street. Though this may be overstatement, the truth it conveys is clear enough. Whatever kind of work we do, of great importance or small, grand or humble, we can do it cheerfully and to the best of our ability and to the glory of God.

May 6 & 13, 1973

In Defense of Rest

Recently, I was in the office of a man whom I admire not only for his considerable ability but also for his sturdy common sense. I was therefore somewhat startled to see hanging on his office wall a sampler which read "To rest is to rust." Not only is that sentiment a foolish one in my opinion but it is also manifestly un-Christian. I thought at once of that magnificent collect in the Prayer Book (*BCP* 832) which, quoting Isaiah, says that "in returning and rest we shall be saved." In spite of my friend's sampler, rest is important not only to our physical welfare but to our spiritual health as well.

Surely that motto is the work ethic reduced to an absurdity. In the restless, striving world in which we live, there are probably many people whose spirits are troubled by any thought of rest. Several years ago at the airport on

Thanksgiving Eve, I ran into a high school classmate whom I had not seen for all the intervening years. We stood and chatted as we waited for our plane; he was taking his family to New Orleans for a long holiday weekend. He told me, rather proudly I thought, that this would be his first vacation in fifteen years, "and by Saturday morning I'll be climbing the wall." What really shocked me about his comments was that he seemed to be inviting my admiration for his busy life. I was not surprised to read in the paper two or three years later that he had died suddenly of a heart attack in his early fifties.

In Janice Holt Gile's novel *Shady Grove*, a hilarious but also very wise story of people in the Kentucky hill country, one character remarks of another, "The preacher . . . is a well-intentioned man. I've got no doubts of that. But I a little doubt he is a very good example of what we'd like our young ones to be, with his jangled-up nerves and his to-ing and fro-ing across the face of the earth. He don't know how to set still and just enjoy being a child of God."

There is a sentiment which would be much more appropriate as a wall-hanging in my friend's office. Or another possibility is a brief quotation from the first section of Eliot's "Ash-Wednesday."

> Teach us to care and not to care
> Teach us to sit still.

September 2, 1984

The Church

"Our aim must be a society so ordered that its members are not
the objects of injustice and oppression." (GC, October 6, 1996)

The Church

The Church as an institution has perhaps rarely undergone such vigorous and thorough re-examination as it is now undergoing in the 1960s. From the learned journals to church periodicals to the popular press, there seems no end to the comment. There is every reason to ask tough questions, never allowing the Church to become smug and satisfied and turned in upon itself.

But unless we have in our minds some reasonably firm notions about what the Church should be and do, we cannot very well profit from the searching criticism. There are of course many ways to state the Church's basic aim and pur-

Interior of St. Paul's Church: Banded red brick, gothic windows, stained glass, wrought iron, an arched wood ceiling, native stone, and an ornate, Italianate marble altar give the church color and elegance.
Photograph by Susan Smartt.

pose but it seems difficult to improve upon the formulation made by Fr. Huntington of the Order of the Holy Cross. He suggested the Church's purpose is threefold:

1. To glorify God. This is the beginning of the Church's mission, providing the focus for everything else it does. As an aim, this one is sometimes spoken of as though it were narrow and even selfish; to the contrary, it is so broad as to be all-inclusive. Quite properly it begins with worship, because the church must be a worshiping Church if it is to accomplish anything. We offer in worship the best that we have to the glory of God: in liturgical form, in music, in architecture, in attitude and whole-minded devotion. But of course we must also glorify God in the whole corporate life of the Church, in all of its concerns and tasks and missions. In all we do, as a Church we seek to glorify God; if what we do is unworthy of that aim, then it is also unworthy of the Church.

2. To save the lost. We cannot abandon this term to those who use it in rather narrow ways. The lost are all about us, but they are seldom lost in the spectacular sins that Christians and the world can easily identify. They are often lost in pride and greed and respectability. We can quite as easily be lost in the country club as in some more spectacular spot.

3. To sanctify the faithful. To make a saint does not mean to put him or her under glass for observation as a perfect specimen; it means making the Christian steadier and increasingly more committed to the Gospel and to its meaning in one's life and in the world.

Fr. Huntington's statement may seem dated, and indeed it does have none of the current jargon. But it is not easy to find a better measure of our corporate life, a better idea of what the Church should be.

January 28, 1968

The Church's Duty

Recently I have been reading Alan Paton's little book called *Instrument of Thy Peace,* a series of meditations based on the familiar prayer ascribed to St. Francis of Assisi (*BCP* 833). The book is excellent for its purpose, almost infinitely illuminating and suggestive. It seems to me a splendid book to read as Election Day 1996 draws nearer.

In the third meditation, Paton writes: "To be the instrument of God's peace is not to confine oneself to the field of personal relationships, but to concern oneself also with problems of human society, hunger, poverty, injustice, cruelty, exploitation, war." For many of us, this sentence states a truth so obvious that it seems hardly necessary to put it into words. But for many Christians, it is the business of the church only to make better individual Christians, not to concern itself with questions that are essentially political, or social, or economic. It is the conviction of these people that when the affairs of the world are managed by better Christians, the state of the world will inevitably improve. And surely all of us would agree that it is an important part of the church's mission to send us into the world to do our work in ways expressive of the Christian faith.

But the church cannot properly stop there. Many Christians see as part of the church's function not the devising and support of specific social and economic policies but the responsible judgment of our society from the Christian point of view. Wherever our society falls short of the kind of organization that facilitates the growth of Christian character, surely the church has the right and duty to say so. The organization of our society has enormous influence upon its moral tone. Paton quotes William Temple: "More potent than school or even the home as a moral influence is the whole structure of society and especially its economic structure." The structure of society itself is thus of deep Christian concern.

The church is not faced with a simple choice between making better Christians or trying to build a better society. Its task is both. Our aim must be a society so ordered that its members are not the objects of injustice and oppression. Such a society will not depend only upon the secular work of good Christians but also upon the church's continual and responsible criticism of that society.

October 6, 1996

Centennial of William Temple

Next Wednesday, October 15, 1981, is the hundredth anniversary of the birth of William Temple. Readers of this page already know, by my frequent references to and quotations from him, that Temple is one of my abiding heroes.

William Temple, Archbishop of York (1929-1942), October 1940. Later Archbishop of Canterbury, 1942-1944.

Someone told me a year or so ago that in the recent past these back-page commentaries have tended to grow more personal. I suppose that's true, I hope not in a negative sense. I am certainly speaking personally when I say that Temple has been one of the greatest formative influences of my life.

For two different assignments recently, I have been thinking more than usual about Temple, his life and work. Those who come to know him in the future will do so almost entirely through the written word, through his own books and those written about him. At the moment there is relatively little of his own in print, and much of what is available is inordinately expensive. But I am confident that at least a few of the best books (*Readings in St. John's Gospel, Christian Faith and Life*, and *Christianity and Social Order*, for examples) will continue to be reprinted from time to time.

I am especially grateful, if I may continue to be personal, that I was able to interview in a visit to England in 1961 a number of people who were closely associated with him. I have a much clearer sense of the man because of these conversations. Mrs. Temple helped me to understand how so busy a man managed to do as much as he did; he never wasted even bits and pieces of time. The book on St. John he wrote in odd moments between appointments. Dorothy Howell-Thomas, who had been his secretary at York and Canterbury, told me what it was like to have the Archbishop do a continuing exegesis of the Book of Job for her at breakfast following Matins in the Chapel. Ian White-Thomson, who had been his Chaplain, spoke to me of his endless patience, his excellent memory and his vigorous sense of humor.

Despite all of the busy activities and manifold accomplishments of his life there was a simplicity about Temple which characterized his whole life. It is interesting to see his memorial in Canterbury Cathedral. Amidst all of the ornate splendor of that great Cathedral, one is deeply moved to see the simple marble altar in the Chapel of St. John the Evangelist with simple lettering before it: "REMEMBER IN CHRIST WILLIAM TEMPLE ARCHBISHOP." Let us remember him with thanksgiving.

October 11, 1981

John XXIII

When an elderly cardinal named Angelo Roncalli was elected pope in October 1958, a great many people smiled knowingly. "A caretaker pope" was the judgment even of some expert observers. But when Pope John XXIII died almost five years later, it was already clear – and it has since become increasingly clear – that this was a profoundly mistaken judgment. The new pope turned out to be a mover and shaker, and the Roman Catholic Church will never be the same again.

But neither will the whole Christian Church, the Body of Christ to which all of us who are called by His name belong, nei-

Pope John XXIII (1958-1963).

ther will this universal Church be the same again. John XXIII helped to shape our attitudes and expectations more than we sometimes realize. He gave to the world not only a new understanding of what the pope can be, how broad his sympathies and how pervasive his influence, he gave us renewed confidence in the best kind of Christian leadership.

Speaking to his electors on the very day that he became pope, John asked the blessing of God on "his very humble office of Shepherd." And in the sermon that he preached at his coronation, which, as one authority noted, was "quite unexpectedly and against all tradition," the pope sounded this same note; he spoke of "that wonderful Gospel picture which St. John gives, in the words of the Savior Himself, of the Good Shepherd." It was soon after John's coronation that Geoffrey Fisher, then Archbishop of Canterbury, decided this was one pope on whom he could call without compromising the Anglican Communion. His visit to the Vatican was the first by an Anglican archbishop.

Even if one were competent, it is too early of course to try to render the judgment of history on John XXIII. But some things do seem very clear. His whole reign was given over to the kind of work which one might expect of the man who wanted to be the Good Shepherd. He made special point of visiting the old and sick and the prisoners; he cut down on official audiences, which are often arranged for the sake of somebody's ego; he cut down significantly on the pomp and ceremony which usually attend the papacy.

One can look at his photograph and see in his rugged face the marks of simplicity and faith. He opened windows in his own Church that nobody can close; the current dialogue between Anglicans and Roman Catholics is part of our inheritance from him. We should think of him with gratitude and thank God for this remarkable shepherd.

March 2, 1975

Archbishop Ramsey

Arthur Michael Ramsey, hundredth Archbishop of Canterbury, died recently in England at the age of eighty-four. He had a distinguished career in the Church and a long and useful life, and he will be very greatly missed. Church historians often characterize former archbishops by a single aspect of their careers. As William Temple was known as the prophet, Ramsey is known as the scholar. He was Archbishop of Canterbury from 1961 to 1974. Since his retirement, he had lived quietly, his main activities writing and lecturing.

It is a matter of thanksgiving for me that I carry for the rest of my life two vivid memories of Archbishop Ramsey. The first – and more important – is the memory of his enthronement in Canterbury Cathedral on June 27, 1961. I spent six weeks in England that summer doing research on William Temple; one reason I had chosen that summer was my hope that I might be able to see the new archbishop enthroned. (Ramsey of course succeeded Geoffrey Fisher.) Mrs. Temple told me the right man to address for a ticket and allowed me to use her name. So on that memorable afternoon I found myself among great throngs of people to witness the most impressive ceremony I have ever seen. It was a great ecumenical occasion as well as an Anglican one, and I found it deeply moving to be present for a ceremony attended by so many representatives of Church and state.

The second memory is much closer to home. Archbishop Ramsey was visiting Sewanee in October 1978 and Joel Cunningham and I drove up to hear his address one evening; I think we were both deeply impressed. I wrote in my journal, "It was a splendid speech and I was delighted to be there. [The archbishop] has great presence and charm. I must confess that I have no memory of his subject or anything he said, but I felt a great sense of confidence and reassurance just in his appearance."

Several years ago the Episcopal Book Club distributed an anthology of daily devotional readings called *Through the Year with Michael Ramsey*. I used it once for an Advent series on this page, and ever since I have found it a book to go back to with pleasure and profit. When I heard the news of his death, it was on my bedside table. Ramsey was a deeply spiritual man and Anglican to the bone. We all have cause to thank God for his life and his work; may he rest in peace.

May 29, 1988

Sister Mary Anselm, C.S.M.: An Appreciation

In recent festivities at St. Mary's convent in Sewanee, Sister Mary Anselm observed and celebrated the fiftieth anniversary of her life as a member of the Community of St. Mary. Half a century devoted to the service of Christ and His church is an impressive record, but the words hardly suggest anything of the richness and fruitfulness of the life of so remarkable a woman. The life of a religious order does not commend itself to everyone in the outside world; even faithful and intelligent lay people can make obtuse remarks about the waste of a life in a monastic vocation. Alas, such people have not had the good fortune to know Sister Mary Anselm.

A significant part of Sister's years in the Community were spent as a teacher of English and Latin; it was that assignment which brought her to the mountain, and to St. Mary's School, a great many years ago. But to know Sister is to know that in all the years both before and after the school was closed, she has made an enormous impact on the lives of people almost without number. As conductor of retreats and quiet days, as speaker, as

Sister Mary Anselm, C.S.M., Christmas 1992. Photograph by Charley Watkins.

intercessor, as scribe for the Sisters at Sewanee, she has bestowed her love and concern and compassion on a vast company of people, some of whom do not even know her name. Those of us who enjoy the privilege of her friendship owe her an incalculable debt of gratitude.

Obviously anyone celebrating her fiftieth anniversary is not a young woman. But in the twelve brief years that I have known Sister Mary Anselm, I have never thought of her as elderly, as indeed anything except vibrant and eternally youthful. No doubt many aspects of her life contribute to this impression, but I am especially aware of three. First, she has in abundance the capacity for friendship, for a vital interest in the lives and fortunes of other people. If a gathering of all her friends were ever to be arranged, a very large hall indeed would be necessary. Secondly, her intellectual interests are undiminished; reading is one of the passions of her life, and she reads an astonishing variety of things.

The third quality I cherish in her is a wonderful sense of humor. One small example: When she was in Great Britain a few years ago, she saw in St. David's in Wales the tomb of a bishop called Anselm *le gros*. (For those whose French is hazy, the bluntest English synonym for *gros* is simply *fat*.) Though she hardly fits the title, she takes pleasure in signing an occasional letter "Anselm *le gros*." Like hosts of others, I remember her at this special time with love and thanksgiving.

June 19, 1988

On the Ordination of Women
Speech at the Convention of The Diocese of Tennessee, January 1976

I begin with an epigraph, taken from the introduction to the book entitled *Doctrine in the Church of England*. Published in 1937, the book contains the final "report of the commission on Christian Doctrine appointed by the Archbishops of Canterbury and York in 1922." The introduction, written by the greatest Anglican of modern times, William Temple, comments on the spirit of good will that characterized the work and the meetings of the commission, which was of course composed of Anglicans of all persuasions and points of view. My epigraph is a brief quotation from Archbishop Temple's words:

> It is a sad reflection upon the sincerity of Christian discipleship
> that so often in the history of the Church controversy has been
> conducted with bitterness and has been associated, as both cause
> and effect, with personal animosity. It is truly said that to become
> bitter in controversy is more heretical than to espouse with

sincerity and charity the most devastating theological opinions; and by this standard the "orthodox" are condemned as grievously as their opponents. Progress in apprehensions of the truths of the Gospel must chiefly come by the intercourse of minds united in friendship, so that they can do that most difficult thing to which St. Paul refers as though it ought to come naturally – "speaking the truth in love."

I hope that in all the deliberations that lie ahead, not only in this convention but also in more informal settings and conversations among Church people and perhaps supremely in the sessions of the General Convention itself, I hope that in all of these circumstances Archbishop Temple's wise and winning words will be remembered: "to become bitter in controversy is more heretical than to espouse with sincerity and charity the most devastating theological opinions."

Before addressing myself to the question at hand, I should like to make three simple observations that form a kind of necessary background to what I wish to say. First, this is not a debate and I have no desire to win debating points in this discussion. Secondly, I think there is a strong argument to be made for the ordination of women and I shall make it as well as I can; but I must be frank to tell you that I do not regard this as one of the really crucial issues in the life of the Church in this last third of the twentieth century. I am certainly not prepared to take to the streets on either side of this question. Thirdly, nothing in my remarks must be construed as being said in admiration or support of the so-called Philadelphia eleven. No doubt these ladies have many virtues, but a sound sense of strategy is not one of them. Nor is loyalty to the canons of the Church. Nor, for that matter, is a sense of humor. I believe they have done immeasurable harm to their cause.

It is certainly not my purpose to survey, pro and con, all that has been said or written on the subject of the ordination of women; the limits of my competence, your patience, and our time will certainly prevent any such attempt. As we are all aware, the question has had its share, more than its share, of attention; wise and foolish things have been spoken on both sides. Learned articles have been written, sometimes answering questions which almost nobody has asked. Ordinary lay people have also been heard from. Some of the comment in the Church press has been helpful; some of it has bordered on hysteria. Sometimes, almost in despair, I have thought of the Prayer Book collect 'for quiet confidence,' which reminds us that in "returning and rest we shall be saved, in quietness and in confidence shall be our strength." The memory of that prayer has made the voices seem more strident.

The strongest arguments for the ordination of women to the priesthood finally in my own mind resolve themselves into two, one positive and one negative. The positive argument is that women have given so generously and so variously of their talents and abilities through the history of the Church that the opportunity should be opened to them to serve in the ways which the priesthood alone makes possible. I think we can no longer say to women, thus far but no further.

Consider the role of women in the kinds of parishes that we know best in this diocese. I have a friend who is fond of saying that without the Jewish constituency in the average American community, there would simply be no cultural life in that community. Though perhaps it is a little overstated, I think the contention is true: without the leadership and energy and imagination and support of Jewish citizens, the cultural life in many communities would sadly languish. Precisely the same thing can be said of the role of women in the average parish. Certainly the parishes I have known well – the two in which I have been a communicant and the ten or twelve that I have observed at close enough range to have some grasp of the quality of their common life – certainly these parishes are difficult to imagine without the work, the leadership, and the unflagging energy of the women. Surely there must be few left who doubt the wisdom of the canonical revisions which made possible the service of women on Vestries, although it is worth remembering that this was a privilege granted with misgiving and difficulty.

No doubt we do well to be skeptical towards a too easy generalization about the evolution of the role of women in the life of the church, but it does seem clear that the history of women in the church has been the history of their progress from the status of inferiority to the status of equality. I am not claiming that the victory is fully and finally won, but I am saying that the thrust of history is in that direction, and rightly so. Let us remind ourselves of certain first century assumptions. A few weeks ago I happened to hear a fundamentalist minister on the radio dispensing easy answers to hard questions, mainly Biblical. One puzzled male listener telephoned to ask whether it was true that women must keep silent in Church, even to the point of not asking questions of their husbands. Yes, indeed, said the minister, though I must say that he seemed to speak more in sorrow than in triumph; they must ask at home. "They can't even ask on the way home?" inquired the caller plaintively. "No, the Bible says at home," replied the authority, I thought a little sheepishly. I looked up the passage for myself and he is certainly right: "If there is anything they desire to know, let them ask their husbands at home" (I Cor. 14:35 RSV). I thought of that little drama being played out by some of the couples of my acquaintance; I thought especially of wives I know, whose IQ must be at least fifty points better than their husbands', humbly asking them to explain some point of doctrine.

St. Paul's stern admonition is a nearly perfect illustration of the attitude towards women in the ancient world; surely his advice on this matter is difficult for the contemporary Christian to take seriously. If this setting aside of a clear command from St. Paul raises problems of Biblical authority, then I for one am grateful to remember that earlier in that same epistle he distinguishes between what he is saying on his own authority and what he is saying on the authority of Christ himself. I am not suggesting that he means for his distinction there to apply to everything he says in the entire epistle; but if he can make the distinction in chapter seven, I will dare to make it for myself in chapter fourteen. It is for me quite impossible to imagine our Lord's saying anything so foolish as St. Paul's injunction to womanly silence in the Church. Surely we can all agree that one of the things that our Lord clearly demonstrated in his own life was a loving concern for women as fully accredited human beings in the Christian scheme of things. Is it possible, indeed, that for our taste our Lord made too little distinction between the status of male and female?

A brief quotation from that remarkable woman Dorothy L. Sayers may throw some light here. The passage occurs in *Unpopular Opinions*, though I am quoting from the little anthology called *A Matter of Eternity*, published in 1973. Thus Miss Sayers: "I think I have never heard a sermon preached on the story of Martha and Mary that did not attempt, somehow, somewhere, to explain away the text. Mary's of course was the better part – the Lord said so, and we must not precisely contradict Him. But we will be careful not to despise Martha. No doubt, He approved of her too. We could not get on without her, and indeed (having paid lip-service to God's opinion) we must admit that we greatly prefer her. For Martha was doing a really feminine job, whereas Mary was just behaving like any other disciple, male or female; and that is a hard pill to swallow."

To believe in the right of women to be ordained priests in the Church of God is in my opinion simply to believe in their right to behave like any other follower of our Lord. Such a follower, male or female, has no automatic "right" to be an ordained priest; but male and female ought to have the same possibility to receive a vocation and to act upon that vocation in whatever way the Church in its corporate wisdom will allow. Some reactions to women's ordination seem to arise from the suspicion that if such a possibility is granted, we shall suddenly be overwhelmed with female priests. Surely one may reasonably doubt the likelihood of that circumstance. God still calls individuals, not groups, to the sacred ministry of His Church; and it will surely be a simple matter, with a modicum of

Prayer Book revision, to pray that the Bishops and Pastors "may lay hands suddenly on no man or woman" to serve in that ministry. After all, the Church does have clearly defined procedures for ratifying and validating individual vocations, and this fact should provide some reassurance to those who feel that the foundations are about to be destroyed.

There are of course other misgivings. I can only say that I see nothing in the nature of women – biological, intellectual, psychological, or emotional – to rule out their being ordained to the priesthood. I cannot think of any argument about the inappropriateness of certain assignments for women; I cannot think of any such argument without seeing at once a parallel argument touching on the ordination and assignment of certain men. I do not doubt, for example, that there are women who ought not to serve as rectors of parishes; but I have known one or two male priests of whom the same could be said. (Nobody here, of course, but in foreign dioceses.)

Finally and briefly, I turn to the negative argument. Thus far, I may have given the impression that I am wholly ignorant of the fact that there is considerable opposition to the ordination of women precisely because they are women and, so the adherents of this view believe, the priesthood is by divine decree a male enterprise. I must tell you that I am quite aware of this view. Briefly, but I hope fairly summarized, the position is this: that the incarnation itself was male and our Lord chose males as his apostles and also, so far as we know, as members of the seventy. Therefore, it is inherent in the nature of things and clearly our Lord's intention that the priesthood be exclusively male. I understand this argument as an intellectual formulation, but I must confess to you that it is an argument in which I find it almost impossible to discover any significant meaning. Of course the incarnation was male, and of course the apostles were male. In the world in which the incarnation took place, in the world in which our Lord's earthly ministry was exercised, anything else is beyond imagination. I would argue that this is true not on the ground of cultural conditioning of some sort but on the more pragmatic ground of feasibility. Somewhere recently (and this is not fake scholarly vagueness; I simply cannot supply the documentation) somewhere recently I encountered a statement from the Archbishop of Canterbury in a discussion on quite another subject. He made a point which seems to me supremely relevant here: Any person reaching out in evangelical zeal to influence other persons must use methods which are appropriate and acceptable to those other persons. That excellent principle seems to me to explain why in the first century the incarnation and the fellowship of the apostles were male.

I rather doubt that St. Paul would expect to be called as a witness in such a case as I am attempting to make, but nevertheless I call him. In a brief passage which certainly identifies and celebrates the liberating influence of the Christian gospel, Paul wrote in his epistle to the Galatians, "For as many of you as were baptized into Christ have put on Christ. There is neither Jew nor Greek, there is neither slave nor free, there is neither male nor female; for you are all one in Christ Jesus" (3:27f). I am not sure that Paul in his own thought always faced up to the full implications of that ringing statement, but his words may serve as a rallying cry for those who believe that women ought to be eligible for ordination to the priesthood. To argue that there is neither male nor female in Christ is not to argue that men and women do not have each their unique contributions to make to the life and worship of the Church. If the language and customs and liturgical forms of the Church have been too exclusively male, as I incline to think they have, the granting of fuller rights and opportunities to women will certainly help to redress that balance. The result will be a richer and fuller corporate life for all of us as children of God and as brothers and sisters in the body of Christ.

The subject of the ordination of women is a complex and many-faceted one. I have tried briefly and simply to address myself to the central issue and to say why I think the ordination of women is a matter of prudence and of justice. I am quite aware that many Church people hold very different views; God grant that I not consider them therefore as less Christian or less wise than myself. The Body of Christ is large and all-embracing; in it is room for many and diverse views. No matter how vigorously we debate this question of the ordination of women, let us do so in the spirit of charity and with a genuine longing to discover and to do God's will.

As I began with one quotation from William Temple, I close with another. Preaching the opening sermon at the Lambeth conference of 1930, he ended his remarks with the deepest truth which you and I can acknowledge: "While we deliberate, [God] reigns; when we decide wisely, He reigns; when we decide foolishly, He reigns; when we serve Him in humble loyalty, He reigns; when we serve Him self-assertively, He reigns; when we rebel and seek to withhold our service, He reigns – the Alpha and the Omega, which is, and which was, and which is to come, the Almighty."

January 1976

The Parish

The Family and the Parish

In an extremely interesting recent column in *The Chattanooga Times*, Max Lerner described a late summer gathering of his own family and then went on to discuss briefly the significance of the family in modern life. One paragraph contained the essence of his position:

> . . .[F]amilies remain crucial, however mobile and shifting their forms may be. What are we as a society? We are mainly three clusters of relationships. One is the family cluster, held together by love, children, kinship and by the rhythms and necessities of daily life. One is the cluster of work and school groups, and the looser groups banding voluntarily for common aims. A third is the friendship group, fleeting or long-range, for breaking bread and for exchanging experience and ideas.

One thing that struck me about this paragraph is how much, by implication, it says about the Church. I suppose in Lerner's view the Church would belong in the second category, "the looser groups banding voluntarily for common aims." And there is some logic in that placement. But we also, as the Church, partake of the nature of both of the other groups. If we take seriously St. Paul's view of the members of the Body of Christ as members one of another, the bonds which bind us can hardly be less strong than those of blood relationships. We too are bound by love and kinship.

We are also, let us hope, a "friendship group," preferably long-range rather than fleeting. In a double sense, we gather for the breaking of bread together: the bread of Holy Communion and often, in small groups or large, the bread of social intercourse. Surely our common life is strengthened in both ways; both are means of reminding us that we are members one of another. (It is therefore a matter of rejoicing to note that in the life of the parish we have an occasional luncheon or dinner.)

Just as the family retains its importance as a structure, so does the parish. There are those gloomy prophets who foresee the end of parish organization as we know it. This seems to me at least a little doubtful. Certainly many things in modern life militate against the traditional concept of the parish, but much also works in its favor. For most of us surely, the parish is still one of the vital centers of our life.

October 5, 1975

Ordination of David Parker

O God, because without you we are not able to please you, mercifully grant that your Holy Spirit may in all things direct and rule our hearts and minds; through Jesus Christ our Lord.

Bishop William Sanders, David Parker, and GC.
David's ordination, January 6, 1985.

By way of preface, I want to say a brief word of thanks and gratitude to David Parker for giving me the privilege of participating in this memorable occasion, a Feast of the Epiphany I shall never forget. Even more, perhaps, I owe Bishop Sanders my thanks for his ready acquiescence. I have known David and Jean for almost twenty-five years; I have known David in many relationships, beginning when he was my student in his undergraduate days at the University of Chattanooga, and including a period when we were colleagues in the administration of the University of Tennessee at Chattanooga. My admiration and affection for David and Jean are virtually without limit. I am deeply honored to be a part of this glorious service.

For a text, a single verse from the gospel: "I am the good shepherd. The good shepherd lays down his life for the sheep." Perhaps there is no metaphor in Holy Scripture which describes so vividly and convincingly the relationship between the Christian leader and those who follow, whether that leader is a priest or a bishop or a seminary dean or a monastic or whatever. Of course all of these persons – indeed all of us who profess and call ourselves Christians – are in some sense surrogate shepherds for the Good Shepherd who speaks in the text, that is, for Christ Himself. But today, on this occasion fraught with so much significance and so much joy, this great high holy day of the spirit, our understanding of this passage is more narrowly focused. We are thinking of the shepherd as the priest; more specifically still we are thinking of David Parker, holding him in our most earnest prayers, as he comes to be ordained to the priesthood of Christ's Holy Catholic Church. We can hope for him nothing better than that in this fold he will prove himself a Good Shepherd.

If we think of the leader as shepherd as one of the great metaphors of the Bible, as it clearly is, as one of the great implied comparisons in other words, we must also realize that it is for those of us living in the latter third of the twentieth century often a somewhat weakened metaphor. This is true mainly for two reasons. The first is that the metaphor has become overly familiar, has been worn smooth through repetition. What is probably the most familiar of the Psalms begins with the simple statement, "The Lord is my Shepherd." And hardly less familiar are the great words of our Lord to which we have just listened in the gospel. Certainly throughout the Bible there are plentiful references to shepherds and to sheep.

The second condition which has weakened the metaphor is the simple fact that most Christians live quite remote from anything so elemental as the tending of sheep, so basic as the role of the shepherd. If it is true, as I am assured it is, that in at least one large municipal zoo in this country there lives among wilder and fiercer animals a quite ordinary cow; if, as I say, this is true, the fact merely dramatizes how distant we are from our agricultural and nomadic past. The most vivid metaphors are those which come from ordinary and familiar human experience, and it is only too clear that the tending of sheep is one experience about which most of us know next to nothing.

But the solution to this problem is not to abandon the metaphor, which has in any case the sanction of our Lord's own usage, but to find ways in which it can be reclaimed, renewed, refurbished. Such a task is by no means impossibly difficult. A little reading, a little thought, a little meditation can help us to make new the force and effectiveness of this familiar metaphor. The claim, for example, that the sheep know and trust the voice of the shepherd was wonderfully renewed for me by a brief passage I encountered a few years ago in *The Interpreter's Bible*. Commenting on the beginning of the twenty-third Psalm, the expositor writes: "Travelers have told us how various flocks may be sheltering in a common fold, and when a particular shepherd comes to the gate and calls, a shivering movement can be seen here and there among the sheep; in little groups of two or three they turn toward the gate and edge their way through the other herds. No sheep

of another flock will move; but these know the voice and straight make answer."
Even so brief a comment redeems us from our ignorance and gives us renewed
understanding of the metaphor of the Good Shepherd.

I believe this metaphor of the Good Shepherd allows us to say almost
anything necessary about the priest and the congregation committed to his charge.
Of the many things one might say, I suggest three things, three qualities, which
that priest, that Good Shepherd, must have: he must be patient; he must be imaginative; he must be faithful.

A good priest is patient. In the present state of the world, patience is not
often looked upon as one of the truly important qualities in human life. But
when St. Paul discusses the fruit of the spirit in the fifth chapter of Galatians,
patience is right there in the list, along with love, joy, peace, kindness, goodness,
faithfulness, and the like. Patience is not a small and inconsequential virtue; it is
a necessary and significant part of the Christian life. Another expositor in *The
Interpreter's Bible* says that ". . .a shepherd worthy of the name is the most patient
of men." So it is of a priest of Christ's Holy Catholic Church. While it does not
use the word *patience*, surely the prayer for Quiet Confidence is a prayer for
patience: "O God of peace, who hast taught us that in returning and rest we shall
be saved, in quietness and in confidence shall be our strength: By the might of
thy Spirit lift us, we pray thee, to thy presence, where we may be still and know
that thou art God . . . ." Surely when we use this lovely collect, we are praying
for patience.

When the supremely great Christian poet of the twentieth century, T. S.
Eliot, writes towards the end of the first section of "Ash-Wednesday," "Teach us to
care and not to care / Teach us to sit still," he is quite obviously praying for
patience. In the frenetic circumstances of the modern world, where we are likely
to be – to quote Eliot from another context – "distracted from distraction by distraction," our very health and sanity depend upon patience, upon the ability to sit
still, upon the insistence that there must be enough rest, enough silence, enough
quiet thought – in short, enough patience – to keep us human and aware of our
total dependence upon God.

A good priest is imaginative. He recognizes that although the faith was
indeed once delivered to the saints, the task of understanding it, interpreting it,
working out its relevance in our own time and in our own circumstances is the
task of a lifetime. A good priest holds before us continually the important truth
that the Christian faith is not a tight little compartment, shut off by itself and
unrelated to the teeming events and pressing concerns of the world around us.
I think often of one of the most frequently quoted and most profoundly true of

William Temple's statements: "It is a great mistake," he wrote in *The Hope of a New World*, "to suppose that God is only, or even chiefly, concerned with religion." This is little more than a restatement of one of our Lord's clearest teachings. In a passage dealing with the downtrodden and dispossessed of the earth and with the right attitude towards their needs, Christ reminds us, "Truly, I say to you, as you did it to the least of one of these my brethren, you did it to me." One cannot read the New Testament and suppose that the faith is concerned mainly with what we may call religion; it is concerned with all of human life.

William Sloane Coffin makes in his book *The Courage to Love* this bold statement: "There is no way that Christianity can be spiritually redemptive without being socially responsible." We live in a particular world at a particular time, and we must somehow find the imagination that will permit us to act in that world, morally, socially, and politically, in obedience to and in conformity with Christian principle. This is an area of great complexity, and we cannot seek to discharge our Christian responsibility by the use of pious and simplistic slogans. Cain's ill-tempered question, "Am I my brother's keeper?" is a persistent question in the Bible, and the Christian answer to the question is, "Yes, I am my brother's keeper."

When Joseph Bernardin was installed the Roman Catholic Archbishop of Chicago in August of 1982, he gave new heart and hope to all the clergy and people of his archdiocese by defining priesthood in bold and persuasive ways. "The priesthood is a passionate commitment," he said, "a fiery-eyed vision and an insatiable thirst for holiness and practical justice. The priest is called to be challenger, enabler, life-giver, poet of life, music-maker, dreamer of dreams." Those imaginative words seem to move the priesthood to a place clearly above the mimeograph machines, the computer, the interminable meetings of many committees. I am not denigrating these things as quite necessary parts of parish administration. I am saying that the priest – any priest but especially this priest who is being ordained this evening – must have the imagination to hold before his people a lofty view of the holiness of God. This is a task far more important than more "practical" concerns. Years afterwards one of the participants in a retreat which William Temple conducted for his ordinands remembered vividly the quality of the occasion: "It was never a time for practical hints; he showed us the Lord, high and lifted up."

A good priest is faithful. Here is an adjective almost infinitely rich and suggestive. The related noun *faithfulness* is another of those qualities St. Paul lists as fruit of the spirit in Galatians 5, a fact more apparent in two or three modern versions than in the King James. For the adjective *faithful*, the *American Heritage*

Dictionary lists among others these synonyms: loyal, true, constant, steadfast, devoted, trustworthy. Obviously to ask that a priest be all of these things is to ask a great deal of him, but what priest worthy of his hire would want us to ask less? A good priest dramatizes in his life the kind of faithfulness, the steadiness, which wins the confidence of those who know him. Like the shepherd who is not a hireling, he is always loyal to his sheep, always deserving their trust and their confidence.

Very little prophetic insight is required to realize that we live in a broken world, a world beset with tragedy and suffering on every hand. This is simply another way of saying that we live in a sinful world. What the Christian must avoid, and certainly what the Christian priest must avoid, is the sin of despair, the feeling that nothing is of any real consequence or offers any real hope. I once knew a college chaplain who was fond of preaching from a text from the eleventh Psalm: "If the foundations be destroyed, what can the righteous do?" His thunderous response to this question was always the same: "They can go right on being righteous!" We are likely to smile a little at such simplicity, but what other answer is there? The same point is perhaps more felicitously made in a plaque located in a church near London:

> In the year 1653, when all things sacred in the kingdom
> Were either profaned or demolished,
> This Church was built by Sir Robert Shirley, Baronet,
> Whose singular praise it was
> To do the best things in the worst times
> And hope them in the most calamitous.

I know nothing else of Sir Robert Shirley, but this 'singular praise' is enough. Let us apply this 'singular praise' also to the priest who, in spite of all the vicissitudes and uncertainties of life, stands faithful and steadfast.

The Anglican heritage to which we belong offers to all of us, clergy and laity alike, the means for holding ourselves steady and faithful. All of the richness of our tradition is summed up in a brief passage in the third of T. S. Eliot's *Four Quartets*, a passage in "The Dry Salvages" which one critic has called the basic passage of the *Quartets*. The whole work deals of course with the great theme of time and especially with those moments at what Eliot calls the 'still point' when time and eternity intersect. In the passage to which I refer, he comments on these fleeting moments when we have our brief glimpses into ultimate reality. And then he writes:

These are only hints and guesses,
Hints followed by guesses; and the rest
Is prayer, observance, discipline, thought and action.
The hint half-guessed, the gift half understood, is Incarnation.

In those five nouns is to be found the essence of Christian faith and practice: prayer, observance, discipline, thought and action. What more certain way could one possibly find to faithfulness and steadfastness?

David, after a long and happy friendship, I can with absolute confidence commend you to the Church, to our Father-in-God the bishop, to the congregations which now and in the future will be committed to your charge. You bring to the priesthood first-rate gifts of character and intellect, of energy and imagination, of devotion and determination. Not least of all, you bring a sense of humor which permits you to recognize the spurious and the pretentious, to realize that even the faith – especially the faith – has its moments of high comedy.

We hold you in our prayers and our affection, praying God to keep you steady in purpose, lively in faith, a loving shepherd and a faithful servant of that Good Shepherd who is our Lord Jesus Christ. God bless you and keep you steadfast in the work that is given you to do.

Almighty and everlasting God, by whose Spirit the whole body of your faithful people is governed and sanctified: Receive our supplications and prayers which we offer before you for all members of your holy Church, that in their vocation and ministry they may truly and devoutly serve you; through our Lord and Savior Jesus Christ.

January 6, 1985

The First Quarter Century
St. Peter's Episcopal Church (1957-1982)

St. Peter's Episcopal Church, 1959.
"The large inverted cross standing in front of the Church, just outside the narthex, has received
considerable attention. Given to the glory of God by members of the F. P. Kendall family, the cross
is inverted of course because of the ancient tradition that St. Peter was crucified head downward."

The establishment and growth of the Episcopal Church in the Chattanooga area is first of all the story of St. Paul's Church. Founded in 1853, eight
years before the outbreak of the Civil War, St. Paul's has played a distinguished
role in the community and in the life of the Church. At the time St. Paul's celebrated its hundredth anniversary in 1953, Dr. Edwin S. Lindsey wrote in his
Centennial History, "St. Paul's Church is the 'mother parish' of all the Episcopal
parishes and missions in the Chattanooga area. This is the central fact in St. Paul's
story. . . ."

Now, thirty years later, it is necessary to modify this statement only slightly in order to say that every Episcopal parish in Chattanooga is either the daughter or the granddaughter parish of St. Paul's. Beginning with the establishment of
Grace Church in 1887, St. Paul's gave its support to the creation of ten parishes,
of which St. Peter's Church is the eighth. The first organizational meeting in
founding St. Peter's was held at St. Paul's on February 7, 1957. But the idea of a
Church to be located somewhere north of the existing city limits had been discussed for a number of years. Immediately following World War II, there had
been considerable expansion of the residential area northward, especially in areas
bordering Hixson Pike.

Further impetus was given to this northward expansion when the Rev.
John H. Bonner, Jr. became Rector of St. Paul's in January 1956. He saw the
potential of the residential developments north of the city limits and expressed

keen interest in "the establishment of new Churches in the city and county." The Rev. Thomas H. Carson, Jr. joined the staff of St. Paul's in January of 1957 to be Vicar of the prospective mission. Twenty-five years later, it is difficult to imagine that Dr. Bonner could have found a clergyman more fitted by temperament and personal qualities to do the hard work of beginning a new operation. Coming to Chattanooga from St. James' Church, Greeneville, Tennessee, Fr. Carson was thirty years old, married, and the father of three children. He was well-endowed with energy and persistence, intelligence and charm. He had hardly arrived in Chattanooga when he began a vigorous program of calling upon prospective parishioners in the area the new mission was meant to serve. By the time the organizational meeting was held in early February, Fr. Carson had enlisted the interest of a gratifying number of persons and more than eighty attended the organizational meeting.

Even before the organizational meeting, the name of St. Peter's had been chosen for the new mission, in honor of the parish in which Dr. Bonner had grown up in Washington, North Carolina. The secretary appointed for the organizational meeting was Rev. Hallie D. Warren, Jr., then assistant to the Rector of St. Paul's. (Thus unobtrusively does Fr. Warren make his first appearance in the history of St. Peter's.) He noted in the minutes that each person at the new mission was asked to buy a prayer book and hymnal at the cost of three dollars. The minutes ended: "Mr. Carson noted that St. Timothy's had offered the loan of a portable altar and altar rail. The Mission is in need of a piano and someone to play it." Four days later, on February 11, the Mission Council held its organizational meeting at the Vicar's residence, a rented house on Oakland Terrace in Red Bank. Arrangements were shortly worked out for the mission at a nominal cost to use designated facilities at the Red Bank High School.

The first service, attended by 147 persons, was held on Sunday, March 10, 1957, the first Sunday in Lent. What would have been the natural happiness of such an occasion was diminished by the sudden and unexpected death on the previous evening of Walter Rodger Beckert, the seventeen-year-old son of Mr. and Mrs. George Beckert, charter members of St. Peter's. His death was the first in the family of the new mission. The beautiful processional cross at St. Peter's was given in his memory.

Services continued to be held in the Red Bank High School auditorium until mid-December of the following year. Though members of the mission were of course gratified to have secured a central location for the holiday services, the arrangement was not entirely felicitous. Equipment had to be stored after each Sunday's use or else taken home by someone and brought back the following week. Provision of simple refreshments was difficult in the summer, requiring chests of ice for cooling beverages. The auditorium floor slanted forward, a condition which made kneeling for prayers uncomfortable and almost impossible. After a few Sundays, most people simply adopted a more feasible posture for prayers.

From the outset, members of the mission were sustained by the determination to erect our own building at the earliest possible time. On April 24, 1957, the council voted unanimously to employ Preston McIntosh of Atlanta as the architect for the initial buildings. Meanwhile, an anonymous donor at St. Paul's gave the necessary money for the purchase of a tract of land on Ashland Terrace, a location which the mission council regarded as extremely propitious. The original tract was 2.75 acres; subsequent acquisitions increased the size to something over seven acres. A master plan was presented to a congregational meeting on October 29 and was enthusiastically accepted by the 175 persons present.

The figures for the operating budget show something of what has happened to the economy in the twenty-five years of St. Peter's existence. A total of more than $15,000 was pledged to the operating budget in the fall of 1957. The figures for the clergy are especially instructive; including salary ($4,500), auto allowance, rectory rent and utilities, pension fund, and health insurance, the total came to slightly more than $7,800. In the building fund campaign held a few weeks later, more than $33,000 was pledged over a three-year period.

Fr. Carson urged the congregation unrelentingly toward that goal of achieving parochial status. He was not a man to be intimidated by obstacles or even seemingly to be aware

Groundbreaking ceremony on June 8, 1958.
Fr. Thomas H. Carson, Jr. and Bob Bracewell.
Fr. Tom was rector from 1957 to 1964.

177

of them. On January 23, St. Peter's was duly admitted to parochial status at the 126th Annual Diocesan Convention.

The building program dominated Vestry discussions over the next several months, at least for the first half of 1958. Fr. Carson never allowed the Vestry and the congregation to forget that anything like full effectiveness for St. Peter's depended upon the completion of the first phase, the building of two connected buildings – the parish hall and the office and classroom buildings. A package was assembled for the financing of the first phase at a total cost of about $140,000. In addition to a gift of $25,000 from St. Paul's and the building fund pledges of $33,000 over a three-year period, it was necessary to borrow an additional $90,000. A ground-breaking ceremony was held on Sunday, June 8, at 4 p.m. with the Rt. Rev. John Vander Horst, Suffragan Bishop of Tennessee, as officiant.

While construction was under way, several men in the parish were using their considerable skills in woodcraft and the like by making some of the appointments for the nave, originally designed also to be the parish hall, and for chancel and sanctuary. A number of parishioners made unique and invaluable contributions to St. Peter's. James P. Browder, Jr. crafted the altar with its admirable proportions and beautiful carvings; he was assisted by George F. Brown, who made the Chi Rho symbol for the front. As a part of his devoted work at the time the building was erected, Mr. Browder, who had made the lectern during St. Peter's occupancy of the Red Bank High School, made the litany desk. He went to great lengths to ensure that all the appointments were of matched walnut.

"The magnificent wooden cross that hangs above the altar" of St. Peter's.

In addition to his assistance with the altar, George Brown constructed the pulpit (with the help, as he recently noted, of many people in locating suitable materials), the Bishop's chair, the Rector's chair, and the base on which the baptismal font rests. Clarence Wilson, assisted by Jewell Weese and Carl Tucker, made the altar rail. Perhaps the most striking object in the sanctuary is the magnificent wooden cross that hangs above the altar. The cross was made by, and was the gift of, Clarence Sutherland, Jr., the father of the Rector's wife, Jane S. Carson. Mr. Sutherland, a manufacturer of custom millwork in Nashville, selected and preserved the wood to be used; he also fashioned the metal ring which passes through the transverse piece; the joining of the perfectly circular ring is concealed inside the wood.

The large inverted cross standing in front of the Church, just outside the narthex, has received considerable attention. Given to the glory of God by members of the F. P. Kendall family, the cross is inverted of course because of the ancient tradition that St. Peter was crucified head downward. But this tradition did not seem to be widely known among those many persons, especially in the weeks immediately following completion of the building, who drove up and circled the driveway, often pausing to examine the cross more carefully. One wag suggested that a small sign should be erected beside the cross saying "Yes, we know it is."

The women in the parish were no less active in producing for the necessities of worship. Under the leadership of Mrs. J. R. Bracewell, they made a set of vestments which were the admiration of all who saw them. They also made robes for choirs and acolytes. The important and significant work of the Altar Guild has been another of the women's contributions. The need for a piano and someone to play it was fulfilled: a piano was provided, and Jean Fields, a charter member of St. Peter's, was pianist. She organized junior and senior choirs in the first year of the mission's existence. The new buildings made possible a more appropriate and attractive musical program, which was enhanced by the generous and welcome gift in the spring of 1959 of the small pipe organ, a gift by the Wilburn C. Hailey family.

The first services were held in the new building on the fourth Sunday in Advent, December 21, 1958. Our parish was pleased to have a home. A service of dedication was held on the afternoon of the first Sunday after Epiphany, January 11, 1959, presided over by Bishop Barth, assisted by Fr. Carson and all the Episcopal clergy of the community. As the service moved toward its climax, the choir and capacity congregation sang during the vesting of the altar "Christ is made the sure foundation."

Another significant milestone was marked by the action of the Vestry at its meeting on June 15, 1959, in signing the necessary documents for the acceptance of Charles Christopher Clements as the first Postulant for Holy Orders from St. Peter's. The son of Mr. and Mrs. C.G. Clements, Chris later graduated from General Theological Seminary in New York and was ordained deacon at St. Peter's on June 29, St. Peter's Day, 1964. At this writing, he is Rector of St. John's Church in Johnston City.

With increasing Church attendance and with a widening range of activities in the parish, the Rector and Vestry were soon giving their attention to the need for expanded facilities and therefore a second building program. When the Church school year began in September 1960, Fr. Carson pointed out to the Vestry that the Church school enrollment was 200 in a space designed to accommodate approximately half that number. Bids were taken in mid-summer, 1962, and the new educational building was completed early in 1963.

This expansion of facilities was made desirable by the quite remarkable growth of St. Peter's during its first few years. At the time St. Peter's achieved parish status, there were 204 communicants. During the year 1958 transfers and confirmations brought this figure up to 265. Less than four years later, at the Vestry meeting of May 14, 1962, the Rector was able to announce that with the previous day's confirmations, the communicant total stood at 531, precisely doubled since 1958.

Through the various arrangements for parochial cooperation, St. Peter's has been able for all its history to participate in the work of the Church in the Chattanooga area. One of the most significant projects has been the establishment of the St. Barnabas complex, including the apartment house for the elderly and the nursing home. The new education building also made possible a significant outreach in the larger community. Quarters were made available at quite nominal cost, for example, to the Cadek Conservatory of the University of Tennessee at Chattanooga for children's piano lessons. Other non-profit organizations use the facilities at no cost or for a small contribution toward out-of-pocket expenses: Alcoholics Anonymous, Al-Anon, Chattanooga International Summer Village, and the Girl Scouts. Since 1966 St. Peter's kindergarten has occupied a considerable portion of this building for its daily program. The Vestry has always taken the view that the Church buildings ought to be available seven days a week.

During 1962, Fr. Carson discussed with the Vestry on several occasions the possibility of a priest associate to be added to the staff of St. Peter's. The need for an additional clergyman was widely recognized and accepted, by the Vestry and by the congregation. The problem was, as almost always, where was the necessary money to come from? The Vestry was able, by prudent management of resources, to budget $2,000 for 1963 for the services of a priest associate to begin on September 1. The Vestry was quite aware of budgetary limitations and also of the fact that implicit in the arrangement of the priest was the commitment to provide the money for the following year. The minutes of a special called Vestry meeting of January 8, 1963, conclude:

> The Rector expressed the views of many when he noted that all that had been done at St. Peter's had been done at some risk and on faith.

The Rev. Charles E. Rice, Rector of St. Phillip's Church in Donelson, Tennessee, accepted the Rector's invitation to come to St. Peter's as priest associate. He would be in charge of Christian education activities throughout the parish, and he served a year in that capacity.

Perhaps the greatest trauma of St. Peter's early history was the resignation of its first Rector in May of 1964. In what Fr. Carson said was possibly "the most difficult letter that I shall ever have to write," he informed the Vestry that he had received a call to become Rector of Christ Church in Greenville, South Carolina. A calling committee was immediately appointed to begin the task of finding a new Rector. During the remaining weeks of summer, a number of priests were considered and visited. On August 13, the calling committee reported its deliberations and laid before the Vestry the names of three prospective Rectors. After full discussion of the qualifications of these three, the Vestry voted to extend a call to the Rev. Hallie D. Warren, Jr., Rector of Grace Church in Waycross, Georgia. Fr. Warren accepted the call and took up his duties in mid-October.

As Fr. Warren had been assistant to the Rector of St. Paul's at the time St. Peter's was organized, he was already known to a goodly number of people of St. Peter's. The newsletter at the time commented in the following words:

> Those who knew Fr. Warren when he was at St. Paul's do not need to be convinced of our good fortune in having him here; those who do not yet know him will also quickly discover his warm and engaging manner, his deep devotion and sincerity as priest and pastor.

The new Rector set the tone for his incumbency. Referring to his first sermon at St. Peter's, Fr. Warren wrote in the church newsletter:

I began my ministry here at St. Peter's Church on the note "Be unto me a Father and a Priest." (Taken from seventeenth chapter of Judges.) This was the request of the wealthy man, Micha, which he made of the Levite that became his Priest. It is my sincere desire that each of you will allow me this relationship and that I may also, as did the Levite, become as one of your own family…. You have gone far and beyond the call of duty in making me and my family feel welcome and we thank you for being yourselves.

Fr. Hallie Warren and his wife Dixie, 1972. Fr. Hallie was rector from 1964 to 1993. Fr. Carter N. Paden, III became rector of St. Peter's in 1994.

The mention of the Rector's family is far more than mere politeness. The simple truth is that in any parish the Rector's wife is hardly less crucial than the Rector himself. St. Peter's has been very fortunate in Jane Carson and Dixie Warren, each of whom brought her own charm and talent to the life of the parish. One prominent laywoman at St. Paul's suggested a number of years ago that a Vestry should call a good wife and accept whatever comes with her!

At the Vestry's annual planning meeting, held at the DuBose Conference Center, Monteagle, in January 1965, Fr. Warren raised the possibility of a daily kindergarten at St. Peter's, perhaps "the first step at a parochial school." The committee appointed to investigate the possibility of the kindergarten found the idea increasingly attractive as they visited other local kindergartens and considered the possibilities for St. Peter's. Ever since its opening in September 1966, the kindergarten has been a continuing success and a valuable service to the parish and the community.

The persistent need for an additional clergyman in the parish was made somewhat less urgent by a development in the late sixties whereby selected lay persons were authorized to administer the chalice at the Eucharist. Originally each parish in this diocese was limited to two such persons, and upon nomination of the Rector, Bishop Vander Horst approved two chalice bearers for St. Peter's: Dr. Robert Boatwright and Samuel H. Payne. The first occasion of their serving in this capacity was Sunday, January 14, 1968, a milestone in the life of the parish. Since it was no longer necessary for the celebrant to distribute both the bread and the wine, the length of the service was significantly shortened.

Any effort to judge St. Peter's as a parish must take into account its response to the liturgical innovation in the late sixties and seventies. The first service for trial use was authorized in 1967 and introduced at St. Peter's on November 12 of that year. Inevitably there was a certain amount of trauma involved in seeking to modify in any way what many consider the incomparable *Book of Common Prayer* of 1928. Some of the liturgical experimentation seemed, to put the matter as acceptably as possible, somewhat awkward. But St. Peter's followed faithfully and conscientiously the instructions of our Bishop to use the trial services in order that we might understand the work of the Church's liturgical commission. Those in favor of liturgical change argued that a Prayer Book in the vernacular assumed periodic change since the language itself is subject to change, and they sought to devise a service in contemporary language in which people would feel comfortably at home.

As a result of the various efforts at revision, the *Proposed Book of Common Prayer* authorized in 1976 for a three-year trial use was essentially a compromise between the traditional and the contemporary. At St. Peter's, the *Proposed Book of Common Prayer* was accepted without great controversy. The proposed book was used punctiliously throughout the trial period, and thus when it became legally adopted as *The Book of Common Prayer* by the action of the 1979 General Convention, the people at St. Peter's by and large felt at home with it. The largely traditional service of "Rite I" in the new book and the contemporary service, which is "Rite II," provide the variety that many parishioners welcome.

Clearly the 1979 Prayer Book does bring to the life of the Church new emphases. One such emphasis is upon the Eucharist as the central act of Christian worship, an emphasis which has been implicit in the life and worship of St. Peter's Church from the beginning. Another emphasis is upon lay participation, both in the services and in the life of the Church; the new Prayer Book makes quite clear that in a very real sense every person is a minister: "The Church carries out its mission through the ministry of all its members" (Catechism, p. 855). At the same time, it is clear that some things in the life of the Church can be done only by the ordained clergy. St. Peter's has continued to welcome any reasonable opportunity for augmenting the clergy staff, for example, the use of seminarians from the School of Theology at Sewanee. Since the early seventies one or two young men have been assigned each academic year for Sunday duty at St. Peter's. Typically, they have taught Church school classes, worked with young people's groups, participated in aspects of the Church services, including preaching, and have in general made themselves useful in the work of the parish.

Certainly throughout its brief history St. Peter's has had its share of problems and difficulties. During the stewardship campaign of 1973, one parishioner wrote the campaign chairman a letter detailing some of the common concerns and suggesting that a Committee be appointed to inquire into them. Five problem areas were suggested for the committee's examination: (1.) Declining attendance at Church and Church functions; (2.) declining growth in spite of considerable population growth in the area; (3.) reluctance of parishioners to accept assignments in Church activities, such as teaching Church school classes; (4.) lack of evidence of good stewardship; (5.) a growing fringe area in the membership. The committee saw as its purpose "to accumulate facts and figures; to study, analyze, and evaluate; to make recommendations to the Vestry . . . ." The Committee membership was widely representative of the various organizations and activities of the parish, and during the next several weeks committee members collected and evaluated the information on which their report would be based.

The Committee's report, submitted on April 1, 1974, comments on some obvious weaknesses in parish life and makes some useful suggestions for improvement. The committee recognized the manifold demands made upon the Rector's time and energy and suggested the consideration of an assistant rector qualified in youth work. The report concludes with a broad recommendation: "Time after time throughout this report *involvement* is the key word. Our simple recommendation is total involvement for the entire Parish of St. Peter's Episcopal Church."

Two months later, at a special executive session of the Vestry on June 2, the Rector made his own report and recommendations in response to the findings of the Committee. Fr. Warren felt that decline in attendance, for example, should be viewed in the light of diocesan and national figures. He noted that a recent Gallup poll had shown that Church attendance nationally had declined by seventeen percent since 1958. He felt that the role of the national Church and of St. Peter's should be studied in the light of the current trends. He made a number of specific suggestions for a better organized parish life, including better communication and better coordination between himself and the committees and between the committees.

Whether it can be ascribed in whole or in part to the work of the Committee, the life of St. Peter's in the latter half of the seventies and into the eighties improved in tone and spirit. Not least significant among developments is the fact that it has been possible to supplement the staff. In 1974 Sam Payne began studying for the priesthood in a diocesan tutorial program with the expressed purpose of becoming a non-stipendiary clergyman on the staff of St. Peter's. He pursued this program for the next several years and was ordained deacon in 1978 and priest in 1979. His first celebration of the Eucharist took place at St. Peter's at 7:30 on the morning of June 17, 1979, and the whole congregation then attended an elegant breakfast in his honor. The newsletter commented on the occasion of the Eucharist and the break-

Plaque of the dedication of the George Connor Library and Conference Room, St. Peter's Episcopal Church, June 1, 1987.

fast: "Those of us who have come to know and love Sam Payne rejoiced to be a part of that celebration. As the Rector noted in his remarks, by whatever measure one uses, Sam sets very high standards in service as he gives himself and his time and talents to the work of this parish and the worship of God in this place."

At its December meeting in 1978 the Vestry took action to honor three persons who were especially active in the formative years of the parish. For sixteen years following its construction, the education building had been called simply that, and the large assembly room on the first floor was called "the big room." The Vestry voted to name the building Carson Hall in honor of our first Rector, and the large room the Bracewell Room in honor of Mary Kittye and Bob Bracewell. As the Bracewells have tirelessly pointed out, they were by no means the only lay people who were extremely active from the first day of St. Peter's life. But for those who have observed over the years the growth and development of St. Peter's, the Bracewells epitomize the kind of devotion and hard work which have built the parish.

Considerable time and energy during the year 1979 at St. Peter's were invested in a fairly elaborate self-study, for which the Rev. Harry Pritchett, then Archdeacon for the Diocese of Alabama, served as consultant. The study involved questionnaires, a series of cottage meetings to which all members of the parish were invited, a parish meeting, and various other devices aimed at identifying suitable parish goals.

A great deal which this document envisions and recommends has been accomplished, if not all of it quite within the two-year limit. The first objective listed, for example, is the establishment of a mission. Under the leadership of representatives of ECSET, St. Paul's, St. Thaddaeus', and St. Peter's, a new mission was organized in the Gold Point area, canonically a parochial mission of St. Peter's. The Rev. William T. Patten accepted appointment late in 1979 as the Vicar of the new mission, later named St. Alban's. Another goal listed in the self-study involved the appointment of a full-time program coordinator for the parish. Nancy Wallace, a communicant of St. Martin's Church, who had most recently been part-time Christian education director at Grace Church, accepted the appointment as program coordinator. She has brought her considerable energy and ability to bear upon many parts of the parish life, most notably Christian education and the work with the young people.

The third goal had to do with improvements to existing buildings. A number of improvements were projected, many of which have been completed since the self-study – new furnishings in the lounge, new carpeting in the nave and the offices, new furnishings in the EYC Room, built-in cabinets in the office, and numerous other improvements. A special project undertaken by a group of women headed by Ann Boyd and Peggy Gentry has provided needlepoint kneelers for the altar rail and for the sanctuary. Much of the improvement to the nave, the narthex, the lounge and other areas has been the work of the Beautification Committee, of which Norma Mills has been chairman.

A fourth goal had to do with new construction. A building program would have included a new parish hall and kitchen, the urgently needed enlargement of the sacristy, and outside storage facilities. The state of the economy and recent building costs have suggested the deferment of these plans. Periodic discussions include the possibility of a new nave slightly to the north of the present buildings (toward Ashland Terrace). In the summer of 1978, a consultant from the national Church met informally with the Vestry to discuss the possibility of a new building. In the questionnaire which preceded the 1982 finance campaign, sentiment in the parish was quite clearly negative about the building of a new nave at that time.

One recent development in the life of the parish demonstrates quite clearly that the world has changed in this first quarter century of St. Peter's existence. Early in 1981 upon the enthusiastic recommendation of Fr. Warren, the Vestry agreed after much discussion and investigation to purchase a micro computer for use at St. Peter's. In early May there was the glad announcement that a more versatile computer had become available; it had already been delivered and named Leroy. Since that time the computer has been used for an increasing variety of

186

tasks, and even the skeptics have conceded that it was a good investment. Moreover, it has provided the Rector with a toy of incomparable fascination.

The election late in 1982 of Norma Mills as the first woman to be senior warden of St. Peter's is evidence of the profound cultural change of the past quarter century. That change, affecting the whole Church, is clearly reflected in the life of this parish. No one who observed the beginnings of this parish can ever forget the truly monumental contributions of the women. Their determination, their hard work, and their financial contributions were all crucial to the development of St. Peter's from the very first. But here as elsewhere, in the decade of the seventies, the women truly came into their own. In 1970 Betty Painter (later Radford) became the first woman to be elected to the Vestry of St. Peter's; a goodly number of women have followed her in that service. Women have also been lay readers and chalice bearers. These matters are surely welcome signs of progress in the decade when the national convention (1976) authorized the ordination of women as priests.

It is not possible to give attention to the importance of women in the parish without due regard to the three women who occupied the position of parish secretary during these first twenty five years. Alice Boyd was the first of the three, serving from late 1958 to mid 1962. Mary Arthur Clements became parish secretary in February 1965 and served until her retirement in June 1982, when she was succeeded by Jean Johnson. The position of parish secretary is of absolutely primary importance, and St. Peter's has been fortunate in the contribution of these three women, and especially of Mrs. Clements in her long tenure.

Another person who has been crucial to the life and well-being of St. Peter's is David Blackwell, who has served almost continuously as Sexton since the buildings were erected. He has not only taken pride in the cleanliness and appearance of the buildings; in his devotion he has always gone far beyond the exact demands of duty.

For the year 1982 the Vestry appropriated a thousand dollars to be used in the observance of St. Peter's twenty-fifth anniversary to be held during that year. On March 14 a festival Eucharist was held as near as possible to the anniversary of the first service held in 1957. Special guests included Bishop Sanders, who was the preacher for the occasion; the Rev. Thomas H. Carson, Executive for Stewardship in the national Church and the first Rector of St. Peter's, who was the celebrant; and the Rev. John H. Bonner, Jr., Rector of St. Paul's.

The twenty-fifth anniversary celebration was concluded on Thanksgiving Day in the presentation of pledges for 1983 and in giving thanks for what has been accomplished at St. Peter's in its first twenty-five years. At the March 14 luncheon the senior warden had quoted a prayer ascribed to Sir Francis Drake, a prayer which seemed to express the spirit of all the celebration held in 1982:

> Almighty God, when thou givest to thy servants to endeavor any great matter, teach them also to know that it is not the beginning but the continuing of the same until it be thoroughly finished which yieldeth the true glory.

By its very nature, of course, the work of the Church can never be "thoroughly finished." In *The Screwtape Letters*, C.S. Lewis speaks of "the Church as we see her spread out through all time and space and rooted in eternity, terrible as any army with banners." Faintly as we may perceive it at times, that is a picture of the Church which we must never lose. In this time and in this place, we are called to the service of this Church as it is manifested in St. Peter's Parish. With whatever imperfections and limitations, with whatever talents and devotion, we experience here the beginning of our relationship to the Body of Christ.

A Tribute to Fr. Hallie Warren

> Like as the waves make towards the pebbled shore,
> So do our minutes hasten to their end.
>
> from Shakespeare's "Sonnet 60"

Few things in human life perhaps are more poignant than our minutes 'hastening to their end,' than some significant era of our lives' drawing to a close. But of course this is precisely the situation in which we find ourselves at St. Peter's: Hallie Warren became the Rector of St. Peter's in October 1964 and he lays down these duties at the end of June 1993. In her kind and generous letter to the parish several weeks ago, Dixie Warren helped us to see and give thanks for so much that has happened in these almost thirty years.

Whatever else we have learned, surely we have learned that any well-regulated parish is first of all a community of faith, a community of Christ. It is into this community that our children have been born and brought up, baptized, confirmed, married. But beyond these rites of passage, surely we have all learned a great deal; in sickness and in health, in life and death we have learned about our responsibility one to another. We have learned a lot about what it means to belong to the community of Christ. We have learned that it is not a question of

mere slogans, no matter how pious they may be. It is a matter of genuine
Christian conviction expressing itself in the deepest and most unsentimental way.

"What's past is prologue," Shakespeare tells us, and it will always be wise
to give him our attention. St. Peter's this year is a scant thirty-six years old, but
many years remain in our parish history that most of us will not live to see. And
these future years will come, and we will build for them by what we have done in
the past, what we have learned, sometimes by the hard knocks of adversity, sometimes not. No parish history is comprised of a miscellaneous series of disconnect-
ed episodes. What will be done here as long as these buildings stand will owe its
beginnings to what has taken place here in even so brief a history.

"So do our minutes hasten to their end." We cannot forever postpone the
inevitable. So what shall we say in gratitude to the Warrens and to the Carsons
before them? To all those almost countless lay persons who have contributed to
the parish in ways beyond our numbers? Is there an adequate way of expressing
our thanks? Yes, I believe there is. A passage which shows up in a good many
books of Anglican spirituality are those words from the 14th century mystic,
Dame Julian of Norwich, as filtered through the 20th century genius of T. S. Eliot:

> And all shall be well and
> All manner of thing shall be well
> By the purification of the motive
> In the ground of our beseeching.

June 20, 1993

On Criticism of the Clergy

During the Lenten series on this page, I did one column on a particularly
provocative question from Martin Smith's book *Reconciliation:* "Do you appreciate
the work of others, especially that of priests and other ministers, or are you
always on the lookout for opportunities to criticize?" (All columns had to do with
our life in the Church.) A number of people, *not* including our own clergy at St.
Peter's, have mentioned that column to me, so it was clear that the column struck
a raw nerve. I heard enough reactions to that page to make me feel that it is
worthwhile to come back to that subject once again.

A priest friend who is a faithful reader of this page has taken the trouble
in the past to write me several notes of appreciation for things said here. In
response to that column for Lent, he wrote, "People complain to me constantly
about one thing or other in the church and say 'there is not the respect in the

church anymore.' I agree and there is certainly little respect from the complainers." If there is a note of exasperation in those words, I can certainly understand and sympathize. From all the evidence I know, he is a first-rate priest and pastor and a very hard worker. That he should be obliged to listen to constant complaining is certainly well beyond the call of duty. Frankly, I think the complainers should be ashamed of themselves.

I wish the complainers knew one of my dearest friends who is a lifelong Roman Catholic. She takes the faith seriously and she works at it, in her parish and in all her relationships. She and I discuss religion a good deal, and I have never once, not one time, heard her criticize a priest of her own church. I have never heard her complain about any of the changes in the Catholic Church that followed from Vatican II. We all know Catholics who have been in mourning, for example, ever since the Mass began to be said in English; not my friend. I don't want to make her sound so meek and mild as to convey the wrong impression. When the Catholic bishops recently retained a public relations firm to help with their opposition to abortion, she was appalled. Like almost all Christians of whatever stripe, she is opposed to abortion, but she is not prepared to listen in silence to the gospel according to a public relations firm.

Life is surely hard enough for the clergy or anybody else without making it harder by frequent criticism. We all know the old joke: Why are the clergy so often unsatisfactory? Because they all come from the laity. One question the bishop asks the congregation at an ordination is to the point. "Will you uphold him in this ministry?" The answer to that question is, "We will!" Let us remember.

June 10, 1990

To Understand More Fully

"We need to remind ourselves over and over again that the intellect
is also a part of our religious lives . . . ."   (GC, January 3, 1964)

Religion by Slogan

A number of years ago John Erskine wrote an essay called "The Moral Obligation to Be Intelligent." As I remember his argument, he developed the thesis that it is never enough simply to behave well; to be a good person, one must be a thoughtful person as well. He was perfectly aware of differences of intellectual endowment; his contention was that it is immoral not to use whatever ability

190

one has as well as one possibly can.

We need to remind ourselves over and over again that the intellect is also a part of our religious lives, that it is clearly sinful to operate on the assumption that the practice of religion does not require the hard discipline of thought. One thing we might well think about is the effort to reduce religion to the level of a slogan or a spot commercial. One can hear these days on local radio stations absolutely unbelievable spot announcements on the subject of religion. One spot suggests that family happiness will greatly improve "if God is installed in your household." This makes God sound rather like a color television set or some other gadget.

Other spots promote Sunday School attendance by calling the Sunday School "God's training ground for youth." Surely this is a bit extravagant. One syrupy spot admonishes us to "make God's love a part of your daily lives; you'll be richly blessed for it." This is the substance of the argument, stated or implied, in most of these spots: worship God not because it is our duty, because we are made in His image, because it is the chief business of our lives to worship Him; worship Him because He will make everything all right. It is nonsense, of course, and it is heretical nonsense. The copy writers have not read the book of Job recently.

Perhaps the silliest example of this mentality is the bumper sticker: "We still believe in prayer." Whatever this is supposed to mean, it suggests that sinister forces have somehow sought to banish the practice of prayer. One suspects this is a comment on Supreme Court rulings; if it is, it would be useful for us to discover what the court has actually said about prayer in the schools. The relationship between religion and the public schools is vexed and complicated. As Christians we are doing no service by displaying mindless slogans.

January 3, 1964

A Parable to Ponder

A parable, according to *The American Heritage Dictionary,* is "a simple story illustrating a moral or religious lesson." An even simpler definition is one that almost everybody seems to have learned in childhood. According to this formula, a parable is "an earthly story with a heavenly meaning." Like many definitions, these fall somewhat short of the reality they seek to convey. Both certainly contain some truth (though the second is a little too neat!), but they give no idea of the richness and radical importance of parable. A really good parable, one theologian has written, turns our world upside down. He points out that the father in the Prodigal Son behaves as no Jewish father would have dreamed of behaving.

191

A few weeks ago I had a letter from a young friend who is a seminarian. For a while this summer, he found himself involved in construction of a church building. "I had a wonderful moment as I was banging nails with one of the carpenters that had been hired. He allowed that church was a strange 'bidness.' For example, he told me of getting into a brawl with another man at a highway tavern and a week later meeting the same man and buying him a beer at the same place. He said that he had gotten into an argument with someone in his church and that person hadn't spoken to him in ten years. So it goes. . . ."

That comment certainly meets the requirement of "a simple story illustrating a moral or religious lesson." I believe that if we ponder this little story, it is quite capable of turning our world upside down. Most of us are not quite prepared to accept the fact that the relationships centered in a tavern (or a bridge club or a country club or whatever) can be, at least sometimes, more Christian than the relationships which center in the church. So it was in my friend's story. We can all think of times when deep and lasting enmities have had their roots in some disagreement within the Body of Christ. Strange "bidness" indeed!

We have it on the authority of St. John of the Cross that "when the evening of this life comes we shall be judged on love." And we have it very clearly on the authority of our Lord that we are not to forgive seven times but seventy times seven. Only the most literal-minded can suppose this is a formula of some sort. In the Body of Christ there is no such formula.

October 5, 1986

Dr. Donald Harbuck

After a long and gallant battle against very nearly insuperable odds, Dr. Don Harbuck died on June 4, 1985. He came to Chattanooga in the summer of 1983 to be pastor of the First Baptist Church, but his severe illness forced him to resign that post on January 1 of this year. His tenure, therefore, at First Baptist was heartbreakingly brief. His resignation and his death were grievous blows not only to his own church but to the religious life of Chattanooga. Few clergymen have come to this city in my lifetime with Don Harbuck's credentials.

He first came to my attention in an interview with Ruth Robinson in *The Chattanooga Times* in the late winter of 1982 when he was at First Baptist to do a Bible study series of some sort. In that interview he made a brilliant distinction between fundamentalism and orthodoxy, terms which unfortunately many Christians use interchangeably. I used this page at the time for a lengthy comment on his views, and several of the quotations seem to me very much worth

192

repeating: "Fundamentalism is a development within the Christian stream in which certain belief patterns are rigidified and frozen and given a kind of eternal validity. Fundamentalism is not really a theology. It is a spirit, a spirit of judgment."

And even more to the point: "Fundamentalism is a kind of tyranny, a tyranny over the mind and the spirit." I think that statement says a great deal about what is least attractive in the religious life of this community. Fundamentalism is really intellectually bankrupt, no matter how many spokesmen it is able to maintain. Don Harbuck understood this very clearly, and he lent the weight of his position to an understanding of the faith and of the Bible which avoided the narrowness and restrictiveness of fundamentalism.

In the providence of God, his influence is not lost to us. Our lives and our understanding of the faith have been enriched by his insights. Because of the patience and courage which he demonstrated in his last long illness, even those of us who knew him briefly and almost casually will never forget the wisdom of his faith and the brightness of his spirit. I bid your prayers for his eternal welfare.

June 23, 1985

According to Swaggart

A few weeks ago a friend sent me an undated Catholic newspaper clipping having to do with certain utterances of Jimmy Swaggart, the electronic evangelist (if that is the right term). I quote one paragraph from the article: "Swaggart, a fundamentalist, has criticized the Catholic Church and most Protestant denominations for advocating false beliefs. He has said that priests are leading people 'to hell' and in a recent attack claimed that Mother Teresa would go to hell unless she accepted Jesus as her personal savior."

Commenting on these statements involves for me certain difficulties. One difficulty is how to deal with Mr. Swaggart while still remaining within the boundaries of that Christian charity which ought to characterize all our relationships. A second and greater difficulty is to try to determine whether one is most put off by the ignorance or the arrogance of Mr. Swaggart's quoted comments. According to some television rating figures, Mr. Swaggart has been seen by 731,774 household in 183 markets; from these figures one can easily see what trifles were the Sermon on the Mount and the feeding of the five thousand.

But as I ponder Mr. Swaggart's opinions, I am convinced that it is chiefly his arrogance which one finds so distasteful. No Christian labors under the assignment of deciding who is going to hell and who isn't; fortunately for all of us, that matter is in quite other Hands. I think we can safely leave Mother Teresa to the mercies and judgment of God. Yet I can't quite do so without wondering what is meant by the phrase, accepting Jesus as her "personal savior." Two evangelical friends have recently helped me understand what seems to me a very curious and even offensive phrase. My friends tell me that these words are meant to describe a conversion experience, the kind of conversion experience that Mr. Swaggart finds essential to salvation. But in this view, as in the other views which he dispenses with such abandon, Mr. Swaggart speaks outside of the mainstream of the Christian faith.

Surely there is no question but that television opens up opportunities for Christian proclamation of the gospel far beyond any other possibilities. But the presence of the television cameras does not confer wisdom, still less humility, and we would do well to remember that fact when we hear some of the charlatans who dispense what they call religion.

May 6, 1984

A Remarkable Life: Nathan A. Scott, Jr.

One of the great scholars in the academic field of religion and literature is Nathan A. Scott, Jr., whose fruitful and productive career was spent mainly at the Divinity School of the University of Chicago and later at the University of Virginia, from which he retired as Kenan Professor Emeritus of Religious Studies. The most recent issue of the journal *Christianity and Literature*, Winter 1994 (scholarly journals tend sometimes to be a bit slow), contains two items of great interest: an address by Professor Scott acknowledging the Lifetime Achievement Award given him, last December 1994, at the annual meeting of the Conference on Christianity and Literature; and a long and fascinating interview with Scott conducted by Ralph C. Wood, professor of religion at Wake Forest University, himself a figure of great stature in the field.

Scott is a man of remarkable background. His father, born in 1874, was the child of former slaves. He says in the interview, "As a young man my father made his way on to Selma University in Selma, Alabama. It was but a 'normal school' . . . which had been established by Yankees, by people who were products of Harvard and Brown and Yale who undertook to offer their black pupils what they had been formed by – namely, a classical curriculum. Though some might judge this to have been a piece of foolishness, nevertheless that's what they did." Still commenting on his father, a bit later in the interview he says, "He contributed more to my formation than anybody else has ever done! Foolish as the program of instruction devised for his generation by their Yankee instructors might seem, he was indelibly marked by it. He was my great *teacher*. . . . I consider him to be the author of whatever there may be in my life that is worth paying attention to."

The father was a Congregationalist, but Nathan Scott, Jr. had made another choice which he waited till his father's death to carry out. He felt he had to "stay put until he had passed from the scene, and then I immediately entered the Episcopal Church and undertook preparation for holy orders." During this tenure in Chicago, he was canon of the Cathedral there, a regular preacher and celebrant, and in charge of continuing education programs for what he called "the reading clergy" (a fine classification but not all-inclusive).

The interviewer asks him what poetic lines come into his mind during "solitary moments and pensive moods." He apparently didn't have to stop and think: "The [*Four*] *Quartets*. The Hopkins of 'The Wreck of the Deutschland' and much else. Many passages from Wordsworth, Keats, Whitman, Yeats. Many of the poems of Richard Wilbur, many of the poems of an old friend now dead, Robert Hayden. . . . A year never goes by when I don't reread, slowly and carefully, Eliot's *Quartets*. They have become for me material, in the Catholic sense, for spiritual meditation." If anyone in the parish is working on his own continuing education program, here are plentiful suggestions.

At the beginning of the interview in *Christianity and Literature*, Professor Wood recounts his surprise when he had first learned that Scott is black, asking whether he found such surprise "complimentary or condescending." Rather a naive question, I think. A moment later he says to Scott that "when I found out you were black it came as a delight. I hope that in studying with you I might atone, in some very small way, for the sins of my own ancestors." Scott's reply is almost brusque: "There is nothing you can do in the way of atonement for the sins of the fathers: those are their sins, not yours."

And yet, I thought of a line from a poem of Richard Wilbur, one of my favorite poets as well as one of Scott's. The line comes from a poem called "The Pardon": "I dreamt the past was never past redeeming." While it is true that Wood, or anyone else, cannot atone for the sins of the past, for the cruel treatment of the black in American history, in some sense at least Wood can use the past as a means for shaping the future. Those of us who are white can certainly resolve that we will do everything in our power to see that everyone of minority status will receive the justice and fairness that is due him or her. While we do not have to take upon ourselves the guilt for the sins of slavery, we can certainly use the consciousness of that guilt in constructive ways.

One thing the interview makes clear is that not only has Scott achieved impeccable scholarship in religion and literature but also that he is a man of uncommonly common sense. Wood asks him in the interview, "What do you make of churches whose worship prohibits any reference to God in masculine metaphors? Jesus, for example, is called God's child." And here is a goodly share of Scott's answer: "I shudder. I believe, of course, that whenever and wherever it is possible to sanitize the common tongue so far as sexist usage is concerned, it should be so sanitized. 'Man,' for example, is not an appropriate generic term for mankind. But I fear that we are handling much too carelessly the received Biblical metaphor when we cast it all aside merely for the sake of a decent regard for the sensibilities of contemporary feminists. I should be aghast if the concept of the Fatherhood of God were to be generally relegated to the discard. I am not at all averse to efforts at discerning a feminine principle in the Godhead. We should be open to revisionist reflection of this kind. But simply to discard a biblical metaphor that has come to be deeply regulative of theological discourse and of liturgical discourse – we're then risking heresy."

August 20 & September 3, 1995

Incomparable Book

There is now available to us an almost bewildering variety of versions, editions, translations, and paraphrases of the Bible. If we really take the Bible seriously as the central book of our religious tradition, we can find no adequate excuse for not growing continually more proficient in reading, understanding, and using it. But where, amongst the plenitude now available, does one begin?

For liturgical use, that is for use in the services of public worship, there are many of us who feel that the King James Version has no equal. Surely for beauty and sublimity of language, it has none. For more than three-and-a-half centuries, the King James Bible has profoundly influenced language and literature in the English-speaking world. One may hazard the guess that whatever sales records develop, no versions will ever rival the prestige of the King James.

But for the purposes of private devotion and study, the King James needs at least to be supplemented. For this purpose, one can do no better than turn to the Oxford Annotated Bible, Revised Standard Version. (There is a closely parallel edition of the New English Bible, and much that can be said of the RSV can also be said of the NEB.) This version is a kind of model of what intelligent and enlightened Biblical scholarship ought to be. It gives the reader all the aids he or she is likely to require short of detailed technical study, but it is all done so well and so concisely that one doesn't feel overwhelmed by editorial matter.

There are brief introductions to both Old and New Testament that help to give the reader a kind of review of what that portion of the Bible seeks to do. Then there is a short – usually about half a page – introduction to each separate book, commenting on authorship, date, and historical context. Difficulties or complexities in the text are dealt with in clear and sensible footnotes. Brief supplemental essays are also included, one of them consisting of sound advice on how to read the Bible. There is also an excellent set of maps.

When Fr. Chuck Murphy was here at St. Peter's for a preaching mission a few years ago, he strongly urged us to make it our invariable custom to get up early enough in the morning to include in our devotions some serious attention to the Bible. By using the Oxford Annotated, we can go a long way in our mastery of this incomparable book.

September 4, 1977

On Reading the Bible

One of my own graduate professors was fond of saying that the only way to be a good teacher of literature, or even an adequate one, is to saturate oneself in that literature. Among the few pedagogical principles to which I swear allegiance, this is one: to saturate myself in the literature, to read, mark, learn, and inwardly digest the literature. But I begin with this cherished principle mainly in order to confess how extraordinarily difficult I think it is to manage any real sort of saturation in the Bible. To saturate oneself in this vast and complex book, to know all of it or most of it really well, is the work of a lifetime. Meanwhile, one simply does the best one can.

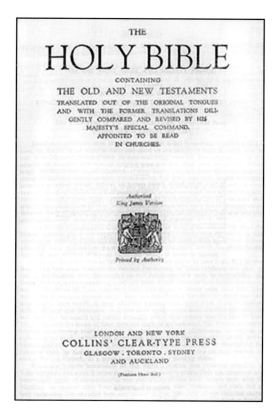

I begin also by acknowledging my indebtedness to those who have helped me to a fuller understanding of the Bible, and indeed of the Christian faith. The list is a long one and I shall certainly not attempt any really complete acknowledgment of those whose lives and writings have nourished me. My own fascination with the Bible undoubtedly began in my childhood when Bible stories were read to me; my interest has grown and flourished in the encouraging companionship of a large number of persons. Of these I must single out three for specific mention: the Rev. Thorne Sparkman, that priest and scholar and former rector of this parish for whom this School of Religion is so appropriately named; the Rev. Professor Fleming James, Old Testament scholar and sometime dean of the School of Theology at Sewanee; and thirdly, a man whom I have known only in the wealth of his writing, Archbishop William Temple, surely the greatest Anglican of the twentieth century, perhaps of any century. What I owe to these three men, in very different ways, is beyond calculation or expression. I shall try to identify specific indebtedness, but there is much that I have gleaned from these three men and from many others whom I cannot identify and document. It is enough to say that other men and women have labored, and I have entered into their labor.

Before we turn to the Old Testament and begin to examine some of its most significant and pervasive themes, I should like to discuss some principles which we ought to bring to the reading and interpretation of the Bible. First, it is necessary to comment on those two words, *reading* and *interpretation*. A good many years ago I was present when a visiting clergyman admonished an audience of high school students with these words: "Whatever you do," he told them, "you must not interpret the Bible; you must simply read it." He then proceeded for thirty minutes to interpret various Biblical passages for them. But what else could he have done if he wished to speak about the Bible at all? It is clearly impossible to read without interpreting; by its very nature, reading *is* interpretation, whether we are reading a traffic sign or an Old Testament prophet. If you doubt this, I ask you only to recollect some time when you have read the simple words of a traffic sign – say on a busy freeway – but have been completely puzzled about the meaning of the sign. Of course there is a certain kind of writing, which we can label broadly as scientific, which aims to be as clear and unambiguous as possible; I say it aims at this, it does not always reach this desirable goal. A recipe, or the instructions for assembling some household gadget, or the directions for a chemistry experiment – these are examples of writing in which the words are chosen, or ought to be chosen, with a view to being as clear and unambiguous as possible. But of course the language of the Bible is not the language of science; it is often, again broadly speaking, the language of poetry. Often the poet will choose the suggestively ambiguous word because it serves his purpose better: in *King Lear* when Gloucester naively calls Edmund his "loyal and natural boy," Shakespeare surely intends us to take *natural* in both its senses, as meaning illegitimate (which of course Edmund is) but also meaning 'according to nature,' that is, a son who shows his father the affection and loyalty "natural" to their relationship.

The Bible confronts us continually, persistently, with the language of poetry. When the Psalmist says, "The folds shall be full of sheep; the valleys also shall stand so thick with corn, that they shall laugh and sing" (65:14), he is not making a scientific statement. If I read that verse literally and scientifically, it is the merest nonsense. But if I interpret Psalm 65 as an exuberant expression of pleasure in the world which God has made, manifested especially in the plentitude of the harvest, then it is clear that the Psalmist's language is by no means nonsense.

When Isaiah attempts to convey to us his magnificent vision in the temple "in the year that King Uzziah died," he is surely not essaying a careful, literal description of the scene such as a movie camera might have recorded if one had been available. He is seeking in the language of poetry to give us some understanding of the beauty and significance of that occasion. I take as one more example a single verse from what the scholars call II Isaiah: "For you shall go out in joy, and be led forth in peace; the mountains and the hills before you shall break forth into singing, and all the trees of the field shall clap their hands" (55:12). I cannot be an adequate reader of these passages unless I bring to them the most disciplined and imaginative use of whatever intelligence I have. In other words, to read is to interpret.

I realize that the clergyman whose advice to the students I have quoted is not an isolated or unique example of the literal mind at work. I am aware that for many Christians, the chief principle employed in the reading of the Bible is that it must be taken exactly as it is, without interpretation. Since this is clearly impossible, I think what they mean is that the interpretation must agree with their own, an interpretation which somehow arises inevitably out of the very words themselves, an interpretation which all right-minded people will accept as the correct and only possible one. But again it is simply not in the nature of the Bible, the nature of the language of symbol and imagination, of poetry, to lend itself to any such treatment.

But of course not all readers take such a view. It seems to me fair and reasonable to say that there are basically three possible positions which we can occupy with respect to the nature and validity of the Bible. Of these positions, the two extremes are fairly easy to characterize. At the one end are those who take the Bible as literally as it is possible to take it, those who feel that somehow any interpretation does undermine the Bible's integrity. For these persons the Bible is not only the inspired word of God but, according to the notion of plenary inspiration, the text of the Bible is protected at every stage of transcription, translation, editing, or whatever, insuring that no human error could at any point have entered in. At the other extreme are those who think the Bible is great literature in just the same sense that Shakespeare's plays or Dante's *Divine Comedy* or Milton's epic poems are great literature. They are willing to say that the Bible is inspired only in the sense in which these and other great literary works are inspired. The adherents of this view do not suppose that the Bible deals with any sort of divine revelation because they have usually only the faintest belief in the Deity and none in revelation itself. Surely if a serious practicing Christian had to choose between these two positions, he or she would unhesitatingly choose the first. Whatever we may think of the naiveté or inadequacy of the literalist view, at least its adherents believe something; whereas those who talk vaguely about the great literature of the Bible, and only that, seem to believe very little.

But fortunately it is not necessary to choose between those extremes; it is possible, and for most of us quite necessary, to take some position between those extremes, but a position in no sense a compromise between them. Such a position I believe most Anglicans occupy, but of course there is no position so bizarre or so extreme that some Anglicans cannot be found who hold it. But in attempting to delineate these positions, I am certainly not talking about denominations; I am talking about points of view towards the Bible. These different views cut across all sorts of denominational lines. The holders of this third, this central, position recognize the diversity and complexity of Biblical literature, and they try to make upon each book or each portion they read the demands which are reasonable and appropriate to that book or that portion. They do not read the story of creation in the same way they read the story of the life of David; they do not read the Book of Jonah in the same way they read the prophet Hosea. They believe that the Bible is indeed the inspired word of God, but they do not conceive of inspiration as a process which absolutely precludes and makes impossible any sort of human error.

They do not believe, in other words, that divine inspiration supersedes the human limitations of the individual writer, that it somehow gives him an infallible mastery of his material, a total and communicable understanding of the nature of God himself. It does not seem to have been the design of the Holy Spirit to select just any man to be a writer of scripture; divine inspiration seems to have touched those persons whose capacity for truth was greatest, who by their intellectual and spiritual gifts were the likeliest vessels of divine revelation. But as one of my own teachers was wont to say, Amos could get only an Amosfull of the understanding of God; he could not go beyond his own capacity. And then when he came to communicate this Amosfull to us, he was obliged to use the frail and unsatisfactory medium of language. In order to read with any real comprehension the book which bears his name, we must see as clearly as we can Amos the human being, his own abilities and qualities, his own limitations; and certainly we must seek to understand the social and political background against which he wrote. And we must also have a lively appreciation of the limits and vagaries of language.

Moreover, to read the Bible well we must also have some grasp of the literary conventions of the age in which the writing was done. One of those conventions has to do with a certain love of hyperbole, of overstatement for the sake of emphasis; in the ancient mind, this use of hyperbole was often coupled with a fondness for good round numbers. It is to be doubted, for example, that the Greek forces who sailed for Troy to return Helen to her rightful husband occupied so many as a thousand ships, though that is the traditional number. By the same token, one can afford to be a little skeptical about the longevity of the Old Testament patriarchs, or the number of Israelites slain in one day during their desert wanderings (e.g., Exodus 32:28). Another ancient tendency was to attach to heroes or central figures details which are clearly legendary. I should myself suppose the story of Moses' infancy is such an instance, or David's killing of Goliath. Both of these stories are certainly within the realm of possibility, but they are the kind of legend which attaches itself very easily to an attractive hero. I think it is both possible and desirable to read much of the Bible without bothering one's head about historicity, that rather pedantic word which merely means historical reliability or authenticity. Sometimes the question of historicity seems neither relevant nor especially significant. I cannot see that it really matters, for example, whether the infancy story of Moses is factual or legendary, and the question need hardly arise when one is reading the Mosaic narrative.

But the question of David and Goliath is rather more complicated. It is of course one of two explanations in the narrative for David's introduction into the court of Saul. I do not believe these two stories can be reconciled without a great deal of fancy intellectual acrobatics, though some people like to get their exercise that way. In I Samuel 16, David comes to Saul as a court musician whose skill with the lyre may help to ameliorate the mental illness from which Saul was beginning to suffer. This account includes the following: "And David came to Saul and entered his service. And Saul loved him greatly, and he became his armor-bearer. And Saul sent to Jesse, saying, 'Let David remain in my service, for he has found favor in my sight'" (21-22). The very next chapter contains the rather lengthy account of David's slaying of Goliath, and several verses at the end of that chapter make it abundantly clear that Saul sees David as he goes to battle and as he returns, and Saul clearly does not know who he is. It seems to me more honest and even more reverent to say, there seems to be a contradiction here, rather than by various twisting and turnings to try to devise an explanation proving that both stories are equally factual.

Two points are worth making here. First, let us put ourselves in the role of the redactor, the editor responsible in some degree for weaving together a continuous narrative from two or three sources. What would we do if we were faced with two stories dealing with some important element of the narrative, two stories which seemed contradictory and irreconcilable? I think our instinct might very well be to use both, to discard neither, lest in doing so we might lose some insight or reflection of great value. And that seems to me almost always to have been the instinct of those redactors for whom just that situation was very real. They give us both stories and let us make of them what we can. The second point is that nothing in the Bible – and I am following William Temple on this point – should be discarded or rejected or set aside without our first saying to ourselves: What did the writer think he had hold of here? We may feel pretty certain that he was mistaken, but what vision of the truth did he find in the story?

Surely it need not bother us to realize that legendary material had a way of attaching itself to great heroes. Earlier I said that this sort of thing happened easily in ancient literature, but one need not go back very far in our own history to find striking parallels. I doubt that many of us regard the story of George Washington and the cherry tree as sober history, and one can label that story as purely legendary without for a moment doubting the historical reality of George Washington. There are of course many of our fellow Christians who feel that if they allow themselves to cast doubt on one phrase of the Bible, the whole book is inevitably lost. But surely such a view is unrealistic and untenable. Anyway if we are labeling something as legend, we are not really discarding it; we are putting it on some other level than the purely factual. The legendary stories themselves are usually typical of the person about whom they are told. Take a quite modern instance: one writer has noted the story given circulation during World War II that General Eisenhower, when he was Supreme Commander in Europe, would approach an enlisted man, thrust out his hand and say, "My name's Eisenhower." The story is pure legend, but the point is that it is the kind of legend told about Eisenhower; it seems like the sort of thing he might have done, even if he never did. Nobody made up any stories about Douglas MacArthur introducing himself to enlisted men.

The principle I am endeavoring to articulate is this: the question of strict historical accuracy is not equally relevant to every portion of the Old Testament narrative. I am certainly not saying that it is never relevant: it is the merest truism to say that both Judaism and Christianity are rooted in history. The exodus of the Israelites from Egypt is in the bloodstream of Judaism, just as the crucifixion and the resurrection are in the bloodstream of Christianity. What I am saying is that the historical reality of these events is not threatened or undercut by the fact that there are fanciful and legendary details in the Biblical narrative.

Perhaps our responsibility as readers and interpreters of the Old Testament becomes somewhat clearer if we remind ourselves of what the Old Testament primarily is. There is always considerable hazard in reducing great complexity to a simple statement or formula, but, carefully used, such reduction can also have great value for us. Perhaps the simplest way to describe the Old Testament is to say that it is the record of God's revelation of Himself to the children of Israel; or, to put it the other way round, it is the record of Israel's slowly developing understanding of the nature of God. The task, therefore, of all of those who contributed to the making of the Old Testament was nothing less than to convey in finite language the nature and majesty of the infinite God. In seeking to carry out this mission, the makers quite naturally turned to all the devices available to them for explanation and description. There is therefore in the Old Testament sober history, as in the narratives of the kings of Israel; there is parable, as in the story of Jonah; there is highly imaginative poetry, as in the book of Isaiah. And of course there are mixtures of all of these elements in almost every Old Testament book. Whatever the method, the device, the kind of literature, the aim is always the same: to make as clear as possible to weak, foolish, and fallible men the nature and being of the Most High God.

March 10, 1976

On Prayer

"What exactly are we trying to do when we pray?"
(GC, March 7, 1965)

Little Children

A friend who belongs to a suburban Methodist Church told me recently a quite memorable story. Before the chief prayers in the morning service, the pastor had read a list of the ill, bereaved, and otherwise troubled, and he asked, "Are there other concerns we should remember in our prayers?" Without a moment's hesitation, a small boy arose to say, "My dog is sick." A little girl said her hamster had died, and another girl reported the illness of her cat. These children clearly dominated the prayer requests.

The wonderfully innocent and unselfconscious behavior of the children must be an important part of what our Lord meant when He said, "Unless you turn and become like children, you will never enter the kingdom of heaven" (Matthew 18:3, RSV). What mattered to these youngsters at that moment was the welfare of their pets, and they had no hesitation about speaking out on their behalf. I suppose children of that age have only the sketchiest of theological convictions about prayer, but even if it had been otherwise, I doubt they would have been deterred on this occasion.

Is there a defensible theology of prayer, which can take animals into account, domestic or otherwise? I certainly believe there is. At the veterinary hospital where a friend and I find ourselves from time to time, I noticed at the last visit something new had been added to one wall of a treatment room: a prayer written by Albert Schweitzer, whom Frederick Buechner has called "one of the great near-saints of Protestantism." It is a prayer to God in His mercy to remember our friends the animals, to keep them from harm, to see that they are treated kindly and humanely. If Schweitzer, then why not the children at my friend's church?

I remember once reading in a very good book about prayer that if children are being given some gradual understanding of what prayer is, there is no reason a little girl should not pray for her broken doll. We all have to learn early that our prayers are not always answered as we would wish, that things don't always happen because we ask for them on our knees – or in some other prayerful posture. A prayer for a broken doll might be answered by timely repairs or by some other means. Surely God does not expect us, at whatever age, to put aside the pain of a broken heart and think only of spiritual things. The children in my friend's story seemed to have an instinctive understanding of that point.

February 11, 1990

"Where Prayer Has Been Valid"

In his regular column in a recent issue of *The Christian Century,* Martin Marty wrote about Thomas Merton's view of the Trappist monastery in Kentucky where Merton spent roughly the last half of his life. Not long after his arrival at the monastery, Merton wrote: "This is the center of America. I had wondered what was holding the country together, what was keeping the universe from falling apart . . . . It is an axle around which the whole country blindly turns." And, as Marty notes, Merton thought, "There may be other such places." There *are* other such places of course, and surely most of us can number among our experiences the discovery and enjoyment of such places.

One such place I was able to add to my own list when I went with a Catholic friend to visit the Trappist monastery in Conyers, Georgia, a few miles east of Atlanta. We were able to spend only a longish afternoon there, ending with Vespers in the Abbey Church just at sunset. Through other people's descriptions, in books and conversation, I had some knowledge of the Monastery of the Holy Spirit (its formal name), though I had never visited it before. We spent time in the bookstore, the guest house, at the side of the lake where ducks abound and where some of Flannery O'Connor's peacocks, or their descendants, are to be seen. We spent a good deal of time walking back and forth on the long entrance drive between two rows of lovely magnolia trees.

For me, I think also for my friend, it was a beautiful day of peace and quiet and reflection and prayer. When I see a monastic community at such close range, I truly marvel at those people who seriously question the point and value of the monastic life. The tradition is a very old one, and the monastics have the excellent precedent of our Lord Himself, who drew apart from the crowds to rest and pray. The Trappist monks find their vocation in prayer and meditation and labor. Their lives have integrity in the root meaning of that word and one cannot be among them even briefly without sensing the fruits of those lives.

When we were kneeling at Vespers and when the monks were chanting the Psalms, I thought of a fragment from the first section of T.S. Eliot's "Little Gidding." The voice of the poem says to the pilgrim who has arrived at the restored chapel of an Anglican religious community that flourished briefly in the 17th century: "You are here to kneel where prayer has been valid." I felt that my friend and I on a Saturday afternoon in the Monastery in Conyers had also knelt where prayer is valid.

January 4, 1987

Prayers Out of a Book

There is an old story (alas, almost certainly apocryphal) that Episcopalians love to hear and to tell. The setting is an ecumenical meeting of clergy in a small

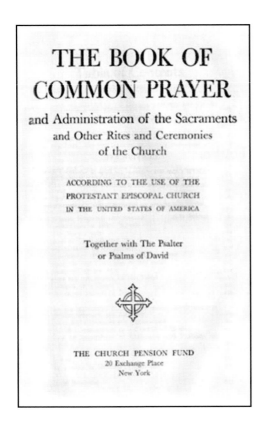

THE BOOK OF COMMON PRAYER

and Administration of the Sacraments
and Other Rites and Ceremonies
of the Church

ACCORDING TO THE USE OF THE
PROTESTANT EPISCOPAL CHURCH
IN THE UNITED STATES OF AMERICA

Together with The Psalter
or Psalms of David

THE CHURCH PENSION FUND
20 Exchange Place
New York

southern town. The presiding officer says to a young Episcopal priest, with only a trace of irony, "Will Father Blank be good enough to say one of his set prayers for us?" "Certainly," says the young priest: "Our Father, who art in heaven . . . ." Apocryphal or not, the story makes an important point.

While the use of set prayers, "prayers out of a book," is not one of the burning issues in my own mind, I have thought a good deal about it recently. An old friend wrote to me and told me that he had been to an Episcopal funeral and asked me a question or two about it. I haven't answered him yet, though I have every intention of doing so. First, I think I'll telephone him and ask, "How much do you really want to know about this?" And I'll offer to send him a Prayer Book because he can learn more by careful attention to the prayers than by almost any other way. Also, I take the view that every literate Christian household should include a copy of *The Book of Common Prayer*.

Moreover, I saw a quotation in a local church newsletter that, as far as I know, I had never seen before, and the quotation made a point that I had never thought about. C.S. Lewis was suggesting an important reason for set prayers: that their use protects us from the dangers of heresy. I looked at that quotation with the shock of recognition; I did not need to wonder whether it was true or not. Since I encountered the quotation, I have heard the truth of it confirmed a number of times, most recently by a young man whose prayer in a local gathering thanked God for allowing us to use His wisdom in dealing with our problems! Not too frequently, I fear. The prayer was not spectacularly inept, but it did ask for the most incredible assortment of virtues and blessings for his group.

Earlier generations were often required in their Church School classes to memorize the collect for each week. I think it is a pity that this custom has fallen out of favor. Obviously, we could still learn a great deal by memorizing those collects; none of them is routine or pedestrian and a good many of them are magnificent in thought and in language. We should never be apologetic about the use of set prayers. A friend in the parish told me of a recent meeting over which she presided, a dinner meeting which would certainly have included a variety of denominations. At the outset she read from the Prayer Book a collect on education and followed that with a familiar grace before meals. A few moments after she concluded, there was laughter in one corner of the room. My friend learned that one gentleman had said, "That's an Episcopal blessing; there wasn't a Baptist word in it!" Well, that's not quite accurate; surely we haven't taken over the whole Christian vocabulary.

January 12, 1995

The Lord's Prayer
A Series of Reflections

Our Father, who art in heaven,
   hallowed be thy Name,
   thy kingdom come,
   thy will be done,
     on earth as it is in heaven.
Give us this day our daily bread.
And forgive us our trespasses,
   as we forgive those who trespass against us.
And lead us not into temptation,
   but deliver us from evil.
For thine is the kingdom, and the power, and the glory,
   for ever and ever. Amen.

To overstate the importance of the Lord's Prayer in the life and thought of the Church is next to impossible. There is no prayer that is given the liturgical emphasis this one receives; it is a fixed part of every Prayer Book service. But even more important, there is no prayer which approaches it as a model of what Christian prayer ought to be and a standard by which our own prayers can be measured.

Some reflections on the nature and substance of this prayer, then, seem especially appropriate for the Lenten season, the time when we seek to sharpen and deepen our religious perception. This page will therefore be devoted during the next several weeks to a discussion of this basic Christian prayer. It is a wide and inexhaustible field, and we cannot hope to do more than suggest lines of thought. Certainly these reflections will contain nothing new or original. As someone has said, we need to be reminded oftener than we need to be taught.

Before we look at the Lord's Prayer intelligently, we must have some theory – however rudimentary and inadequate – of what prayer is, of what, in other words, we think we are doing when we say our prayers. It is perhaps easier to say first what we are not doing. We are not seeking to inform God of what He does not know. We are not seeking to bribe Him or to strike a clever bargain with Him. No doubt at times we allow ourselves to pray in such a way as to suggest that we are trying to do some or all of these things; but the more sincerely we try to pray as our Lord taught us to pray, the further we are from any attempt to misuse our prayers.

What exactly are we trying to do when we pray? Perhaps one of the most helpful answers to this question is also one of the simplest. When we pray, we are seeking to understand the will of God and to make every part of our life conform to that will. In our prayers we are not seeking to appropriate God's power for our purposes. We are seeking to lay ourselves open to His grace and guidance, asking Him to use us for His purposes.

The Lord's Prayer is important in Christian tradition simply because it is so lofty an expression of the heart and purpose of all prayer. The more fully and deeply we apprehend the spirit and teaching of that prayer, the more confidently can we discipline and strengthen our own prayer.

"Our Father"

Our Father: these familiar words at the beginning of the Lord's Prayer are perhaps not so simple as they look. Indeed they are quite complex, not because they are difficult to understand but because each of them carries suggestions of fundamental Christian truths. It is easy of course to say this prayer without giving a thought to these truths; but they are quite clearly there, whether we regard them or not.

Perhaps it is not too pedantic to point out that the possessive pronoun is plural; it is hardly too much to say that most of the great possessive pronouns in our lives are plural. The minute we begin to think of my Father, my Church, my Rector, we are at the very least promoting verbal confusion. If we are "members incorporate in the mystical body of Thy Son," then we are involved in countless ways with the lives of other people. At least in principle, it would seem quite impossible to be a Christian in isolation from other people. Certainly our relationship with God is so interwoven with our relationship with our neighbor, one can hardly imagine love of God without love of neighbor. All this and more we are acknowledging when we say "Our Father." Even at our most solitary moment, even when we would prefer to escape the awful responsibility implicit in that pronoun, we say "Our Father."

When we call God by the title Father, we are of course using a metaphor. But this does not mean that the word is simply a poetic flourish; we use a metaphor for the purpose of describing one thing in terms of another. When the finite being looks for language with which to characterize infinite Being, one is at a loss; there is no language clear enough, comprehensive enough. So we do the best we can: we apply to God the loftiest and best language we can think of; we use a metaphor. As the Psalmist saw God as a shepherd, so the Christian sees Him as Father. And there is little point in worrying about what this metaphor does not say, when after all it does say so much. The wisdom, the providence, the loving kindness, the tender regard of the father for the child – all the qualities of human fatherhood at its best at least suggest to us the nature of God our Father. Something of these things should be on our minds as we pray this greatest of all prayers.

"Who Art in Heaven, Hallowed Be Thy Name"

When we direct our thoughts at the beginning of the Lord's Prayer to our Father "who art in heaven," we are not seeking to place Him geographically. Certainly we are not trying to suggest that He is "out there" somewhere, remote from our needs and concerns and prayers. Whatever else heaven is, it is surely outside of the realms of time and space as we know them. We cannot suppose that God is in any way bound and limited; the very freedom from the limits of time and space seem to us of the essence of the nature of God.

"Hallowed be thy name." This is actually the first request that we make of God, the request that His name should be held in honor and reverence. The prayer begins, then, with our minds quite firmly fixed on God, not on ourselves; on His eternal and unchanging nature, not on our own whimsical and capricious natures. And of course we are not merely asking that His name itself be respected but that He Himself should be glorified. For the Jew the name of the Deity was a sacred symbol of the Deity itself, so sacred that it could never be completely spelled out or spoken. So we are not only asking here that His name should not be used trivially or profanely; we are asking also that God Himself be honored and glorified.

But what is the point of asking God that His name be hallowed, Himself adored? To answer this question is to discover a basic key to the meaning of the Lord's Prayer: we are simply asking God to give us the grace and strength to honor His name. We are not asking Him to perform some great miracle, or series of miracles, by which His own glory will be made evident. We are asking Him to use us, to make us good enough for use, for His own glorious purpose.

From one point of view at least, this is the essential truth about this great model prayer which our Lord taught His disciples. We seek to make ourselves fit children of our Father so that His work may be done through us. His name will be hallowed in the world to the extent that you and I hallow it. That thought should induce in us a certain Lenten humility.

"Thy Kingdom Come, Thy Will Be Done"

In one view, the Lord's Prayer is basically a means of asking God to accomplish His purpose in the world by using us. This truth is especially evident when we come to the next unit of thought in the prayer: "Thy kingdom come, Thy will be done, on earth as it is in heaven." Surely we cannot suppose that these are matters which God can somehow perform in the world, regardless of what we are doing meanwhile. These are things which can be done in and through God's weak human creatures and in no other way.

"Thy kingdom come." It is possible to have learned theological disputes about whether the kingdom can ever be established in this world, or whether it must belong to eternity. Such discussions have their place, but it does not seem likely that our own behavior as Christians will be much affected. Whether the kingdom is established in this life or in the world to come, we know that it can be established only when we put aside our own selfishness and weakness and make ourselves agents of God's purpose.

Indeed the next phrases in the prayer belong, logically and grammatically, to the same thought: "Thy will be done, on earth as it is in heaven." To the extent that His will is done, His kingdom will be established. To the extent that the obedience of men in this world is as firm and certain as the obedience of spiritual beings in eternity, His Kingdom will come.

We are tempted sometimes to look at the sinful chaos of the world, the poverty and strife and selfishness, and wonder why God doesn't "do something about it." But surely the New Testament makes clear that God rejects every means of accomplishing His purpose except the freely given allegiance of men; He will not overpower us, He will not divest us of our own freedom to reject Him. So when we pray for the coming of His kingdom, we are asking God to give us grace and strength to rid ourselves of everything that works against that kingdom.

"Thy will," not ours. If we can pray for God's will, and mean it, we need never be afraid of selfish prayer, of prayer too much concerned with ourselves. If we say to God, "Thy will be done," and if we mean it, then we certainly purify and discipline our motives and desires.

"Our Daily Bread"

"Give us this day our daily bread." Perhaps for most of us, especially those of us who are not far advanced in our prayer lives, the dominant note in prayer is petition. Give us this, do that for us, make it possible for thus and so to happen. If self-concern is at the center of our lives, then it will inevitably be at the center of our prayers also. It is not, however, at the center of the Lord's Prayer.

If we look at this great prayer again and again from the point of view of what it can teach us about the nature of prayer itself, then we must surely notice several things about this request for "daily bread." First, we come to pray for it only after we have fixed our minds on God, on His eternal and unchanging nature, on the establishment of His kingdom which will result from the doing of His will. All this we remind ourselves of, and we remind ourselves of the responsibilities which these things lay upon us as followers of our Lord. Then, and only then, we pray for bread, for the physical means which sustain our lives and give us the strength to do what is ours to do.

We must not of course be so literal-minded as to suppose that we are praying only for bread; we are praying here for all the necessities. But we must be equally careful in defining for ourselves what the necessities are. Nobody who has read the New Testament with any care at all can suppose that God is very much interested in our possessing things for their own sake. God is interested in sons and daughters, not consumers.

All the same, it is perfectly proper to ask in our prayers that our physical needs be met. It is commonplace to say that Christianity is the most materialistic of all religions; it never shuts its eyes to our physical nature, to our material needs. Christ fed the hungry (as the New Testament clearly reminds us). He healed the sick; He turned water into wine for the sake of wedding guests. These are not the acts of Someone who discounts the material world.

So we pray quite naturally that our physical needs be met. At the same time, we remember to keep these wants under Christian discipline. Even when we ask for bread, we are asking for the physical means to do His will.

211

"Forgive Us Our Trespasses"

"Forgive us our trespasses, as we forgive those who trespass against us." We have fixed our minds on God; we have asked Him to further the establishment of His kingdom (which is to say we have asked Him to use us for this purpose); and we have prayed for our physical needs. Now we ask for the forgiveness of our sins, though even here our request is a conditional one.

Surely it is not without significance that we pray for several other things before we mention our sins. We ought not certainly to be morbidly preoccupied with our sins, so engrossed with thoughts of them that our prayers will have room for little more than a recital of misdoing. Several years ago a visiting preacher was described in the local newspaper advertisement as having been "redeemed from a life of outstanding sinfulness!" This pride in spectacular wickedness seems a long way from the spirit of the Lord's Prayer, which does not ask us to magnify the errors we have made.

On the other hand, there is no reason to suppose that we can gloss over or ignore our sins, those trespasses which prevent us from giving ourselves wholly to the establishment of God's kingdom. Surely of the things that might be said about prayers for forgiveness, the most certain is that we are freely and gladly forgiven when we turn to Him in genuine penitence. Nothing in the New Testament is clearer than this; witness the parable of the lost sheep or the prodigal son.

Secondly, even though God waits and longs to forgive us and to restore the broken relationship which trespasses have caused, this does not mean that His forgiveness is cheap, that He is saying "oh, your sins don't matter at all." They matter enough that the Son was crucified for them.

Thirdly, we are asking God to forgive us in the same way, and to the same degree, that we forgive those who sin against us. So if I nurse grudges, if I say rather proudly that I'll forgive but not forget, if I cherish the memory of the wrong done to me, then I am putting quite definite limits on the forgiveness that God offers me. It is not easy to forgive those who abuse and mistreat us; indeed for us it is impossible. But if we ask God to give us grace to forgive them, and to forgive us to the extent that we forgive them, then we learn again that with God all things are possible.

The Lord's Prayer Concluded

"Lead us not into temptation, but deliver us from evil." For many people, this is the most puzzling request in the Lord's Prayer, puzzling because it seems so utterly unlikely that God would lead us into temptation. Why should we even bother to ask Him not to do so?

At this point perhaps, the New English Bible throws a helpful light on the prayer; it translates this sentence: "And do not bring us to the test, but save us from the evil one." It is simply a matter of common sense that if we are making an honest effort to order our lives as Christians, we should wish to avoid temptation, avoid the very occasion out of which evil conduct may arise. And if we ask God to meet other of our most pressing needs, why should we not ask Him to spare us from temptation, not to bring us to the test?

Someone has said that this petition is like what a child might say to his father, walking with him in the dark. The child might put his hand in his father's and ask the father to shield him from harm. He asks not because he thinks the father is likely to do otherwise but because it is a natural and reassuring thing to do. And so no doubt it is with us, as the children of God.

"For Thine is the kingdom, and the power, and the glory for ever and ever." This doxology with which the prayer concludes was almost surely not originally a part of the prayer which our Lord taught His disciples; it came to be used in much the same way that we use the *Gloria Patri* at the end of the Psalms. For whatever its origin, this conclusion is a useful reminder that the prayer is centered on God and not on us. As we begin by fixing our mind on the nature of God, so we end in the same way.

For the early Christians, these words were the expression of a vital faith and hope, not always sustained by the immediate historical circumstances. The kingdom and the power seemed most often to belong to the secular order. But the Christians saw beyond the difficulties of the moment and ascribed to God what is rightly His. All these things – kingdom, power, glory – do belong to Him. The Lord's Prayer is one means of offering ourselves to Him in love and faith so that He may find us usable in the work of His kingdom.

March 7-April 28, 1965

The Liturgical Calendar –
Advent, Christmas, Lent, Easter

"By our observance of the Church's feasts and fasts, days and seasons,
we are continually rehearsing for ourselves the great truths of the faith."
(GC, December 8, 1996)

A Note on the Liturgical Calendar

One of the advantages of the liturgical reform and renewal of the past twenty-five years or so is a clear improvement in our attitude toward – and vocabulary about – the season in which we have now arrived. The common name formerly for the Sunday following Easter was Low Sunday. According to Massey Shepherd's commentary on the 1928 Prayer Book, nobody seems quite sure where the name came from or exactly what it meant. But what the linguists call a kind of folk etymology sets in, and we make our own definitions, consciously or unconsciously. Among other things, Low Sunday seemed to mean low attendance and low enthusiasm.

But the Prayer Book of 1979 no longer classifies the next several Sundays as Sundays *after* Easter, but instead as Sundays *of* Easter. The difference is not a trivial one. We are not trying to crowd the celebration of the Resurrection into one lone Sunday but we extend our observance through the next several Sundays, indeed right through what we call the Great Fifty Days – in other words, from Easter to Pentecost. This year Pentecost is May 22, which pretty well divides the liturgical calendar into two halves, the first half beginning with Advent and ending with Pentecost. It is perhaps a bit simplistic but still useful to say that about half the year is given over to following once more the events of our Lord's earthly life; the other half we spend in contemplating the relevance of His teaching to the world we live in.

The Christian calendar pivots on the two great festivals of Christmas and Easter. Important as Pentecost is in the Christian scheme, it is not quite co-equal; nor is there really a Pentecost season, as there are Christmas and Easter seasons. (It is useful to note that the designation of Sundays following Pentecost are properly called Sundays *after* Pentecost, not *of*.)

One of the things I find myself repeating on this page is the significance and value of the liturgical calendar as a teaching device. But I am only moderately penitent about these repetitions, and I am always glad to confess that I am reminding myself quite as much as I am reminding the reader. In his message to the most recent session of the School of Religion at St. Paul's, Thorne Sparkman wrote, "We all need constant return to the fundamentals." It is a simple reminder contained in those words, but full of meaning and significance for all of us.

April 10, 1988

Advent and Christmas

"Work of Peace"

The Bishop Barth Bible Class at St. Peter's has been using this fall the little devotional book by Alan Paton called *Instrument of Thy Peace*. The book is composed of a series of meditations based on St. Francis of Assisi's familiar prayer. One of the nicest features of the book is the prayer with which almost every meditation ends, each of them including a note of real immediacy: "And may I this coming day do some work of peace for Thee."

Surely for most of us, this note of immediacy, almost of urgency, is a very useful thing. There are few of us who do not have in mind some good things ("some work of peace") we will do when it is convenient, or when we can get around to it, or surely before another month is past. But, alas, such intentions have a way of getting lost, of getting postponed almost indefinitely. The months and even the years pass, and the good work remains undone.

Advent is surely a good season to come to grips with this problem, to ask earnestly in our prayers that we have some opportunity for works of peace and charity and to do them faithfully and promptly. About three weeks remain until Christmas; we ought to use some of this time to plan and to do some special works of goodness and kindness. In the bustle and hurry of the season, it is easy enough to neglect those things in which we really invest ourselves, in which we give of our time or talent for the real welfare of another person.

In one of Robert Frost's poems, he speaks of "A love that wanted re-renewing." There are few indeed of us who do not know such loves, such relationships which have weakened and declined not because of conscious decision or effort but largely because of the tempo of modern life. Looking toward Christmas, the Advent Season would be a good time for such renewal. We ought to make a real and effective search for the lonely, the neglected, the ill, the aged; and we ought to do something about some specific people.

Such a deed will take more time than the conventional Christmas card or gift. It will cost us some trouble. But if we take Advent and Christmas seriously,

215

we will count the trouble as of no importance. Let us all find "some work of peace" to do.

December 8, 1974

Advent I: Prayer

In this season of Advent, we turn to T. S. Eliot's magnificent poems on the spiritual life, *Four Quartets,* and more specifically to a passage used before from "The Dry Salvages." After several lines in which he has discussed special moments of understanding and spiritual insight, he continues:

> These are only hints and guesses,
> Hints followed by guesses; and the rest
> Is prayer, observance, discipline, thought and action.

These five nouns give us an excellent summary of the elements of our spiritual lives, and it is to those words that this page will be addressed during the weeks of Advent – with one additional column for good measure.

The order in which Eliot places these words is of course not accidental. It is fitting that our Advent meditations begin with the notion of prayer because, properly understood and practiced, prayer is so much at the heart of our lives as believers and members of the Body of Christ. Surely prayer is the most pervasive of all Christian activities; in a very real sense our whole lives are given over to prayer. William Temple makes the essential point in *Christian Faith and Life*: "There ought to be no sense of spiritual transition as we pass from any occupation which is our proper occupation at the time to the thought of God. We should feel, whether it be in performing the duty He has given us or in remembering Him Who gave us the duty, that we are always seeking to deepen our union with Him. But the moments when we concentrate upon this purpose particularly are our times of prayer."

Advent is a good season to strengthen and deepen our prayer lives. (After all, this is the beginning of the Christian year.) We can approach the task in almost countless different ways, but whatever way we choose, we must begin with the resolution to work on our prayer lives. Just as tennis or bridge or the violin demands serious effort in their mastery, so does prayer require the same. There are books to help us, one of the best being C. S. Lewis's *Letters to Malcolm: Chiefly on Prayer*. There is the great model prayer which our Lord taught the disciples, a fit beginning of almost endless meditation. But the main thing is the will to improve our prayer life and our determination in these few weeks of Advent to set aside the time to do it.

December 1, 1996

Advent II: Observance

The second word in the list of five nouns that summarize our spiritual lives in T. S. Eliot's "The Dry Salvages" is the word *observance*. In an excellent little book *Meditating on* Four Quartets, Dr. John Booty, former dean of the seminary at Sewanee, comments interestingly on this word: "Observance is the disciplined, regular observance of the church year, of feasts and fasts, in the context of the Eucharist, prompting meditation upon and response to the life, passion, and ultimate self-giving of Christ and of the myriad saints following in His way."

It is a happy coincidence that our attention falls on observance at the very beginning of the Christian year. We are not, I think, sufficiently grateful for, nor attentive to, the liturgical year as a means of education and participation in the Body of Christ. The calendar is the way in which we remember the great events in the life of Christ and examine the meaning of those events in our contemporary world. All of us carry in our heads special calendars of one sort or another; John Henry Newman is said to have ever afterwards regarded as a day of grace that day upon which he was summoned to Oriel College at Oxford to be installed in a fellowship which had been granted him. All of us have our days to celebrate and to remember, and the liturgical calendar is the Church's remembering and celebrating.

Once on the weekend before Thanksgiving I saw a newspaper picture of two very happy children. The cutlines solemnly informed us that the Christmas season had been inaugurated that weekend with a parade somewhere. The most charitable thing one can say is that the person who wrote the cutlines was confusing the Christmas season with the Christmas shopping season, quite a different thing! Those of us who live by the Christian calendar know that the "Christmas season" begins at midnight on Christmas Eve and not a moment sooner.

By our observance of the Church's feasts and fasts, days and seasons, we are continually rehearsing for ourselves the great truths of the faith. We are nourished by that calendar and made better and more faithful Christians.

December 8, 1996

Advent III: Discipline

Perhaps *discipline* is not a word we often think of in the practice of our faith, but the reality that lies behind that word is of essential importance. A faith without discipline can hardly be called a faith at all. As Eliot remarks in an essay, a religion that does not sometimes require us to do what we prefer not to do and also sometimes refrain from doing what we prefer to do is a religion hardly worthy of the name.

As Anglicans we certainly have enormous freedom in the practice of the faith, but this fact does not mean that our life as Christians can be free of discipline. In one of the most familiar collects in the Prayer Book (Collect for Peace, 57), we acknowledge to God that our service is "perfect freedom." The Latin from which the collect was translated is literally "whom to serve is to reign." In our "perfect freedom" as Christians and Anglicans, we freely take upon ourselves the discipline necessary to our faith. Not to do so is a serious failure of our own responsibility.

Take what is perhaps the simplest possible example: If we are serious about the faith, we accept the discipline of coming regularly to church and of making our communion. Whether we should come to church is not something we debate each time the occasion arises; we take it as a matter of course that our responsibility begins with regular and faithful attendance. Unless we do accept and practice this discipline, we cannot possibly avail ourselves fully of those means the church provides for our nurture and growth. We cannot ignore the church's life of prayer and sacrament and expect to fulfill our own Christian destiny.

Certainly also unless our moral lives are bought under discipline, we are likely to be living in chaos. "Although the Word is common to all," Heraclitus wrote, "most men live as if they had each a private wisdom of his own." But we have no such private wisdom; the Word is indeed "common to all" and we are under discipline to hear that Word and act accordingly.

December 15, 1996

Advent IV: Thought

We come now to thought as the fourth element of the faith. Eliot has arranged the words in a kind of natural progression, although of course each element pervades and undergirds all the others. I wonder how true it is that thought, for many Christians, is the least obvious of these elements of the faith. I think often of a friend who remarked to me several years ago that he never remembered hearing a sermon on the subject of loving God with one's whole mind, as we are clearly commanded by our Lord to do (Matthew 22:37). If we do not realize that exercising our intellectual faculties is an important part of the faith, we are not paying attention.

To say that the faith was once delivered to the saints is, of course, perfectly true; but the task of appropriating that faith, making it genuinely our own, is the work of a lifetime. And the most important part of that work is thinking carefully through the faith, discovering as fully as we can its relevance to our own lives. We must not delude ourselves that this is an easy task. Twenty years ago Richard Poirier, an American scholar, published a brilliant critical book on Robert Frost, the subtitle of which is *The Work of Knowing*. The author argues, very persuasively, that Frost has often been underestimated as a poet, that at his best he deserves to rank with the greatest poets of our time. To read Frost well enough to understand this is hard work; to understand well almost anything – and certainly the Christian faith – is hard work.

We seem to be seeing a resurgence in recent years of the notion that any Christian will have no difficulty in understanding and interpreting the faith. There are no hard questions, according to this view, for anybody, say, who reads the Bible. To call this view simplistic is the most charitable thing that can be said of it. The Bible is no intricate rule book which we have only to master to know precisely what we ought to do in any circumstance. Of course it is our Christian duty to read and ponder the Bible carefully, but there still remains the hard work of thinking out, for example, how our Lord's plain commands are to be applied in specific circumstances. Hard, careful thought is certainly an essential of the faith.

December 22, 1996

Christmas Meditation V: Action

"The rest is prayer, observance, discipline, thought and action." These five words from T.S. Eliot's "The Dry Salvages," summing up the elements of the

Christian faith, have been the subject of these meditations during the weeks of Advent. Now that the Christmas season is here, it is perhaps especially appropriate that we focus on the final meditation in the series on the element of action. It is in action that our faith most fully manifests itself, in action that it is tested and tried for its depth and sincerity. To use more homely language, the proof of the pudding is in the eating; or, as our Lord Himself put it, a tree is judged by its fruit.

We can of course talk about Christian action on many levels, but here I am thinking of it on the very personal and individual level. I am thinking of the faith we profess in the most ordinary and routine duties and relationships of our lives. The man in Robert Frost's beautiful lyric poem "Stopping by Woods on a Snowy Evening" cannot remain indefinitely to drink in the beauty of the woods, "dark and deep," because he reminds himself that he has "promises to keep." All of us who are members of the human covenant – and surely that is all of us – have promises to keep, duties to perform, obligations to meet. "Charity begins at home" is probably too often used as an excuse for letting it also stop there, but there is truth in those words. Surely our first obligation is to those who are closest to us in ties of love and kinship. But our duty does not stop there.

The starving and the downtrodden and the dispossessed of the world also have a claim upon us. If we truly take the faith seriously, our Christian action reaches out far beyond the limited orbit of our own lives. Obviously we make our choices carefully and intelligently; none of us can possibly respond to all the charitable appeals that are made to us in any given week, especially at this time of year. But to dismiss them all is certainly not the Christian answer either.

As Dr. John Booty points out in his little book on *Four Quartets* in Lancelot Andrewes' image, "The Christian becomes the willing conduit of divine grace in the world." Or, as someone else has said, Christ has no hands but ours, no feet but ours, to do His will.

January 12, 1997

Lent

A Lenten Rule

The Christmas Feast is already a fading memory,
And already the mind begins to be vaguely aware
Of an unpleasant whiff of apprehension at the thought

Of Lent and Good Friday which cannot, after all, now
Be very far off.

These lines from W. H. Auden's *For the Time Being: A Christmas Oratorio* remind us that time is passing and Ash-Wednesday looms ahead. But we need not panic: because Easter is relatively late this year, occurring on April 15, we still have about a month to prepare for Lent. In any case, despite Auden's rather whimsical words, we ought not to regard Lent with dread. On the other side of Lent awaits the most exultant season in the Christian calendar, the Great Fifty Days from Easter to Pentecost.

Lent is a very positive and important and valuable part of the life of the church and of our own individual lives. Unless we experience growth in our spiritual lives, we are going to be living in stagnation. Not a very happy prospect. We ought to be growing constantly in the life of faith, but Lent is perhaps the most fruitful period in the calendar for us to work on that growth, to improve our understanding and practice of the faith. That is the kind of Lent that makes a genuine and lasting difference. It is not too much to say that, if we observe Lent properly, our lives will never be the same again.

All of us should fashion for ourselves a Lenten rule – clear, specific, and not so demanding that we cannot possibly live up to it for the forty days. Others may make suggestions about our rule but only each individual, with appropriate help where it is needed, can fashion that individual rule. Certain elements should be included in the rule, but again, the way the various elements are designed is a matter of individual choice. Most people would say the chief elements include the following: (1) increased devotions, corporate and individual; (2) an appropriate discipline of self-denial; (3) a feasible program of good works, applying the Christian faith to our human relationships; and (4) study and learning.

All of these four elements are available to all of us in a great variety of ways. If every one of us in the parish made a Lenten rule, it is quite possible – indeed likely – that no two would be exactly alike. The chief point is that these weeks of preparation and penitence give us the opportunity to develop in the faith, to welcome the great festival of Easter with increased rejoicing.

February 4, 1990

Incisive Questions: Lent I

According to custom, the columns during Lent will comprise a unified series. For this purpose I turn again, as I did a few years ago, to Martin L. Smith's book titled *Reconciliation*. Father Smith is an Episcopal priest who is also a member of the monastic order called the Society of St. John the Evangelist (most often called the Cowley Fathers) whose American headquarters are in Cambridge, Massachusetts. When I say that I "turn again," I do not mean that I turn to the same material. Late in the book there is plentiful material for the examination of conscience, and I use this time a wholly different section, this one called "The Unity and Equality of God's Sons and Daughters."

Father Smith quotes a single verse from the New Testament following it with a series of questions. I include here the first two of those. "'There is neither Jew nor Greek, there is neither slave nor free, there is neither male nor female, for you are all one in Christ Jesus' (Galatians 3:28). How unreservedly do you accept this strict equality and act in accordance with God's all-embracing care? Do you harbor racism in your heart or practice it in word or deed, or consent to it by cowardly silence or inaction?"

This single verse from Galatians is a radical claim for the equality of all people; by "radical" I mean going to the root of things. Surely in this verse St. Paul is faithful to the divine love which embraces us all and treats us with "strict equality." I shall not of course attempt to answer these questions except for myself, and I remind the readers of this newsletter that any sternness in the questions is Father Smith's. But all of us should certainly face the questions

GC's notes on a page of Reconciliation: Preparing for Confession in the Episcopal Church *by Martin L. Smith. Cowley Publications: Cambridge, MA, 1985.*

honestly and squarely, giving careful thought to answers that are borne out by our behavior.

One does not have to be a profound social critic to realize that racism is a corrosive and deeply un-Christian element in American society. I am not sure that there is a greater social evil confronting us, and we do well to ponder Father Smith's second question with the greatest care, to ask ourselves whether we practice racism by word or deed. Any time we use a derogatory term for a racial group or use jokes that denigrate their humanity, we are indeed guilty of racism. But I suspect that most of us are more often guilty of the "cowardly silence or inaction" of Father Smith's question. I think often of something told me by a friend who was a member of the Chattanooga school board at the time the board was struggling with integration of the schools. My friend had made a speech to a civic club to which a good many of his friends belong; one of the speaker's oldest friends told him later that he regretted that he could not say a word in the speaker's defense when he was submitted to severe verbal abuse after the speech. That is the "cowardly silence" indeed. And when one thinks of the unbelievable hatred that very small black children were subjected to in such places, for example, as Little Rock and New Orleans, it is even yet heartbreaking.

In the penitential season of Lent, we can do no better than to examine our own lives for the sin of racism.

February 29, 1994

Bias and Prejudice: Lent II

"Do you scorn people of other cultures or religious traditions, and
show prejudice and bias?"

from *Reconciliation* by Martin L. Smith, SSJE

Several years ago one of the summer courses at Kanuga was called "The Parables of Flannery O'Connor," an excellent name for the study of a number of notable stories by that remarkable writer. One of her most incisive stories is "The Displaced Person," which examines exactly the problem that Father Smith's question poses: prejudice and bias against other cultures or religious traditions. "Displaced Person" is a term which the post-World War II generations may not recognize; it was a term that came into use following that war and designating those persons who were uprooted from their own society and cast adrift.

223

O'Connor's story of course dramatizes the issues involved; it is not a sociological essay; it is a parable. A Polish family of Displaced Persons arrives, by previous arrangement of course, at a dairy farm where the father is to be tenant farmer, along with another white family and two black men. The owner is Mrs. McIntyre, who at first is delighted with such a productive worker. But all too soon suspicion runs riot and everybody, with the possible exception of the two blacks, turns against the Polish family.

We get an early hint when Mrs. McIntyre is showing the white tenant farmer's wife the house the Polish family will occupy and points out that the curtains on two windows in a given room are of different colors. Mrs. Shortly (the tenant) says, "They can't talk. . . .Do you reckon they'll know what colors even is?"

The Roman Catholic priest (one of only two I can remember in all of O'Connor's fiction), who has arranged for the Polish family to come to America, soon is out of favor with Mrs. McIntyre; she can tolerate conversation with him only after she fortifies her ginger ale with "at least a finger of whiskey." All the common prejudices focus on the family of Displaced Persons: they are Polish, they are Roman Catholic, they are "different." Mr. Shortly even thinks that he recognizes in the Polish father an enemy soldier who had thrown a hand grenade at him when he was fighting in Europe, but Mrs. McIntyre points out to him that Mr. Guizac is Polish, not German. "It ain't a great deal of difference in them two kinds," Mr. Shortly replies.

It is easy enough in this story to see how destructive bias and prejudice are. But do we see it equally well in our own ordinary lives? Or is it hidden from us by a lot of comfortable attitudes, familiar to us as an old shoe? One of my university colleagues once had a paper from a freshman who wrote, "He is from Mississippi so I knew he was prejudiced"!

Here is the first collect from the Good Friday service in *The Book of Common Prayer*: "Almighty God, we pray you graciously to behold this your family, for whom our Lord Jesus Christ was willing to be betrayed, and given into the hands of sinners, and to suffer death upon the cross. . . ." It is a prayer we would do well to remember and use frequently.

February 27, 1994

The Practice of Sexism: Lent III

> "Do you practice sexism or consent in any way to the treatment
> of women as inferior to men, or project stereotypes onto members
> of the opposite sex?"
>
> from *Reconciliation* by Martin L. Smith, SSJE, 89

Here is a matter about which all of us, men and women, should certainly examine our consciences and ask ourselves quite seriously whether we are guilty of sexism. The word has two definitions in the *American Heritage Dictionary*: (1) "discrimination based on gender, especially discrimination against women; (2) attitudes, conditions, or behaviors that promote stereotyping of social roles based on gender." If we contemplate those definitions carefully, we can certainly identify, in ourselves and others, at least something of the attitude that manifests itself in prejudicial treatment of persons of the opposite sex.

Probably most of us do not pay enough attention to the use of language which fosters and reinforces prejudice against members of the opposite sex. Provided that we do not allow ourselves to forget the beam that is in our own eye, perhaps we learn most from observing the language and attitudes of others. (Surely we ought to be able to modify our conduct at least as much through the observation of others as through observation of ourselves.) Some years ago I knew a couple who married fairly late in life; their respective spouses had died several years before. Mainly because we patronized some of the same retail stores, I encountered them fairly frequently. In those encounters I cannot now remember one single pleasant and gentlemanly comment from the husband. He consistently addressed his wife as though she were a moron, though I think her native intelligence was far greater than his.

Not surprisingly, the husband's sons from his earlier marriage for the most part treated their wives abominably. One of them used to complain to me bitterly about his wife, who worked in the family business. I tried never to miss an opportunity to pile irony upon irony in responding to his comments: "Why don't you divorce that woman, Jack? Nobody in the world but you would put up with her laziness and incompetence! Nobody else would show the patience you show to her." Since the patience he showed her was absolute zero, he quickly realized the true intent of my words and at least for the moment stopped his abuse. When she died a few years ago, he was inconsolable, but it was a little late to show her the respect and gratitude he certainly owed her.

One of the worst things we can do in all of our social relationships (using "social" in its broadest sense) is to project stereotypes onto others, male or female.

Certainly the Christian faith requires us to treat every human being as a child of God, unique and precious in God's sight. We must as Christians work and pray to see all human beings as individuals endowed by their Creator with talents and abilities strictly their own. If we feel that there are flaws in others requiring our Christian charity, we can always hope and pray that others will show the same charity toward us.

March 6, 1994

Our Plain Duty: Lent IV

"Do you try to 'get inside the feelings' of the desperate, the needy, and the neglected in society?"

from *Reconciliation* by Martin L. Smith, SSJE, 90

One of the ways we "get inside the feelings" of those whose lives are very different from our own is by a deliberate exercise of the imagination, perhaps through reading, perhaps through observation. This question of Father Smith's easily reminds us of the parable of Dives and Lazarus (Luke 16:19-31). George Buttrick has memorable words to say about this parable in a book published many years ago: "Dives was not unscrupulous; the story gives no hint that he came by his wealth dishonestly. . . . He was not cruel in the word's accepted meaning. . . . Dives dispensed the customary charities; he was no more unfeeling than fifty other men in his town. But his love (if such it could be called) was so thin and perfunctory as to be almost an offense. He passed Lazarus several times a day, but he never really saw him. He felt no genuine compassion" (*The Parables of Jesus*).

Dr. Buttrick once pointed out in a personal letter that he felt the book had been superseded by more recent scholarship. Even so, these are powerful words that not only help us into the meaning of that parable but suggest to us our own duty: we need really to see what is before us. We do not have to be cruel and unfeeling to miss the human drama all about us; we have only to be careless and superficial. We have only to be so habituated to suffering and hardship that we don't make any genuine emotional or intellectual response.

I had a friend once who used to excuse any failure to do some perfectly obvious good deed by saying, "I'm just not a thoughtful person." Anyone capable of saying that might have been expected to be on the way to becoming thoughtful. Surely we ought to be able to put ourselves into the shoes of someone suffering hardship of some sort; we cannot allow ourselves to be so concerned with ourselves that we, like Dives, simply do not see the suffering around us.

More than one fairly recent poll has suggested that the American people are becoming bored with the problems of the homeless and the disadvantaged. If that is true, I cannot imagine a more un-Christian response to the world we are living in. Surely a concern for the poor and downtrodden is one of the most pervasive themes of the Bible. We are under the clear biblical mandate not only to take notice of the problems of others but to concern ourselves with the alleviation of those problems. As Christians it is unthinkable that we should be bored or indifferent in such matters. We have our Lord's clear statement of the case in the parable of the sheep and the goats: "Truly I tell you; anything you did for one of my brothers here, however insignificant, you did for me" (Matthew 25:40, *Revised English Bible*). Our duty could hardly be made clearer.

March 13, 1994

"On Earth as in Heaven": Lent V

> "God is the champion of those whose rightful claims in the community
> are neglected or denied, such as the widows and orphans, the destitute
> and underpaid, the outcasts and strangers on whose behalf the prophets
> cried out: Do you sincerely pray for God's will to be done on earth as in
> heaven?"
>
> from *Reconciliation* by Martin L. Smith, SSJE, 90

All of us surely know how easy it is to say the Lord's Prayer by rote, sometimes thinking little about what it means, about what tremendous things we are asking and committing ourselves to. Think of what we are asking in this petition: "Thy will be done on earth as it is in heaven." It is virtually impossible to think of heaven as other than a place where God's will is perfectly obeyed by "angels and archangels and all the company of heaven." What we ask in the prayer is that those of us still in this life will be equally obedient, equally attentive to carrying out the will of God in our lives and in the society in which we live.

At the moment many billboards over the city carry this admonition: "Commit a random act of kindness." I take it that the sign is meant to amuse us, at least slightly, as well as give us advice. I'm all in favor of acts of kindness and if they can be only random acts, I'll still rejoice in them. But the *American Heritage Dictionary*, without which I could hardly manage my life, defines *random* as "having no specific pattern, purpose, or objective." If the advertising people, or whoever, are going to do a campaign urging kindness upon us, I would prefer the campaign to have pattern and purpose. Why shouldn't we, for example, resolve to be polite and thoughtful toward other motorists? And let us not forget the pedestrians, either; they too deserve a break.

But these are the manners of life and not the morals, and surely the words of the Lord's Prayer strike deeper than that. Indeed the prefatory note quoted at the head of this page includes these words also: "Both the Law and the Prophets and the New Testament summon believers to become the champions of the weak, to be 'hungry and thirsty for righteousness,' in the words of the Beatitudes." There is hardly a theme of the Bible more pervasive than this one. A concern for the poor and downtrodden of the earth runs like a thread through the Bible, both Old and New Testaments.

We should make it our business to quicken our consciences by reading, by meditation, by sacrament and prayer so that we can realize how much work we need to do in this world to further obedience to the will of God. We should be especially observant of how we spend our money, in the hope that thus we can do more for people in need. When we ask, "Thy will be done on earth as it is in heaven," we are not asking God to perform some series of miracles; we are instead asking for the grace and strength to do what is our clear duty.

March 20, 1994

Questions to Ponder: Lent VI

"Do you take delight in others' failings or misfortunes? Are you quick to judge or condemn, in spite of your own many failings?"

from *Reconciliation* by Martin L. Smith, SSJE, 92

These questions seem so obvious, but how difficult it is for most of us to remember our own frailties when we are censorious of others. Surely if we are truly honest with ourselves, we can remember to our shame what we can ourselves be capable of. Then how in all fairness can we be harsh and unforgiving toward others because of their failings? C. S. Lewis says somewhere that knowing himself as he does and still thinking that in some sense he can be called a Christian, how can he bring himself to condemn others? It is a question for all of us to ponder.

One of the best things we can do in the examination of our own consciences is to read carefully and prayerfully some great passage from the New Testament, such as I Corinthians 13, St. Paul's great hymn to Christian love. Though the cadences of the King James Version are without parallel, we do well to read the passage in a modern, less familiar translation. Here is a crucial paragraph from the *Revised English Bible*:

> Love is patient and kind. Love envies no one, is never boastful, never conceited, never rude; love is never selfish, never quick to take offense. Love keeps no score of wrongs, takes no pleasure in the sins of others, but delights in the truth. There is nothing love cannot face; there is no limit to its faith, its hope, its endurance.

For most of us surely it would be extremely difficult, in the echo of those words, to "delight in others' failings or misfortunes." It is easy enough to note the failings of others, but do we dare to conceal or disguise from ourselves our own failings? It is a part of our Christian duty to find the means of seeing our own sins as clearly as we can, asking forgiveness for them, and being kindly in our attitude towards others. We need to give careful attention to Father Smith's second question at the head of this page.

Do we hasten to judge and condemn? Surely one of the clearest of our Lord's commands is "Do not judge others." Obviously there are times when we must make some kind of judgment in order to manage our affairs and do our work as we should. If we have any kind of administrative responsibility, for example, we must give some thought and attention to those who are delegated to do this task or that one. But that is a kind of limited judgment which certainly does not presume to make any sort of ultimate assessment. I still remember with some horror a comment made by someone many years ago who had some considerable right to think of herself as a Christian. "When you come right down to it," she said, "there are not more than a handful of good Christians in all of Chattanooga." None of us who heard that comment dared ask her who the others were. We are not called upon to make that kind of judgment; quite the contrary.

March 27, 1994

Easter

The Risen Christ

"If Mass could only be, every morning, what it is on Easter morning! If the prayers could always be so clear, if the Risen Christ would always shine in my heart and all around me and before me in His Easter simplicity! For His simplicity is our feast, this is the unleavened bread which is manna and the bread of heaven, the Easter cleanness, this freedom, this sincerity" (Thomas Merton, *The*

Sign of Jonas).

    In the message sent recently to the final session of the Thorne Sparkman School of Religion at St. Paul's by the priest for whom the school is named, the simple point was made that "We all need constant return to the fundamentals." And one of the things which enable us to make this "constant return" is the liturgical calendar, emphasizing for us the two great festivals of the Christian year, Christmas and Easter. (Pentecost is of course the third feast of major importance.) If we think of life as a spiritual journey, then every Lent is a new experience in discipline, every Easter a new discovery and exultation.

    We come to Easter morning in a kind of triumph, as Merton's words clearly indicate. After the long weeks of Lent, after what must surely be for most people a renewed attempt to understand the faith more deeply and to practice it more obediently, we come to what Merton calls elsewhere "a plateau in the spiritual life." Surely it is one of the greatest of God's gifts that we can experience in the great festivals the simplicity of Christ, a simplicity which rejoices the heart and strengthens the will. The liturgy is more meaningful, its impression more indelible, than at any other time in the Christian calendar. Everything secondary and inessential seems swept away by this Easter cleanness, this simplicity and sincerity.

    As we are all aware, there are those persons who make their way to church on Easter and hardly at any other time. I think we ought to be very patient with such people, making no judgment, not even thinking any criticism, much less voicing it. It seems to me unlikely indeed that they come, as often suggested, to show off their Easter clothes; there are much better settings for that. Surely they must come out of some longing, some desire to be in touch with something real and vital that once perhaps they knew. God grant that they may discover here the Risen Christ shining in all our lives.

April 3, 1988

230

Part IV

Country and Service,
Community and Citizenship

"We strive for justice and decency in quite specific and practical ways; we do not
simply pray for these things and then feel that we have done our duty."

(GC, July 1, 1987)

S/Sgt. Connor, London, July, 1945.

Country and Service

"For the Human Family"

O God, you made us in your own image and redeemed us through
Jesus your Son: Look with compassion on the whole human family; take away the arrogance and hatred which infect our hearts;
break down the walls that separate us; unite us in bonds of love;
and work through our struggle and confusion to accomplish your
purposes on earth; that, in your good time, all nations and races
may serve you in harmony around your heavenly throne; through
Jesus Christ our Lord.

The Book of Common Prayer

It is probably not possible for most of us to read the words of this prayer
just now without recalling the television series *Holocaust* which was recently
viewed by millions of American citizens. The kind of hatred and inhumanity
upon which Nazi brutality was based is the very antithesis of the "bond of love"
for which we pray here. It is hard to believe now, a generation after World War II,
that a nation so civilized as Germany had been, a nation with some claim to being
called Christian, could be involved in the murder of millions of Jews.

I ought to confess that I was not among those who saw *Holocaust*. I am
so much opposed to violence and cruelty and bloodshed that I cannot bear to see
instances of these things dramatized, no matter for what purpose. But I felt that I
could refrain from looking with clear conscience because in 1945 I had my own
opportunity to witness the result of Nazi policy towards the Jews. Only a few
days after Buchenwald came into Allied hands, I was one of a small group of
Americans given a complete tour of that particular version of hell. I have never
forgotten that afternoon, and I never shall forget it.

Once a few years after the war, I saw General Eisenhower quoted on his
reaction to Buchenwald. I do not remember his exact words, but his point was
that in looking at that camp, he felt he was witnessing the end to which racial
prejudice always comes. I felt precisely the same thing. No matter how harmless
racial slurs and jokes may seem, racial prejudice ultimately manifests itself in
senseless cruelty and hatred.

And so how natural it is, and how necessary, to ask God to "take away the
arrogance and hatred which infect our hearts" to the end that all of us finally serve
Him in complete harmony.

May 7, 1978

Meditation for July Fourth

One of the great prayers in *The Book of Common Prayer* is one called "For Our Country" (820). The prayer is too long to reproduce here, but I quote the beginning as a reminder: "Almighty God, who hast given us this good land for our heritage: We humbly beseech Thee that we may always prove ourselves a people mindful of Thy favor and glad to do Thy will." It would be an excellent observance of Independence Day to read and contemplate that prayer.

One of the clear advantages of the Prayer Book is that by giving us the language of corporate prayers, it helps to teach us the basic attitudes which ought to underlie our prayers. Surely no area needs this instruction more than the area of our attitude to our country. We need to think clearly about what our Christian view ought at its best to be. Too many religious spokesmen have contributed to a kind of civil religion in which we tend to see God as sort of super-American with a very special love for these United States. The prayer "For Our Country" is a very powerful corrective for any such self-satisfied view.

In this very first petition with which the prayer opens, we are reminded of the gratitude which we ought to feel for this "good land." But we show forth that gratitude "not only with our lips but in our lives," to quote from a quite different prayer. We ask that we "may always prove ourselves a people mindful of Thy favor and glad to do Thy will." And to do the will of God as citizens of this country surely means, among other things, that we seek to build here a society in which all people can live in dignity and justice. And this means that we strive for justice and decency in quite specific and practical ways; we do not simply pray for these things and then feel that we have done our duty.

Robert Penn Warren says somewhere that anybody who loves his country totally is out of business as a writer. Such a person is also in danger of being out of business as a Christian citizen. It is our responsibility to recognize the ways in which our society falls short of the will of God, to see our failures and shortcomings as reminders that we are not doing our duty as Christians. "America: Love it or Leave it" is from the Christian point of view stupid and even blasphemous. We must love our country enough that we work continually to make it the sort of country in which persons find their fullest development as the children of God.

July 1, 1984

World War II – A Letter Chronicle

"The heroes aren't particularly remarkable people in themselves;
they are often, it seems to me, quite ordinary people who have
been challenged, by circumstances, to do the impossible and have
done it."   (GC, May 26, 1945)

Sonnet for Heroes

For Bill, Gaines, and Otis*

O splendid dead who died in fire,
Whose blood stained red the sands
Of barren desert and mingled with the mire
Of swamplands far from home, who yesterday
Made glad our hearts with laughter and with love
Forever silent now, do you think we live
As always, or that we can ever rise above
The desolation of the heart and give
Ourselves to music and to play, forgetting you?
O, young and valiant heroes, whose very names
Are images of sorrow in our hearts, it is not true!
We may in time return to dancing and to games,
But always we shall see our world with misted eye,
Remembering the nameless graves wherein you lie.

September 1943

On Army Life and Friends: To Isobel Griscom
from Fort Riley Kansas, November 14, 1942

For the first time since last Sunday, I can settle down to my own affairs,
entirely sure that my time is my own for a few hours. The only thing that makes

---

*Bill Lowery, Gaines Milligan, and Otis Schoocraft were all from Chattanooga and had attended
Central High School with GC. Each died in separate plane crashes in 1943.

the scrubbing and polishing in preparation for Saturday morning inspection at all worthwhile is that it is the certain harbinger of a half-holiday. I never thought I would see the time when an hour or two in which to write a letter would seem as priceless as it does now. By far the worst thing about the army, so far as I am concerned, is the absolute impossibility for rest and quietness, for reading or writing. This communal life has made me miss, more than almost anything else, the opportunity to go to my room and close the door and collect my thoughts. That always seemed like such an ordinary thing, not at all a luxury or anything to be especially grateful for. By the time I get through with my class in the evening and polish my shoes and clean my equipment,

Pvt. George Connor, 9th Armored Division (Signal Corps), December 1942, Fort Riley, Kansas.

it is almost time to go to bed. Sometimes I read a magazine or the *Times* (which brings Stuart Taylor and Jennie Watkins to me in this outpost!) for a few minutes. As a result of this hurried life, I always have a vague feeling of unrest, of not knowing exactly what goes on, of not seeing the situation clearly as a whole.

As a matter of fact, the difficulties which I am having – and all of them are mild – are not at all the difficulties which I expected to have. I expected to be unduly awkward in marching, the manual of arms, and such like. *Marabile dictu*, I turn out to be something of a model in both. I expected to waste away from sheer physical exhaustion; while I never go to bed in any state except complete weariness, I have held my own with boys who have led really rough and tumble lives. On the other hand: I expected to bring with me such a strong memory of the things I have been doing and loving that I thought I should miss them only slightly, that I would seldom feel entirely a refugee from the good life.

Unfortunately, hardly a day goes by that I don't wish I could have fifteen minutes conversation with any of my friends. It is a feeling I cannot describe never to be able to have any real conversation, to talk about books, or poems, or ideas with anybody equally able (or better able) to discuss them. I don't mean, of course, that there is no one to whom I am disposed to speak or with whom I am glad to discuss the army and our milieu, but I am unspeakably weary of limiting my conversation to the military horizon. There are three boys in this company who are my closest companions. All three of them are good-hearted, affable, refined, kind-hearted. It is worthwhile to associate with them if only to be called by one's first name, or to be with someone who knows enough to say "please" and "thank you," or to be with someone who is considerably above average in morals and intelligence. But they are people with whom I would be hardly more than on speaking terms in civilian life; they are people of very limited insight and imagination and interest. I know well that I am lucky even to have these people nearby, but that hasn't stopped me from wishing every day that I could see and talk to somebody who knows more and thinks straighter than I do.

Being continually with people who are less able than I am in most ways has other disadvantages. Our training is divided about equally between drill, rifle practice, manual of arms, physical conditioning and hiking, on the one hand, and classroom lectures on the other. Those lectures, covering such diverse subjects as chemical warfare and defense against gas attack, first aid, military discipline and a hundred and six other subjects, are quite naturally geared to the average intellect in the company. As a result, the lecture periods are to me a purgatory in which my blackest sins can be washed white as snow! We take a section of material and go over and over and over it until the stupidest individual can grasp it. The general orders which every soldier is required to memorize before he can go on guard duty are explained twice a day. The Articles of War, which are about as difficult to understand as the directions on the average box of aspirin, have been read and minutely explained to us four times! I have been told how to take a bath so many times that I fully intend to spit on the next person who begins to tell me how to take one. Yesterday we went to see a required movie. The purpose? To instruct us how to brush our teeth! I think I can say, without committing the sin of pride, that I have known for a long time how to brush my teeth. But, of course, most of these people are amateurs at bathing and tooth brushing and it is unfortunately true that the rain falls both on the just and the unjust. This part of the training is made more difficult by the incompetency of the officers as instructors. The army seems not to know that to teach properly one must have not only the particular knowledge he is supposed to impart but also a technique for imparting it. They rush through the lectures and then they pad and pad to fill up the time; it is singularly disgusting.

I knew it was a mistake for me not to take shorthand last summer. If I had, I could send you one of the Chaplain's sermons verbatim. They are the worst I have ever heard, and I make the statement carefully and thoughtfully. I may have written you some of my reactions to the Chaplain in my last letter. His sermon last Sunday was the last word. The thesis: be glad to give your life for your country. The sermon depressed me less because it was poor than because it betrayed such a complete lack of understanding of the men whom it is his job to serve. The men, with almost no exceptions, are without moral and religious convictions of any kind. They are in the army because they are required to be; their only thought, as regards the army, is that they'll be glad to get out of it. Their lives are simply quite devoid of conviction, of strength, of spiritual fiber. Now the Chaplain's job, under such circumstances, is simply terrific. He is obliged to do what he can against the will of the persons for whom he is working. So he begins by telling them not to mind getting killed. It seems to me that people ought to be taught the things that are worth living for before they are asked to die for them. Willingness to give one's life for a cause seems to me to be the very end of a life of devotion, to be the very finest and highest manifestation of allegiance to principle. This is, I know, of no immediate interest to you; I simply had to say it to somebody and I haven't been able to as yet.

I don't know whether I said anything to you in my letter about the possibility of a Christmas leave. I have issued various communiqués on the subject, the last one being that the chances for leave were reasonably good. The final word has now been spoken. Nobody inducted after September 1 will be allowed to leave until, probably, March – unless, of course, one lives near enough to home to go in three days. As it is, we will get Christmas Eve and Christmas Day – which we intend to spend in Kansas City, the idea being that the post won't be any too festive. I regret not being able to come home, of course, but in my heart of hearts I didn't really expect to get leave so soon after coming here.

You said in one of your letters that you hoped I wasn't writing pleasantly about the army to spare my friends from suffering for me. Far from it. As I say, there are plenty of difficulties, but none so grave or so painful that they cannot be withstood in good order. I am learning tolerance and patience from the bottom up. In every way, I grow stronger day by day. I have learned to keep quiet when I was aching to speak out, to be calm when I am inclined to be disquieted. I have learned that I have never worked hard enough on the things I should have worked hard on, that in many ways I have shirked the obligation which is mine by the virtue of my having special abilities. I may never be the most valuable member of the army, but when the glad day of peace comes, I will certainly be a vastly improved individual. . . .

I must close – the noise is so great, so distracting that I can hardly form a sentence. You will never know how much I enjoy your letters. They are my best reminder that the details with which I am daily concerned are not the only elements in my life.

Devotedly,

George

Appointed Chaplain's Assistant: To Fr. Thorne Sparkman from Fort Riley Kansas, January 7, 1943

I'm not at all sure that I have just now either the time or the strength to write all the things I have to say, but I'll do the best I can. So much has happened of late that I have been quite at a loss for the time to write anything akin to decent letters. Most of the hectic activity has been the result of our basic training being well over, thanks be to Heaven. It was ended with two days of exams, both written and oral, by the toughest bunch of officers I ever hope to see. I made a very decent score on all of them, but when I remembered that they were designed to fit the average mind in the regiment, I was not tempted to pride in my own rating. However, I was very glad to do them well, because one never knows just what sort of condition he may find himself in from one day to the next, and it may very well be that some opportunity might open to me tomorrow which would make me very grateful for my score on the exams.

Now that basic is over, I have taken my job with the chaplain. When I was classified on the evening of my arrival here as a chaplain's assistant I was naïve enough and unaware of the army set-up enough to imagine that all I had to do was sit back and wait to begin assisting. Fortunately, I was jarred out of my complacency early enough to make continuous effort to keep the job open for me. And it required no little effort, because this is one of the most sought-after jobs in the regiment. (I think a number of the lads were convinced that it was the softest job, too; little do they know.) Too, there was the problem of persisting toward this end despite the attractive offers from other quarters for jobs of various kinds. The personnel of the army is hitting such rock bottom level just now that anybody who can read is regarded as a pretty remarkable creature, and anybody who can write legibly and perhaps even type is considered as being only slightly lower than the angels. Consequently, I have had insistent offers from the company's first sergeant to be his orderly and do his desk work and like offers from a dozen places to be a clerk of some kind. But I have remained steadfast in my determination to do just what I am doing, and finally managed to convince the proper people that I intended to do nothing else.

My final assignment is with the regimental chaplain, for which I have cause to be much more grateful than two months ago I thought I could be. You may recall that I wrote you about a possibility of my being transferred to another outfit to assist a Presbyterian chaplain, whom I admired very much. Fortunately, I found out two things about said chaplain just in the nick of time: first, his theology is definitely the God-is-a-pink-cloud variety (the image is yours) and I frankly had rather work for a rank fundamentalist. At least, the fundamentalist believes in something. But the second discovery was such that would have prevented my working with him regardless of his theology or anything else; the discovery, made very painfully, was that his private life is far from exemplary in the worst possible way. It was a great disappointment to me because he seemed like such an able, brilliant young man, but I was certainly glad to see the light while I could still bow out gracefully.

This job turns out to be about three times as tough as I thought it would; I'm very glad, though, because I should hate for it to be a half-hearted sort of thing. With so many people giving every ounce of strength to the army, I should hate to do any less. The chaplain's assistant is, in reality, his secretary, his clerk, his ambassador to the men, his chauffeur – and just about everything else. I write all of his letters – and they are legion; it is amazing the number of things the chaplain is consulted on – make all of his appointments, keep all his reports. And as you know if you've ever had any contact with the army, it simply thrives on reports. We must keep an accurate record of all the services he holds and the exact number of soldiers attending, the hospital calls he makes, the guardhouse visits, the interviews – in fact, records must be kept of just about everything he does. Besides this, it is my job to supervise details of prisoners who clean the chapel, to see that it is always ready for services and to see that the property is kept in order and always clean enough to pass inspection should the adjutant drop in. My chauffeuring activity consists in driving the chaplain's peep anywhere he doesn't want to drive it himself and to use it on any long errands of my own and to see that it is kept clean and always in good running order. (In case you didn't know, a peep is a jeep in the armored force; the only difference is the name.) A great deal of this work, as you can easily deduce, is the sort of work which anybody of slight intelligence could easily do, but part of it requires such tact and special abilities as I hope to develop as I progress. There is a great deal of opportunity for service to the men, and a great opportunity to get to know them well and to face all sorts of circumstances. It is, as I hoped it would be, a job which will be of tremendous value to me.

The task of deciding whether to apply for officer training has been something of a problem to me. A great many people, including my company commander, have urged me to apply. My position has been that since the job I have is such a good prelude to the one I will have after the war that I would do better for myself and the army to stay in it. As I may have explained to you in an earlier letter, I don't feel that I have any real natural talent for soldiering; so long as I pay attention to instructions and work like the devil, I can do creditably enough, but it is just about there that my ability ends. But one of the chaplains in the division says that this is nonsense, that the real need is for officers who understand men, who can win and hold their sympathy, and who can be really reliable as leaders of men. Perhaps; I don't know… What I have now decided to do is this: since it seems very likely that the division will be in garrison for several more months, I think I shall sit tight for at least three months in the job I have. There is no particular rush for a decision, and three months would give me an opportunity to know enough about the army, its organization and function that I would make a far more intelligent officer than I could possibly make if I applied for training right now. I'm not sure that I will apply at all; I just can't see myself as a competent officer. If I could apply for training as a special service officer, or an intelligence officer, I would do so without any hesitation, but applicants for those jobs must be physically unfit for line duty. I would be very grateful for your advice on this subject; I'm at my wit's end.

I am getting to know a great many of the Episcopalians on the post and am beginning to feel considerably more at home than I have felt heretofore. Steve's fellow-seminarian, Chaplain Man, who is stationed at the post hospital, is really a fine priest and a grand chaplain. The job at the hospital is back-breaking and he is doing a magnificent piece of work. I have gotten to know him very well and to like him very much. I go down to the hospital to chat with him at my every opportunity (none too frequent) and to some extent it compensates for not being able to talk to you. You have no idea how much I miss coming in to see you; there is seldom a day which passes which doesn't bring some new problem I'd like to talk to you about. There is also another Episcopalian in the Division, Chaplain Brendilmihl, from the Diocese of Eau Claire. He seems to be a brilliant man and a very able one, but unfortunately, he is leaving shortly to become chaplain for a division of ski troopers which is training in the Colorado mountains.

Through Chaplain Man, I have met at least one contemporary, an Episcopalian, who can converse at length without the use of either profanity or obscenity, and you can take my word for it that that is no common accomplishment in the army. The boy is from Philadelphia, belongs to St. Alban's Church (which church were you curate of? Was it St. Alban's, by any chance?) and is an extremely interesting chap. Unfortunately, he is now in the guardhouse, has been for four months, doing sentence for talking back to an officer. Chaplain Man says, however, that he was not to blame at all, and the fact that the officer involved was defrocked, or the military equivalent, seems to indicate that he wasn't. However, military law says that a soldier charged with willful disobedience to an officer must be sentenced; and they consider six months a token sentence! Fortunately, the boy was strong enough to survive without any bitterness whatever, so far as I can tell. And that is something, considering the humiliating treatment to which military prisoners are subjected. He is now paroled, which means that he sleeps in the guardhouse but that he is not guarded while on the job. Chaplain Man got him the job of caretaker at the Catholic chapel at the main post, and he is like a new person. I go down every Sunday afternoon and talk to him; it's the only time he has off and is permitted to receive visitors. It's a little ironical that I should have to go to the guardhouse to find a suitable companion, but he is much less suited for the guardhouse than innumerable men in my company who aren't there.

On last Monday evening, I went up to Topeka to see the Ballet Russe. While I was there, I went around to see Grace Cathedral and to meet the Dean, who turned out to be a very charming man and a good friend of Bishop Hart's. Have you ever seen this cathedral? It is very lovely; I believe it has the best stained glass windows I have ever seen. Unfortunately, it has a mural above the altar which could easily be used on the cover of the *Ladies' Home Journal*, but apart from that it is magnificent. The Dean invited me to come spend a weekend with him and I probably will.

I am glad to report that thus far I have done very well with my private devotions. I haven't neglected them a single night since I've been here, although I certainly can't say the same for my reading. I am anxious to read a good comparison of the R C and Anglican brethren; what would you suggest? Dr. Yerkes recommended one to me while I was at Sewanee, but I have forgotten the name of it.

I really must close; I know you haven't an afternoon to devote to reading a single letter. I hope this finds you well and happy and with the parish in full control. You said in your last letter for me not to quit writing if you were slow to answer; I don't expect you always to answer. I know how busy you are. But I am nonetheless glad to hear from you when you have a few moments to spare. Give Genevieve my kindest wishes and the same to Mrs. Sparkman.

Affectionately,
George

Longing for Home: To Fr. Thorne Sparkman
from Fort Riley, Kansas, January 18, 1943

Your letter came more than a week ago and, as always, I was delighted to hear from you. I deduce that your Christmas holidays must have been terrific, and I was a little surprised that you had rallied so soon. I was pained to hear that the cigarettes were so slow in reaching you; apparently the week I had allowed them to get there in was not enough time with the mail so crowded.

Written on the back of his photograph: "Dressed for an afternoon of frolic in the snow. Note rubber boots." Fort Riley, Kansas, winter 1943.

Today I have found myself unusually nostalgic for Chattanooga and the so-called "sunny south." We are having a thoroughgoing blizzard, with snow falling more heavily by the hour and the thermometer at something like ten below zero. What makes the weather almost unbearable is the terrific wind which blows here night and day. I suppose the army knows what it's doing in keeping me at Fort Riley, but I don't know what earthly use a frozen soldier is going to be to them.

Since I've gotten more or less caught up with my work in the Chaplain's office, I have a little free time every day for reading. It is the Chaplain's point of view that so long as I'm up with my work, my time is better spent in reading than in doing some unimportant task just to appear busy. Of course, I hasten to agree with him. My good friend, Chaplain Man, has just lent me a splendid book on prayer, which I am reading and enjoying very much. It is George S. Stewart's, *The Lower Levels of Prayer*, an English book published several years ago. In it, he deals with such simple things as preparation for prayer, the physical circumstances, dealing with interruptions and distractions, and such like. It reminds me considerably of Mr. Barth's course on prayer at Kanuga.

I wonder if you have given any careful attention to the current issue of *Forward Day by Day*? This is the first one of them that I have followed and used in daily devotions, although I have always read them. I think this one is particularly good; whoever wrote it manages to say more in a few words than most people can say in fifteen minutes.

In a few days I will have been in the army for three months; not, of course, a very long time, but already I have begun to realize how tremendously valuable my experience here is going to be. I believe my usefulness as a priest will be increased a dozen times for my having had this opportunity to know men from the ground up. I doubt that I am "changed" very much as yet, but I am bound to be changed if I stay here much longer. The course open to me – and to everybody else like me – is to deal with all sorts of people and see above and beyond their faults and the great limitations in their lives. It is certainly not an easy lesson to learn, because it would be far easier to dismiss them as impossible and to become ruthlessly intolerant. But with patience and tolerance, they can be borne with, even loved – and it is in such a way that I'm convinced one must progress. There is no other way. I have heard much too much about how much the army can teach one; as a matter of fact, unless a person has learned to think in Christian patterns, he is not in a position to learn here much of anything worth knowing.

I see in Saturday's *Times*, which arrived today, that Bruce was (to be) ordained on Sunday. I would certainly have liked to have been there. I surely do envy Bruce his opportunity to serve his deaconate with you; I hope he will be half as valuable to you as I know you will be to him. I hear from numerous sources that Eric is doing very creditably at Sewanee and I am so glad to hear it. He has had such a tough time all his life that he certainly deserves smooth sailing by this time.

Although I don't want to be overly optimistic (how bitterly I have learned not to be!), I think the time until I see you again will be much shorter than the time since last I saw you has been. At least, I devoutly hope so.

With best wishes always,
George

The Beating of a Black Soldier: To Isobel Griscom from Fort Riley, Kansas, July 9, 1943

There is so much to be said that I have no hope of finishing this at one sitting. But I will start it now and finish it some time before I go downtown to Church on Sunday morning – since it is then that I want to mail the letter. It will probably surprise you to know the reason for my wanting to mail it in town: it is quite probable that my outgoing mail is being carefully looked over by the intelligence office. As I have implied in earlier letters, I am working in cryptography, the code in which the most secret army messages are sent. The F.B.I. investigated me for weeks before they would allow me inside the cryptographic room. Every day I encode and decode messages concerning movement of hundreds of troops, and were I disposed to reveal any of the information, could certainly do great violence to the war effort. Needless to say, I attend to the whole job with utmost care and secrecy. My family doesn't even know what I'm doing. It is my opinion that the intelligence office will read my outgoing mail for several weeks to make sure I'm not selling out to the Germans! As for incoming, naturally it isn't read, I'm quite certain, since we get it almost directly from the Junction City Post Office.

All of which provides a more melodramatic introduction to the letter than is justified. I merely want to write about certain things which I would not care to be involved in, were the intelligence office to become aware of them. I don't know just where to begin, but perhaps I had best do so by saying a word about Military Police. I don't know whether I've ever given you any insight into that tribe, but they are usually the strongest and toughest and most unprincipled of available soldiers. On this point, it is fairly easy to avoid any reprimand from them, but if one is reproved (for having a button unbuttoned, for example), he is wise to take the reproof quietly, even though he is likely to be cursed for such a trivial thing. One does not "talk back" if one is smart, because life can be made miserable by the MP's. I have heard wild stories about how the guardhouse is administered, how the most ignorant and brutal of them tyrannize the prisoners and exact tribute of unbelievable sorts and kinds from them. Last night for the first time I saw and heard them in action. I forget whether I mentioned that the barracks in which we are now quartered is next door to the guardhouse and is separated from it only by a narrow court. Since we are on the second floor, we can look easily across and into the windows of the cells. Last evening, several of us went to the late movie and came home about ten-thirty. We were sitting in front of the windows trying to enjoy a facsimile of a breeze when suddenly, the air was split with the most blood-curdling screams I've ever heard. For a long time, we could see nothing, but we could hear the shouts of some Negro, obviously in pain. And three or four angry voices. Then the lights went on in the basement and we could see several MP's beating on the Negro with clubs, while he was screaming for mercy. The only thing I heard him say distinctly was, "Oh Lord, if you're going to torture me all night, why don't you go ahead and kill me?" He must have fallen then, because we heard one of the MP's shout, "Get up on your feet, god damn you." The better to provide a target, I suppose. After a few minutes, three MP's and a prisoner came out and drove away in a truck. One of the

244

boys in the detachment came in and told us that there had been "a big fight" in the guardhouse and that the MP's had just taken one prisoner to the hospital. This morning I got up and looked out of the window quite early to see if there were blood on the ground, and there was plenty of it. While I was getting dressed, two MP's came out and washed the truck out and swept gravel and dust over the blood on the ground.

What seemed even worse to me than the terrible beating given the Negro was the attitude of resignation with which everyone accepted the whole affair. The more atavistic among us said, "Well, that will teach those damned niggers to respect *us*"!!! Others said, "Well, it's too bad but nothing can be done about it." When we came to work this morning, I asked the janitors here, paroled prisoners, what started the fight. They said that the Negro was in solitary confinement, that one of the MP's teased and cursed him, until finally he called the MP an unflattering name, whereupon, the MP summoned *five* of his fellow MP's and the fight was on. Each MP was armed with a blackjack, and each fell on the Negro and beat him without mercy. I made up my mind that I was not going to admit that nothing could be done until I had tried and failed. Naturally, in a case like this, the person to wage the fight is a person with weight, which he can throw around if need be. There are only two persons available to the enlisted man for help in such affairs, the inspector general and the Chaplain. Since I knew him, I chose the Chaplain and went to call on him this noon. Whether he is really concerned or not, I cannot say. I have always thought him a little stuffy and I thought he was especially so this morning. Every sentence sounded like an oration. Well, yes, it sounded deplorable, but we must realize that some men must be punished brutally. Perhaps, but not when they are *provoked* into fighting and then attacked by *five* MP's. The final upshot of it was that he promised to look into it, to talk to the prison officer and see what can be done.

What I'm afraid he'll run into is this: all of the maltreatment, the whole stinking business is going on with the knowledge and implicit consent of at least part of the officers in charge of the guard house. The Provost Marshal himself is aware of it all, I'm afraid, and whoever sets out to see justice done is going to have a fight on his hands. My reasons for thinking so are two: the general riot last night didn't stop, although I'm certain it was heard by the MP sergeants in the front office – I know two or three of them and they are very decent young men and I feel certain that they would have stopped this disgraceful affair if they had felt the support of their officers. The second reason: I heard a story last winter which, if true, indicates a very sad state of affairs. It seems that one of the prisoners told the Provost Marshal himself to go to hell. The major (the Provost

Marshal) handed the boy over to the MP's and told them to punish him fittingly. Hence, he very cleverly relieved himself of the guilt of the crime. I don't know whether he publicly washed his hands or not. But he put the matter in very good hands. The boy was taken out each day for seventeen days, chained to a rock and in zero weather stood at attention for eight hours a day! Twice a day, because of the magnanimity of the MP's, he was given bread and water! Whether this story is true, I do not know, but I heard it from several independent sources. A great many other stories I have heard I would not inflict upon you. If the Chaplain cannot get results, I'm going to talk to the Inspector General. The reason I hesitate to do this is that if an investigation were ordered, I would almost certainly be involved in it. And the MP's would never relent in their efforts to get me behind bars, once they knew I had asked that the matter be looked into. But I think I will never forget that Negro's screaming and the sound of the blows as they fell on him. It was the clearest insight I've ever had of life under the Gestapo. And this is the United States – founded, strengthened and preserved by men who believed in justice enough to die for it. Well, I haven't reached the be-still-my-soul-and-see-injustice-done stage yet!

Saturday Morning

It developed last night that I was not the only person who slept poorly after the riot on Thursday evening. Last night one of the boys came home very well oiled and did considerable talking. He is a rather intelligent person, from a small town in Missouri, rather rough and tumble and not one whom I would expect to be too upset by Negro baiting. I have been amazed more than once at the way in which a few drinks utterly divest some of the boys of their swagger and proud pretenses, of how their real reactions come to the surface of their minds and are voiced with almost embarrassing honesty. I always feel, especially felt last night, that I was taking an unfair advantage just to listen. The boy came in about eleven, and was terribly grateful that I had made up his bed (which I did less out of altruism than out of a desire not to be awakened by his trying to do so if he should come in around two or three). He simply didn't understand how I, a servant of God Almighty (this was the first time I heard him use divine names with even the slightest respect) a follower of Christ, a shepherd of the lost (!!!), could bother with him, a drunkard, a complete no-good, who never had, never would amount to anything. Oh, he admired me terribly for saying prayers – and apologized for the time – unknown to me – when he interrupted me. After ten minutes of this, he was quiet for a while, and then said, "you know, I can't stand much more of this." "Much more of what?" "This damned brutality – that's what it is, beating that poor black Negro – I couldn't sleep last night for thinking about it. I ask you, are we fighting for democracy or are we fighting for the Gestapo? I tell you I can't stand to hear anything like that again." So – we live and learn. Some day I may even have enough sense to stop trying to predict what is going on in other people's minds. . . .

On Racism: To Fr. Thorne Sparkman
from Fort Riley, Kansas, August 10, 1943

. . . Last Sunday, when it was 112° in the shade and 170° in a cassock, I said my first service of morning and "preached" my first "sermon," or, as I should say, for the first time preached one of your sermons. The affair went off better than I expected on the whole. All the dear old ladies looked steadily out the nearest window during the "sermon" and told me afterwards it was quite fascinating. I thanked them just as politely as though I believed them. . . . The rector is taking his vacation and no other priest is close at hand to pinch hit and he hesitates to close the Church for two Sundays because so many soldiers come – hence, the invitation to me. I suppose the situation was desperate enough to warrant asking me, but I'm not sure. Eric told me in June about your advice to him as to what sort of sermons he should attempt this summer, and I used the advice as faithfully as if it had been given to me.

The central idea, to which I referred often enough to keep it really central (!), was that reform, for the Christian, begins with himself, that he does not seek to improve society primarily by trying to improve some group, but largely by trying to improve himself. As a point of departure, I used the two-fold Commandment, saying that it was really the basis for all Christian betterment. Then, I'm afraid I trod on rather dangerous ground – I tried to show what would happen were we to apply the Christian technique of reform to the question of the Negro problem. The point was that we ought to wish well for the Negro because in the second part of the Commandment we are commanded to love our neighbors. To establish that the Negro is our neighbor, I referred, of course, to the parable of the Good Samaritan, which is safe ground, especially with Dummelow in one's footlocker. I did have sense enough to steer clear of trying to advocate any solution to the Negro problem (not the least reason being I don't know any). The chief point of this part of the sermon was that our attitude towards the Negro is the thing that needs most to change – that it is better to think of him as a Child of God and a brother to us and even to insist that he be segregated than to grant him total "social equality," that is, seats beside us on a bus or tables in a restaurant, and still resent him. Out of understanding and love will come at length a good solution, but a violent change in *mores* without a change in heart will result in chaos. Need I say that I am not sketching the "sermon" for your instruction but for your criticism.

Perhaps in a different situation, in a quieter moral climate, I might have stayed entirely clear of such a discussion, but I have been so occupied with thoughts about race relations that I could not keep them out of my remarks. I thought I knew what race prejudice is when I was in school, but what I knew before I came to the army is a pale, inconsiderable fifth cousin to what I have met here. Day after day, week after week, I listen to the foulest, filthiest attack on the Negroes, the Jews and the Japanese – no one of which constitutes anything like a problem on this post. The Negroes are unusually quiet and well-behaved; there is a rather great number of Negroes here and I have never seen the slightest clash between white and colored troops. As for the Japanese, there are about a hundred of them living in the same barracks with us, and I have never seen quieter, more humble people. In fact, their humility, which is obviously their answer to preju- dice against them, sometimes makes me want to apologize to them for my own race. Despite the fact that both Negroes and Japanese go out of their way to get along with us, a day seldom passes that someone doesn't suggest they should all be sent to Concentration Camps, or just murdered. For the first time, I am begin- ning to have some idea of hatred so bitter that it becomes self-destructive. One hears so much, and regrets it bitterly but hears it in silence, because what can one say? . . .

Happy vacation – give Mrs. S. my best wishes.

As ever,

George

A Soldier for One Year: To Isobel Griscom
from Fort Riley, Kansas, October 22, 1943

. . .Today I am able to say that I have been a soldier for a year, since it was indeed a year ago today that I was called up for active duty. It has been a strange- ly fascinating year, bringing so many new people and so many new situations into my life, breaking the limitations which have bound me and leaving me little power to say exactly what the year has meant. If I had to ascribe one word to it by way of description, I think I would say that it has been a victorious year – victory over myself and the fears and complexes which my environment placed upon me. It is unnecessary to remind you of what things I mean; it is obvious to you, who misses nothing, that my early influence was towards a quiet and inactive sort of life, with a minimum of freedom of any kind. When I knew that I was coming to the army, I thought that the experience – so filled with everything of which I had always been afraid, would either make or break me. I speak of the year as victorious because it has not broken me, for five minutes even, and it has gone far towards making me. Frankly, I expected last fall that with hard work, I would be a fair soldier – that I could, with great effort, achieve the minimum. Is it any wonder, really, that I felt triumphant when I found that I could fit into such a strange new existence and fit well from the start? I still remember with amazement the first few weeks, when I had expected to be miserable, spent almost hilariously. I'm sure that many people were convinced that I lied in my letters, that I was simply too proud to say I hated the army, and I understand their skepticism, but it was unfounded. I was sparing nobody.

I had often wondered exactly what foundation my life was built upon. I know too well with what things the structure was weakened, and I had a terrible fear that once in the midst of such an alien and undesirable life as the army, the structure might collapse. My brother once told me that I lived on my conceit, but I think the past year has belied that statement. Surely I met no encouragement anywhere for any conceit, and yet I survived to tell the story. If my life had been built on conceit, then the dressing downs I have taken in the last year would have left me comfortless, but they didn't. I have shed the cloaks of scorn with no trouble at all. I think you will know what I mean when I say the year has been a triumphant year, because you know very well what was there to be triumphed over. If I confessed to some people that I felt my year of army life was a great victory, they would wonder what I meant. I haven't gotten a promotion in a whole year, nor found myself a really suitable job – but how minor those things are. Being able to remain a private for a year with a minimum of regret (but, hope still springs eternal) and being able to do a menial task to the best of my ability with a minimum of complaint are parts of the victory.

The worst thing about the year has been the paucity of "good people," of possible friends. In the sense that I had good friends in college, none I have known in the army can qualify. I have had friends, pleasant and casual, who were and are nice people to drink coffee with in the PX or go to town occasionally, but I can't say that I would have any regret never to see any of them again. Sometimes, I have a tremendous longing to be able to say to someone that I like to read poetry, that an idea appeals to me, that such and such an essay is worth reading;

but, the opportunity for such happy conversation is non-existent. It is this area of human relationships which is apparently closed to me for the duration. It is this element for which I must depend on my letters, and it is for that reason that I am forever indebted to you for your kindness for writing so regularly and, chiefly, for remembering that I did not shed my deepest interests along with my white shirts with button-down collars.

Despite my lack of close friends – or perhaps because of it – I have made, I think, considerable progress in my human relations. I have never been, am not now, and never expect to be "one of the boys." Simple and harmless as it is sometimes meant to sound, this fraternizing seems to me usually to call for nothing less than the abdication of our deepest convictions. Certainly in the army, where prevailing tastes, ideas and morals are so abominably low, to try to be 'one of the fellows' is certain suicide. . . . Certainly there lies in the past of each of us many things which we might, with pleasure, recall. But there are, I venture to guess, many things also which we would prefer to see buried forever. I am struggling to say what I mean – conversation for a year with my compatriots has, I fear, dulled my ability to express an idea. Perhaps it can be said this way – that what we wish from the past is the security and peace and happiness, which it seems in retrospect to have given us. We are wishing for a happy sort of world, and I see no reason for looking backward to find it. It is only by rejecting a certain amount of the past that we can hope for any tolerable life in the future. It seems to me to be a childish and a fatal error to tell ourselves that our happiness for the future depends strictly on our recapture of the past. It induces a silly and futile sentimentalism which for a hundred reasons will do great and inestimable damage. . . .

First Days of Combat: To Isobel Griscom
from somewhere in France, January 13, 1945

I have wanted for a long time to tell you something of our first days of combat, and I hope this time to manage to finish the letter. I do not intend, of course, to write about military aspects of the operations; that would undoubtedly be dull and repetitive for you and impossible for me. I want to try to tell you something about the people, how they behaved, how they managed to persevere in an almost impossible situation.

It would surprise you, I think, to know how slowly the whole situation of a large-scale German offensive became known to us. One cold winter morning towards the middle of December, a messenger from my crew drove two of us up through a series of lovely little towns in Luxembourg. We were trying to retrieve a certain piece of equipment we had lent to a unit which had left our control. We drove through towns filled with our troops, artillery and tanks in force, and I remarked then that I couldn't understand why the Germans weren't shelling those positions, inasmuch as they were in easy range of German fire. Next morning, we had the answer: they began shelling those very towns with everything they had. That was the beginning. Next day we moved up to assume tactical control of certain of the division units which were slugging it out already with the enemy. That was the day, I believe, when the U.S. was told that a real counter-offensive was under way. It is strange to me how actual participation in the war narrows one's perception of its scope: you have no idea of a general front line from Aachen to Belfort, you concentrate your attention on a few bridges and a road junction and a wooded draw. And these few things assume such immediate and obvious importance that any more remote action seems unreal and unrelated to your own activity. It was at least four or five days before a copy of *Stars and Stripes* found its way into the headquarters and we read of the encirclement of Bastogne and knew, for the first time, that the offensive was a widespread and powerful German thrust.

But to go back to the first day we moved up. We were in the middle of things so quickly, and so deeply, that I still cannot remember the order of events for the first two or three days. On the day the shelling began, one of the officers in the headquarters (whose emotional maturity is as low as his rank is high) said, in high good humor, "Damn, I had a wonderful time this morning – really got shot at for the first time. Wonderful day." But 24 hours later, he looked old and weary and very much wiser than he had been the day before. I thought his remark was painfully stupid and certainly the days that followed bore me out. There is no way to describe those days; it is possible only to mention facts from here and there, to give you some scattered idea of what went on. I am anxious not to misrepresent the facts: I am making no attempt to write about the war from the point of view of a person actually fighting in the front lines. Nobody in a headquarters knows what that is like, but, too, we were uncomfortably close to the fireworks and even though our experience was more or less vicarious, it was nonetheless, strong and unforgettable.

One's chief contact with the front is through liaison officers, messengers, commanders who come into headquarters from time to time for conferences. In all my life, I never realized that the mere sight of persons closely involved with fighting could affect anyone as they did me those first few days. Men came in looking so completely worn out, so thoroughly incapable of the fighting you knew they were going to have to do shortly – and without any sleep – that one almost wept to see them. Perhaps you can see what I'm driving at if I make an effort at comparison. To me, it is painful to see persons who have suffered great personal bereavement. There is something shocking and disquieting to see a familiar face bearing the imprint of grief and sorrow. It was that feeling, more potent and overwhelming than I ever felt it, that grew more and more unbearable, strong and terrible during those first few days. I wish it were possible to tell you how completely mad the world seemed. Friends came in I had known since Fort Riley days, laughed and joked with through a good many common experiences – and their tired, drawn faces, their overwhelming weariness so obvious in every movement of their bodies, was heartbreaking. One company commander (whom I admire as one officer whom every soldier would be glad to serve under) lost a dozen men or so, and day by day his face grew more taut until I wondered how much longer he could endure. A battalion commander, who more than one day found himself with his back against the wall, looked like the personification of death itself. I shall never forget the faces of some of those men.

I had often wondered, in days before the breakthrough, how American troops ever made good soldiers. We are so unsuited to soldiering, from the point of view of habits and outlook, so fond of pleasure and skeptical of hardship, how can we wage war effectively and wholeheartedly?

I have learned a good deal about that, although it seems impossible to put much of it into words. I have learned that necessity is the mother not only of invention but of a lot more things, such as nerve, and gallantry and devotion to duty. If one *must*, absolutely must, hold a bridge or defend a hill or kill a squad of Germans, he will do it. The heroes aren't particularly remarkable people in themselves; they are often, it seems to me, quite ordinary people who have been challenged, by circumstances, to do the impossible and have done it. Yes, one can do whatever is necessary. We discovered that in my own crew, where during the first week three hours sleep was a luxury and more than three unheard of. I wouldn't have thought it possible, but it was necessary and it was done. And I was amazed to discover how nervous energy would last long after the body was worn out. I woke a number of times after two hours sleep feeling equal to going back to work again. And after the first hectic period, I felt a good deal of pride in what we had accomplished – pride in the men in my own section, in the staff and the headquarters, in the troops attached. And since the *Stars and Stripes* announced it yesterday, it is revealing no military secret to say that the accomplishment was this: Combat Command "A" of the Ninth Armored Division held the Germans in Luxembourg for ten days, preventing the recapture of Luxembourg City.

It is almost midnight (hence your dinner time) and in a few minutes, I shall be going to bed. (Another useful talent I've acquired is the ability to sleep soundly on a hard floor or anywhere else. I need only one thing in order to sleep – space to put my bedroll.) Your letter of December 30 arrived today and, as usual, it was good to hear from you. I'm glad you enjoyed Bart's letters and Archbishop Temple's essay – which I thought very absorbing. (I'm afraid it will be a long time before the Church has such another valiant saint and warrior as he. I've never known who succeeded him.)

In the same mail with your letter came the October 1 *Times* (current, isn't it?), which provided some comic relief. In the magazine section there appeared this optimistic headline: "Speedy End to War, Better Postwar City Is Goal of Sutton Jones, Rotary President." It was a large order, even for the Rotarians, but I wish they could have succeeded.

We're back in France – in a very snow-covered France. Parts of it are lovely, but it is so terribly cold one's enjoyment is curbed. Fortunately, we're always in buildings – I can't imagine a pup tent in this weather! Yesterday, in a small town, a boy about 9 spoke in very precise English: "How do you do?" "Well, how do *you* do?" I countered. "God damn," said he, loudly and cheerfully, exhausting, no doubt, his American military vocabulary. . . .

On Germany and the German Military:
To Martha E. (Jones) Gundaker, April 26, 1945

I didn't realize how deplorable my correspondence situation was until I realized that I owe you one and perhaps two letters. Things are really bad. You don't mind, do you, dear, if I throw E. Post to the winds tonight and write you in pencil? My pen has behaved normally by going dry on me, and since it is 3:30 AM I do not feel like looking for ink or using the typewriter, thus awakening the barred and leaved people sleeping near me.

I wish I could tell you what an exciting time I've had since we crossed the Rhine in March. I'm sure that never again will I be so closely involved in the making of history, or rather with the people who were making it. For those of us who have waited so long for the evening of the score, the disintegration of the German armies in the West is deeply gratifying. That I saw it first hand I would exchange for nothing. I love to remember now the arrogant Nazis in newsreels, goose-stepping their way to what they thought was world conquest. What a different picture now, with long columns of prisoners, broken, bedraggled, for the most part ridiculously old or young for fighting. How wonderfully complete is their reduction from the world's masters to the defeated remnants of what was once an army! I still appreciate the intelligence of the American engineer company which erected in the midst of the ruins of Aachen the quotation in both German and English – from *Mein Kampf*: "Give me five years and you will not recognize Germany again!"

The country is really lovely. Even when we were most deeply involved in the fighting, I enjoyed the country itself immensely. April has been such a fine month, clear and beautiful – and at times, within range of German artillery, the war seemed remote and incredible. Week before last we traveled for miles and miles between rows of blossoming cherry trees on either side of the road. And the gardens are lovely – there are always pansies and jonquils and tulips in profusion, and huge bushes of japonica delight the eye.

Currently, we're in something like a rest area, and after a whole month with very little time for relaxation, it is most welcome. I have about caught up on my sleep and I'm about ready to launch into an orgy of reading. I have a couple of books Izzy sent me and also the new Henry James anthology of his ten short novels. I don't know James very well and I'm anxious to dive in and see what it's like.

Recently, while we were deeply involved with the Master Race, we received for distribution to our battalions the Army Cook Book. (So useful, you know, when 88's are flying overhead!) Have you seen it? If you haven't, you owe it to yourself to locate a copy because it is choice! My two favorite passages are these:

Boiled Eggs
Ingredients: Water, boiling
Eggs

Jam Sandwiches
Ingredients: Jam

These are the pure and undefiled works of genius!

More anon. Write when you can, and I shall do likewise.

Love,
George

The End of the War: To Isobel Griscom
from somewhere in Czechoslovakia, May 9, 1945

Since the hours attending the end of the war have been among its busiest, this is my first real opportunity to send you any report of how and when and where the end came for us. Here the war ended in such overwhelming excitement and confusion, a full account is not possible. But, chronologically, I will note a few of the more important moments we have lived through. No one would deny, I suppose, that the first week in May was the most news-packed week of the whole war. The death of Mussolini and Hitler, the capture of Berlin, the surrender in Italy and the northwest pointed so surely to an early end of the fighting that we expected the news almost hourly. It was almost in an atmosphere of carnival, then, that we moved into Czechoslovakia on Sunday, the 6th, to launch our final attack in the European theater. I was delighted to come here for two reasons: first, I wanted to be in the middle of things when the end came, not sitting in a rest area miles behind the lines. Second, I was glad to come to Czechoslovakia to be a part of the force which liberated her from the ignominy into which democratic betrayal forced her in 1939. There was something dramatic and deeply satisfying about ending the war not by bringing "balm from Gilead" (remember that lovely sonnet?) but bullets from the United States, which made up in effectiveness what they lacked in poetic appeal.

Sunday's fighting was tough, and I would never have guessed that total capitulation was so near. The resistance was spirited, and some of us began to wonder if the southern redoubt wasn't to be a tougher nut to crack than we had thought. The attack began again at dawn on Monday, the 7th, and things got off to a good start. The rain and clouds which had made Sunday a miserable day had disappeared, and the sun shone brightly – and so did our hopes when every report from the battalions indicated that almost nothing stood between us and our objective. In our vehicle we always listen to the radio net which the headquarters uses to co-ordinate the fighting. At about eight o'clock, one of the battalion intelligence officers said he had picked up a Nazi soldier who told him the German radio had told them the war was over and bade them go home. Perhaps the war was over, I remarked, and we might not know it for days. (I was remembering the division's crossing of the Rhine, when for days we didn't know our bridgehead at Remagen was the only one!) But I was wrong, and for once we were to know what went on before the world knew it. At nine o'clock, the tank battalion operations officer informed the headquarters that the German garrison in one town was assembled and waiting to surrender when they entered the town. It was good news, and we began to realize that indeed all resistance was crumbling. At about 9:15, the operations officer called the Colonel, who was near the leading elements at the head of the column. "I have an urgent message for the Combat Commander," he said. We waited breathlessly, wondering what had come up. My first thought, remembering the past, was that perhaps our aircraft had sighted strong opposition ahead. After a delay, the Colonel answered the call, and the operations officer gave him the message: "The following word has been received from higher headquarters – Cease all aggressive forward movement. Further instructions later." We looked at each other. "This is it," I said, in my excitement forgetting to say something epigrammatic or quotable. We were between two towns when the word came, and as soon as a hotel could be cleared for us in the next town, we moved into it and awaited "further instructions."

They arrived in the early afternoon. The Germans, we were told, had signed unconditional surrender early that morning and that it would become effective at midnight last night. Soon after that word came, we learned what it means to be a unit in the front lines when the fighting ceases. High ranking German officers began appearing to surrender their units and to arrange for their evacuation – and ever since, German generals have been a dime a dozen. Konrad Heinlein (spelling uncertain!) who organized Nazis here in the Sudetenland gave himself up at the headquarters last night. Every hour has brought some new excitement.

I have seen the German army in the throes of total and very bitter defeat. I can't imagine any Germans who can believe this time that they were technically undefeated. Last night a friend and I walked through this lovely old Czech town, across the bridge which spans the river on the eastern side of the town. There was parked a German hospital convoy, a group of eight or ten vehicles loaded with their sick and wounded. They were awaiting an American escort before moving on through the town and to hospitals. When the escort came, we watched them move across the bridge and through the town. I shall never forget the sight. The vehicles were packed with medics, equipment, nurses, everything they could get into them. Some of the men looked barely alive – their faces all were taut and drawn, unutterably weary and sad. They had the look of a beaten army, and certainly no one who sees them can ever again see this German military machine as a thing of glamour and power. The roads are filled with German convoys, thousands and thousands of German troops moving back to the rear areas and into our selected points of assembly for them. As an army, they have been totally and completely conquered.

And how do we feel about the end, now that at last it is here? Very pleased, very happy, but unbelievably weary and let down. For myself, I think I felt very much as I expected – not elated, or terribly excited, or overwhelmingly happy. I felt that a very interesting but a very trying and demanding time of my life had ended. In the months I've been in the E.T.O., I've seen too much misery and suffering, too much cruelty and injustice to imagine that the problems ended with the war. The taste of the Buchenwald Concentration Camp is too recently in my mouth to permit now any feeling of elation. I'm not saying I wasn't happy to know the end has come – but the happiness is deep inside, and it's shadowed and modified by a hundred regrets. There were among us no wild celebrations; nobody got drunk except one or two individuals, although almost everybody had set aside a bottle of something for the V-E celebration. Some of us had saved three bottles of very excellent champagne, and we drank toasts to the end of the war. Mine was simple, perhaps sentimental, but heartfelt: "To the memory of a great American, who did not live to see the end of the war which he did more to win that any other single individual." And surely Franklin Roosevelt's death must have stood between a great many people and a hilarious celebration.

Now that it's over, we can relax and congratulate ourselves that we weren't hit by artillery, or bombed, or strafed, or sprayed with gas. I feel as though I had been walking on the edge of a cliff, and prevented from falling only by the grace of God and an inestimable and disproportionate amount of good luck.

This is merely a sketch – I'll no doubt be on this subject for a long time.

Yours ever,
George

End of the War and Visit to Buchenwald:
To Fr. Thorne Sparkman, May 17, 1945

I am desolate that ten days after the shooting ended, I still haven't sent along any notes about the end as we saw it. My seeming negligence I can explain only by saying that the end of a war is not quite the same thing in the front areas as it is in New York, or London, or Chattanooga. No telephone directories got torn up and thrown around, not only because none was handy but largely because there just wasn't time. During the past two months I had announced frequently and feelingly that upon hearing that the Germans had gotten enough, I intended going to bed for at least three days. How naïve that hope was the past ten days have clearly shown me. There has been a tremendous amount of work connected with the denouement which I hadn't quite expected and which has kept us busier, even, than we were during certain parts of the operations themselves.

After the division pulled back from the Mulde in late April, I had a horrible premonition that when the end came, we would be so far removed from the fighting that we would get in on none of the excitement. This would not have been to my liking; I feel quite naturally that I have seen a fair amount of the war and I wanted to see the end of it from the best possible point. I had my wish. When the end came, we were fighting in just about the only place left to fight, Czechoslovakia. When SHAEF's "cease fire" order came down on Monday, the 7th, we were very much involved in the war. At about noon on that day, we moved into a hotel in Elbogen, which is near Karlsbad and on the main road to Pilsen. It was from this very lovely spot that we witnessed the tremendous drama of disintegration which the German army staged. I have never seen anything quite like it, and I shall never forget it. The end was received about as I expected. Naturally anybody who has fought the war for any length of time meets the end of it with certain feelings of happiness and elation, which are, however very strongly modified by fatigue and loneliness and the realization that the end of the war is the beginning of a lot of problems. Even the least thoughtful and observant cannot have seen what they have in Germany without realizing that we were witnessing the collapse of more than an army. One feels, nevertheless, a certain sort of self-congratulatory feeling, a sort of rejoicing that the German air force and artillery and infantry have done their combined worst for us and we have still survived; one feels a little as though he had walked on the edge of a cliff and had somehow, by the grace of God, managed not to fall. But there were no unrestrained celebrations, and so far as I know, although liquor was fairly plentiful at the time, nobody in our own group got wildly drunk, as many had threatened. All of which pleased me very much, not so much because it foreshadows an improvement in morals but because it seems to indicate a willingness to face reality, which seems infinitely more necessary now than during the war itself.

During the two days which intervened between the surrender and the official end of the war, we had good opportunity to watch a good deal of the drama at very close range. Since we were 'in contact' at the time of cessation, naturally the initial job of rounding up the remnants of the *wehrmacht* fell to us. We had German units and high headquarters off our telephone switchboard and an hilarious time was had by all. I must record that the spirit attending most Allied-German conferences which I saw during this time was a little too festive to suit me, and I note in the *Stars and Stripes* that Gen. Eisenhower felt the same way. There was much too careful attention to the letter of the law regarding military courtesy, especially in the light of the behaviour of the German army when it was on the other side of the conference table. I was very pleased to hear what the celebrated commander of the Third Army had to say on the subject. It seems that a German field marshal wanted to give up his whole command, but would surrender to no one except Gen. Patton. When word was passed along to Georgie, he said, leaving out the more violent language, "If they want to surrender, they will surrender to the field commander nearest them. If he isn't good enough for 'em, to hell with 'em. I'd rather make PW's out of 'em, anyway."

To feel in any way kindly or tolerant towards the Germans, military or civil, I have to forget much of what I have seen during the past two months. Late in April, I went to see the Buchenwald Concentration Camp at Weimar. I thought perhaps all the stories of atrocities had been exaggerated, and I wanted to see for myself just what went on in such places. I saw, and I shall never forget it. There are no words adequate to describe the horror of it, but I promise you that none of the newspaper accounts I have seen has been exaggerated. But you cannot, I believe, realize the cold and calculated horror of the thing until you see it. I have read numerous accounts of Dachau and Lublin, but all the reading I had done gave me no idea how cold the blood would run when I walked into the room in which giant furnaces had consumed human lives by the thousands. Somebody described Buchenwald as an assembly line of death, and that description is not in the least excessive. (*Time* magazine in the Apr. 30 issue contained a very masterful summing up of the place, which I recommend to you if you haven't already read it.) What existed there was so obviously not the isolated acts of a few strong-minded young men; it was the carefully designed and scientifically managed system for the extermination of human life. And the Jewish professor, a native of Prague, who conducted us through the camp kept reminding us that of the twelve prison camps he personally had been in, this was one of the more humane! It was a paradise, he said, in comparison to the camps in Poland. Some of the inmates were still in Buchenwald, in the hospital wards, and we saw and talked to some of them. There is no way to describe how they looked, except to say that they looked like they were living somewhere on the other side of death. I am glad I went to see Buchenwald, because otherwise I think in years to come I might have begun to think that Nazi cruelty was blown up by the press for its own use. I know now what depths they sank to. (An interesting footnote to that visit was that it occurred on April 30, and the indefatigable Russians, in the midst of all that misery and suffering, were erecting flags and maypoles and all sorts of decorations for a riotous celebration of May Day!)

Since the war ended, and before, I have talked to a rather considerable number of British and American soldiers who have been prisoners of war. I had a particularly long conversation on VE day with six British lads who had been captive since the fall of France. They spoke quietly, and with typical British understatement, but it was plainly evident how greatly they had suffered at German hands. The spokesman deemed it necessary to beg my pardon for calling the SS chief who had been in charge of the camp a "bastard of bastards." How thoroughly British, I thought, that he should find it necessary, after five years at the mercy of the Nazis, to beg my pardon for calling one of them by a name doubtless much too good for him. The large groups of liberated war prisoners are among the most moving sights of the war. Some of them seem gay and terribly happy to be free, but most of them look beaten and hungry and, worst of all, as though long ago they had given up any efforts to have normal human feelings. It is an appalling thing, and while I have no doubt that in time they will recover, one is enraged that their treatment has been such as to leave them the way they are. In dealing with Germany now and in the future, I think we will be very wise to remember Buchenwald and Dachau and these liberated prisoners of war. I don't pretend to know the answer to the German riddle, although I hope to know before I leave here, but I am sure that we err in making a strong distinction between Nazis and non-Nazis. The calmness with which these non-Nazis seemed to have looked the other way so much of the time seems to make them equally guilty, in my opinion.

Thank you very much for your letter of April 25 which arrived about a week ago. I can assure you that my Russian was not equal to the demands put upon it. However, these demands were slight because I saw only a handful of Russian officers. They came into our CP one morning a couple of days after the fighting stopped, and it would have done your heart good to see the Park Avenue boys rushing around to find Scotch to drink with them. Never did I expect to see what I saw that morning: a vestryman of St. Thomas', New York, drinking with a Communist!

To show you how lightly the war sat on me, I am enclosing a recent snapshot. It was taken on Low Sunday, at about the time you were rushing around getting people confirmed. Our column was halted and waiting for a pontoon

S/Sgt. Connor on the banks of the Weser River, May, 1945.

bridge to be built across the Weser. The picture was taken on the bank of that beautiful little stream. In case you think that's a riding crop in my hand, you're right. But I hasten to add that it isn't a permanent fixture.

I am naturally pleased to report that we are living now in the luxury that becomes conquerors. We are quartered in a beautiful and very modern hotel, which besides having excellent office space gives most of us private rooms. This is the first privacy I've ever had in the army, and I simply revel in my wonderful room, with large soft mattresses and running water and comfortable chairs and radio. I knew there must be some advantage in being a staff sergeant, and now I'm sure. And although you won't believe it, the hotel staff here is intact, and we aren't even obliged to make our own beds. So you can concentrate your prayers now on my spiritual well-being, since the body is being well taken care of. . . .

As always,
George

End of the War and Buchenwald: To Ben Kramer from Coburg, Germany, May 26, 1945

Your letter of May 3 arrived more than a week ago, and as much as I appreciated getting it and was delighted to hear from you again, other duties have prevented my answering it earlier. The ending of a war is not quite the same thing for the people involved as it is for those who are removed from the scene. As much as some people may have felt like celebrating the end, more mundane tasks claimed all our time and attention. I think the ten days following VE day have been the busiest I have had in the ETO. More about this later. . . .

For me, the war ended on a note of drama and poetic justice. We were fighting in Czechoslovakia, about the only place left to fight. This combat command was attached to the First Infantry Division and was attacking towards Karlsbad, on the main road to Pilsen. The headquarters was in the column immediately behind the attacking tank battalion on the morning of May 7. At about 9:30 we heard on the radio, tuned to the command channel, our operations officer say he had an urgent message for the combat commander. When the general was finally gotten to the radio, the message was read. Coming from the commanding general of the First Infantry Division, the message said; "Cease immediately all forward and aggressive movement. Take local security measures and await further instructions." Turning to the lads in my vehicle, I said "This is it," forgetting in the supreme moment to say something profound and quotable. At the time I didn't feel particularly excited, but since then I have not been able to think of that moment without getting chills. It was the moment the world had been waiting for so very long, and it seemed particularly appropriate that we should be in Czechoslovakia, where for many of us the war started with the betrayal of Munich. Do you remember Edna Millay's sonnet ["Czecho-slovakia"]: "If there were balm in Gilead, I would go / To Gilead for your wounds, unhappy land. . ."?

Since we were in contact (another of the army's little euphemisms!) at the end of the fighting, the task of processing, collecting and moving to rear areas the remnants of German units in that sector naturally fell to us. As soon as the cease-fire order came down, we moved into Elbogen, a lovely little town on the high hills above the Eger River, which flows almost completely around the town. We were in a hotel there, with a terrace in the rear which looked out over the river and miles of valley. We were there in that lovely spot for six historic days. I shall never forget what I saw during those days. For what seemed like endless time, the beaten and weary Germans moved through our lines to assembly areas. I have never seen so clearly the effect of total military defeat. They certainly cannot claim this time that their armies were technically undefeated. You remember of course the notorious Henlein who organized the Nazi regime in the Sudentenland. He was, I suppose, our most notorious take, since he gave himself up at our head-quarters. Later, he committed suicide, as did so many of the others. I wonder if in the whole history of mankind a regime has ever fallen with so many suicides, so much violence of every sort.

I hope sooner or later to achieve some sort of objectivity and philosophic detachment in regard to the Germans, but I have not achieved it yet. I profess not to know whether there are any 'good Germans,' whether the nation as a whole, or only a large part, or a small minority is responsible for the sins against humanity which Hitler has committed for twelve years. Right now, I am in the mood to say that to a large extent, the whole German people is responsible and that they must not only be punished but must be re-educated, given somehow a new set of val-ues, a new chance to prove themselves worthy of being in the family of civilized nations. I am in this sort of mood because I have seen, since coming into Ger-many on February 28, too much of their handiwork. Late in April, I went in a small group to see the Buchenwald Concentration Camp near Weimar. I had wondered sometimes if the reports from concentration camps had been exaggerat-ed in the newspapers in the United States. Although surely the evidence against the Nazis has always been overwhelming, I suppose I had the typical American skepticism which prevents our totally believing anything which seems to lie a little outside the reasonable. I shall never be in doubt again. The trip made me ill, as I knew it would, but I wanted to go and see for myself what went on in such places. I saw. I shall never forget it. There are no words to describe what and how one feels. I have read a dozen accounts of such places as Dachau and Lublin, but all the reading in the world couldn't have done to me what the sight of the huge furnaces, in which countless lives had been extinguished, did to me. My blood ran cold, and I could find no way in which it seemed suitable to react to such barbarism. The whole filthy, slimy mess at Buchenwald will live with me for the duration of my life. Some of the inmates were still there, in hospital wards undergoing treatment by our medics. There is no way to describe how they looked, except to say paradoxically they looked as though they were living on the other side of death. And the Jewish professor, from Prague, who conducted us through the place told us that of the twelve or so camps he had been confined in, Buchenwald was one of the *more humane*! I think we dare not forget Buchenwald. It is the complete culmination of the Nazi regime. It is not an isolated spot of evil, where a few SS men are creating their own terrorism unknown to the authorities. It is the carefully planned and scientifically executed means of obliterating human lives, which a ruthless state has declared undesirable. And the whole thing goes on with the approval and backing of the state, and certainly with some sort of indifference or approval on the part of the German people. If their resistance is so passive that such horrors as Buchenwald can exist under their very noses without their effectively opposing it, then surely they cannot but be jointly guilty with the state. (In trying to place the blame for such things correctly, I thought: who is to blame for the treatment of the Negro in the South? Most to blame are those who actively mistreat him, who lynch him and burn his body. But they are also guilty who pay him disgraceful wages and keep him in filth and poverty all his life. But there are also large numbers of us who are guilty because we see these things year after year and yet never raise an effective voice against them. There is practically nobody in the South, or for that matter, the whole country, who is not in some measure responsible for the Negro's position.)

Another thing I do not wish to forget in dealing with the Germans is their treatment of prisoners of war. Two or three days after final collapse, I talked at length one morning with a group of British lads captured and held since Dunkirk. The lad in charge of the group told their story, and he was shy and diffident and spoke with typical British understatement. But it was so difficult for him to underplay the suffering he and his fellows had been through, so obvious was it that the Nazis had been their usual repulsive selves. He spoke of the SS leader of their camp, and found it necessary to beg my pardon for calling him a "bastard of bastards." How thoroughly British, I thought, that after five years of imprisonment and suffering they should find it necessary to beg MY pardon for calling an SS man an appellation I am in the habit of reserving for my best friends. My conversation with these people was difficult beyond description. I gave them a box of rations and a carton of cigarettes, and their gratitude was so touching, so genuine and so vocal. They insisted over and over again that I had done so much for them, and all the while I kept thinking that while these people had been in prison I had still been at home, eating thrice daily and sleeping soundly between white sheets, far from suffering and bloodshed. When they thanked me so profusely, I literally could not reply. Some things one cannot put into words.

Since the end of the shooting, we have moved back into our zone of occupation in Germany. It is centered in Coburg, a beautiful little Bavarian town of about fifty thousand people. We are installed in a hotel here which is surprisingly modern and spacious, and life is very serene for the time being. For once, I have my own room with a soft bed, a radio, plenty of closet space, hot and cold water. Small details? Yes, no doubt they are, but after weeks and weeks of almost continuous movement, of never settling down anywhere for more than a few days, after throwing books, letters, dirty laundry, muddy boots into my duffel bag, it is simply wonderful to settle down, to get things put away and cleaned up. And to have the privacy of a room of one's own seems very good indeed to me after so much of the army's community life!

This much more about the end of the war: it came, very much as I thought it would, quietly and with little drama for us. I don't think undisciplined exuberance is an emotion of which those of us who saw so much of the war at first hand are capable. We are happy the war is over, but it is a happiness considerably modified by weariness, and loneliness, and a realization that the problems which confront us now are much tougher than mere military problems. And certainly for me, as for countless others, one other fact made a celebration hollow and empty. When we drank toasts on the evening of the seventh to the end of the war, mine was sentimental but sincere: "To the memory of a great American, who died on the eve of the victory for which he was more responsible than any other man." And surely Franklin Roosevelt's death stood between many of us and any real celebration of the victory when it came. We were in the midst of combat, literally speaking, when I heard the broadcast of the President's funeral. (I have never known whether it was the actual broadcast or a resume later in the day.) When the celebrant read the majestic, ancient words of committal from the Prayer Book, I could not keep the tears from my eyes. What a loss humanity suffered when he died. I wonder if ever again we shall see the likes of him.

I have not made wide publication of this fact, but I want to tell you. I managed to acquire a Bronze Star with an unusually generous citation for "meritorious service in connection with military operations against an enemy of the United States in Germany, March,

S/Sgt. Connor receiving the Bronze Star, April 1945.

April, 1945." I hope you know that I have retained enough balance not to take this too seriously, but for one reason I was proud of it. I never pretended that the army was my game, but I have learned to play it with some skill. My job has been routine and unspectacular, but like every other job in the army at times the lives of thousands of men hinged on the job being done right. Whether I had gotten the Bronze Star or not, it was enough to know that the General and the staff were satisfied that the job was done adequately. . . .

Waiting to Return Home: To Fr. Thorne Sparkman from Coburg, Germany, August 9, 1945

If during recent weeks, I have wondered what interests you were pursuing to the exclusion of writing letters to your apostates, I certainly wondered no longer when extensive clippings arrived yesterday from the Sunday *Times* of July 29. To think you had joined, however briefly, the wonderful estate of Stuart Taylor and Fred Hixon, et al, and I didn't even know about it to say some extra special prayers on your behalf. But I take it you survived the assignment in commendable manner. I enjoyed the article very much, especially where I thought I saw touches of the Sparkman humor here and there. (The most outstanding example of your restraint being the statement that the Chaplains' drill was a little less polished than the Baylor/McCallie version.) The pictures and the captions are delightful. "The Rev. Mr. Sparkman found the chow at the chaplains' school to his liking." Possibly, but that is *not* the expression he wore when the Rev. Mr. Sparkman ate steaks at Tomlinson's.

Things have moved on here about as usual since I last wrote you. I was away for about a month, during which time I spent eight days in London, two in Paris, and seven in Le Havre – or just north of Le Havre. Travel on the continent these days is incredibly complicated, but certainly the holiday in England more than compensated for the inconvenience involved in getting there. I had forgotten how tired I was of army routine until I got away. I enjoyed London tremendously. Of course, it seems wonderfully revived and rejuvenated now that the lights are really on again. I dislike sweeping conclusions made on short visits, but it seemed to me this time that the good will built up between ourselves and the British is simply incalculable. The American soldier, I believe, has in almost every case revised his opinion of what he once considered an effete and silly people. The British, in turn, have apparently disabused themselves of the idea that America is nothing but a vulgar province, the reaction which I'm told was common between the two wars. It seems to me that common understanding and sympathy between ourselves and our allies is one of the prime necessities of a decent world, and I think we've made a lot of progress with the British in that direction.

When I got back to Coburg, the disintegration of the division had already begun. The division is returning to the U.S. in October for deactivation, less most of us who have less than 85 points. Most of my friends have already gone, and I remain constantly ready to start packing. I want only two things – to go to the CBI [China-Burma-India Theatre of Operations] via the U.S. and to do a job there bigger and harder than I did here. I hope my combat experience will enable me to do some sort of work which really matters, because I've no desire to sit the next one out. Now that we have the very gratifying news that Russia has come in, plus the atomic bomb, perhaps we can hope that a year will see us through in the far east. In the light of these events, the intolerable possibility of getting shipped directly to the CBI seems a little less horrible.

The policy of non-fraternization has been virtually scrapped, as you no doubt know, although certainly few people here thought it was being obeyed while it was in effect. But those of us who make some effort to obey orders are having our first real chance to meet some of the Germans, to talk to them and try to see what goes on in their minds. I have been pleased by some of the things I have observed. I was afraid there was no conscience left in Germany, but apparently I was wrong. Some people do seem bitterly ashamed of what happened, and I don't mean the professional "nichts Nazis" we met when we first began the chase in Germany. But I am still convinced that to some degree *all* Germans are guilty for the crimes of the Nazi regime, not only those who beat the Jews but those who looked the other way. And it seems to me obvious that drastic measures for re-education must be employed, of what sort I do not pretend to know. I am sure, however, that AMG [Allied Military Government] is not capable of saving the German mind and soul. And I hope sooner or later, the Russians, the British and our own government will get around to giving the Germans a decent chance to recover from the past 12 years – for the world's sake more than for Germany's.

This is the army: as you may have read in the newspapers, the venereal disease rate has risen tremendously since V-E Day. Many frantic schemes have been thought up to lessen it, none more alien to reality than one instituted in the division a few days ago. At 11 pm (or 2300, since you learned the 24 hour system when you were a chaplain) an officer peers into every bed to make sure its occupant is there. If he isn't in by 11, he must be marched to the dispensary for preventative treatment. This scheme seems based on the idea that it is impossible to contract VD before 11 o'clock in the evening – an idea not without its charm but just a trifle naïve. One of the sillier aspects of the whole business locally is that we must have our beds labeled with our names to facilitate the task of the inspecting officer. Since I live in a single room alone, and since there is but one bed in the room, I thought it might be presumed that I sleep in that bed. But, No, said the master minds, each bed must be labeled. I complied as follows:

> Here lies the body of S/Sgt. Connor,
> A happy young man, not without honor.
> He fraternizes from nine to eleven
> Then sleeps soundly till morning at seven.
> Eight full hours in bed he relaxes
> Wholly without benefit of prophylaxis.

I forgot to mention that the lifting of non-fraternization has allowed us to be entertained by Germans. We go regularly to hear the Beyreuth symphony, which is an excellent orchestra. A string ensemble plays Viennese waltzes in the mess in the evenings, the Coburg Opera Company is in operation once more, and it is wonderful to hear good music again regularly. The audience at the Coburg Symphony last night was terribly cosmopolitan: the Americans, of course, a few British people, mostly Royal Navy, some French, a few Russians and Lithuanians, and several hundred Polish officers and men who have just arrived here with a cavalry brigade. And, thanks to the music, international relations were very smooth. But as one of my German friends (late an officer of *Wehrmacht* artillery!) has put it, "Art is international. Beethoven, Shakespeare. Did I not break my own teeth on Mark Twain?"

Always the optimist, perhaps I will see you before too long.

As ever,
George

Still Waiting to Return Home: To Fr. Thorne Sparkman from Coburg, Germany, August 21, 1945

Since I wrote you a couple of weeks ago, the complexion of the world has changed considerably. If you have not already done so, you may disregard all my comments about possible service in the Pacific and allied subjects. That is a fate from which I have been saved by the kind cooperativeness of Hirohito. A week has passed now since VJ Day, and I am none the less happy or optimistic about the future. It is impossible at this early date, of course, to predict with any accuracy just when I may expect to be free from these chains, but it seems to me, taking all things into consideration, that early summer is a safe guess. With a little luck, it is quite possible that it will be much earlier. I have only 60 points, but there are vast numbers of people with less service and less combat service than I, and their points are consequently very low. At any rate, 60 doesn't seem the hopelessly low score it seemed two weeks ago. Anyway, believe it or not, I am not straining at the leash now that I know it is just a matter of time. I can wait with patience, or with something that will pass for patience to those who don't look too carefully. The only really important thing is that I shall be home in time to enter seminary next September, and I think there is no possibility, or next to none, that I won't be. If it does seem that I am going to be a little late, I can always try throwing my weight around a bit to get out early. I'm sure people like Gen. Frazier and Charlie Coleman will be only too glad to see what they can do for me.

As for the immediate future, I am very much in the dark. The division has been alerted for shipment but so far we do not know whether those of us not yet eligible for discharge will come back with it. About the only chance, I think, will be for some lieutenant colonel to say the division can't possibly disband without us, since a certain number of 'essential men' can be taken back. I do not feel very strongly one way or another about this, except that I am very hopeful of getting a job somewhere which will involve some work. Nothing could be worse than sitting around for several months waiting for a discharge and having nothing to do. I do not mean to sound like an eager beaver, but I have found the army's long waiting periods the most nearly intolerable spots of my army career.

I should like very much to know what your opinion is on the matter of a seminary. Do you think Sewanee is still the place, or would you recommend another? I know when I was home last, it seemed possible that almost everybody there might resign in a year or so. I don't imagine that I got to know the place well during my three weeks there, but it seemed to me that Dr. James and Dr. Yerkes made up the seminary; I cannot imagine the place without them. What would you say to Virginia, or has it too suffered during the war years? I have no opinion since it has been only for the last few days that I have been minded to consider this problem at all. One thing worth noting is that this time I shall be much more independent financially, in my own right, than I was before. And I hope I do His Grace of Memphis no injustice when I suggest that that fact may be of prime importance. Do you think I should write the Bishop and tell him that I am still of the same mind about the priesthood? Are there any details you can think of which I ought to look after in preparation for taking up where I left off? I'll be grateful for your expert advice in any or all fields. . . .

This is meant to be only a note. There are a great many things I wish to write about in detail, but they must wait for the present. I hope you and Mrs. Sparkman enjoyed your holiday in Wilmington, and that you had better weather than we have had in Bavaria for the past two weeks. It has rained steadily.

As always,
George

On England and the English: To Fr. Thorne Sparkman, from somewhere in England, September 2, 1945

Despite your excellent advice about French ports, we spurned them all – as yet – and have settled down in England. I find that more satisfactory naturally, and despite the difficulties of the accent and the coin system, I expect to be well oriented very shortly. Of course, I can't tell you exactly where I am, but it is a good spot, and I think Sir Cecil Rhodes would approve of my location. The country hereabouts is lovely, and even with the English climate, I believe we should have a happy time here. There hasn't been much time as yet for getting around, but I'm hoping to get to London sometime soon. Some of our confederates have already been there and have come back with glowing stories of what can still be had to eat and drink, even after five years of war. I'm afraid that they may have missed some of the important points from their reports, but I suppose one cannot expect too much from those who consider England merely a poor and somewhat rustic facsimile of the United States. A good many of the lads were reassured, however, about the progress of English civilization when they discovered that they do have buses and trains "over here"!

So long as we remain here, I will apparently have no difficulty in finding appropriate churches. The RC's are already clearly stunned by the altogether unorthodox fact that the stateliest and loveliest churches do not emit Latin. We are within easy distance here of some very beautiful churches and at least one celebrated cathedral. The church closest to my barracks is small and extremely lovely; the altar is among the best I have seen anywhere. I discovered this little church purely by accident; I was walking one evening and came upon a clear cut path (perhaps once a bridle path) through a dense forest. Following it for about 75 yards, I came upon the church, almost hidden from view. At that time, a conference of American and British chaplains was going on there, and Evensong was in progress. This was my first sight of British chaplains. I had always been under the impression that their chaplains wore ordinary clerical garb, but, as you may know, they wear the full army uniform except the shirt. In its place, they wear their clerical collars and shirts. They certainly make a better impression, as a group, than our chaplains do.

Perhaps what makes me particularly grateful for the plethora of services is my experience on the ship. The ship chaplain was a Southern Baptist, sub-Huff variety – and to find him the chaplain on that particular ship was like finding Bob Jones installed as Dean of Canterbury, if you get what I mean. Although there were regular Anglican chaplains and service aboard, the time and place for any one of the services were never published. The Reverend Chaplain contributed immeasurably to the happiness of the troops by forbidding poker playing on the ship. He was quoted to me as having said that the army makes evangelism almost too easy. To stamp out sin, you simply forbid it!?! Neat, isn't it? Needless to say, all the poker players were in a state of grace when we landed. . . .

Department of Americans Who Aren't Quite On To It All, As Yet: all the barracks here are named with horribly unpronounceable English names. Also each back entrance, leading into the wash rooms, is labeled "Ablution." Recently one very insular young man lost his way on the post, and when the he inquired his way of an MP, he was asked the name of his barracks. The answer was quick and inevitable: "Oh, I live in Ablution 4"!

Please give all the staff, Genevieve and Mrs. S. my kindest regards. I hope your curates are behaving themselves properly, and that all goes well in your golf and with the lesser aspects of the Lord's work.

With best wishes,

George

Military Citations Re-visited, A Memoir (1970)

Though I don't really believe the calendar, in a few short weeks I'll be observing the twenty-fifth anniversary of my separation from the Army of the United States after an honorable, but undistinguished, career as an enlisted man in World War II. My army friendships have long since dwindled to a few notes exchanged at Christmas time. Since I rarely see anyone who can corroborate my memory of events, a certain air of unreality pervades my own recollections.

Occasionally, something in the news recreates that whole unbelievable army world for me, and some distant event is suddenly made vivid again. Two such news stories have been reported in the past few months. The first was the story of the hapless general whose citation for bravery, unhampered by dull facts, seems to have reached unprecedented imaginative heights in that limited but fascinating genre. The whole story brought back to me the weeks immediately following the Battle of the Bulge.

During that period I became something of an authority on military citations. There was a time when I thought I might – to use a phrase from the academic world – "do something with" the material I had collected. I think this period was the least tolerable in my whole military service: Everybody was edgy, the weather was miserable, quarters were crowded and inadequate. Only the officers in the headquarters in which I served rose above these limitations; they gave their time and talent to writing citations about the courage and gallantry each other had displayed during the battle. One had to admire the system. It would have been intolerable of course for Colonel X to write an account of what a splendid hero he had been; it was quite another matter for Major Y to write the account for him. Colonel X was then only too happy to reciprocate. One had only to be careful not to praise one's friend so highly as to diminish the glory of one's own achievement.

Since these masterpieces were turned over to enlisted clerks for typing, their texts, or at least generous excerpts from them, circulated freely in the headquarters. Though they were the works of several hands, there was a certain sameness. The prose was like nothing else in heaven or earth. Perhaps the most descriptive comment is to say that much of it read like what is called in *The New Yorker*, Rich, Beautiful Prose. After all these years, I remember only one elegant example. For unadorned eloquence and force, it can hardly be surpassed. In an account of a skirmish at a roadblock in Luxembourg, there occurred the beautiful climactic sentence: "At this point in the action, Lt. Colonel Smithfield personally threw a hand-grenade."

The second recent dispatch in which I found personal delight was the story of the dog who had been recommended for military decoration. The account indicated that this had resulted in great indignation, but I ascribe that to the fact that he belonged to a sergeant. People who served with me were apparently much more broad-minded.

In the late fall of 1945, I was stationed for a time in Maxhütte, a very small southern Bavarian village. There was absolutely no work to be done, everybody was bored to the breaking point, and about the only recreational facility was an enlisted men's club where we could drink beer, write letters and play cards or chess. One evening I was sitting there writing a letter amidst fogs of ennui when the door opened to admit several soldiers who were apparently an honor guard for the handsomest German Shepherd I think I have ever seen. He was enormous, very dark in color, with a finely shaped head and highly intelligent eyes; he walked with the dignity that his station in life obviously required. He wore on his person ample evidence of the general idleness and boredom of the troops: someone had made for him a perfectly tailored Eisenhower jacket. On his massive chest were rows of ribbons to elicit the envy of the most distinguished combat veteran. On either side he wore the chevrons of a staff sergeant. I felt constrained to describe this magnificent creature to my correspondent and to note that here was one staff sergeant concerning whose parentage the common allegation could hardly be denied.

My most vivid and satisfactory memory of a military citation comes also from the occupation period in Germany. Properly speaking, it has to do not with a military figure but with a civilian, an American Red Cross field director attached to our unit throughout our service in Europe.

The incredible and galling fact was that he had directed his generous attentions mainly not just to officers but to field grade officers. He seemed never to miss an opportunity to be of help to majors and colonels and even more glorious beings. I have a sharp memory of Christmas Eve 1944, during the Bulge, when he came into our headquarters building carrying a case of cigarettes. Nobody had any cigarettes left at that point, and the hearts of the steady smokers leaped up. He disappeared into the staff room where there were perhaps a dozen officers, mainly field grade; when he returned to our area, he was carrying no cigarettes whatever. But he did toss on my desk three packages of chewing gum and wished all seventeen enlisted men present a merry Christmas. Even with all the recent advances in linguistic candor, I am unable to quote here any of the comments these greetings elicited.

In the late summer of 1945, a directive appeared authorizing unit commanders to recommend for military decoration certain civilians who had not previously been eligible; understandably this included Red Cross field directors. (I hope it also included the Red Cross women, most of whom genuinely deserved such thanks.) Anyway, our field grade officer friends did not forget their kindly benefactor; they simply fell over each other getting a citation written to submit to division headquarters. Its eloquence made up in fervor what it may have lacked in verbal felicity. They were not an ungrateful bunch; I'll say that for them. After many days of revision and re-typing, the citation was thought to be worthy of its object.

One of my jobs was message center chief, and I was therefore responsible for materials going to and coming from division headquarters. I was up early one morning after a stint of night duty and thinking I might as well get an early start on the day's work, I began going through the materials intended for division. And what should I find on top of the heap but the Red Cross man's proposed citation. Suddenly I realized that fate was tapping me on the shoulder.

I was too prudent not to think out my situation: the division was almost ready to leave for the U.S.; I was about to be transferred to another outfit for further duty in Germany. It was six o'clock in the morning and nobody else was stirring. I went out to the incinerator and tore that citation into a thousand pieces. I have never struck a match with greater pleasure. It was my finest hour.

Published anonymously in The Chattanooga Times *on Christmas Day, 1970*

Politics and Religion

"There seem to be a good many people, locally and nationally, who forget
that there is a considerable distinction between the imperatives of the
everlasting Gospel entrusted to the Church and the current program of any
political party or special interest group."

(GC, May 25, 1980)

Republican or Democrat?

Since we are now in the midst of a political campaign, it may be a useful time to remind ourselves that there are Christian principles which are relevant to such occasions. Indeed if our religion is what we claim it is, it ought to offer us some guidance in every department of our lives.

One sometimes hears the statement that the Church should not "mingle in politics." If by this is meant that the Church as such ought not to sponsor or endorse political candidates or specific political measures, surely few would disagree. But if one means that the Church has no concerns in the political realm and should make no effort to influence political thought, many of us would vigorously dissent. Given the Christian doctrine of man as the child of God, it seems that at least three principles can be suggested as relevant to a political campaign:

1. We are expected to make the best use we can of the intelligence that God gave us. This means that we will, so far as we are able, substitute hard and careful thought for empty political slogans. It means also that we will not be led like sheep by any group, organization, neighbor, relative or friend; God gave us minds to use and we should use them.

2. In any campaign, we should be as unselfish as possible in deciding whom to support. This is easy to say and hard to do, but surely we ought not to pick our candidate on the basis of narrow personal or professional concerns. Our country faces increasingly difficult problems in an increasingly complex world; we have no moral right to choose for positions of authority only those persons who are most sensitive to our own interests.

3. All human institutions are imperfect and under judgment, including political parties; they are never more than imperfect instruments, though necessary instruments in a free society like our own. We ought to remember that they are fallible, that they do not contain within themselves everything necessary to our salvation, no matter how exuberantly we talk at election time.

No Christian can stand aloof from politics. If one does, one is doing one's bit for mediocrity and dishonesty in government, and surely no Christian wants this on his or her conscience. One's conduct in politics and elsewhere should demonstrate the application of Christian principles.

October 14, 1962

No Easy Answers

Several national columnists have commented recently about the ways in which religion has been injected into the current presidential primary campaigns. Surely not since 1960 have the religious views of the candidates been so much discussed and debated. One candidate has made very strong statements about the depth of his religious convictions. The recent local appearance of another candidate read in the newspaper accounts more like a revival meeting than a political rally.

James Reston wrote recently that the questions put to some of the candidates sound more as though we were choosing an archbishop than electing a president. Certainly those who are Christians as well as citizens have every right to pay attention to the candidates' religious views, but we would be mistaken to use religious faith as the chief criterion for making our choice. It is surely not enough that one believes in God and that one be a practicing Christian; if one is to be a fit president, he or she must also be possessed of the knowledge and skill and prudence required to execute the high office. Not many of the great issues which we face as a people lend themselves to easy solution simply by reference to Christian principles.

There is at least one thing that can be very disquieting in a candidate's embrace of the Christian faith: some versions of that faith seem to tempt their adherents to a feeling of omniscience. There are certainly religious temperaments which regard all questions as essentially simple, as susceptible to a plain choice between right and wrong. But a little serious reading of history ought to convince anyone that the most difficult times for any leader are those in which he or she must choose between undesirable and often sinful alternatives. Any version of the faith which glosses over this point is potentially dangerous in a political leader. One thing that gives Lincoln his stature in American history is the moral agony he felt over the Civil War.

Unless we have some magic means for isolating ourselves, we are all in for several months of political discussions. It is our responsibility as citizens and Christians to make the best choices we can. To do that, we must not only be faithful to our religious beliefs, but we must think clearly about the actual arena in which political decisions are made.

June 6, 1976

A Word about Politics

Fairly early in William Temple's Church career, he joined the British Labor Party. He did so because he thought that on the whole its aims and programs were nearer the Christian view than those of other parties of that era. But his official biography makes abundantly clear that he was always extremely careful not to allow Labor politics to become a substitute for Christian ethics. While he was Bishop of Manchester, he began to feel some dissatisfaction with attitudes of the Labor Party and he resigned from it. He is emphatic in his book *Christianity and Social Order* that the Church as such, or Christian leaders as such, must not embrace any particular program of social or political action.

I have been thinking a good deal recently about this aspect of Temple's career for a very simple reason: there seem to be a good many people, locally and nationally, who forget that there is a considerable distinction between the imperatives of the everlasting Gospel entrusted to the Church and the current program of any political party or special interest group. I recently heard a radio sermon – I heard only a small part, but it was quite enough – which would have done very nicely for a partisan political speech. Not too long ago in a local gathering I heard a long prayer in which a local clergyman instructed God in the virtues of free enterprise. I don't find free enterprise as one of the primary emphases of the New Testament, and I am astonished by those who seek to make it so.

Lately there has been an increased stirring of overt political activity by evangelical and fundamentalist Christian groups. Any citizen is free, of course, to embrace any view one wishes and to advocate that view as vigorously as he or she can. But whether Church leaders have the right in their official capacity to lend their support to specific political causes is another question, and a much more complicated one. I find such groups often espousing religious and political views that are quite unacceptable to me, and I resent any implication that as a Christian it is my duty to follow their lead.

Surely the basic point to remember is that every political, social, and economic view is under judgment – all of them imperfect, none of them fulfilling completely what could be called Christian aims. As Christians, our permanent citizenship is not of this world, and we do well to remember that fact in any political campaign.

May 25, 1980

The Will of God

Between now and the presidential election of 1988 we will be confronted with a good deal of imprecision in thought and in language. This will certainly be nothing new, but we seem to be in for more confusion in religious thought than we have witnessed in a single presidential campaign. One religious term is already being used in a loose and almost impossibly ambiguous way; I refer to "the will of God."

Already I have encountered, I believe three times, a statement obviously arising from discussion of the potential presidential bid by Pat Robertson. The writers have made the point that some Christians (usually designated as fundamentalist or evangelical or whatever) think it is possible to know the will of God.

Surely all Christians suppose it is possible, in some sense, to know the will of God. If we say in our Lord's own model prayer, "thy will be done," surely we are among other things suggesting that it is possible to know what that will is.

But like most religious and theological language – or any other language for that matter – the term "will of God" can mean quite different things to different people. Some Christians find it possible to speak of the will of God as though they have a direct connection which makes impossible any ambiguity or misunderstanding. Some years ago a member of what I should certainly call a religious cult told me that God guided him quite specifically in every detail of his life. If it was God's will for him to buy a new car, God indicated to him what make and what color. When the present Miss America was enthroned, I was interested to read that her grandmother felt that her selection had been the will of God.

That the Creator of the universe should concern Himself with such mundane details as the choice of an automobile and the choice of Miss America rather boggles the mind. But surely few of us who attempt to live out the Christian imperatives in our lives are willing to abandon the term "will of God" to those who use it so trivially. If members of the religious right, for example, make sweeping claims for their ability to know the will of God, what other Christians must do is to think and speak as clearly as possible about their own Christian responsibility.

In the report of a doctrinal commission in the Church of England published in 1938, William Temple suggested that a great deal of human misunderstanding arises from two related conditions: We use the same words to mean different things and we use different words to mean the same things. We need very much to keep this point in mind as we brace ourselves for the rhetoric and maneuvering aimed toward the presidential election two years hence. As I have suggested, there is plenty of ambiguity surrounding the question of what we mean when we speak of knowing the will of God. It is an important Christian concept, and it must not be abandoned (as other terms have been) to those who use language carelessly and sometimes sweepingly.

One prospective candidate's public utterances seem to suggest that he is in direct communication with the Throne itself. If this is true, what he needs with three million signatures on petitions is not entirely clear. One is almost cynical enough to suppose it has to do mainly with fund-raising. Reports of these confident utterances have several times included a reporter's statement that Christians (often qualified by an adjective) think it is possible "to know the will of God." Yes, indeed we do. We know that it is God's will that we love our neighbor, that we do our duty, that we behave righteously. But those are broad concepts and applying them to specific decisions and situations is by no means easy or automatic.

William Temple, in a famous preaching mission at Oxford in 1931, recounted an experience of his own, asking the audience not to regard him as "egotistic" in doing so. He was faced with an important career decision. He was doing work which he enjoyed and which he felt to be of value; he was invited to leave that work and take up a new position. Everyone he consulted suggested that he should stay put. He thought the matter over as carefully as he could. He writes, "having come to no conclusion at all, I began at eight o'clock in the evening to say my prayers, and for three hours, without pause, I tried to concentrate all my desires on knowing clearly what was God's will for me." And he concludes this account with two sentences which underline his point: "Each man has to find his own vocation. Every man is able to find that out if, quite sincerely, he will seek to do, not his own will, but God's." Let us not give up this concept though it is sometimes voiced in strange and wonderful ways.

October 19 & 26, 1986

Leaders

Hubert Humphrey: The Bedrock Essentials

Whatever one's politics, a recent lengthy news story about Hubert Humphrey should have spoken to all of us as Americans and perhaps even more especially as Christians. After a long, notable career in politics, Humphrey of course failed in his chief ambition, which was to be President of the United States. Moreover, he is now recovering from major surgery for cancer, with the threat which it always poses for the future. In his reaction to all this, he seems to have reached a philosophical position which any of us would do well to emulate.

Two points in the news story are paramount. One is Humphrey's attitude toward the prayers and good wishes for his recovery following the surgery. "I could feel it in my body," he said, "the warmth, the friendship, the prayers. It was really like a healing balm. I know it sounds almost irrational, I can't explain it, but I knew something was happening to me and I was getting strength from it." None of us could explain it, but there are few surely who have not had something of this same experience in ways large and small. When we enter into any dark valley, who is wise enough to assess the value of the intercession of our friends – or indeed of total strangers who pray in many lands 'for the whole state of Christ's

Church and the world'?

The other notable point is Humphrey's recognition that time is not on his side (surely any of us past a certain age must recognize this) and his acceptance of this fact and condition. Judging from the news story, one gathers that this is giving Humphrey a philosophical calm and resolution which allows him to immerse himself in his present work with no regret and little thought for what might have been: "That doesn't mean that you have to rush as if there are no days left. But you use each day and you can't afford to spend any time in self-pity." Surely if we try to live as Christians, that is the attitude we seek to achieve.

There is a question which we as Christians should sometimes ask ourselves: when everything secondary and superficial is stripped away, what is left as the bedrock essentials in our lives? Humphrey's attitude in the twilight of his life certainly helps to provide a good part of the answer.

February 13, 1977

Gene Roberts, Mayor

On more than one occasion I have quoted on this page a very useful comment by the late Bishop Theodore N. Barth. He was fond of saying that while Christians are not permitted to take pride in anything, lest we commit sin in doing so, it is permissible for us to feel "holy satisfaction." No doubt all of us in St. Peter's Church took that "holy satisfaction" in Gene Roberts' resounding victory at the polls on May 1st. The city government of course is entering a wholly new era, and it seems absolutely essential that we have the best possible leadership. I have every confidence that in Gene Roberts, that is exactly what we will get.

Gene Roberts, (ca. 1980).
Mayor of Chattanooga 1983-1997.

In his compelling little book called *Christianity and Social Order*, published in the midst of World War II, William Temple discussed the role which Christians, both individually and collectively, ought to play in public life. He argued that the Church does indeed have a role in politics, but perhaps its most important task is to develop Christians who will take their part in the work of governance. And

279

beyond that he wrote of "the pervasive sweetening of life and of all human relationships by those who carry with them something of the Mind of Christ, received
from Christian upbringing, from prayer and meditation, and from communion."

In this transitional period in city government, I am especially grateful to
see a person of Gene Roberts' Christian conviction in the post of chief executive.
It is, after all, the local government which has the greatest and most obvious
impact upon the life of the citizens. The great social and political questions facing
the city certainly call for the best in Christian thought. There are Christian principles to help us devise all policies for education, for dealing with crime, for economic growth, for the kind of civilized city which all of us would like to see. We
understand well enough that it is difficult to translate Christian principle into
political policy, but I for one want the assurance of knowing that there are those
in office who believe that Christian principle is relevant.

I have known Gene Roberts for forty years, and I have absolute confidence in his integrity, his thoughtfulness, his concern for all kinds of people.
Here at St. Peter's, where we claim him as one of our own, we should hold him
and his family especially in our prayers, knowing that the task he faces is daunt-
ing. I am glad to remember that among his attributes are the qualities of kindness, gentleness, and toughness. He will need all three.

May 12, 1990

In Praise of an Idealist: Jim Rouse*

In the May 12, 1991 issue of *Parade*, one of the feature articles was about
James Rouse, whom all of us should contemplate and, in my opinion, greatly
admire. Rouse, now 77 years old, is the retired president and founder of the
Rouse Company, urban planners, builders, and developers. The company has
some spectacular projects to its credit, including Columbia, Maryland, a city
between Baltimore and Washington that was carved out of farms and swampland.
Columbia is the kind of place which makes us realize what cities could be like if
we took the necessary effort.

But the focus of the article was on Jim Rouse's life since his retirement.
He created the Enterprise Foundation to help build the kind of housing which he

---

*On September 29, 1995, President Clinton presented Jim Rouse (1915-1996) with the Presidential
Medal of Freedom, the nation's highest civilian honor, to recognize his humanitarian service. "James
Rouse was a creative and passionate advocate who did more to revitalize America's cities than any-
one this century." – Donna E. Shalala, Secretary, U.S. Department of Health and Human Services

thinks the inner-city needs if our country is to be a truly great country. This is a project which commends itself to us as Christians. We cannot ignore the poverty and squalor which characterize the lives of the downhearted and the dispossessed. We cannot afford to abandon the inner-cities to drugs and poverty and crime. We surely proved in the Persian Gulf war that whatever we think is important, we can find the money to support. Rouse believes that we can also find the money, public and private, to make our cities decent and habitable again. We cannot only afford to do it; we cannot afford not to do it.

The Church of the Savior in Washington asked Rouse's advice and help in providing decent housing. The *Parade* article makes it clear that his work with that church changed Rouse's life, but it doesn't really explain how central to his life that church has become. (I have that from other sources, absolutely unimpeachable sources.) People call Rouse a visionary, and he reminds me in this regard of Pope John XXIII, who was said by one American writer (an Episcopal priest, by the way) really to believe in "the breathless promises of the Gospel." Rouse is pleased to agree that he is an idealist: he believes that anything that ought to be, can be.

Gene Roberts made a speech several years ago in which he paid some considerable attention to the nay sayers in the community. We certainly have our share. Every time they hear of some exciting new possibility for the city, they rush to their typewriters to explain to newspaper readers that it is hopelessly naive, wrongheaded, expensive, *etc.*, *etc.* It is the duty of our leadership of all kinds, including certainly the church, to remind us from time to time of people like Jim Rouse.

May 26, 1991

Community and Citizenship

"Every time we go into the voting booth, we should act
to make this a more just society."

(GC, June 23, 1996)

Meditation for Independence Day

From the conference held here several weeks ago called Chattanooga by Design, two notable statements quoted in *The Chattanooga Times'* coverage deserve to be remembered. The first is by Dean Jaquelin Robertson of the school of architecture at the University of Virginia: "Good cities are always acts of will. They don't just happen." The second is from Mayor Joe Riley of Charleston, South Carolina: "We can make our cities what we want them to be." In a real sense Dean Robertson and Mayor Riley are saying the same thing – that the city, any city, is a human construct, a work of art which we can make what we will.

Perhaps there is no better way (I use the word "perhaps" to avoid the appearance of dogmatism) to observe and celebrate the Fourth of July than by giving some thought to the nature and growth of the American city. In the dean's statement, the second sentence might well have read, "Cities need not just happen." Even casual observation is sometimes enough to show that cities, or a great part of cities, do indeed "just happen." Can anyone, for example, look at the strip development on Dayton Boulevard, or Brainerd Road, or Broad Street, and suppose that any of this took place as a result of careful and thoughtful planning?

Those of us who live in Chattanooga, most especially those of us who grew up here, are grown so accustomed to the magnificent beauty of this area that we become very casual about it. Few cities indeed are set in the kind of geographical splendor which we simply take for granted. Given the natural beauty which God has bestowed upon us, it is all the more incumbent upon us to build a city which is, in every way we can manage, worthy of its setting. As another speaker at the conference pointed out, "We are all designers of America. We are all responsible for what is ugly, and inhumane and derelict . . . ." Every act of carelessness or thoughtlessness or selfishness which leads to the demeaning of our environment is an immoral act.

Many years ago I presided over a television program which featured a discussion of the appearance of this city. It was my polite and neutral duty to listen calmly as one participant (I have mercifully forgotten who it was) explained to us that the billboard is essentially a work of art. How often it is when we are exploring some human enterprise, we find ourselves confronted with simple greed. In the prayer "For Our Country" (*BCP* 820) we thank God that He has given us "this good land for our heritage." Let us give some Independence Day thought to the kind of cities we are providing as our response to that heritage.

July 3, 1988

What Is It That Makes a City Great?
Chattanooga Arts and Education Council, Annual Meeting

As I think about the beginnings of The Adult Education Council and all the hard work that so many men and women have invested in it, I am very mindful of the significant relationship which I think we always saw between this city and the educational program which we were working to establish. And perhaps it is worth underlining that the full corporate title of the organization was The Adult Education Council of the Chattanooga Area. So when I use the word "Chattanooga" I am not talking about the corporate city limits; I am, of course, talking about the whole metropolitan area.

Robert Penn Warren says somewhere that "A man who loves his country totally is out of business as a writer." I kept thinking of this quotation during a panel discussion in the recent Conference on Southern Literature; I understood at least some of the participants to be saying that it is in good part out of the tension between the world as it is and the writer's hope of what it can become that he or she finds the incentive to write. I would paraphrase Warren and say that a person who loves his or her city totally is out of business as a citizen. One of the most useful functions such an organization as this can perform is to give us new ways to look at the city and to make judgments about it.

I remember with both pleasure and profit a leadership institute in 1954 in Racine, Wisconsin. The afternoon discussion group I chose had as its focus the nature of the American city, what things make it livable and attractive. Each person in the group was asked to assume that he or she was changing jobs, that he or she had two equally desirable and lucrative offers in two different cities. By what criteria would one choose between one city and another? This very useful device forced us to think about what we ourselves really require in a city, about what standards we should use in judging it.

Whatever our individual private index is to the quality of the city, I suspect that there is widespread agreement among us that certain conditions are essential to a city's greatness. Not total agreement, of course, but surely a strong consensus.

Whatever else we want, surely we want a stable and prosperous economy, a government – or in our case, alas, governments – enlightened and responsive to the public will, strong educational systems and institutions, racial justice and equality, the necessary facilities and mechanisms for the maintenance of the health and welfare of the citizenry. I think we would all agree that these things are minimum essentials without which it is impossible to think of civilized community life. And I believe that by and large in most of these areas, there has been measurable improvement over the past generation. Unfortunately the new Jerusalem is not yet arrived, and all of these areas require our continued watchfulness and dedicated effort. It is because of this need as well as others that all of us should rejoice in the establishment of Chattanooga Venture.

Beyond these things there are at least three aspects of the city which seem to me of enormous importance, aspects concerning which the Arts and Education Council is in an excellent position to further the public understanding. The first of these is the appearance of the city. Surely none can doubt that in the past generation we have come a long way in this regard.

Persons who have once lived here or who often visited here and who come back after a long absence are astonished by the appearance of the downtown area. Of course, a part of their reaction is to the architectural improvements, exciting building programs in parts of the central city. But they are also responding to the redesign of Market Street, the appearance of trees and other greenery which does so much to refresh the spirit and to soften the impression of endless asphalt and concrete. Surely Provident Insurance has taught us all that it is possible to enhance the aesthetic appearance even of parking lots. These returning visitors are responding also to beautifully restored buildings which are an important part of our heritage. The community has made substantial progress in its concern for its own appearance.

But the task is by no means finished; surely that fact is clear to all of us. The point has been made repeatedly that Chattanooga is extraordinarily fortunate in its natural beauty. We are so habituated to the unsightly strip development, the hideous neon, the raucous, ubiquitous billboard that we have come to accept them as a way of life.

Obviously, it is not enough merely to concern ourselves with the appearance of downtown, important as I believe that to be. We must be even more concerned with the economic vitality of the central city; we must not abandon the city in the headlong rush to the suburbs and the shopping malls. The city has really been the crown and focus of Western civilization as we have known it; it is quite impossible to think of that civilization's being sustained by an endless pattern of shopping malls. Valiant attempts are being made to deal with this problem in Chattanooga, and I hope this organization will do all it can to continue lending support and encouragement to this revitalization.

Another absolute essential in a city which aspires to a cultivated and civilized life is a wide variety of informal educational opportunities. Perhaps there is no idea which has so consistently informed the goals and activities of this organization, and certainly of many others, as the simple but crucial idea that education is life-long. There is never a time when any of us can say, my education is complete, I know all I want to know or need to know. To be alive is to be learning, to encounter new experience, to chart new paths. I believe this point is far clearer in the consciousness of this community now than it was when this council opened its doors.

Certainly in that hypothetical situation posed in the discussion group in Racine, one would not for a moment have considered locating in a city without something like a first-rate library. In the founding and development of this organization, the public library played a leading role. It is almost impossible to overstate the case for the library as an educational institution. One of the best ways to judge any educational program is to ask how much it increases the use of the library.

It is possible, of course, to be very narrow and parochial in making judgments about the city and what makes it the city it is. I hope you won't accuse me of such parochialism if I say that UTC and UC before it have played a crucial role in their civilizing influence on this community. Certainly since the merger of 1969, the university has found a wider and more diverse clientele and the resources to serve that clientele. I cannot imagine living in a city which did not have the kind of educational opportunity the university makes possible.

University of Tennessee, Chattanooga, 1969. Courtesy of the Chattanooga-Hamilton County Bicentennial Library.

Nor can I imagine living in a city without access to public television. I am quite aware that we owe some gratitude also to commercial television as an educational instrument, but its successes seem to me to be relatively few and its failures and shortcomings all too plentiful. I should hate to live in a city where one did not get the variety of political and social opinion which *The Chattanooga Times* makes available to us. I should hate to live in a city without an art museum, without the most diverse possible cultural opportunities. If we are not aware of these things as our blessings in Chattanooga, we are not paying attention.

But the most important thing about any city, I should think, is the people living in it; in the long run, it is the residents of the community who make it civilized or not, inhabitable or not, a curse or a blessing. In his essay called "Civilization," Emerson says: "The true test of civilization is, not the census, nor the size of cities, nor the crops, no, but the kind of man the country turns out." (I know his language is shockingly old-fashioned, but unless we are to revise everything written before, say, 1960, perhaps we can remember that the word "man" is being used here generically.)

Emerson of course is right that in judging a civilization, the quality of the human beings involved is infinitely more important than anything else. What finally makes Chattanooga an attractive and satisfying place to live is the presence here of enough of the people whom C. S. Lewis characterizes somewhere as the "people who really bear the burdens and ring true." When we think of an educational program and the city in which it functions, we are thinking most of all of the individuals involved, of what takes place in their hearts and minds, of what sort of commitment they are able and willing to make.

In preparation of these remarks, I reread the history of the Council's first six years which I wrote in 1958. I concluded that history with a quotation from a special report written earlier that year about a very ambitious project called Basic American Issues. Because I think these words are relevant to virtually everything the Council has done in all its 33 years, and because for me they make a supremely important point, I conclude with them:

"The most important question of all can probably never be answered with any assurance. How much influence will the project have on the life and thought of those persons who share in it? What difference will the project ultimately make in the individual's understanding of himself or herself and the world one lives in, in one's commitment to the great moral and intellectual tradition of Western society? The question can only be rhetorical, but my own confidence in the long, slow, difficult process of education persuades me to believe that we have every reason to be hopeful."

July 11, 1985

The Value of Taxes

A few weeks ago Public Works Commissioner Ron Littlefield held a meeting with representatives of businesses and apartment complexes to discuss the issue of dumpster pick-ups. I don't know where justice lies in this matter, and I can see plausibility in arguments on both sides. What caught my attention was a single comment from one of the participants. A representative of a downtown club was quoted in *The Times* as saying, "city services is the sugar that makes the bitter pill of taxation palatable." (Reagan himself always manages, as he did in his most recent press conference, to make taxes sound inherently evil.)

Surely it is a truism to say that taxes are the price we pay for civilization itself. Like any other taxpayer, I am always happy to see officials at every level of government spend money as prudently as possible. But I am thoroughly weary of officials and would-be officials whose only conviction seems to be an unwillingness to spend money on clearly essential services. Such timidity and lack of vision will not build here the kind of community most of us wish to see.

Most of us want a reasonable and tolerant religious climate, good schools, a superior public library, a lively recreational program, adequate parks, a vigorous cultural life and so on. These are things that cost money, and most of them are in the public sector.

The plight of the public schools, here and elsewhere, is to a significant degree testimony to our reluctance to pay for essential services.

Having spent a lifetime in education, I am quite aware that our deficiencies are by no means wholly due to a lack of enough money. In public discussion of our educational problems, not nearly enough attention is paid to the influence of our society upon the whole of the educational enterprise. The prestige of that enterprise, not too many years ago, is vastly diminished in our time. Education is a long, slow and hard process, and as a people we are too much inclined to look for the quick fix. So, it isn't entirely a lack of money which hampers the schools. But when one says that, one must also say that the schools suffer from our curious attitude toward taxes.

When I was a student at Central High School 50 years ago, the curriculum was significantly richer than it is now. While we were not then in the depths of the Great Depression, we were still living in its shadow. And yet, in modern foreign languages, we could choose among Spanish, French and German; now there is only Spanish. Then we could take four years of Latin; now there are barely two. We could take two years of speech, an opportunity which I found enormously valuable. No such program now exists. I was told a few years ago when I served on a ten-year evaluation committee at Central that there simply wasn't the money for a speech program. Pity. What makes taxes palatable is the quality of our common life they can make possible when they are wisely used.

November 3, 1987

Thoughts in an Election Year

The opening piece in the Talk of the Town in the current *New Yorker* is written by some anonymous person too young to have watched the first Kennedy-Nixon presidential debate in 1960, but who had recently seen an anniversary rerun on the Arts and Entertainment channel. Though he knew what was said at the time about the first debate, his own reaction was very different from what he expected. "Watching the debate brought home" to him, he writes, "the almost unbelievable debasement of American political discourse in the intervening thirty years." The writer is not uncritical of what he sees in both candidates, though he can also write that "neither man questions the other's integrity or patriotism, suggests that a debate between conservative and liberal points of view isn't healthy for the country, produces a programmed 'zinger,' resorts to a cheap line, delivers a canned speech, or pretends that running a government doesn't mean making difficult choices among competing interests."

One can hardly read these recent words and recall the 1988 debates without considerable pain. And the *New Yorker* piece is a reminder of a book reviewed in *The New York Times Book Review* for October 14: *Pledging Allegiance* by the journalist Sidney Blumenthal, a story of the 1988 campaign. I have read only the review and not the book, but it seems clear that Blumenthal excoriates both candidates equally. His comments on both are "withering," to use the reviewer's adjective. Reading about Blumenthal's gloomy assessment, I was reminded of a letter a good many years ago from an English friend. Why, he asked, in a country which has produced so many able people in so many fields do you get so many mediocrities running for president of the United States? This bipartisan question is one which all of us ought to ponder.

I have at least one clue: I think the electorate has to shoulder a good deal of the blame for the failures of American politics. Who put the incompetents in office but ourselves? (Certainly those who didn't vote at all have NO right to complain.) I think often of a *New Yorker* cartoon of perhaps twenty years ago. On a lonely country road, a poor beleaguered motorist is changing a flat tire in a downpour of rain. His two young children are in the car; they have obviously just made a suggestion to which he replies: "We can't change the channel. This is life!" I am afraid this cartoon is a parable for American life these days. Too many voters think we can just change the channel, or throw the rascals out, or revolt against taxes, or think up an inane slogan, or whatever.

November 4, 1990

Prisons, A Matter of Christian Conscience

A number of years ago, I clipped from *The Chattanooga Times* a column by Anthony Lewis which he concluded with a quotation from one of the great statesmen of the twentieth century. These words were spoken by Winston Churchill in the House of Commons on July 20, 1910, when he was Home Secretary. I have reread these words several times recently, and I have thought of them frequently since the management of the county prison at Silverdale was contracted to a private corporation.

"The mood and temper of the public in regard to the treatment of crime and criminals," Churchill said, "is one of the most unfailing tests of the civilization of any country. A calm and dispassionate recognition of the rights of the accused. . .and even of convicted criminals against the state. . .an unfaltering faith that there is treasure, if only you can find it, in the heart of every man – these are the symbols which . . . measure the stored-up strength of a nation, and are the sign and proof of a living virtue in it."

If Churchill is right, as I think he is, that our treatment of crime and criminals is an "unfailing test" of our civilization, then it seems to me highly immoral that government, at any level, should assign the management of prisons to private enterprise. This is too delicate and sensitive a matter by far to be put in the hands of any person or group who is not politically accountable. If it is true that prisons can be managed more efficiently or more economically by the private sector, then I believe it is the duty of all citizens to inquire in minute detail how this can be done. Anybody who can believe that private corporations are always more efficient than government has not had any problems recently with any corporate computer.

It seems a great pity that only one county commissioner stood his ground recently in the controversy over the renewal of the CCA contract. Saving money is not the highest virtue in life or in government. Civilization is an expensive enterprise, and taxes are the chief means by which we pay for it. It should rest uneasy on any Christian conscience that we have found such a dubious way to achieve efficiency or economy in the management of prisons.

October 7, 1986

The Death Penalty

Surely there must be room, as there is in most questions, for disagreement among Christians about the use of capital punishment in our society. For my own part, I must confess, I see no justification whatever for the death penalty. I have never seen any study that supports the notion that the death penalty is a deterrent to crime. Chief Justice Rehnquist and some of his colleagues on the Supreme Court now profess to believe that a speedier application of the death penalty is necessary to function as a deterrent. Speed and efficiency have their virtues but not here, not in the lessening of appeals and the rushing of convicted persons to the lethal injection. As a nation that likes to think of itself as civilized and even

Christian, surely haste is not the answer.

One of the most unseemly aspects of a sensational trial, such as the recent local sex abuse case, or a notable execution, as in the recent California gas chamber use, is the vocal and vindictive attitude of the friends and family members of those who have been wronged. We can all of course identify with those persons in their grief and pain; we too would suffer if friends or family were the victims of crime. But is there any justification for the kind of raw vengeance that these people so often exhibit in their behavior and comments in the courtroom and in the corridor? I think on Christian grounds we must say, no, there is no justification; such behavior is a violation of everything our Lord had to say about forgiveness. If we forgive as Christians only when it is easy to forgive, what virtue is there in that?

How do we find a truly rational explanation for the increasing violence in our society? The question is very complex and I am sure the answer – or answers – must be equally so. "It ain't complicated enough to be the truth," one character remarks to another in one of Faulkner's fictions. And any real answer here must be many-faceted. The ease with which handguns can be acquired is one factor. The almost casual use of violence in our entertainment, in television and the movies, is another. An old friend of mine, who is one of the shrewdest observers of the passing scene, puts it well, I think. "Violence," he says, "is the pornography of our time." Violence seems to grow apace and the more we see of it, the easier it is to accept and to view casually. I truly wonder sometimes what damage has been wrought by a generation's use of television as babysitter.

In a scene late in Shakespeare's *King Lear*, Lear discusses the vicissitudes of life with his old friend Gloucester, who has been blinded by the King's cruel son-in-law. "You see how the world goes," Lear says to him. And Gloucester replies, "I see it feelingly." And if we don't sharpen our own ability, as Christians and as human beings, to see the world feelingly, it will only grow more alien and more violent.

May 3, 1992

In Time of Crisis:
The Shooting of Black Women On 9th Street

In the magnificent prayer "For Our Country" (*BCP* 820), we pray among other things, "Save us from violence, discord, and confusion; from pride and arrogance, and from every evil way. Defend our liberties, and fashion into one united people the multitudes brought hither out of many kindreds and tongues." None of us who work and pray for a just society can view with anything but outrage the "violence, discord, and confusion" implicit in the recent shooting of several black women on Ninth Street [now Martin Luther King, Jr. Boulevard]. Certainly as Christian citizens of this community we are challenged to do everything we can to reduce the effect of this senseless and brutal act.

The question before us is: what can we do, as Christian citizens, most effectively to combat such violence and to continue to work toward the establishment of a society in which every human being is treated as a child of God? First and most important of all, we can and must continue to pray that "Thy kingdom come, Thy will be done." Obviously, every time we gather before the altar of St. Peter's Church in public worship, we are praying for the peace and welfare of the world. But let us in our prayers be especially mindful of the fears and hopes of our black brothers and sisters in Christ, asking God to use us in whatever way is open to work for racial justice and harmony.

Clearly we cannot simply say our prayers and then sit with piously folded hands waiting for others to do the work which is necessary to the just society. We need to remember often to our soul's health what someone said about prayer: "We pray as though everything depends upon God, and then we work as though everything depends upon ourselves." Our prayers and our work complement each other; either without the other is imperfect and incomplete.

We must do everything we can to strengthen the good and put down the evil in our community. We must stand up and be counted in the cause of justice. But we must not fail to pray even for those misguided people who seek their destiny in the Ku Klux Klan, asking God to give them repentance and better minds. But above all, we must remember that we have it on the authority of our Lord Himself that we will be recognized as Christians because we love one another.

May 4, 1980

Our Plain Duty:
Standing Against the Burning of Black Churches

All of my life I have hated to witness the wanton destruction of things that are not meant to be destroyed. I hate to see what was a perfectly functional automobile being towed away after an obviously serious accident. I was stationed for two months in the fall of 1945 in Schweinfurt, which had been heavily bombed during World War II and where the smell of death was still in the air. There was certainly no doubt in my mind about who should win the war; peace on Hitler's terms would have been unendurable. Nevertheless, I saw enough cruelty and violence in that war to last me a lifetime.

All these intensely personal things I say in order to put into some kind of context what follows. I believe that the vast majority of Americans are sickened by the burning and desecration of black churches in so many places, mainly southern. It seems incredible that on the border of the twenty-first century we could witness such hatred, such vindictive behavior. But how else are we to explain what is happening? I heard recently on National Public Radio a commentator whose normal tone of omniscience I find quite annoying, but in this case it seemed to me he was right. He suggested that there is no real evidence of a wide (or even a narrow) conspiracy, that he tends to think of what has been happening as an epidemic.

But surely we can take very little comfort in that fact because it is clear that so many burnings are possible only when racial hatred runs high. Given the position of the black church in the civil rights movement, the burnings clearly seem like an act of retaliation. These sub-humans appear to feel that it is their sacred duty to turn back the clock. Many thoughtful observers have suggested recently that we are losing – perhaps have lost already – the battle to make this society one characterized by justice and equity for every human being. It seems to me a battle we cannot, we must not, lose.

I believe this Church – I don't mean St. Peter's, I mean the Episcopal Church – must continue to stand up and be counted among those who long for racial justice and tolerance. We should give and give generously to the restoration of houses of worship, whose burning has been devastating to our black brothers and sisters in Christ. Every time we go into the voting booth, we should act to make this a more just society. We have a splendid opportunity in the forthcoming election for school board members. We are in nothing less than a war for justice.

June 23, 1996

Part V

Among Family and Friends

". . . a man with so many friends that you wonder how he has managed to keep up with the whole pack of them for so long. . . ."

Frederick Buechner

GC, Fred Buechner, Doug and Peggy Hale, June 1994.

For Those We Love

In a famous passage by Dom Gregory Dix, we are reminded of the many occasions for which the Holy Communion is celebrated, how many human reasons there are for making our communion with some special intention: "Men have found no better thing than this to do for kings at their crowning and for criminals going to the scaffold; for armies in triumph or for a bride and bridegroom in a little country church; for the proclamation of a dogma or for a good crop of wheat; for the wisdom of the Parliament of a mighty nation or for a sick old woman afraid to die . . . ."

Surely it is rare that we come to the communion service without a special intention of some sort, without coming to say prayers of intercession for some person or persons with special claim on our allegiance and affection. For let there be no mistake about it, it is with such persons that our intercessions begin. It is all very well to invest our concern in large abstractions – the poor, the downtrodden, the sick – but we begin with those people nearest and dearest to us, those who stand in the first two or three circles of our affection. Let us hope we go on to others, but unless we acknowledge our primary loyalties, there is something false and remote in our prayers for the distant and the unknown.

And how shall we make intercession for those we love, for those whose lives are often dearer to us than our own? Once a mother whose daughter was about to make an unsuitable marriage (at least from her mother's point of view) went for a long time to daily mass, in her words, "to storm the gates of heaven with my pleas." It is a poor approach, this approach which assumes for oneself a degree of wisdom almost divine, this approach which seeks to instruct God in what He "ought" to do for us and for those we love. Humility is a beautiful virtue, never more so than when we are praying for others, when we are seeking for them nothing less than the power and grace of God made operative in their lives.

The prayer "For Those We Love" (*BCP* 831) strikes precisely the right note: ". . . we entrust all who are dear to us to Thy never failing care and love for this life and for the life to come; knowing that Thou are doing for them better things than we can desire or pray for . . . ." We think as clearly as we can about those we love, we may even offer specific intercessions; but in the long run we commit them to God, knowing and rejoicing in the fact that they are continually in His care.

March 25, 1973

Sonnet in Memoriam

For My Mother, Isabelle Bible Connor (1890-1920)

To you whose life expired when mine began,
Whose face I have not seen, nor voice heard,
I write these lines and form with childish hand
A message to the dead, a loving word
To the spirit that will not ever die.
O, do not think because I shed no tears
My grief is any less, perhaps that I
Could now forget the lonely, barren years,
For such is not the case. But not always
Shall I abide with grief upon the earth;
One thing alone will keep me in my days:
The strength to live and hope which you gave birth.
It is enough; I with you – know it well! –
Shall evermore in Truth's proud temple dwell.

May/August, 1939

Infant GC with his Aunt Ida ("Aunt Dida"), September 1920.

Letter on GC's Father and Alan Paton's *Too Late the Phalarope*, April 4, 1964

Dear Charles,

    . . . I don't believe I mentioned that the reason I was brushing up on the *Phalarope* was for its use in a session with Herbie Levy, whom I've been tutoring a little. (This was the final session.) He was here this evening and the results were not brilliant, though once I began pressing and probing, he began to see the intention of the novel. But not before some false starts. He thought Pieter's father was quite a good father, "he gave him what he needed and sent him to school." What about the reaction when Pieter's guilt was discovered? Well, of course Pieter had done a *very* bad thing. Of course, I agreed, but the father?

I asked him what he would expect from *his* father if he ever did a "very bad thing"? He saw the point and admitted the old man was cold and cruel.

But you know there were points in our discussion at which I could hardly hold my voice steady. I always dread having to talk about the novel in class; it would be rather awkward to weep in class – especially in the presence of students who think I have ice water instead of blood in my veins! Herbie and I discussed the incident of the phalarope, and I suddenly realized one big reason why the book is so deeply moving for me. It is perhaps because this incident comes so near to showing what the relationship *could* have been, and one is shaken by the waste. For my own father and me, there was never any phalarope, too early or too late, and I suppose this adds to the pathos for me. . . .

Letter to Fr. Mike concerning GC's Father, August 1, 2000

Dear Mike,

According to my promise, I want to give you some notion of what I am asking of you. For one thing, I do NOT want to give you the impression that this is a matter which keeps me awake at night, but it is one I think of almost every day of my life. The problem is grounded in a few biographical facts. My mother died when I was about seven weeks old (she was buried on her 30th birthday). I have no doubt that my father was devastated by that loss, especially since I had two older brothers, but he did not re-marry for almost two and a half years. The pre-nuptial agreement had nothing to do with money and everything to do with his three sons. His second wife graciously agreed to accept into the household my two older brothers, but she wanted it clearly understood that she would not be responsible for the youngest son, then about two-and-a-half years old.

Therefore, I fortunately missed the cold, unloving treatment my two brothers were given. She was cruel to them in unbelievable ways. At the time this woman became my father's wife, Charles would have been just past his 12th birthday and Jim a little past his ninth.

Though I am telling you the plainest truth when I say that I don't lie awake over these matters, I still ask myself why Agnes took the approach she did. My brothers were still children and they too were devastated by our mother's death. The only plausible excuse I can think of is that she assumed children of their age (especially male children) could be very unruly, very hard to manage. Thus she laid down for them the most strict rules and she showed them as far as I could see (or they could see) no kindness or affection whatsoever. Thank God I escaped that treatment by virtue of the pre-nuptial agreement. (I use this term with irony, but the arrangement was simply accepted by all concerned.)

GC's aunts Stella (left), who was called Aunt Johnny, and Ida (right), whom he affectionately called Aunt Dida, a family nickname. Both were sisters of GC's father. Another sister, whom GC called Aunt Lizzie, was the mother of Grace Battle (see Eulogy in this Part). This picture was taken at 1012 Hanover Street, Aunt Johnny's home in North Chattanooga. Buddy, the bulldog between them, belonged to Aunt Johnny.

As for me, I landed on my feet; two of my father's sisters came to my rescue: Ida, who had never married and had helped three of her sisters raise their brood of children; and Stella, who had married Fred Robinson, already well on his way to being a wealthy man. It oversimplifies a little – but not much – to say that Ida supplied the energy and willingness and Stella supplied the money. The household in which I lived for the first seven plus years of my life was made up of my aunt Ida and my paternal grandmother; we lived in Red Bank on the same property which I recently sold after 104 years of family ownership. After my grandmother died in 1928, we were in and out of 1012 Hanover Street in North Chattanooga, the Robinson household. We sometimes spent the coldest months of the winter with them, but the first budding leaf brought us back to Martin Road in Red Bank. The family nickname for Miss Ida was Dida; I never called her anything else, nor did those cousins whom she had helped to raise. By the time of my grandmother's death, she was 56 years old, not an old woman by any means, but she remained unbelievably vigorous for another thirty years. She worked a 12-hour day in her vegetable and flower gardens and in countless other chores.

Of course there was no legal adoption of me nor any legally mandated support from my father. I think I may have been about ten years old when Dida shamed my father into sending her twenty dollars a month for my support. (Of course in 1930 that was more than a mere pittance.) He supplied the occasional present she demanded he give me. Even after all these years I find it difficult to think of him with any warmth whatever. In short, Mike, I do not know what forgiveness I owe him nor how in any case to manifest it. He died in 1950 and his wife survived him by 32 years.

I have been asking myself for a long time what my Christian duty is in this matter. I am not looking for a father confessor who will say to me, "Now, now, don't trouble yourself about all that." I have been looking for someone in whom I could feel confidence and who had the moral imagination to tell me what my duty is. I felt so immediately at ease when we had lunch at the Southside; as I drove away it struck me that you are the very kind of person I have been looking for.

But you must not think that I am looking for a large number of discussions over a long period of time. I don't think I really need that; I think I need only a couple of sessions, maybe only one, of an hour or two. I am fully cognizant of your priestly responsibilities and that they will certainly increase when the U. is in full operation. Moreover, I am even more cognizant of your health problems and the burden they place upon you. So if you tell me on August 7th that you just can't do this, I will not think one iota less of you. I will hope only that if this is the case, that we can have an occasional lunch when we can praise or deplore as the situation seems to require! I'm sorry this grew so long and I look forward to seeing you next Monday: *my* party of course, so let us have no unseemly disagreements in public.

Gratefully,

George

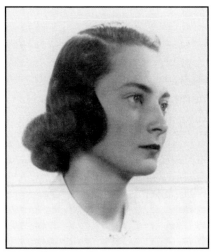

Eleanor Williamson, ca. 1940.

Eleanor Williamson was called "Tis" (with a soft "s") and graduated in 1940 from the University of Chattanooga with honors and a major in biology. GC was very much in love with her (the sonnet following is in her memory), but their lives took different paths. She was accepted to medical school at Vanderbilt, one of two women in her class, and GC attended seminary at the University of the South in 1942 for a month before being drafted in the U.S. Army. Tis later joined her uncle in medical practice in Columbia, Tennessee.

Sonnet in Memory

For E. W., 1918-1962

In that blinding hour when all at last came clear,
And what we guessed and hinted at grew into what you knew,
When you saw Reality Itself in radiant light
And understanding like a cloud enveloped you,
What vision then, my dear, what memory touched you still?
Did you recall our April walks, the hills in flame and snow?
Our praise for any book, our scorn for many another?
Did any knowledge then cause pain to know?
Did any memory burn? Could you grasp then
How, in exile you imposed, I went on loving you
And keeping faith when you urged all release?
Did you see at last that my most lavish words were true?
O in that light forever shining, that Pentecostal flame,
Remember my love, my dearest, remember my name!

1962-1963

Sonnet to a Friend

"There is no way you can calculate the value of a Doug Hale."
                    – Bill Nash, MTSU game, 1/31/73

No, there is no way, neither by the stars
Nor by the Tarot pack, nor by miraculous device
Like IBM or any other. I've tried these ways
With careful formulae, and prayerful and precise.
They do not work; there is no way. Yet driven
By insistent heart, I still forever yearn
To find at least some parallel; but there is none.
The limit of your worth is past my art to learn.

But neither can I trace the bounds for any gift of God:
I take the earth, the sun, the seasons, and the rain,
With simple gratitude, as gifts of grace unmerited,
Beyond my hope to comprehend or to explain.
And thus I take your love that quickens all my days,
A gift of shining grace, beyond my thanks, beyond my praise.

Definition

For C.T., 1963

There was, as best I can recall,
No outward sign at our first greeting
That supernatural forces were at work;
But surely grace was in our meeting.

I would not call it less who know
How few they are whom I call friend.
I'm careful of that simple word
That others love to twist and bend.

I leave others to adore a casual friend
And give themselves linguistic airs;
Such holy language I respect so much
I save it largely for my prayers.

Let others speak of hosts of friends;
My friends are rare and numbered few;
And I insist the very word be rare
To make it good enough for you.

Debased by overuse, the word's inadequate.
I'll turn perhaps to Latin or to Greek
To find, I trust, some useful phrase
To carry all the meaning that I seek.

But I expect too much of words;
The truth endures to my life's end:
There are no words quite good enough to tell
The glory that is mine to call you friend.

Charles Thornbury and GC, July 2002.

Letter on the Death of Bob Lanza's Father, June 25, 1971

This morning at 5 a.m. I left for Memphis to represent our parish at a young man's ordination. I got all the way to Tiftonia before the belt on the alternator broke. I spent almost two hours at the friendly Esso station getting it fixed and it was then too late to continue. So here I am with quite a lot of unexpected time on my hands; the first thing I'll do is write the letter to you that I meant to write yesterday.

In your most recent letter to me you wrote, "what your appearance in Huntsville meant to me I can only hope to understand in the future." What I intended my presence there to do, *inter alia*, was to indicate the concern and affection which are especially difficult at such times to find words for. This letter is in some degree an extension of the same purpose. I gathered from your comments the day you were here for lunch that you are feeling some self-reproach about what you did and didn't do in the last days of your father's life – and perhaps earlier as well. "My own heart let me more have pity on" [Gerard Manley Hopkins]. I know the feeling, believe me. I am not playing games with allusions; that great sonnet is worth pondering. I think what you are feeling is what everybody feels in greater or lesser degree. As one of my wisest friends once wrote me after her father's death, "So we learn at last that prodigality of affection is never enough."

All of us, God help us, fail those we love and to whom we are bound by the closest ties. We do what we can do, and it is never enough. Some things we cannot do because the pain is too great and we simply cannot go on reproaching ourselves for that fact. As one of your (and my) favorite

Carolyn Mitchell, GC's student worker in the mid-1960s, Bob Lanza, in his "We ♥ George Connor" t-shirt, and GC at his retirement gala, 1985.

poets said, "I dreamt the past was never past redeeming" [Richard Wilbur]. And I think in a real sense it never *is* past redeeming because if we are truly open to human experience, our failures give us the knowledge and incentive to redeem the past by words and deeds which are still open and possible for us. A crude example: I did something very unkind once to an old army comrade. It was less unkind than he thought but still damned unkind. (Too long and complicated to explain in a letter, though I will in conversation sometime.) Anyway, I had hardly done this stupid thing when I was overwhelmed with remorse. Though I can't make amends directly, this experience has made me infinitely more careful and thoughtful about treatment of others. In what way I can, I have redeemed that past.

So much for sage advice, not very helpful, I imagine. Better still, I keep you and your father and mother in my prayers. I'm aware this says little to you, but I keep thinking of someone who told his friend that there are more things in heaven and earth than are dreamt of in your philosophy. I am of course *not* suggesting any neat, facile religious explanation of all the pain and sorrow and frustration we are heir to. But there are flashes of light and moments of comfort and I welcome them. "For I greet him the days I meet him, and bless when I understand" [Hopkins]. And when I don't understand, all too often I still remember and believe that

> . . . all shall be well and
> All manner of thing shall be well
> By the purification of the motive
> In the ground of our beseeching.
>   [T.S. Eliot]

Again, I am not playing an allusion game, except incidentally; I am writing out of my heart's blood.

————————

————————

As you well know, there are few student errors that are really amusing. I think I found one of the exceptions yesterday in a freshman theme. I think the young man who wrote it is really quite bright. He was describing the problems of a rock band and toward the end, he wrote: ". . . when you hire a singer, believe an old pro, you've really given yourself a pain in the ass. In almost a month he will think himself to be a pre-Madonna."

Send me a word sometime that you are alive and well. If I can do anything to help, let me know. Do take care of yourself.

Love,

George

Letter on the Death of Hans Bingham, April 12, 1974

Dear Bob [Lanza],

I'm sorry not to have followed up my call sooner but there has simply been no time. Soon after I called you the other night, Carol Bingham called me and asked whether I would read some poems and "say a few words" at Hans' funeral. Naturally I would – but I must say it was about the toughest assignment I ever had. I went out to see Carol Wednesday afternoon and she asked me whether you knew about Hans' death. I told her I had called you and how sorry you were that you couldn't come. She had not supposed you would and understood quite well.

I read Frost's "Road Not Taken" and then quoted a line from two or three others. I'll send you a Xerox of my comments if you like, but they aren't very satisfactory. By grace I managed to keep my voice steady but just barely so.

The funeral was as you know yesterday afternoon. There was a fair crowd and people, I think, from most segments of his life. I think the pall-bearers were mainly early friends; a couple were probably Kappa Sigs. There were many flowers – too many, I think. I gave a book to the UTC Library instead, which I always prefer to do. The coffin was some sort of polished wood, very plain, and I noticed with approval that there was no pall of flowers on it.

He was buried in Chattanooga Memorial Park (where the swans and

Dr. Hans Gobers Bingham Jr. died at age 30, killed in a traffic accident. He was a nuclear physicist with the Atomic Energy Commission at Oak Ridge, TN. He was valedictorian of Red Bank High School, where he was also voted a member of the Pop Warner Little All American Football Team. When he attended the University of Chattanooga, he was President of the Kappa Sigma fraternity, vice president of the student body, a member of Blue Key, and was voted the Bachelor of Ugliness. He held a Ph.D. degree in nuclear physics from Florida State University, and received a prestigious Nuclear Science Fellowship after graduation. "[He] was involved in some of the more exciting basic research at ORNL [Oak Ridge Nuclear Laboratory] – that with the Isochronous Cyclotron."

From the Chattanooga Times *(April 10) and* The Oak Ridger, *April 9, 1974.*

ducks are, you may remember), which is only about a mile from my house as the crow flies. His grave is under an enormous long-needle pine tree and a few yards away the dogwoods, both white and pink, are a riot of bloom. It was a lovely, warm April day yesterday, and that was something to be grateful for.

You know how devoted I was to Hans and you know too then what a sense of loss I feel. But so do you, of course, and so do, I suspect, countless people who knew him. I can't recall whether I've told you that he and Carol came to see me in late February and spent a couple of hours here on a Saturday afternoon. How glad I am for that – and for all the times I had seen him in the last few years.

I hope things are going well for you and that your progress is solid if not spectacular. Happy Easter, or as my Jewish liquor dealer said to me this morning, "Have a nice weekend!"

Yours,

George

Eulogy for Hans Bingham, Jr. (1944-1974)

We are gathered here today to honor the memory of Hans Bingham, to express our love for him and our gratitude for his love and friendship for us, to celebrate the beauty of his life. We shall serve him poorly if we allow our thoughts to grow morbid or unduly sad. We cannot of course avoid an overwhelming sense of loss, but even more we thank God for the high privilege and pleasure of knowing him. Our lives will never be the same because they will be enriched by a knowledge of his goodness, his gentleness, his courage, his love.

Hans had an adventurous and hospitable attitude towards human experience, and the result was a wide variety of interests and enthusiasms. He was a scientist who did not isolate himself in a narrow and limited view of science, foregoing all else. A poem he enjoyed was Robert Frost's "The Road Not Taken," which tells us something about Hans. It is a familiar poem:

> Two roads diverged in a yellow wood,
> And sorry I could not travel both
> And be one traveler, long I stood
> And looked down one as far as I could
> To where it bent in the undergrowth;

Then took the other, as just as fair,
And having perhaps the better claim,
Because it was grassy and wanted wear;
Though as for that, the passing there
Had worn them really about the same,

And both that morning equally lay
In leaves no step had trodden black.
Oh, I kept the first for another day!
Yet knowing how way leads on to way,
I doubted if I should ever come back.

I shall be telling this with a sigh
Somewhere ages and ages hence:
Two roads diverged in a wood, and I –
I took the one less traveled by,
And that has made all the difference.

This poem is perhaps not so much about making a single choice as it is a poem about the necessity for making choices. Any choice we make inevitably involves some loss, the thing we cannot do, the road *not* taken. Hans Bingham kept his choices and opportunities as wide as life itself; he never allowed himself to be fitted into some narrow personal or professional mold which shut out the rest of the world. The laboratory was a kind of natural home for him – but then so were the concert hall, the theater, the library, and perhaps most of all the physical universe that he lived in. One modern poem includes the line, "The greatest poverty is not to live in a physical world." Hans did live in a physical world; he cherished that world and he rejoiced in its beauty.

Most important of all, he gave himself in love and friendship to other persons. He spoke in deeds more than he spoke in words, and his life was a continual witness for Christian charity. His were quiet affections, but they were strong and deep and they were each uniquely expressed. Another poem, a tribute to a soldier killed in World War II, says, "His laugh was real, his manners were homemade." It is a line that could have been written of Hans: everything about him was genuine; almost everything he said and did was distinctively and profoundly himself.

I spoke earlier of what surely all of us must feel: a great sense of loss. We cannot help feeling that, but surely we know also that this is not the whole truth.

At Lincoln's death one of his cabinet members said, "Now he belongs to the ages." And now we can say of Hans that he belongs to the ages, unfettered by the limitations of time and space. Those of us who loved him will remember him always, with affection and gratitude. He will always be part of our consciousness, of our perception of the world we live in. So we have lost him only in a superficial and transient sense. In the hands of God, he belongs to us always. Let us express our thanksgiving for this fact in the words of a traditional prayer:

"We seem to give him back to thee, dear God, who gavest him to us. Yet, as Thou didst not lose him in giving, so we have not lost him by his return. Not as the world giveth, givest Thou, O Lover of Souls! What Thou givest, Thou takest not away. For what is Thine is ours always, if we are Thine. Life is eternal; and love is immortal; and death is only a horizon; and a horizon is nothing save the limit of our sight.

"Lift us up, strong Son of God, that we may see further; cleanse our eyes that we may see more clearly; draw us closer to Thyself that we may know ourselves nearer to our beloved who are with Thee. And while Thou dost prepare a place for us, prepare us for that happy place, that where they are, and Thou art, we too may be; through Jesus Christ our Lord. Amen."

Simplicity: June McEwen

One of the pleasant fringe benefits of teaching, perhaps the most pleasant, is getting to know students as persons and, with some of them, ultimately establishing warm and durable friendships. One such person for me is June McEwen, who came to my freshman class at the university twenty years ago this fall, a wife and mother in her early thirties; both her children then in school, she was returning to college to earn her degree. A few choice spirits among my students I have been able to identify immediately, and June was one of them. The first writing she did for me was an ungraded introductory essay, not only beautifully written but deeply moving. I have been privileged for a long time to call June my friend, one whom I admire almost without limit.

I bring all of this up because June recently published a book, *The Gift of Simplicity* (Broadman Press). The subject of simplicity, a simpler lifestyle, is something she has been thinking about a great deal in the past few years. She is obeying Thoreau's familiar injunction, "Simplify! Simplify!" In the cluttered and overbusy lives that most of us live, it is very good advice indeed. And so is June's book full of good advice and practical suggestions about how one can actually go about endeavoring to achieve simplicity in one's life. She discusses simplicity from a biblical and spiritual point of view, realizing that the conditions under which we live and work have enormous influence upon the quality of our spiritual lives.

One way to judge a book is to take note of the authorities whom the writer quotes in support of the book's theme. Not surprisingly for me, June has chosen her quotations very well. One of the most appealing is from Elton Trueblood, the distinguished Quaker figure: "Most people whom I know are too busy. It is a common experience to see people rushing in every direction, no one having time to contemplate or to speak slowly with friends. At worst, we become a hectic generation, always running to keep up or to maintain our demanding schedules. . . ." Who does not recognize oneself in these words?

I hope a lot of people will read this book and a lot of groups use it for study and discussion. Anything we can do to bring our fragmented lives under discipline is certainly worth doing. In a typical gesture, June is contributing her royalties on the book to World Hunger; may those royalties make that organization very rich.

November 25, 1984

Olan Mills

One of William Temple's briefest but most significant books was a little volume written in the midst of World War II called *Christianity and Social Order*. So far as that order is concerned, Temple asserts in his book that the Church's chief task, though certainly not its only one, is to produce the kind of Christian people who will make all the difference in their personal lives and in their social responsibility. At the outset of his argument he says that "to make good Christian men and women is the Church's most important contribution."

Last week I thought of this passage when I read in the newspaper that Olan Mills had been selected as the recipient of the 1988 Manager of the Year award. The long story in *The Chattanooga Times* not only dealt with the essence of Olan's "management style" but also his wide involvement in community enterprises, corporate and educational and civic. Those of us who know how conscientious and hard-working he is in those responsibilities he accepts certainly felt no surprise in his designation as Manager of the Year. Any surprise we felt at St. Peter's might have been expressed in the simple question, why not sooner? A careful observer will note that prizes and awards often go (not always but often) to those who, sometimes with great cunning, work at getting them. If we had been obliged to wait to see Olan honored in this or any other way until he lifted a hand on his own behalf, we would have a long wait indeed. For all eternity, as a matter of fact.

C.S. Lewis speaks somewhere of those persons "who bear the burdens and ring true." Among the people I always think of as fit objects of that description are Olan and his wife. The life and work of any parish are of course enriched by those who take their Christian responsibilities seriously and do something about them. At St. Peter's Olan and Norma are certainly in this company, and all of us are in their debt.

May 15, 1988

In Memoriam: Jane

A note at Christmas from a friend living in New York brought the sad news of the death of a mutual friend after a long and difficult illness. The three of us were members of a small circle of friends in graduate school. While we have kept in touch, mainly by notes at Christmas time, we retained the sense of shared experiences, and the pleasure of the holiday was diminished by the word of Jane's death. I felt keen regret that I had not known of her illness so that I could have remembered her in my prayers.

But of course, Jane was not the first among friends and acquaintances to suffer in some valley of desolation which I knew nothing about. It is a common human experience to learn about many difficulties after the fact. And I am always glad to remember at such times that we pray in the Eucharist, Rite I, in the prayer for the whole state of Christ's Church and the world (and in parallel passages in Rite II) for "all those who in this transitory life, are in trouble, sorrow, need, sickness, or any other adversity." Those words are so inclusive that we cannot fail to pray for anyone who needs our prayers, whether known to us or not.

More recently I received a copy of the program leaflet used at my friend's memorial service held in St. Paul's Chapel at Columbia, where she served on the faculty of the library school. The service opened with an organ prelude of J. S. Bach selections, beginning with "Jesu, Joy of Man's Desiring." I was a bit startled to note that after the memorial remarks of four friends, there was a vocal solo, an American hymn arranged by Aaron Copeland: "Shall We Gather at the River?" I smiled when I saw that and wondered if I had ever told my friend Jane, herself a tolerant teetotaler, an old story about the fervent sermon by the preacher who regarded alcoholic beverages as one of the Seven Deadly Sins. He warned his flock about the evils of drink, ending with an eloquent promise: "We're going to rid the earth of this stuff. We'll take all the bourbon and throw it in the river.

We'll take all the Scotch and throw it in the river. We'll take all the gin, all the vodka, all the rum and throw it in the river. Hallelujah! Now let us stand and sing that glorious old hymn 'Shall We Gather at the River?' "

Jane was a person one does not forget. Her goodness and kindness, her happy spirit I will cherish for the rest of my life. I am glad to remember now that I was praying for her when I didn't even know that I was praying for her.

January 31, 1988

Emily: A Status Report

For the past several weeks, one of the names on the prayer list at the Sunday Eucharist has been Emily. Like many others on the list – though by no means all – she is prayed for in the anonymity of her first name only. I thought parishioners might like to know more. Emily lives in the Pacific Northwest; I knew about her illness because she is the barely-turned-three-year-old grandchild of one of my all-time favorite students at Chattanooga High School, too many years ago. When Emily was discovered earlier this summer to have a malignant tumor in her thigh, her grandmother wrote me and I'm sure a good many other people, asking our prayers. Thus her name is on the prayer list at St. Peter's.

Emily's tumor was recently removed by a skilled surgeon who was fortuitously available. She has begun a course of treatments both by radiation and by chemotherapy; the prognosis is positive and there is every reason to believe she is on the road to a full recovery. But as long as she is undergoing such rigorous therapy, we ought to keep her in our prayers, so her name will be on the prayer list for yet a while.

I have no hesitation in saying that I lack an adequate theory about what we may expect our prayers in Emily's case, or any other case, to accomplish. I doubt that an adequate theory is necessary, perhaps not even desirable. Another name on the current prayer list is that of an old friend who is presumably dying of a malignancy both inoperable and inevitably fatal. Or at least so we see it from a human vantage point. But I do not explain the impossibilities to God when I pray for my friend. Who knows in what way the divine mercy may touch him?

Surely it is part of Anglican temperament not to feel that we must understand everything about the faith in order to be found faithful. I have quoted on this page before (but not in a long time!) the verse ascribed to Elizabeth I, which, according to Bartlett's *Familiar Quotations* was her "answer on being asked her opinion of Christ's presence in the Sacrament":

'Twas God the word that spake it,
He took the Bread and brake it;
And what the word did make it,
That I believe, and take it.

No doubt that is a very Anglican formulation, but I find it a perfectly satisfying one. As C.S. Lewis writes somewhere, after all our Lord did not say of the
Bread, "Take and understand," but "Take and eat."

By the same token, I do not know what weight our prayers have in the
divine economy, but the New Testament admonitions to pray are certainly to be
taken seriously and obeyed. In praying for thirty or forty people on a Sunday (or
any other time) we obviously leave out of consideration thousands upon thousands. But in all the Prayers of the People in the Eucharist, we are also remembering those we do not name or even know. Perhaps the point is clearest in "the
prayer for the whole state of Christ's Church and the world." Meanwhile we pray,
among others, for Emily.

October 2, 1994

Eulogy for Mae Davis Thornbury (1911-2001)

The Angels
by Paul Ramsey

The angels take approaches. Some enter by root
And others cloud-following, cloud-brightening, come.
Some in street clothes walk a gloomy one or two miles
And do not enter conversations, but watch trees,
City soot, gables that are cracked with many snows,
And limp into a bar, and hear each word which speaks
Even with broken love to cheer them as they turn,
And look into the empty mirrors, and depart.
And there are lovely angels which touch young faces;
These are as necessary to us as breathing
And words rarely capture the approach of their wings.
And there are great angels on great hills when wars come
Who know so much about justice they grow weary
But hold their beautiful adamant swords steady
And have such endurance we have great need of them.

And there are others who can do nothing but stand
In a given place and enter water and trees,
Wooden benches, a turn of weed-fixed light, a stone
White barred with grey and singular in its standing.
At certain hours one can view their plain, their sacred
Countenances. These are the ones whom I know best,
My companions, my intercessors, and my friends.

To speak words of one's own devising on an occasion like this is not for me an easy task. To read Paul Ramsey's beautiful poem "The Angels" is one thing, but it is quite another thing to speak from the heart about this remarkable woman, Mae Davis Thornbury. My mind goes back to the first time I met Mrs. Thornbury. I am reasonably certain it was at the time when Charles was still an undergraduate at the university. He wanted me to visit the Thornbury Market and to meet his mother, who presided over it. My visit lasted perhaps no more than five or ten minutes, but it was time enough to discover, not at all to my surprise, that she was quite as remarkable as I had been told.

Early in my life I came to the conviction that whoever is in charge of any sort of enterprise – business, professional, academic, whatever – that person in charge sets the tone for the enterprise. That visit was longer ago than either her sons or I like to remember, but everything that I observed in that brief visit has been confirmed by every comment I have heard and every direct experience of my own of her hospitality, her warm and genial manner, and her sturdy common sense.

Mae Thornbury, ca. 1985.

William Temple, Archbishop of Canterbury during World War II and the most distinguished Anglican of the 20th century, has given us in his book *Christian Faith and Life*, a perfect parable. The world we live in, he wrote – I am quoting from memory and these may not be his precise words – the world we live in is like a shop window where some mischievous person has changed all the price-tags, so that the really worth-while things have cheap tags while the meretricious and unworthy goods have the high price tags. Mrs. Thornbury has spent her long life in acknowledging what is worthy and desirable. As a single example, she decided that her sons would have the best education she could manage. All three of them are graduates of McCallie School and of the University of Chattanooga, and all three of them have gone on to graduate or professional schools. I don't for a moment mean to suggest that the three sons stood idly by, depending entirely upon their mother for encour-agement and support. Each of them carried his share of hard work. But their mother had the good judgment to recognize the value and necessity of education.

The 31st and final chapter of Proverbs says a great deal in praise of a good woman. Toward the end of the chapter, these words are found in the King James Version: "She openeth her mouth with wisdom; and in her tongue is the law of kindness. She looketh well to the ways of her household, and eateth not the bread of idleness. Her children arise up and call her blessed. Many daughters have done virtuously, but thou excellest them all." The words came from a writer who lived a great many centuries ago, but they provide a quite appropriate tribute for women like Mae Thornbury.

As I am sure is true of all of us here, I have delighted to sit at the tables of some very gracious hostesses, but none of them more gracious than Mrs. Thorn-bury. And I cannot remember in my life any hostess who could compete with what Mrs. Thornbury provided for her guests. Busy as her life always was, she obviously delighted in providing a veritable feast for everybody who sat at her table. I remember writing her a thank-you note once after such a feast, and I felt I had to be honest with her and I told her that as much as I enjoyed the dinner, I did not have quite enough to eat. She had offered her guests that evening only eight or ten vegetables and three or four kinds of meat, and the desserts clearly showed her utter indifference to calories and cholesterol. But several such dinners I shall never forget.

I end with a brief prayer by John Donne, Anglican priest and poet of the 17th century, and dean of St. Paul's Cathedral in London:

> Bring us, O Lord God, at our last awakening into the house
> and gate of heaven, to enter into that gate and dwell in that
> house, where there shall be no darkness nor dazzling, but one
> equal light; no noise nor silence, but one equal music; no fears
> nor hopes, but one equal possession; no ends nor beginnings,

but one equal eternity; in the habitations of Thy glory and dominion, world without end.

February 15, 2001

Canine Observations

The 18th century poet Christopher Smart in his "Jubilate Agno" ("Rejoice in the Lamb") wrote a section beginning: "For I will consider my Cat Jeoffry / For he is the servant of the Living God, duly and daily serving him." For nearly a hundred lines, Smart "considers Jeoffry," detailing how the cat performs a worthy and admirable role as one of God's creatures.

Perhaps if Smart can be permitted to wax eloquent about his cat, I may be allowed one of these commentaries to discuss a young collie named Laird, whom I have owned – loosely speaking – for nearly three months now. Since the subject matter of these pages has always been quite varied, I hope no reader will feel that I take an impossible liberty. Like Jeoffry, Laird is a member of God's created universe, and his response to that condition deserves observation and comment.

Laird is successor to an old and venerable collie named Angus, who went to his reward in mid-summer. He had achieved such dignity that I had forgotten what puppies were like, but I have

Laird of Midlothian, June, 1980.

been reminded. Laird begins every day the way a Christian should begin every day: he welcomes it with fervent joy, the expression of which is almost violent in its enthusiasm. He praises his Creator with boundless energy, with the same happy abandon with which David danced before the ark. David's behavior led to Michal's rebuke; I accept Laird's cavorting with pleasure and even with envy.

I can report to the theologians one modest and not very scientific experiment. One of Angus's most winning ways was his method of expressing contrition. When he had done anything for which he was scolded, or even given the silent treatment, his habit was to sit down immediately in front of me and offer

313

his paw by way of apology. With Laird, I have been very careful not to induce feelings of guilt that might express themselves in a similar way. It has made no difference. On several occasions he has behaved badly and has realized that he behaved badly. While he has not learned to offer his paw, he has clearly shown by ears laid back and head ducked that he realizes that he is a miserable sinner.

To substitute animals for human beings is sentimental and indefensible. But to recognize in animals the work of a loving Creator is one of the ways in which we rejoice in the creation. All the works of the Lord praise Him: even Jeoffry; even Laird.

November 28, 1976

Letter on the Death of Michael, September 1, 1964

Dear Charles,

This will be brief, but I must tell you that yesterday afternoon I was obliged to have Mike put to sleep. He has been having increasing difficulty with circulation, heart, kidneys – and finally everything seemed to bunch up on him.

Dr. Williams said he could probably live at most a month longer, but he would suffer a great deal. So, we took the humane way, but I'm sure I need not tell you how desolate I feel.

Love always,
George

GC with Michael (1963) at 1012 Hanover Street.
Photograph by Jeff Carr.

Letters on Michael and New Puppy Angus, September 2, 5, and 19, 1964

Dear Charles,

It didn't occur to me that I could possibly get a letter from you today, so it was doubly welcome when it did come. I don't know whether you'll get this before you go away for the weekend or not, but I write briefly and hastily for a couple of reasons.

314

First, my note yesterday about Mike must have sounded very gloomy and I don't want you to think I've gone into a permanent decline. Of course I miss him terribly, but I have already got a new dog and so the cycle begins again. He is a four-and-a-half month old collie, but his appearance is very different from Mike's. He has the energy of a whirlwind and about the same behavior pattern. Thus far he is nameless. When I get some done, I'll send you a snapshot. . . .

Herbert called me yesterday afternoon to wish me a happy birthday – I was amazed that he knew, much less remembered! Then when I came home from dinner at the Bradleys', he had left a package – a very fine little wooden figure he had gotten at that Indian shop in the Read House. The card said: "I'm sorry about the unwrapped package. Twenty years from now, I hope we're both around so I may wish you a happy 94th birthday – Herbert." I also got your rude card. (All Thornburys may go to hell.)

I like the picture very much; thank you for sending it. And of course I am grateful for the inscription. In small difficulties and large, the thought of your friendship warms and comforts me more than you can imagine.

More, and better, soon. Meanwhile, have a good Labor Day weekend and take care of yourself.

Love always,
George

September 5th, 1964 . . . I do not propose to make each letter a progress report on the new puppy, but I must tell you that he is flourishing. I never saw such energy! Mike was always so sedate – about the most wicked thing he did was to run through a pile of leaves and scatter them. This boy has his long nose stuck into everything. His kennel owner specified that he should have vitamins – what he really should have is tranquilizers! I haven't fully decided, but I think I'll name him Angus. . . .

This afternoon I cleaned out the dog-house, which hadn't been done since it was moved over here as Mike had spurned it any-way. One thing it yielded up from under the straw was a potato chip bag. I could not keep the tears from my eyes! I'll never be able to open potato chips again without thinking of Mike. There are always of course a thousand ways to remember. C.S. Lewis is right; if one doesn't want to suffer, one should never commit himself, not even to a dog.

Puppy Angus (Laird MacTavish), 1964.

September 19, 1964 . . . I think how strange and how interesting memory is. I've always been fascinated with the little flashes of memory recorded in the *Quartets*. This is also in my mind because of Mike's death and the sudden flash of recollection I have of him. How interesting it is that we see things very differently in retrospect from the way we saw them at the time. I don't know whether I ever told you what led to my having that pen built in the back yard. Three years ago this month he acquired suddenly and without warning a taste for chicken; he brought home two of the neighbor's fryers one Sunday morning. There seemed no solution but to build a pen and keep him there or on the porch except when I was with him. So for six months, until the neighbors sold their chickens, I kept him up. (On his second day of freedom, he was hit by the car.) Anyway, every afternoon for those six months I walked him for at least a mile, often farther. At the time it often seemed a chore and a nuisance, as it did later when we were on Hanover Street, though often, especially in good weather, I did enjoy it! Now, however, I look back on the walks with very great pleasure. No matter how busy I was, the walks had to be done and they became a kind of quiet respite for me. Not very well put, but I'm sure you understand me. I'm thinking of working off some of Angus' excess energy by daily walks, though we'd probably have to walk 25 miles to reduce his energy in any appreciable way.

George Scorey DVM

GC and puppy Tay, four months, a moment of mutual adoration at 3110 Martin Road (1990).

In our Anglican mother Church, Ashland Terrace Animal Hospital, just down the street, would be in St. Peter's Parish. When I recommend – indeed insist upon – my friends' taking their pets there, I am really urging upon them a quite remarkable man named George Scorey. I tell my friends that what Clif Cleaveland MD is to me as my "primary-care" giver (not the happiest of phrases, I think), George Scorey DVM is to Tay of Stirling.

Those at St. Peter's who do not understand that statement have simply not had the privilege of meeting Tay of Stirling. Though meeting Tay is rather like meeting a whirlwind, he has great charm and great beauty. He is my first tri-color collie. If you don't quite know what that means, all you need do is look up the word "collie" in the American Heritage Dictionary (1992) where Tay or his brother or his cousin posed for the illustration. "Gorgeous" is what all women and a good many men call him. George Scorey has been his primary-care giver since Tay's first appointment there in April 1990.

But I must write about Tay's predecessor in my almost fifty-year succession of collies. His name was Laird and he was the Lassie-type collie, the most beautiful golden color of that strain I ever saw. He also of course was George Scorey's patient. It was in Laird's death that George Scorey deepened my gratitude and affection, both for Laird and for himself. Two of my earlier collies had been "put down," to use the British expression, including alas the beautiful Laird. Like all large dogs, he suffered the pains of arthritis. (So do I, not because I am a big dog but because I am an old dog.) On a dazzlingly beautiful morning in April 1990, I brought him to George Scorey for the last time.

One moment of that morning I will never be able to banish from my mind. When George was ready to give Laird the merciful lethal injection, he said to me, "Just hold his head and speak to him quietly" and I managed to say to Laird through my tears "Everything will be all right." But I remember the everlasting sadness of what I could NOT say: Almost every night, when he had settled into his bed I always patted his head and said in the words of Horatio to the dying Hamlet: "Good night, sweet prince, and flights of angels sing thee to thy rest." I could not for a King's ransom have said those words at the moment they would have been not metaphorical but literal. But they are the words I always think of when I remember that bright spring morning when George Scorey's kindness to me was beyond all telling.

October 11, 1998

Eulogy for the Reverend Thorne Sparkman

On the Occasion of a Requiem Eucharist

We are gathered here this afternoon not so much to mourn the death of Thorne Sparkman as to celebrate his long and useful life. Surely we have cause, those of us who knew him, to thank God for his influence not only upon ourselves but upon all those whose lives he touched, both here at St. Paul's and in the larger community. Even those who did not know him, or knew him only slightly, can rejoice in his fruitful ministry as rector of this parish and his leadership in the community from 1938 to 1949.

Rev. Thorne Sparkman, ca. 1940.

This signed picture was always on GC's bureau. "The Reverend Thorne Sparkman of Christ Church, Baltimore," Dr. Edwin Lindsey writes, "was called on September 29, 1938, to be rector of St. Paul's . . . Mr. Sparkman was a man of great ability; a Rhodes Scholar, a brilliant preacher . . . His intellectual powers, incisive reasoning, wit, broad knowledge, and many accomplishments made him especially admired by young men of the church." - From A History of St. Paul's Episcopal Church, Chattanooga, Tennessee, 1853-1953, *Edwin S. Lindsey, published by Vestry of St. Paul's Parish (1953).*

I speak of him first as preacher and teacher. The two functions are linked in my mind for an excellent reason: someone has written somewhere that William Temple found it virtually impossible to preach without also teaching at the same time. It seems to me that precisely the same thing can be said of Dr. Sparkman; I don't believe he made much distinction in his own mind between those two functions. For some years *The Chimes* carried each week a sort of paragraph outline of the sermon of the previous Sunday, and one cannot browse through those sermon outlines without realizing not only how attractive and compelling they make the Christian faith but how much also they enlarge one's knowledge of that faith. Some years ago when Dr. Sparkman was here for a week of noonday Lenten preaching, on one occasion Paul Ramsey and I walked back to the University together, discussing what made his sermons what they were. Paul suggested that his preaching style was clearly unique, and I think that's true. I have heard my share of really good preachers, and certainly there are many ways of being a first-rate preacher. Thorne Sparkman's way was absolutely his own. I remember two things which may throw some light on this matter. I remember Dr. Sparkman's saying that every serious flaw of preaching is a flaw of character.

Perhaps the second memory may throw some light on that statement. I remember his telling a simple story, probably in a sermon, though I cannot be sure. A priest was passing through a town and remembered that a seminary class-mate lived there. He stopped by the rectory and they had a pleasant visit, follow-ing which they went next door to look at the church, accompanied by the host's seven-year-old son. While the two friends stood back in the center aisle admiring the architecture, the little boy climbed into the pulpit. He began a sermon in pantomime; finally in his frustration that he wasn't getting their attention, he waved his arms vigorously above his head and cried, "Look at me! Look at me!" "Oh yes," said the visiting priest to his friend, "I have heard that sermon before." I'm afraid we've all heard that sermon before.

Some adjectives which could be justly applied to Dr. Sparkman's preach-ing style are 'quiet,' 'restrained,' 'understated.' The late Dr. William Masterson was discussing this style once, and he said, "Oh, very occasionally, in great emotional stress, he might lift one finger." If true (and I never saw it happen), that was cer-tainly the exception. He never tried to do with voice or gesture what the thought and the words would not do. He had of course an incomparably beautiful speak-ing voice, but he never tried to play any tricks with that voice.

One more recollection of Dr. Sparkman as preacher and teacher. We had in those days an organization called the Young People's Forum which met on Sunday evening. We did not define 'young people' very strictly; most of us, I sup-pose, were in college, but there were a lot of young professional people and a few of indeterminate age. As a very new Episcopalian, I learned a great deal in the sessions of the Forum, much of it – by no means all – in St. George's Chapel where we began with prayers and brief meditation by Dr. Sparkman. I would give a handsome price for those meditations in any form. Whenever I think of T. S. Eliot's still points in his *Four Quartets*, those moments when time and eternity intersect, I think of those meditations in St. George's Chapel. One of those occa-sions, I can date precisely – Sunday, December 7, 1941, the day the attention of the world was fixed on Pearl Harbor.

Now I speak of Thorne Sparkman as pastor; here too one is obliged to use superlatives. In a letter after he went to Hilton Head more than twenty years ago, he wrote, "I still consider myself more pastor than prophet." As he was a superb preacher and teacher, so also was he a superb pastor. When I think of his pas-toral talents, I think inevitably of my first meeting with him, just about this time of year in 1940. I had come under the church's spell several years earlier and regarded myself as belonging to the soul of St. Paul's, if not to the body, but I had not yet been confirmed. Giving in to the pressure of some of my friends, I made an appointment to talk with Dr. Sparkman in his office. With all the confidence and insouciance of a college sophomore, as I then was, I outlined for him the terms on which I was prepared to be received into the Episcopal Church. He listened to me with perfect courtesy. He did not throw me out of his office; he did not even permit himself to smile in amusement. I joined the confirmation class which began soon afterward, and my life has never been the same.

I know the conditions of life have changed and pastoral calling is far more difficult than it was in those days. But I shall always remember that he visited those who were "in trouble, sorrow, need, sickness, or any other adversity." There were almost countless people in the parish who had stories to tell of his kindness and sturdy support, often well beyond the call of duty. I remember with special gratitude the case of a friend and classmate of my own who was critically ill one summer. He was not a member of the parish nor likely to become one, but Dr. Sparkman stopped in his hospital room almost every day over several weeks. Similar stories abound among members of the parish and indeed in the wider community. After he left St. Paul's and came back for noonday preaching or whatever, it was always interesting to note how many people outside the parish showed up to hear him and to greet him.

The pastoral concern, which was so revealing of the man, was especially manifested towards members of the church staff. Dr. Edwin Lindsey included in his centennial history of St. Paul's statements about the parish from the living former rectors. At the end of Dr. Sparkman's statement, he said, "Lastly, and not as an afterthought, during the years that I have known St. Paul's the best work in it has been done by the parish secretary . . . . One should be as careful as possible in the selection of the clergy, but the best parish will always be the parish with the best parish secretary." Small wonder that Genevieve Ernst's attitude toward Dr. Sparkman stopped just short of idolatry – if it did indeed stop.

One more example of his treatment of staff. When Dr. Sparkman and his family moved to Bryn Mawr in the fall of 1949, Will King, who was then sexton, took a part of his vacation to go with them and help them move. Like Dr. Sparkman himself, Will was an avid baseball fan. While he was in the East, Dr. Sparkman arranged for Will to go to a World Series game in New York where he occupied a box seat belonging, I believe, to the president of Pennsylvania Railroad.

I close with two quotations, which through the years I have found increasingly memorable – and instructive. During Dr. Sparkman's incumbency here, General Seminary in New York was searching for a dean and Dr. Sparkman's name was on the list of prospects. A parishioner asked him whether he would accept the deanship. "I have made it a firm rule," he said, "never to accept any position until it is offered to me."

The other is more personal, for which I ask your indulgence. When I was a student at the University of Chattanooga, in good weather young men took chairs from the commons, as we called it, beneath the Oak Street stadium and sat outside watching the traffic pass and solving the problems of the human race. One fine spring day, I was sitting out there in late morning when Dr. Sparkman drove by. About four o'clock that afternoon, having been to a couple of classes and done other useful things, I was sitting there again – and again he drove by. This time he stopped, and I went over to the car to assure him what a productive day I had had, that I hadn't wasted all my time, *etc., etc.* He was reminded of an incident when he was a Rhodes Scholar at Oxford. A young man not totally devoted to his studies was summoned by his tutor. "Mr. So-and-so," the tutor said, "every time I look out of my study window, you are going out the West gate. What can you say for yourself?" "Nothing, I'm afraid, sir," the young man replied, "except that every time I go out the West gate, you seem to be looking out of your study window."

For all of us here, especially for participants in the Thorne Sparkman School of Religion, for countless people, living and dead, I give thanks for Thorne Sparkman's life, for his example, for the sturdiness and beauty of his faith. For that life and for the gifts which he bestowed upon us, what can we say except, thanks be to God.

February 22, 1989

Eulogy for Grace Loomis Battle (1903-1999)

Good afternoon, ladies and gentlemen. This eulogy for Grace Loomis Battle does not purport to be a disinterested, impartial view of the qualities of this remarkable woman. For that sort of presentation, a different eulogist would have been required. As perhaps most of you know already, Grace and I were first cousins; her mother and my father were brother and sister.

In the last generation or so, it seems to me, the emphasis has shifted in a memorial service like this or even in the burial service itself; it has shifted to become more a celebration and thanksgiving for the life of the departed rather than a mournful recital of the sense of loss and deprivation.

This is the approach that Dr. Dudley took at the graveside service last

Grace Battle on her 90th birthday.

Thursday in Forest Hills Cemetery in his thoughtful and incisive words; and it is certainly also the approach that I shall take in these brief remarks.

I begin with an incident that took place probably about seventy-five years ago but which I remember vividly after all these years. At the corner of 7th and Market Streets in downtown Chattanooga, in the space now occupied by Waldenbooks, there was the most marvelous institution, certainly marvelous in the eyes of a child: George K. Brown's Ice Cream Palace. The name George K. Brown was a substitution and the Americanization of the most unpronounceable Greek names one could imagine. I can still remember the tables which I believe were round with metal legs somewhat like a double corkscrew. I will not pretend to remember to what sort of delicacy Grace treated me, but in those days, it need have been no more than plain vanilla ice cream. I remember that the glass of water was so cold, it made my tonsils ache. I was carrying a little leather change purse, widely used by children of my day; I laid it on the table when we sat down. After we had sated ourselves with George K. Brown's delicacies and were going out the door, the waitress came running after us saying, "Oh, madam, your little boy left his change purse." Grace's answer was swift and emphatic: "He is NOT my little boy!" With a child's intuition, I recognized all the implications of that firm statement and I giggled for some time until Grace said, not unkindly, "That will be enough of that."

I think this is my first memory of Grace, and it not only amuses me to this good day, but even more it reminds me of her kindness and generosity. I cannot remember a Christmas or a birthday since that memorable occasion at George K. Brown's that I did not receive from her some thoughtful gift. And I have seen through all the years that I was merely an early beneficiary of her kindness. She came from a large family; she had eight brothers and sisters, and there have always been plenty of children to be remembered. Did she show any partiality? Yes, she did; she has been partial to girls. She always wanted to be sure that the girls were treated at least as well as the boys.

It seems to me fair to say that this same generosity she has shown to children has characterized all of her giving to charitable causes in which she has been interested. It seems hardly necessary to say that in the competition for the charity dollar, only the extraordinarily rich – the Ted Turners and the Bill Gateses of the world – can respond to all of the appeals or even to most of them. Grace Battle gave to those causes which her Christian conscience commended to her. In the presence of her trust officer and other fiscal experts, I certainly do not wish to leave the impression that she asked my advice about her giving. But in one limited way, I was sometimes a party to her decisions. She would ask me my judgment of this or that organization. Was it effective? Was it efficient? Did I know anybody on the staff or on the board of the organization or organizations she was considering? In such discussions she was mainly thinking out loud and using me for a sounding board.

Grace was committed to the mission of the church to foster justice, peace, and good will in the world. I feel quite sure that all her planning for her own stewardship was grounded in her own church, to which she was intensely loyal. I do not mean that her thinking had to do entirely with the Signal Mountain Presbyterian Church, but rather with the whole Christian enterprise, with the universal church, with the Body of Christ. But for Grace as for all of us "who profess and call [ourselves] Christian," this loyalty begins with our own primary allegiance and spreads outwards. For her the center was the Signal Mountain Presbyterian Church, and I think Dr. Dudley more than confirmed this loyalty by his words at Forest Hills last Thursday morning.

Grace Battle had a real talent – perhaps one ought to say a real genius – for friendship. I have encountered recently in several places the claim that friendship is especially precious in the Judaic and the Christian traditions. Certainly the narratives in both Old and New Testaments would validate that claim. I think friendship is one thing Grace especially cherished here at the Alexian Village in the last few years of her life. These are sometimes called the twilight years, but somehow that does not seem quite to express Grace's approach to her life. The formal name of the painting of Whistler's mother (presumably in her 'twilight' years) was *Arrangement in Grey and Black*; I don't think Grace would have made a very good model for that painting.

She was a woman who was not reluctant to speak her mind, firmly and clearly. When I was a quite new resident and barely beginning to learn the ropes at the Village, someone asked me, "Did you already know some people here before you came?" "Yes, a good many," I replied; "for example Grace Battle is my cousin. You have perhaps heard of her?" The answer was laughter which I could not quite interpret. I should think most people here would be at least on nodding acquaintance with this woman; otherwise why would the handrail between the Brow View and the main building be known as the Grace Battle Memorial

Parkway? (Jack Henry has given me permission to say that he devised the name, originally as the Grace Battle Parkway, but it is now appropriate to call it her memorial parkway.)

It was my pleasure to introduce her to at least three medical specialists of my acquaintance, and to each of them I said, privately, "You must be clear about one thing: you are going to earn your fee. She is a grateful patient, but she will make quite clear what she expects of you." I must say that all three behaved to her satisfaction and the relationship with each was amiable.

I dare say there are not many here who know that she had a police record. No, she was not on any FBI list of the ten most dangerous criminals. I mean something quite different: I mean she expressed herself to policemen with the same force and candor that she used for a lot of other people. I was myself witness to two such occasions. Once when I was still in my teens, Grace and I ran into each other downtown. Both of us were on our way to visit a favorite aunt who lived on Hanover Street across the river in North Chattanooga. Grace of course offered me a ride, which I gratefully accepted. There were then only two bridges across the Tennessee River and she naturally chose the Market Street Bridge. She was in the extreme right lane to turn on Frazier Avenue. In those days there were no traffic lights at that intersection and a live policeman stood there to direct the traffic. He called out to Grace, "Step it up, please! Faster!" She rolled down the window and said to him, "We are going quite as fast as we want to, thank you."

The other incident was rather more heated. It was several years later and it was in that same spot at the North end of the Market Street Bridge. I have forgotten what infraction she was guilty of, but the policeman pulled her over and took out his book of tickets and began to write a citation. When she handed him her driver's license he said, "Are you Dick Battle's wife?" "Yes, I am," she said, and I heard the threatening hostility in her voice. "Why, I know Dick well; I wouldn't think of giving his wife a ticket." "Why, that is ridiculous," she said, "if I am guilty of what you say I am, it is your duty to give me a ticket!" But he waved her on and walked away. She fumed all the way to Hanover Street.

As I warned you at the outset of these remarks, they were not going to be impartial. I am very partial; I had too much affection for Grace, too much gratitude for all the kindnesses she has shown me, quite literally all of my life.

I end with a brief stately passage from John Donne, that priest and poet of the 17th century, and the Dean of St. Paul's Cathedral in London:

Bring us, O Lord God, at our last awakening into the house and gate of heaven, to enter into that gate and dwell in that house, where there shall be no darkness nor dazzling, but one equal light; no noise nor silence, but one equal music; no fears nor hopes, but one equal possession; no ends nor beginnings, but one equal eternity; in the habitations of Thy glory and dominion, world without end. May the souls of the faithful departed, by the mercy of God rest in peace, and light perpetual shine upon them. Amen.

August 2, 1999

Memories of a Friend

When one has had a long and happy friendship with someone, it is perhaps often difficult to remember one's first meeting with that friend. But I remember quite clearly my first meeting with Ben Kramer. The 1940 fall semester at the University of Chattanooga had begun a few days earlier. I was standing with Bill Mills in front of Tomlinson's Restaurant on McCallie Avenue at Houston Street. Ben was in some class with Bill and Bill introduced us. I still remember Ben's saying, "I wish I could talk with you longer, but I need to get down to the Read House," where he and his mother were living.

Bill told me that Ben had just transferred from Washington and Lee in Lexington, Va. The college community is always interested in new faces and new personalities at the beginning of a new academic year. Ben had a commanding presence; he was tall and handsome, with a beautiful speaking voice. (And singing voice too, as I soon discovered.) Ben's arrival coincided with the arrival of Dorothy Hackett Ward as head of speech and drama and therefore also the University Players.

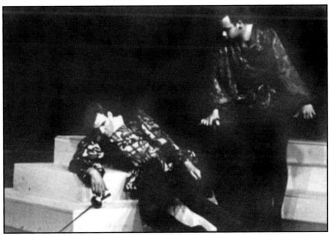

GC as Mercutio (left) in Shakespeare's Romeo and Juliet *(ca. 1941).*

325

Ben was in almost every play during his two years at UC. I remember best his role as Romeo in the first Shakespearean play in Mrs. Ward's long tenure in the department. After graduation he went on to a remarkable career in radio and television. I do not pretend to be an impartial judge because he became my best friend in college. A sentimental song in that era included the words "When other nights and other days / Have found us gone our separate ways." Ben and I certainly went our separate ways, but we never lost touch with each other. In a telephone conversation a year or so ago, he said to me, "Of the people who really matter in my life, I have known you longer than I have known any other person." I found that a very moving revelation.

Early on in his career, the program director of a large radio station in New York suggested that he change his name to Carl King. I think for a time he used the name only professionally, but it soon became so complicated to juggle the two names that he decided to adopt the professional name legally. Once not too long ago, again on the telephone, I called him Ben without thinking. I apologized and he said, "You are perfectly welcome to call me Ben anytime you want to." Perhaps if double surnames had been as popular as they have become, he might have called himself Kramer-King.

I think without question of the UC and UTC people that I know, he had the most varied and distinguished career in radio and television. He began in Chattanooga by putting WDEF on the air in 1941 and worked there, mainly part-time, for the most of the time he remained in Chattanooga. Because of serious and almost fatal surgery in the spring of 1942, he was exempted from military service. During World War II he went from here to Washington, thence to Philadelphia, thence to New York.

In the relatively early days of television, he did a syndicated series of pro-grams called "King's Crossroad." This was the time that the Ford Foundation was heavily subsidizing "Omnibus," a sort of imaginative variety program, much supe-rior to much of the drivel we see on television nowadays. Once I suggested to Carl that "King's Crossroad" was a low budget "Omnibus." Exactly, he said.

My old friend died in North Palm Beach, Florida, on January 16, 2001. Unfortunately circumstances made it impossible for me to go to Florida for the memorial service on January 27, but close to the hour of the service, I went to the chapel at Alexian Village, where I now live, and read the burial office in the Book of Common Prayer. I prayed not only for him but also for his wife Jean, his daughter Melissa, and son Geoffrey, and his infant granddaughter.

As I walked back to my apartment, I thought of a poem by an ancient Greek, Callimachus, the memorial poem to his friend Heraclitus:

They told me, Heraclitus, they told me you were dead.

They brought me bitter news to hear and bitter tears to shed.

I wept as I remembered how often you and I

Had tired the sun with talking and sent him down the sky.

Those of us who knew him best will cherish the memory of Ben Kramer and Carl King.

Spring 2001

UTC English Department Faculty, ca. 1972. Photograph courtesy of Tom Ware. Left to right:

Craig Barrow	*Arlie Herron*	*Robert Vallier*	*Thomas Ware*
Mary Cocke	*Robert Welch*	*John Tinkler*	*Enid Bryan*
Vernon Lattin	*Thomas Preston*	*William Shurr*	*Daniel Jones*
Patricia McAuley	*Harry Glasser*	*George Connor*	
Roland Carter	*Robert Fulton*	*Paul Ramsey*	

Eulogy for George Coleman Connor

Alpha Society Meeting, April 15, 2003

On the occasion of George Connor's retirement dinner in June of 1985, several hundred people gathered in the Crystal Ballroom of the Read House to honor him – but also to acknowledge many of the remarkable contradictions in his character and demeanor. Almost everyone who knew him even casually would come to recognize that he was in many ways a rich embodiment of the best elements of the Chattanooga community and of this university, which he dearly loved and served in a number of capacities for twenty-six years, as faculty member, as chairman of the English department, as executive assistant to the chancellor, and ultimately as Guerry Professor – and beyond that honor, not only the recipient of the UTC Distinguished Alumnus Award but the UT National Alumni Outstanding Teacher Award.

A 1947 graduate of the University of Chattanooga, he came back here to complete his degree after serving in the U.S. Army in World War II, where among other adventures he was in the famous and perilous Battle of the Bulge in 1945, earning the Bronze Star for meritorious service. After several years of teaching in local secondary schools, he became the founding director of what is now known as the Adult Education Council – and later received his Master of Arts from Middlebury College. Always prominently active in community and especially Episcopal Church affairs, he lectured widely on Christian themes and literary topics, also writing essays, book reviews, meditations, and commentaries. Widely admired for extending his generosity, his wisdom, and his depth of spirit in a positive and gracious manner, he carved out a career in Chattanooga difficult to emulate and all but impossible to equal.

But I do not wish to be unduly reverent here, nor would he wish it. Those who knew him best soon learned that despite his formidable bearing, his demand for excellence, and his sometimes thundering eloquence, he was endowed with an especially quick and vivid sense of humor, often at its best when ironic and self-deprecating. The executive editor of the *Chattanooga Times-Free Press* Tom Griscom, at that time a student to George, recalled a moment one afternoon in the chancellor's suite when he saw the great man deeply pondering over some papers. "Gee, Mr. Connor," he said, "that's quite a picture with the light streaming in over your shoulders like that!"

"Young man," George answered, "what makes you think that light is coming from outside?" Tom once stated that it took years for him to consider Mr. Connor a mere mortal. Small wonder.

One of George's favorite stories about himself recounted an incident when he was waiting in the outer office of a friend with whom he was to have lunch. As he sat there, the receptionist stared at him for a time, then asked, "Aren't you Mr. Connor?"

"Yes."

"And didn't you used to teach at East Lake Junior High?"

"Yes."

"You was my English teacher there!" Somewhat taken aback, he was not quite certain he heard her correctly.

"And didn't you used to teach at City High?"

"Yes."

"You was my English teacher there, too!"

Episodes such as that, George admitted, helped keep him humble, although a number of his students over the years would probably not have agreed with that self-assessment. A young co-ed, still chafing from a rebuke she had deserved in one of his classes, found her way to the office of the Dean of Women, to register her complaint. "You must remember," she was told, "that Mr. Connor is a far more decent man than he seems to be."

He was once referred to as a combination of Genghis Khan and Socrates. Indeed, on that occasion of his retirement dinner, the mayor of Chattanooga, Gene Roberts, presented George with a street sign for the driveway up to his house. On one side was the designation Genghis Khan Connor Drive; on the other, Socrates Connor Drive.

I doubt seriously that George ever for a moment considered posting that sign: and I think that he truly was, certainly in his own mind, despite some of his reputation, humble, devout, and deeply grateful for the experiences and the blessings in his life. He died last August 20, at the age of 81. He had been an active member of Alpha since 1959.

In the early 16th century, Robert Whittinton, a grammarian and rhetorician, composed a passage about Sir Thomas More as an exercise for schoolboys to translate into Latin. It reads in part: "[He was] a man of angel's wit and singular learning; I know not his fellow. For where is the man of that gentleness... and affability? And as time requireth, a man of marvelous mirth and pastime; and sometimes of as sad a gravity; a man for all seasons?" A man for all seasons: such also was our colleague and friend George Connor. Take him for all in all, to paraphrase Hamlet's utterance, we shall not look upon his like again.

Dr. Thomas C. Ware
Professor of English, UTC

George Coleman Connor

George Connor was born September 1, 1920, and grew up in Red Bank, Tennessee. He graduated from Central High School (1938) and received his A.B. degree with a major in American literature from the University of Chattanooga (1947). He studied at the School of Theology, University of the South (1946-47), and at the Bread Loaf School of English, Middlebury College, Vermont, where he earned an M.A. in literature in 1955. Susquehanna University awarded him an honorary Doctor of Humane Letters in 1994, "in recognition," the citation reads, "of your exemplary life as a teacher and your dedication to quality in life and literature."

When he was a student at the University of Chattanooga (1938 to 1942), he was inspired by the brilliant teaching of Isobel Griscom and the spirited directing of Dorothy Hackett Ward, a new professor in the Speech and Theater Department. He was a member of the University Players for four years; he performed in 10 plays and received the Phi Mu acting award for his title role in *Cyrano de Bergerac*. His first three years, he wrote articles for the UC newspaper *The University Echo*, and he was editor his senior year. He received *The Chattanooga Times* scholarship and was listed in *Who's Who in Colleges and Universities*.

In his junior year, he was Professor Griscom's student assistant in the English Department. She was, from his first year at the University in 1938 till the end of her life in 1992, his greatest mentor. The day after her death Connor said that "she was the best teacher I ever had at any level. I cannot make the point any more plainly or any more justly than that." "She believed as strongly as anyone I have ever known," he wrote in 1963, "that the teacher's main function is to teach, to give to that teaching the best and truest effort of which the teacher is capable; but her interest in her students as human beings, her concern for them, inside or outside of class, was virtually without limit." They were devoted friends, and Griscom's standards of teaching and her concern for students who cared about learning became his own.

Dr. Thorne Sparkman, who was the rector at St. Paul's Episcopal Church in Chattanooga in the late 1930s and 1940s, was a model for Connor's religious beliefs and spiritual life. Connor was confirmed on March 31, 1940, and two years later he was admitted as a postulant for holy orders. His indebtedness to Sparkman was beyond any tribute he felt was adequate, and in his eulogy in 1989 he said simply what words would allow him: "I give thanks for Thorne Sparkman's life, for his example, for the sturdiness and beauty of his faith."

During World War II, Connor served three years in the United States Army with the 9th Armored Division. Away from the home of his childhood, his understanding of himself and his perspective of American society and humanity matured and deepened. He saw combat duty in the Battle of the Bulge and the crossing of the Rhine River in the last months of the war, and he celebrated VE Day in Czechoslovakia; he was awarded the Bronze Star for meritorious service in Germany in April 1945.

Shortly after he returned to the United States on New Year's Day of 1945, Connor enrolled as a seminarian in the School of Theology at the University of the South at Sewanee, Tennessee for three semesters, but he did not find a vocation as a minister and pastor. As it turned out, being a pastor was not far from being a teacher; as he wrote of Archbishop William Temple – one of his intellectual and personal heroes – he "found it virtually impossible to preach without also teaching at the same time." While Connor's decision not to continue in the seminary was a low point in his life, the inspiration and example of Isobel Griscom and Dorothy Ward allowed that teaching was not so much an alternative as it was a road he had been traveling all along.

Connor was initiated into teaching at East Ridge Junior High, "an assignment," he said later, "that has made almost everything else seem comparatively easy." The next year, he moved to Chattanooga City High School, where, for three years, he taught English, public speaking, coached class plays and Stunt Nite, and was in charge of all chapel programs. "Otherwise I just rested," he said later. In 1952 he was appointed the executive director of the Adult Education Council (now the Arts and Education Council), sponsored by the Ford Foundation as one of a small number of test cities in the United States. The Foundation emphasized that teaching would be the primary goal of adult education in "the development of the whole person." The appointment was a natural fit for Connor; the Foundation was "concerned with developing the ability to think independently and well, not with passive acceptance of ready-made, prescribed opinions." The Council, under his leadership and in collaboration with the Chattanooga community, built a vital organization committed to a program of liberal education for adults. Chattanooga was one of the few test cities to succeed in being self-sustaining after five years of sponsorship.

Connor went to the University of Chattanooga in 1959 as a member of the English Department. In 1963 the senior students presented him with the Ivy Award, the highest honor given by the graduating class. The University yearbook in 1969 was dedicated in his honor and in 1970 he was elected to Blue Key. He served as president of The Alpha Society and AAUP and as a chairman of the

Faculty Council. He chaired the English Department (1963-69) and was executive assistant to the President (later Chancellor) of the University (1967-70) during a period of major transition when the private college of the University of Chattanooga became part of the University of Tennessee system.

Shortly after he returned to teaching, Connor was named Guerry Professor of English in 1973, the most prestigious honor the University bestows upon a member of faculty. His teaching was recognized again in 1983 when he was presented the National UT Alumni Outstanding Teacher Award. When he retired from UTC in 1985, the George Connor Professorship in American Literature was established to honor his 26 years of service as a scholar, administrator, and classroom teacher.

A popular speaker, Professor Connor frequently gave lectures and taught classes in the Chattanooga community. He taught an annual six-week course, Invitation to Literature, at Senior Neighbors and St. Barnabas Apartments from 1973 to 1993. For several decades, he taught a series on Christianity and Literature (and other religious and theological topics) at 15 different churches in Chattanooga, Cleveland, Knoxville and Johnson City, Tennessee. He taught classes at the Chattanooga Bible Institute and Thorne Sparkman School of Religion (St. Paul's Episcopal Church, Chattanooga) and twice chaired the planning committee of the School. From 1988 to 1998, after his retirement, he taught a series of seminars for doctors and their spouses on literature and its relevance to the practice of medicine.

In the community and in his church, he served generously. He was a member of the Executive Council and the Friends of the Bicentennial Library. He was on the Book Review Committee and presented a number of book reviews in the twice-annual series. He was also a member of the Board of Directors, Foundation for Public Education, and of the Conference on Christianity and Literature. When George Connor died, he was a communicant of St. Paul's Episcopal Church of Chattanooga, where he had been confirmed in March 1940. He had served on the vestry of St. Paul's and of St. Peter's Episcopal Church, where he was a charter member in 1957. In the Episcopal Diocese of East Tennessee, he served as chairman of examining chaplains and was a member of the Commission on Ministry.

Besides his dedication to teaching, community service, and his church, Professor Connor published *Education for Freedom: A Six-Year Report, 1952-1958*, of the Adult Education Council of Chattanooga. The "report" was published as a 73-page booklet because the work of the Council was a model for other cities in the United States for an inclusive adult liberal education program. With Professor

Elizabeth Drew of Smith College, he co-edited *Discovering Modern Poetry* (1961). He published *Hints and Guesses* (1982) and *Hints and Guesses - II* (1997); each was a selection of commentaries he wrote weekly for the St. Peter's Episcopal Church newsletter from the late 1950s to 1997. The first collection was published on the occasion of the 25th anniversary of the founding of St. Peter's; the second on the 40th anniversary. As a charter member, a teacher in Bible classes, a member of the vestry and search committees for clergy, he knew first-hand the history of St. Peter's and he was asked to write *The First Quarter Century: St. Peter's Episcopal Church (1957-1982)*.

After Guerry Professor Emeritus Connor retired from UTC in 1985, he published *The First Century: The Public Library in Chattanooga* (1988), which was commissioned by the library board and Friends of the Library for the centennial year. He edited and compiled *Listening to Your Life: Daily Meditations with Frederick Buechner* (Harper San Francisco, 1992). Fred Buechner said of the 366 selections of his writing: "In a way, it seems to me less my book than it does George Connor's."

Throughout his teaching career, Professor Connor preferred to be called "teacher" rather than "professor." To some, he was the rigorous "Guardian of the English Language"; the cut line of another article had it that "Connor Defends English Language From Philistine Assaults." But his "guardianship" had less to do with grammar than with the lazy and imprecise use of language over the expression of clear thinking. In 1973 when he was named a Guerry Professor, a *Chattanooga Times* editorial spoke of him as a "master teacher": "A man of genuine scholarship, Professor Connor expects a commitment to excellence from his students and demands it of himself." One student wrote in an evaluation of his teaching in 1982, "If Gov. [Lamar] Alexander's 'master teacher' is someone who enlightens, enriches, and in rare instances, transforms a life, I think I have met the 'master' of them all – George Connor!" The *Times* editorial concluded that Connor was also "a tireless worker for the best causes on campus and community, a good citizen, a warm friend," and many, many friends, associates, and students felt the same. He died August 20, 2002 and is buried at Chattanooga Memorial Park in Red Bank.

On the occasion of Connor's retirement in 1986, then-UTC Provost John Trimpey eloquently summed up much of Connor's life as a teacher, colleague, and friend: "the University is losing more than a superb teacher and a tireless contributor; it is losing a whole perspective, a philosophy, a view of academe which it shall not likely ever replace.... There will be no more George Connor for us. And that makes me sad. We will hire new, young, brilliant teachers and dynamic researchers, but they won't have the impact on our students that you have had. They won't bring the integrity to their work that you have done. They won't replace your wit, style, and high seriousness. We will miss you for all the English students who didn't have the opportunity to study with George Connor. And I will miss you because, whatever else you are or have been, you are a good man. They are, indeed, hard to find."

Editor's Notes and Acknowledgements

In selecting and arranging *Living with the Word*, I have made every effort to choose the most representative of George's thinking, his ideas, his passions, his beliefs, and "the utter joy of his wit," as Fred Buechner says in the Preface.

I have edited the selections as lightly as possible, some with George's approval before he died and some changes he made himself. Several commentaries that first appeared as two parts are now one essay, for example the one on Nathan A. Scott, Jr. Some commentaries were written at different times (on C.S. Lewis and Alan Paton), but they melded together almost without effort. The booklets *Education for Freedom* and *The First Quarter Century: St. Peter's Episcopal Church*, were too long to print here, but I include edited versions of them because they were significant publications in George's life. I edited *Education for Freedom* rather heavily in cutting large sections and abbreviating paragraphs (I can hear George saying disdainfully, "that's what *The Reader's Digest* does!"), and *The First Quarter Century* less so. If I have left out something that is not faithful to the spirit of the document, I hope I will be pardoned, especially in instances where persons were named in the edited sections.

I began collecting and reading George's speeches, commentaries, essays, letters, and poems, in the summer of 2000. In the first round, I arranged them into ten sections, which made the book unwieldy. By the next summer, I had narrowed the arrangement down to five, which were the major themes of George's life – learning, teaching, Christian faith and life, citizenship, and friendship. It took me some time to cull and re-read all the available documents, and my own illness interrupted the work for over a year. In the meantime, other documents kept turning up, and, after George's death, I went back to the drawing board to select new documents, cut some I had selected, and rearranged the collection to give a larger view the man himself.

I have so many people to thank that if I miss someone, I hope I will be forgiven on the grounds of senility and not ingratitude. I had such astonishing support for this project that I want to thank everyone who asked or talked with me about it. Indeed, I lived with the word for some time, and it was always helpful to talk about the progress of THE BOOK, as Rick Govan so aptly dubbed it.

In the planning stages of *Living with the Word* in September 1999, a committee of colleagues and friends gave me useful suggestions in how to proceed: Dr. J. William Berry, Dr. Clif Cleveland, Mr. Roger Dickson, Mr. Tom Griscom, Mr. Doug Hale, Dr. Jane Harbaugh, Rev. Hunter Huckabay, Jr., Mrs. Olan Mills, Mr. Jack Murrah, The Rev. and Honorable Sam Payne, Ms. Rickie Pierce, Dr. Verbie

Prevost, former Mayor Gene Roberts, Dr. Bill Stacy, Mr. Herbert Thornbury, and Dr. James Ward.

All members of the planning committee were supportive and helpful, but I want to thank in particular Dr. Jim Ward for his advice on getting the book into print, and my brother Herbert for so generously sponsoring the committee meetings. Herbert also gave me secretarial support and made every resource available to me that I needed. Without his goodwill and sponsorship, the book would not have been finished. Dr. Bill Berry, then-Provost and Senior Vice-President of Academic Affairs at UTC made available generous funding from the George Connor Professorship of American Literature. The rest of the financing came from the Lyndhurst Foundation, with Jack Murrah's enthusiastic endorsement.

I want to thank Fred Buechner for his superb Preface. He and George were good friends, truly a mutual admiration society of two, and the Preface makes that abundantly clear. To Doug and Peggy Hale for making available to me many of the pictures and several documents in this collection – especially George's correspondence with Rev. Thorne Sparkman – I am most grateful. Tom Griscom, Isobel Griscom's nephew, made available to me her correspondence with George. Dr. Tom Ware sent me documents and pictures of George in the English Department at UC and UTC. Bob Lanza loaned me his correspondence with George, as did Carolyn Mitchell. Others who loaned me pictures or sent copies include Rev. Hallie Warren, Gene Roberts, Martha Gundaker, Rick Govan, Schaack Van Deusen, Jean Parker, David Parker, Jr., Dick Ramsey, Susan Smartt, and Liz Battle. To all of you, thank you very much.

Librarians and archivists at UTC, the Chattanooga-Hamilton County Bicentennial Library, and The University of the South went out of their way to help me find information and pictures. I especially want to thank Steven Cox, Head Archivist at UTC, who spent many hours searching for pictures and information about UC and UTC. He always responded quickly and searched out information that I would not have found on my own. Church archivists were also most helpful: Chappie Chapman at St. Paul's Episcopal Church and Ruth Vredeveld at St. Peter's.

In the middle and final stages of completing the manuscript of *Living with the Word*, I owe a great debt to Carolyn Mitchell in proof reading. She also insisted that "word" should be in the title, and she was right. Reita Jackson expertly transformed many of the pictures into digital formatting, and she advised me as I worked my way through the project. My two student workers are well beyond their young years in their talents and skills, and I was fortunate in having them assist me. John Rogers culled through and proofed documents and he gave helpful advice on my own writing. Mary Dellenbach is not only greatly talented in computer skills (John is as well) but has a keen eye for detail, style, and clarity. There came a point during the past year where I began to feel she was coeditor. Both have very bright futures ahead of them in whatever endeavors they choose.

My greatest regret in completing this volume is that George is not alive to celebrate the publication of *Living with the Word*. It is a small, but no less splendid, consolation that we now have something of him through his work. As Fred Buechner says in the Preface, "The door now stands open. Come in and make yourself at home."

INDEX

General Index
(See also Index of Subjects and Themes)

Connor, George (continued)

Genevieve [Ernst] – 241, 270, 320
Genghis Khan – 329
George K. Brown's Ice Cream Palace – 322
Germany, Coburg – (see under "World War II")
Gile, Janice Holt – 155
Glaser, Harry – 327
Grace Battle Memorial Parkway – 323-324
Grace Church – 175, 181, 186
Greek Tragedy – 100
Griscom, Isobel – 13, *54-64*, 90, 254
      Letters to – 136-139, 234-238, 243-247, 248-250, 250-253, 255-257
Griscom, Tom – 328-329
Guerry, Alexander – 89
Gundaker, Martha – 55
      Letters to – 253-254

Hailey, Wilburn – 179
Hale, Doug and Peggy – 132, 293, 299
Harbuck, Don – 192, 193
Harnack, Professor – 50
Hart, Bishop – 241
Hayden, John – 195
Heraclitus – 18, 218, 326
Heart of Midlothian – 97-98
Hebrew Prophets – 95
Helen of Troy – 201
Hemingway, Ernest – 34,
Henlein, General Konrad – 256, 262
Henry, Jack – 323
Hersey, John – 17,
Herron, Arlie – 54, 55, 82, 327
Hilton Head – 319
Hirohito – 268
Hitler, Adolf – 255, 262
Hixon, Fred – 265
Hodge, Mary K. – 55
Holocaust – 232
Hopkins, Gerard Manley – 99, 100-101, 195, 301, 302
Hosanna – 145
Howell-Thomas, Dorothy – 158
Huckleberry Finn – 34, 97
Huggins, Lisa – 6
Humphrey, Hubert – *278-279*
Huntington, Fr. – 156

Independence Day – 233, 281-282
Interpreter's Bible – (see under "Bible, The" in *Index of Subjects and Themes*)

Red Bank – 297
Red Bank High School – 176-177, 178, 303
Rehnquist, Chief Justice – 289
Reston, James – 107, 275
Reynolds, Mary Macdonald – 58
Rhodes, Sir Cecil – 269
Rice, Rev. Charles – 181
Richardson, Mrs. W.B. – 22, 31
Riley, Mayor Joe – 282
Roberts, Gene – *279-280*, 281
Robertson, Dean Jaquelin – 281, 282
Robertson, Pat – 276
Robinson, Fred – 297
Robinson, Ruth – 192
Roncalli, Angelo – (see "John XXIII")
Roosevelt, Franklin D. – 108, 257, 264
Rouse, Jim – *280-281*

Saint Alban's Episcopal Church – 186
Saint Barnabus complex – 180
Saint George's Chapel – 319
Saint James' Episcopal Church – 176
Saint John's Church – 180
Saint Martin's Episcopal Church – 186
Saint Maybe – 152
Saint Paul's Episcopal Church – 118, 137, 139-141, 156, 175, 177, 178, 181, 186, 187,
             308, 318, 320; Mother parish – 175
Saint Peter's Episcopal Church – 118, 126, 130, *175-188*, 189, 197, 279, 280, 291, 307,
             309, 316
Saint Peter's kindergarten – 180, 182
Saint Phillip's Episcopal Church – 181
Saint Thaddeus' Episcopal Church – 186
Saint Timothy's Episcopal Church – 176
Sanders, Bishop William – 169, 187
Sayers, Dorothy L. – 75, 152-153, 165
Scarlet Letter, The – 60
Schlack, Natalie – 82
Schoocraft, Otis – 234
Schweitzer, Albert – 203
Scorey, George – *316-317*
Scott, Nathan A. Jr. – *194-196*
Selma University – 194
Sewanee – 53, 89, 160, 161, 183, 241, 243, 268
Shakespeare, William – 51, 70, 95, 100, 189, 200, 267
        Hamlet – 7, 50, 96, 98, 148, 317, 330
        King Lear – 97, 198, 290
        Macbeth – 51

Index of Subjects and Themes

"Habitual vision of greatness" (see *Connor, George*, "Favorite Quotations"
in *General Index*)

Poetry – (see under "Literature")
Prayer – (see under "Christian Faith and Life")
Prayer Book, The – (see "*Book of Common Prayer, The*")
Publishing industry – 17-18, 94

Quality of life – 15-19 (see also "Excellence")

Race and racism – 38, 73, 117, 151, 195, 222, 232, 243-247, 248, 263, 290-292
Reading – (see under "Education" and "Literature")
Relationship(s) – 47, 62, 77, 142, 143, 150, 209, 220
        Dependent upon others – 148
Religion
        and Conversion – 122
        and Higher learning – 66-67,
        and Politics – 273-276, 279-280
        Religious movies – 119, 132
        and "the Whole life" – 141
Religious commitment – 100-101, 124

Service – 77
Simplicity – 119, 229, 306-307
Slogans – (see "Critical thinking")
Standards – (see "Excellence")
Students – (see "Education" and *Communities*, "University")

Teaching – (see under "Education")
Television – 17-18, 285
        Point of View – 36-37
Time – 2, 3, 16, 188, 189 (see also "History")
        Past – 95-96, 102, 189, 195, 250, 301

Unsentimental – 187
Understanding – (see under "Learning")

Violence – 19, 232, 243-247, 251, 262, 290-292
        Cruelty – 97, 151, 157, 195, 226, 232, 257, 259, 290, 291-292, 296

Words – (see under "Language")
Work – 62, 127 (see also under "Christian faith and life")
World War II – 232, 271, 291-292, 305, 325
        American soldier – 252, 266
                (see also "Soldier" under *Connor, George* in *General Index*)
        Communal life of – 235, 264
        Allied Military Government (AMG) – 267
        Army Cook Book – 254
        Articles of War, The – 236
        Battle of the Bulge – 271, 272, 328